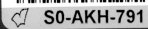
血界戦線

けっかいせんせん

3

― 世 と 世界のゲーム ―
せか せかい

BLOOD BLOCKADE BATTLEFRONT

THE TREMOROUS BLOOD HAMMER

STORY AND ART
YASUHIRO NIGHTOW

TRANSLATION
MATTHEW JOHNSON

LETTERING AND RETOUCH
STUDIO CUTIE

DARK HORSE MANGA

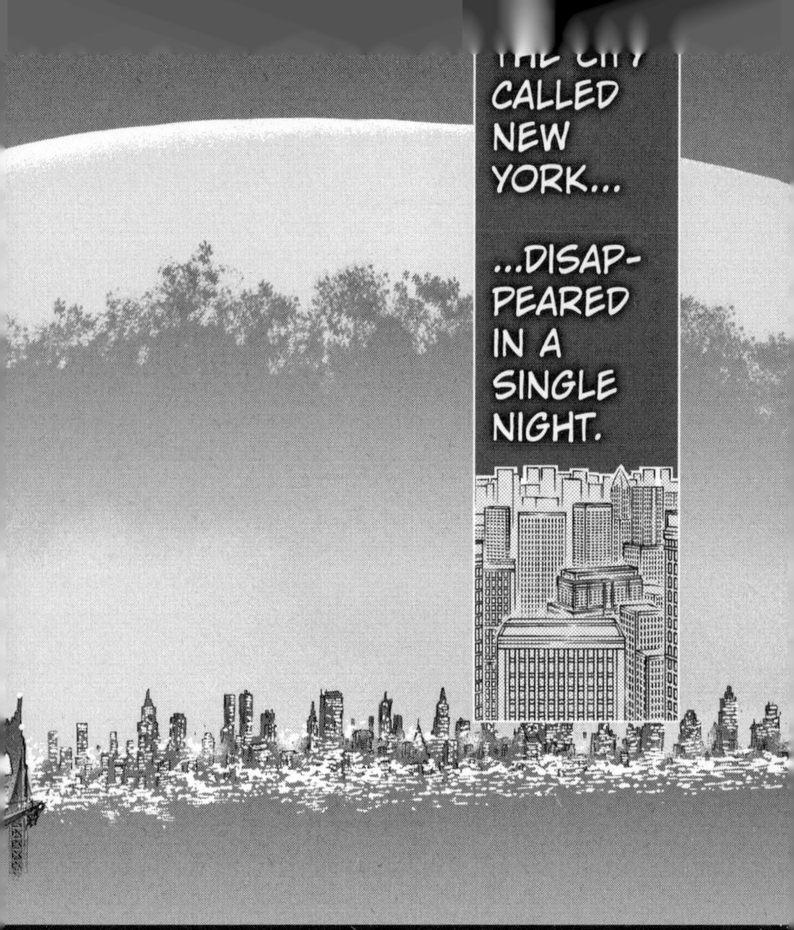
CALLED NEW YORK...
...DISAPPEARED IN A SINGLE NIGHT.

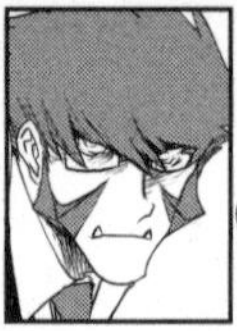

CHARACTER FILE:1

TOP SECRET

Klaus von Reinhertz

Leader of the secret society ***Libra***. He's so strong willed that he's honest to a fault and incredibly strong. While his red hair and large body are very intimidating, he has a calm demeanor and is very gentlemanly.
Master of the Brain Grid blood battle technique.

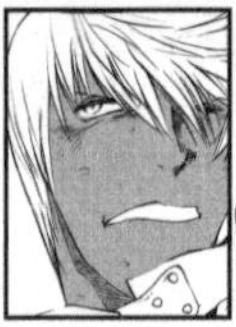

CHARACTER FILE:2

TOP SECRET

Zap Renfro

Member of the secret society ***Libra***. A cheery, silver-haired, suntanned punk. Good at looking after junior members. Master of the Big Dipper style blood technique, in which he manipulates blood into the shape of a sword and then sets it on fire.

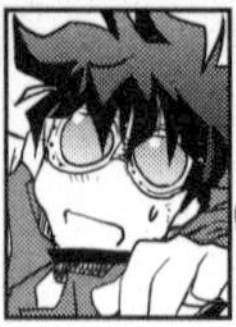

CHARACTER FILE:3

TOP SECRET

Leonard Watch

Member of the secret society ***Libra.*** Though he was a normal young man, he was given "the Eyes of the Gods" in return for the sight of his sister. Not ready for prime time when it comes to battle.

IN ITS PLACE, ***"JERUSALEM'S LOT,"*** THE CITY SHROUDED IN MIST, WAS BUILT OVERNIGHT.

THE CITY IS A BRIDGE BETWEEN REALITY AND ***"THE BEYOND,"*** WHICH HAD FORMERLY BEEN NO MORE THAN THE STUFF OF LEGEND.

THE MAJORITY OF THIS REALM LIES PAST THE BORDER IN A LAND THAT IS STILL UNKNOWN TO MAN, A LAND WITH A THICK, IMPENETRABLE VEIL OF MIST.

AS A PLACE WHERE MIRACULOUS EVENTS BEYOND HUMAN POWER BECOME REALITY, IT IS COVETED AS AN AREA FROM WHICH A THOUSAND-YEAR REICH OVER THE WORLD COULD GET ITS START. IT IS RAMPANT WITH THOSE OF SUCH AMBITION.

YET THERE IS A SECRET SOCIETY THAT WORKS IN THE SHADOWS TO MAINTAIN BALANCE IN THIS WORLD: ***LIBRA.***

THE YOUNG MAN ***LEO*** HAS FOUND HIMSELF A MEMBER OF LIBRA THROUGH UNEXPECTED CIRCUMSTANCES...

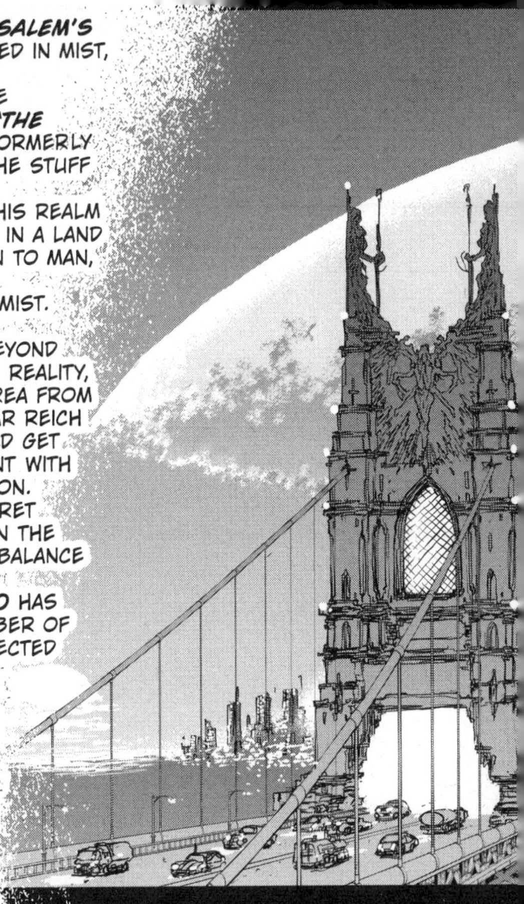

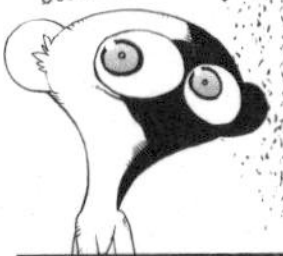
Sonic Speed Monkey

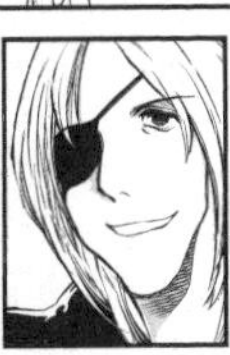

CHARACTER FILE:7

TOP SECRET

K•K

Member of the secret society ***Libra***. A long and thin beauty with superior fighting abilities. She annihilates monsters with her Blood Bullet technique using electric-shock heavy weaponry.

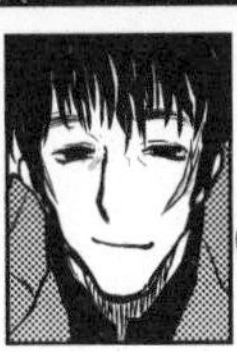

CHARACTER FILE:6

TOP SECRET

Stephan A. Starphase

Member of the secret society ***Libra***. Has a scar next to his eye and wears suits. Acts as Klaus' second in command. Uses the Esmerelda Blood Freeze, a technique that instantly freezes everything with a skillful kick.

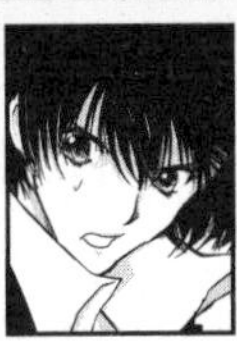

CHARACTER FILE:4

TOP SECRET

Chain Sumeragi

Member of the secret society ***Libra***. Actually an invisible werewolf, Chain can disappear and move at high speeds. Mostly performs intelligence, recon, and pursuit for the society.

血界戦線

―世界と世界のゲーム―

CONTENTS 3

BLOOD BLOCKADE BATTLEFRONT

THE TREMOROUS BLOOD HAMMER

Welcome to
New York

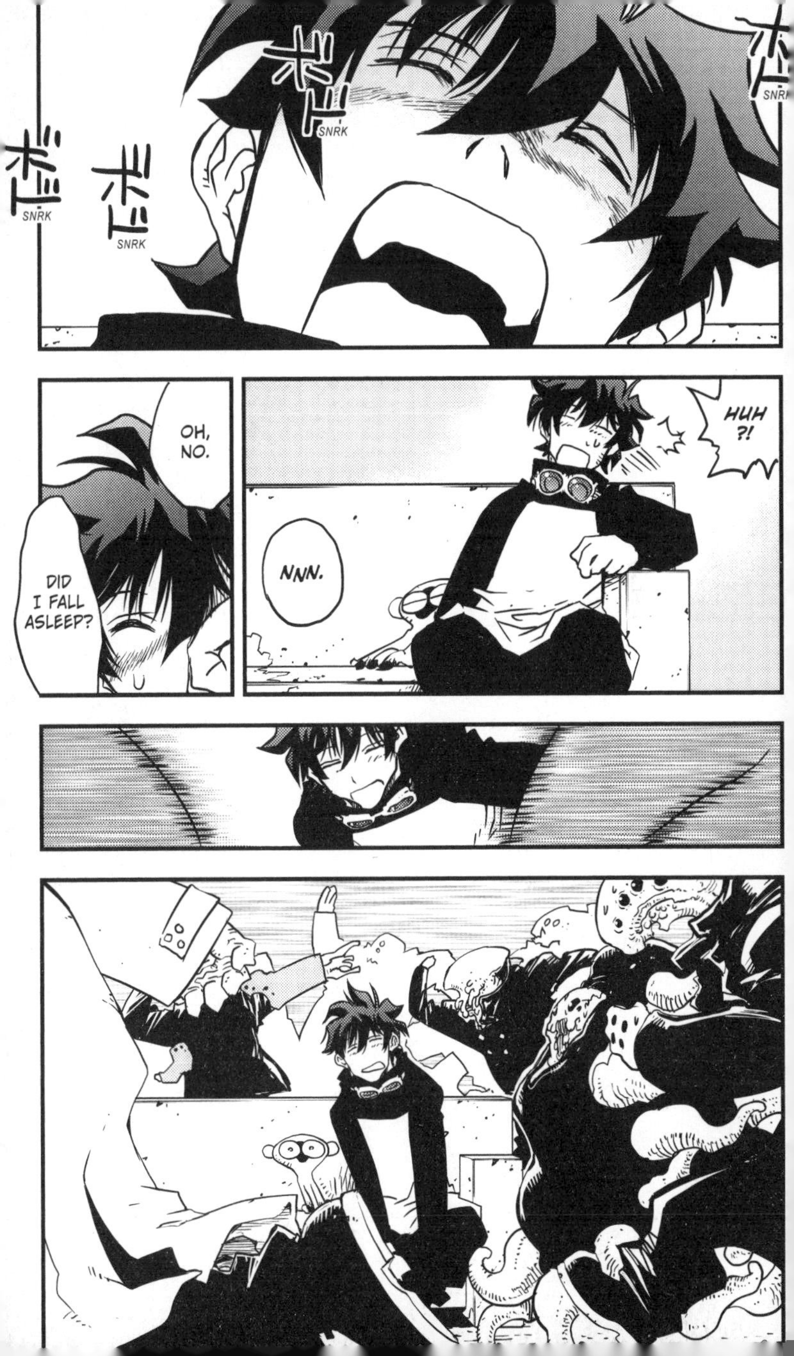
SNRK
SNRK
SNRK
SNRK
HUH?!
NNN.
OH, NO.
DID I FALL ASLEEP?

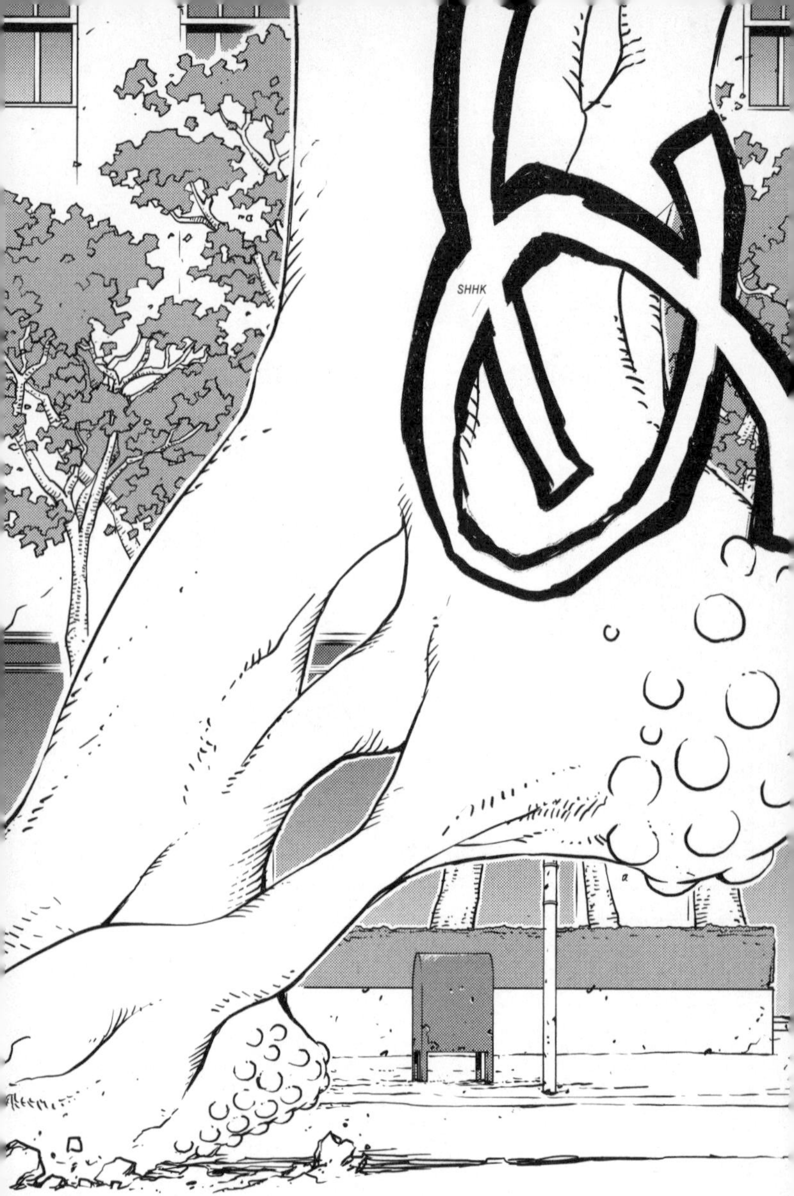
SHHK

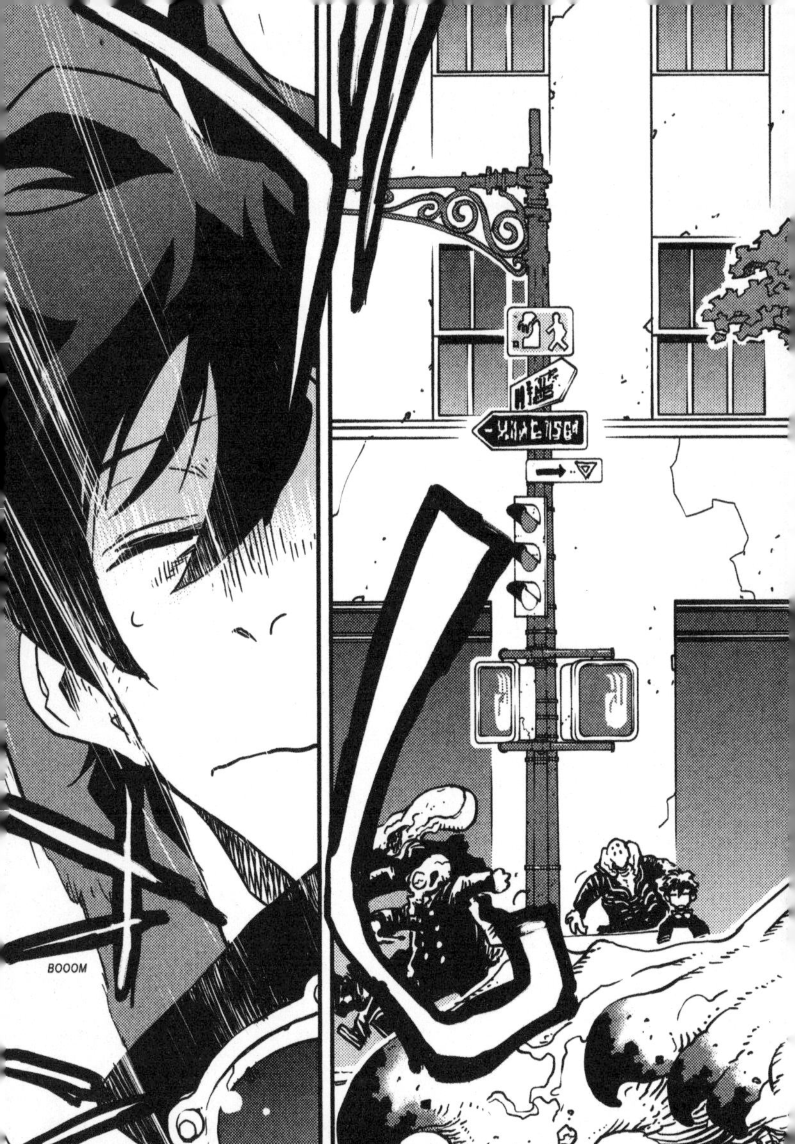
BOOOM

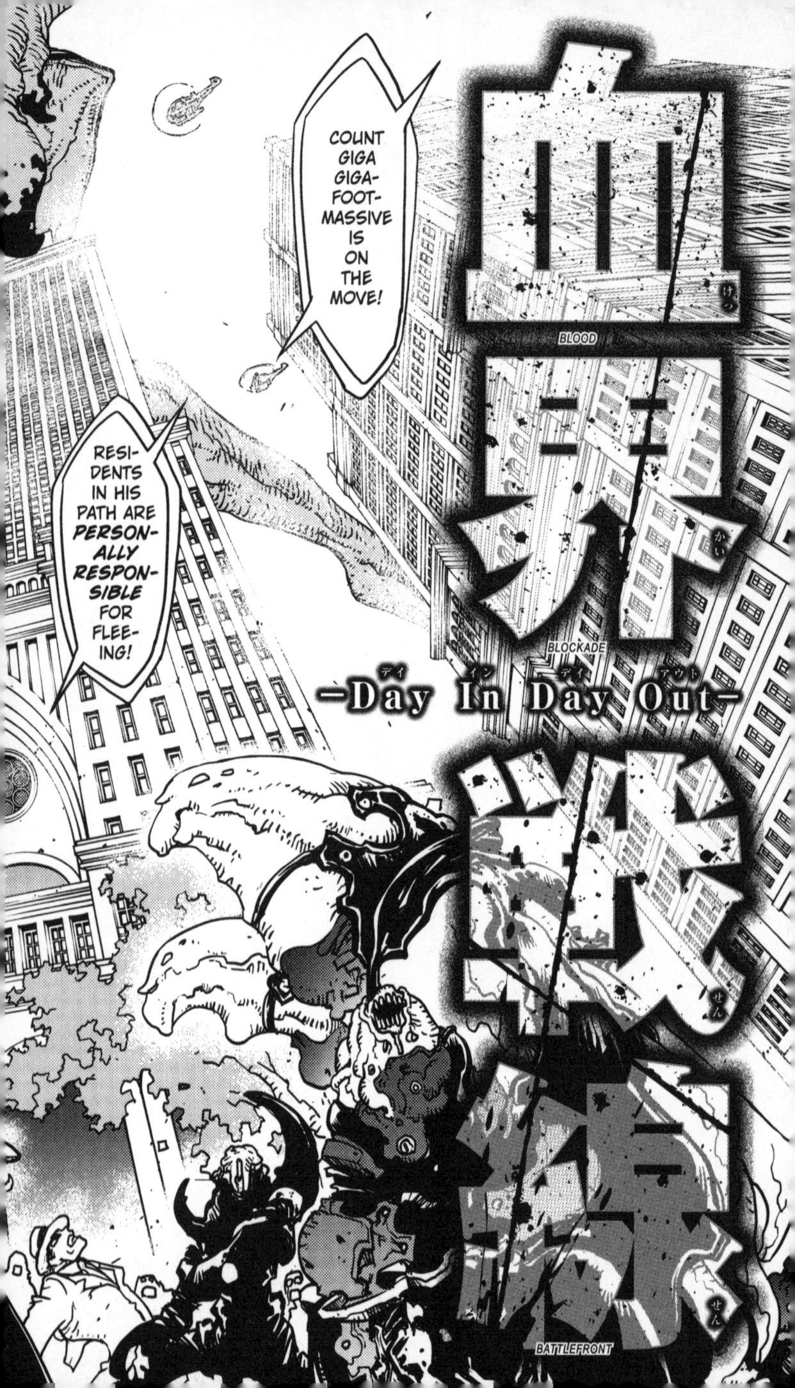
血界戦線
BLOOD BLOCKADE BATTLEFRONT
−Day In Day Out−
COUNT GIGA GIGA-FOOT-MASSIVE IS ON THE MOVE!
RESIDENTS IN HIS PATH ARE *PERSONALLY RESPONSIBLE* FOR FLEEING!

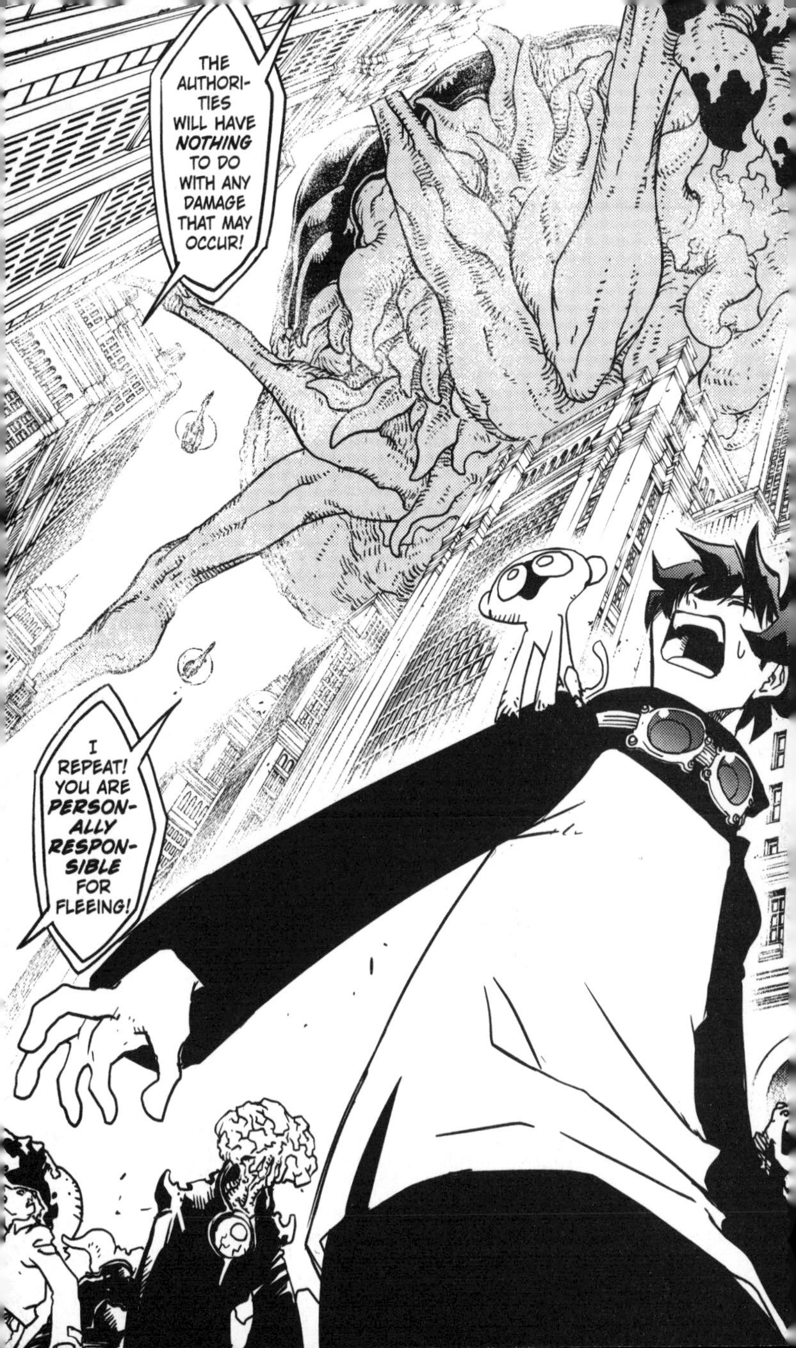
THE AUTHORITIES WILL HAVE **NOTHING** TO DO WITH ANY DAMAGE THAT MAY OCCUR!
I REPEAT! YOU ARE **PERSONALLY RESPONSIBLE** FOR FLEEING!

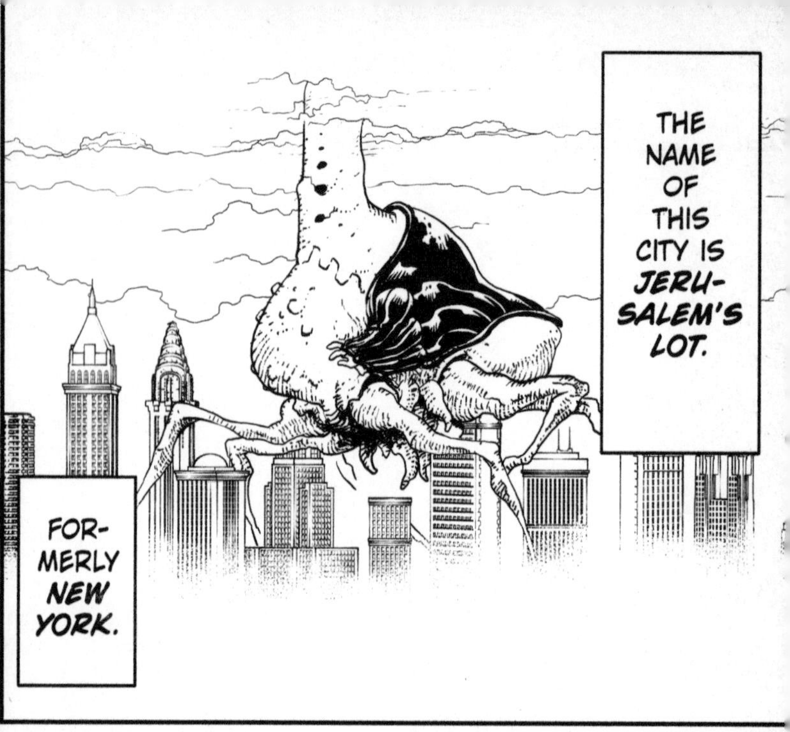
THE NAME OF THIS CITY IS ***JERUSALEM'S LOT.***
FORMERLY ***NEW YORK.***
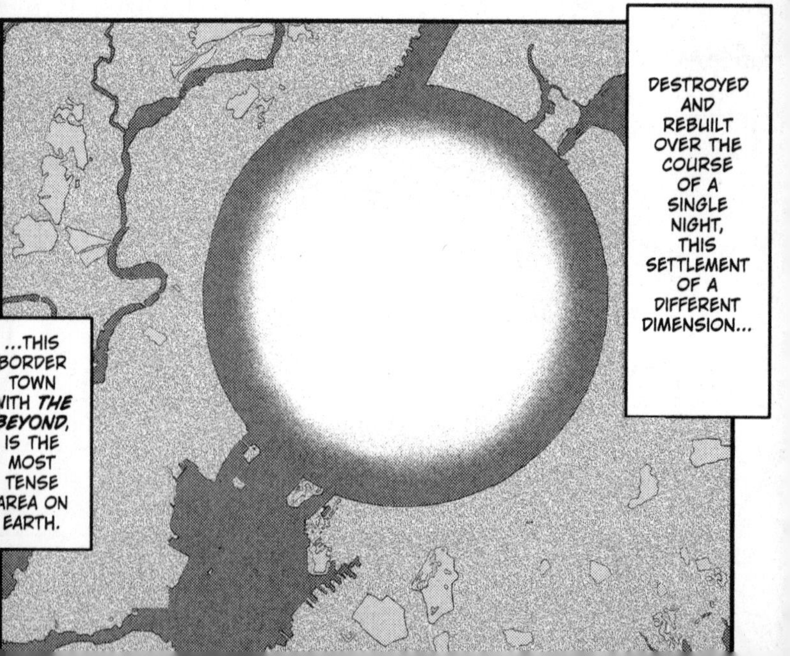
DESTROYED AND REBUILT OVER THE COURSE OF A SINGLE NIGHT, THIS SETTLEMENT OF A DIFFERENT DIMENSION...
...THIS BORDER TOWN WITH ***THE BEYOND,*** IS THE MOST TENSE AREA ON EARTH.

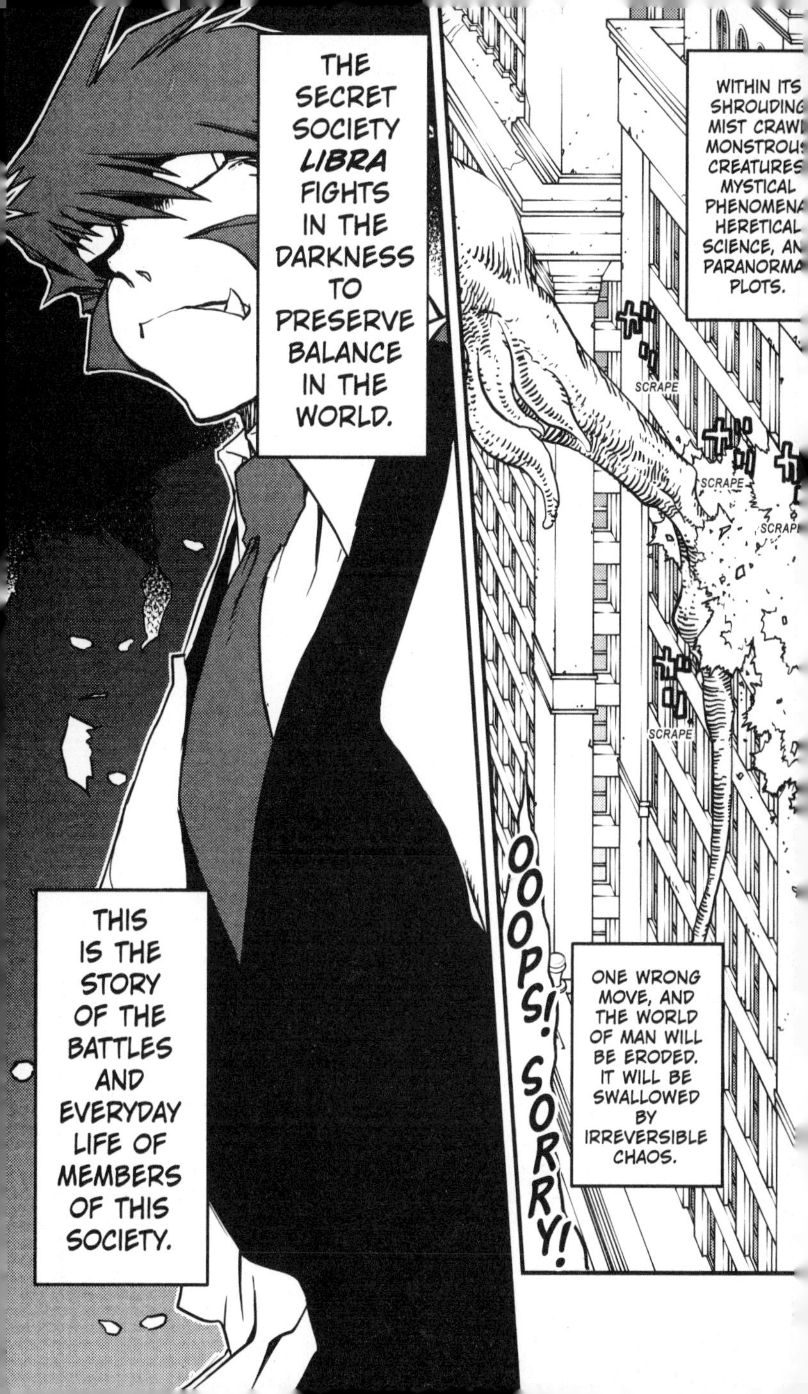
WITHIN ITS SHROUDING MIST CRAWL MONSTROUS CREATURES MYSTICAL PHENOMENA HERETICAL SCIENCE, AN PARANORMA PLOTS.
SCRAPE
SCRAPE
SCRAPE
SCRAPE
ONE WRONG MOVE, AND THE WORLD OF MAN WILL BE ERODED. IT WILL BE SWALLOWED BY IRREVERSIBLE CHAOS.
OOOPS! SORRY!
THE SECRET SOCIETY *LIBRA* FIGHTS IN THE DARKNESS TO PRESERVE BALANCE IN THE WORLD.
THIS IS THE STORY OF THE BATTLES AND EVERYDAY LIFE OF MEMBERS OF THIS SOCIETY.

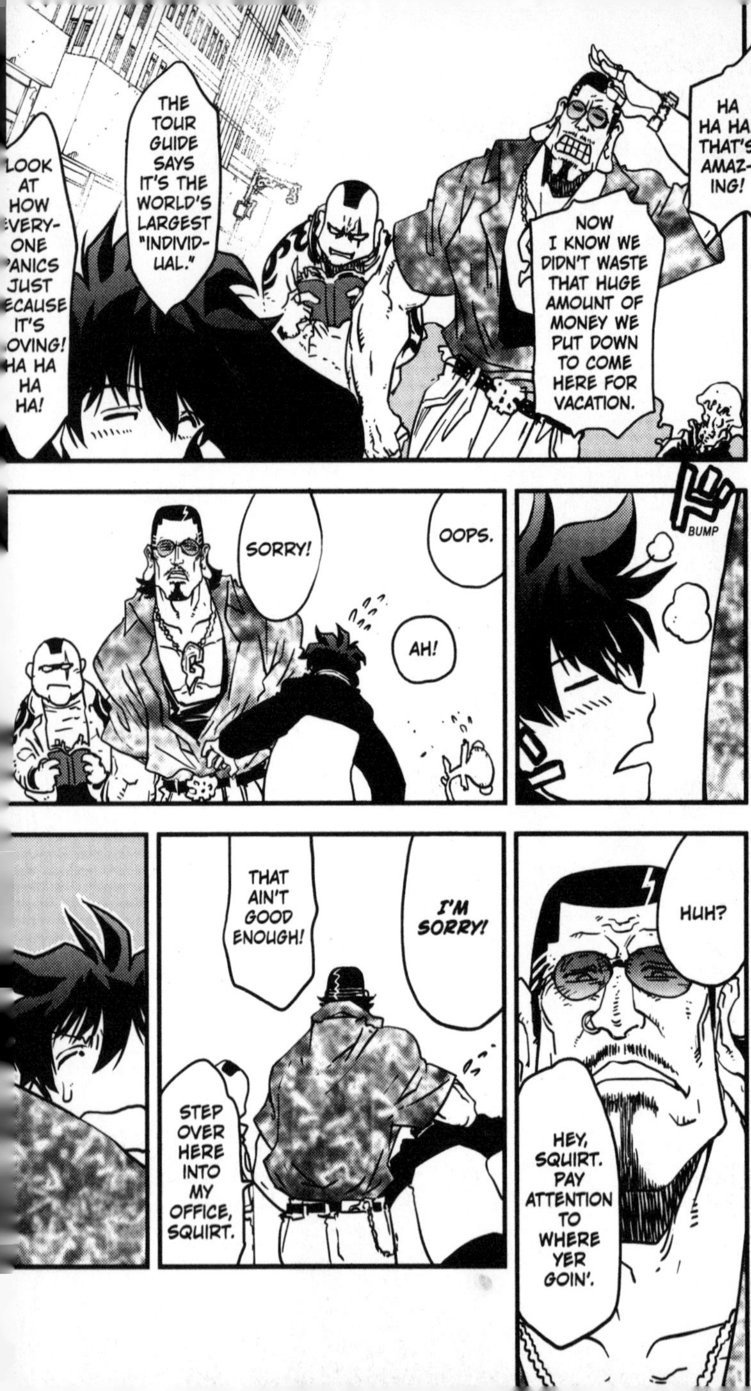
HA HA HA! THAT'S AMAZ-ING!
NOW I KNOW WE DIDN'T WASTE THAT HUGE AMOUNT OF MONEY WE PUT DOWN TO COME HERE FOR VACATION.
THE TOUR GUIDE SAYS IT'S THE WORLD'S LARGEST "INDIVID-UAL."
LOOK AT HOW VERY-ONE ANICS JUST ECAUSE IT'S OVING! HA HA HA HA!
BUMP
OOPS.
SORRY!
AH!
HUH?
HEY, SQUIRT. PAY ATTENTION TO WHERE YER GOIN'.
I'M SORRY!
THAT AIN'T GOOD ENOUGH!
STEP OVER HERE INTO MY OFFICE, SQUIRT.

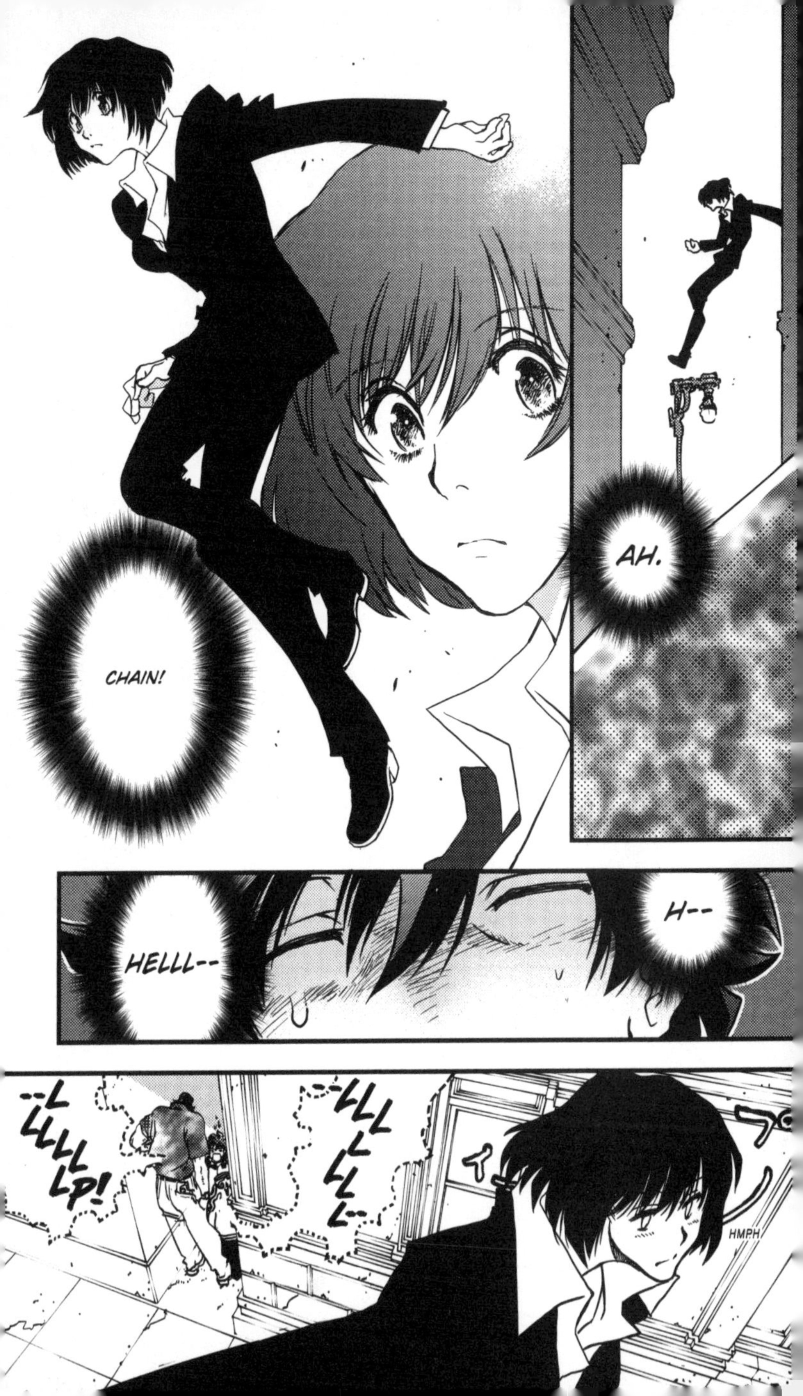
AH.
CHAIN!
H--
HELLL--
HMPH
--LLL
L
L
L--
--L
LLLLL
LP!

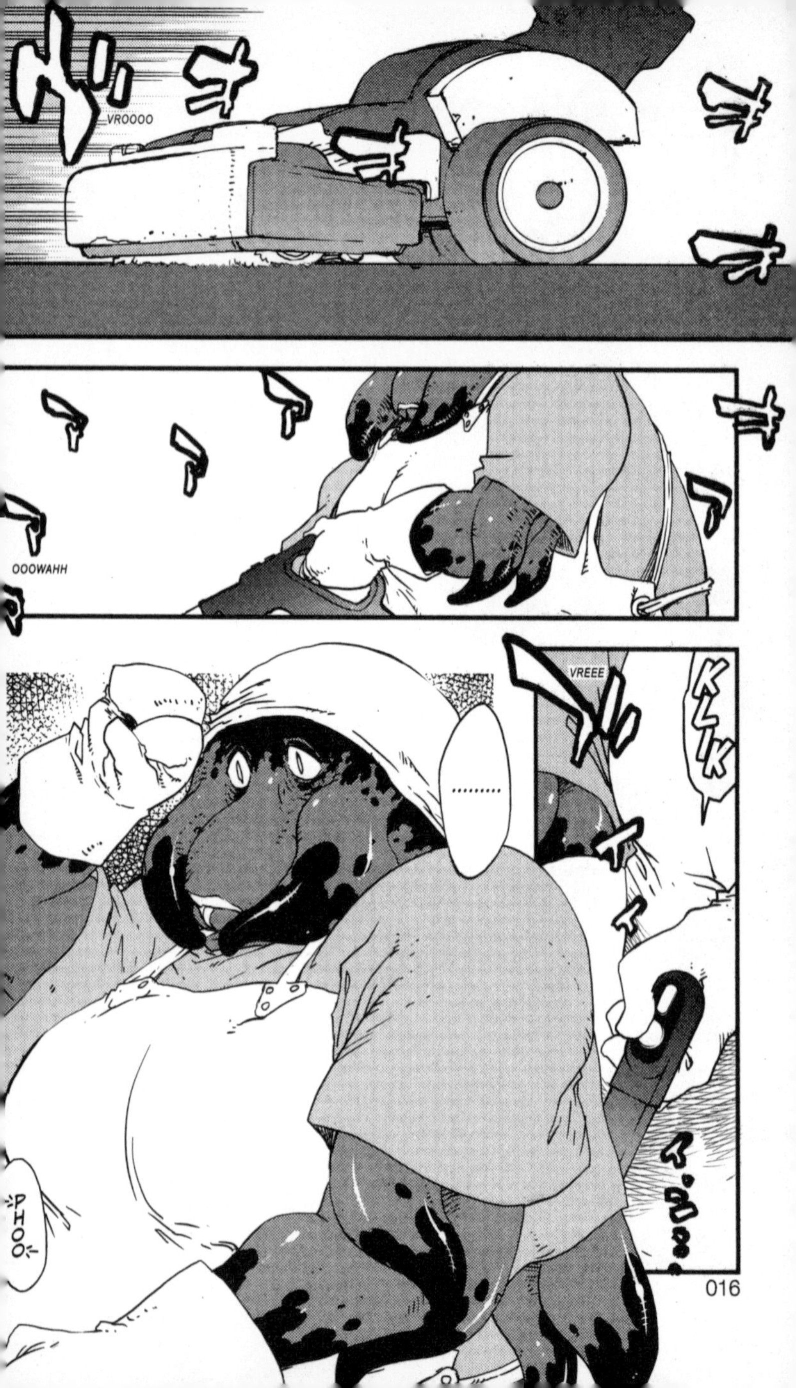
VROOOO
OOOWAHH
VREEE
KLIK
....
PHOO

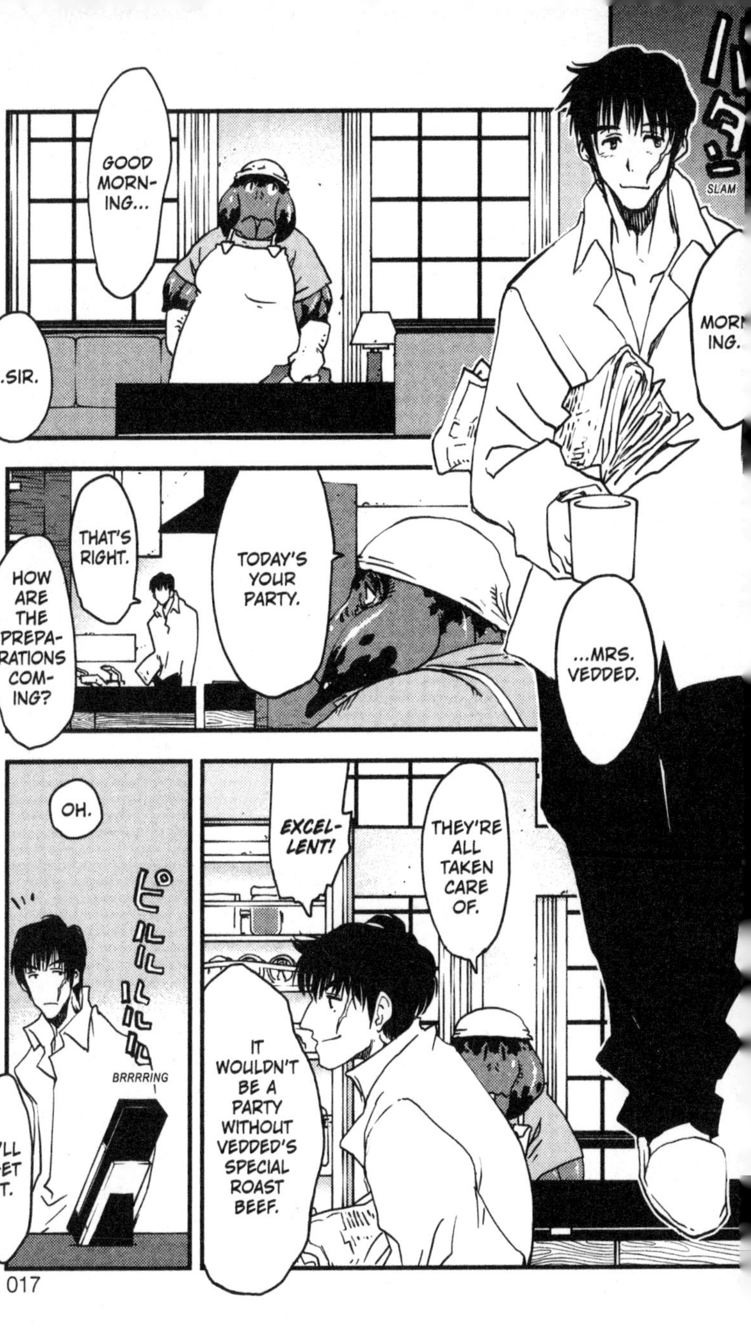
SLAM
MORNING.
...MRS. VEDDED.
GOOD MORNING...
...SIR.
TODAY'S YOUR PARTY.
THAT'S RIGHT.
HOW ARE THE PREPARATIONS COMING?
THEY'RE ALL TAKEN CARE OF.
EXCELLENT!
IT WOULDN'T BE A PARTY WITHOUT VEDDED'S SPECIAL ROAST BEEF.
OH.
BRRRRING
I'LL GET IT.

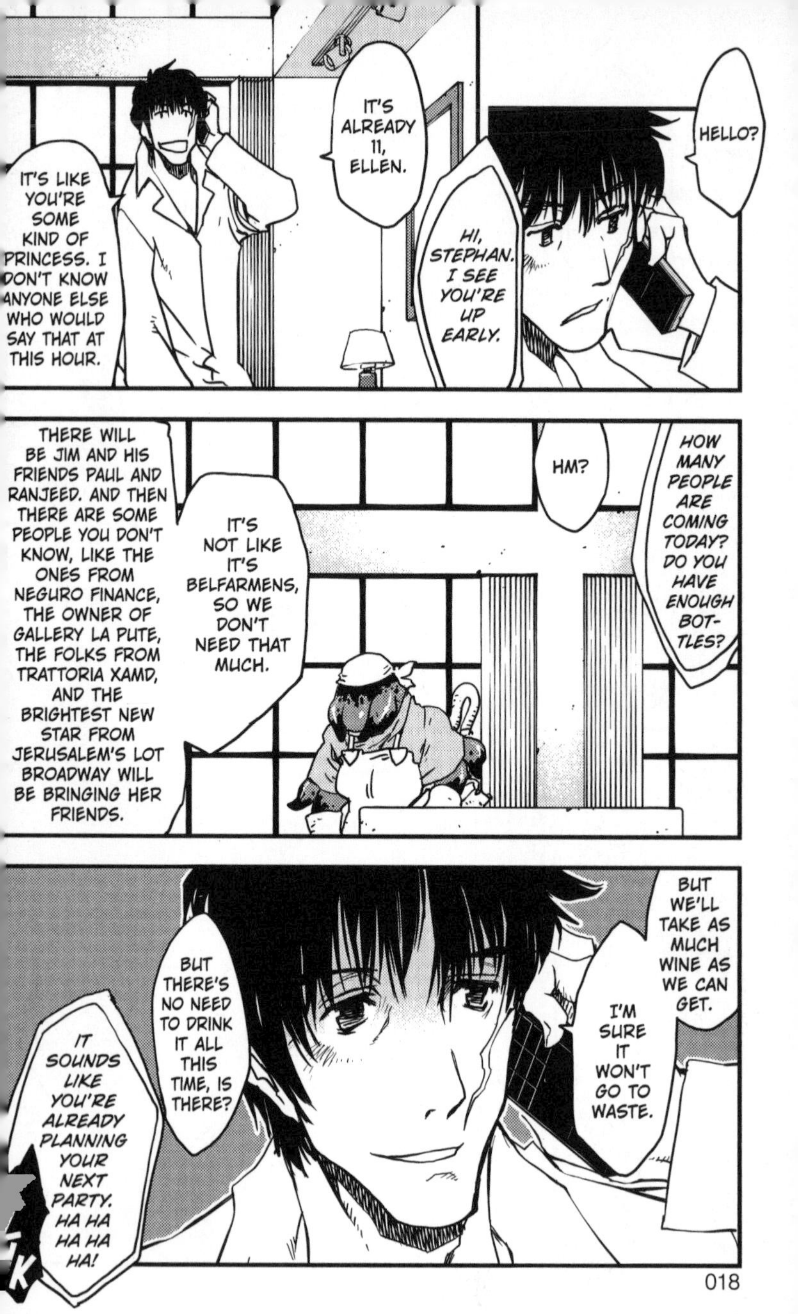
HELLO?
HI, STEPHAN. I SEE YOU'RE UP EARLY.
IT'S ALREADY 11, ELLEN.
IT'S LIKE YOU'RE SOME KIND OF PRINCESS. I DON'T KNOW ANYONE ELSE WHO WOULD SAY THAT AT THIS HOUR.
HOW MANY PEOPLE ARE COMING TODAY? DO YOU HAVE ENOUGH BOT-TLES?
HM?
IT'S NOT LIKE IT'S BELFARMENS, SO WE DON'T NEED THAT MUCH.
THERE WILL BE JIM AND HIS FRIENDS PAUL AND RANJEED. AND THEN THERE ARE SOME PEOPLE YOU DON'T KNOW, LIKE THE ONES FROM NEGURO FINANCE, THE OWNER OF GALLERY LA PUTE, THE FOLKS FROM TRATTORIA XAMD, AND THE BRIGHTEST NEW STAR FROM JERUSALEM'S LOT BROADWAY WILL BE BRINGING HER FRIENDS.
BUT WE'LL TAKE AS MUCH WINE AS WE CAN GET.
I'M SURE IT WON'T GO TO WASTE.
BUT THERE'S NO NEED TO DRINK IT ALL THIS TIME, IS THERE?
IT SOUNDS LIKE YOU'RE ALREADY PLANNING YOUR NEXT PARTY. HA HA HA HA HA!

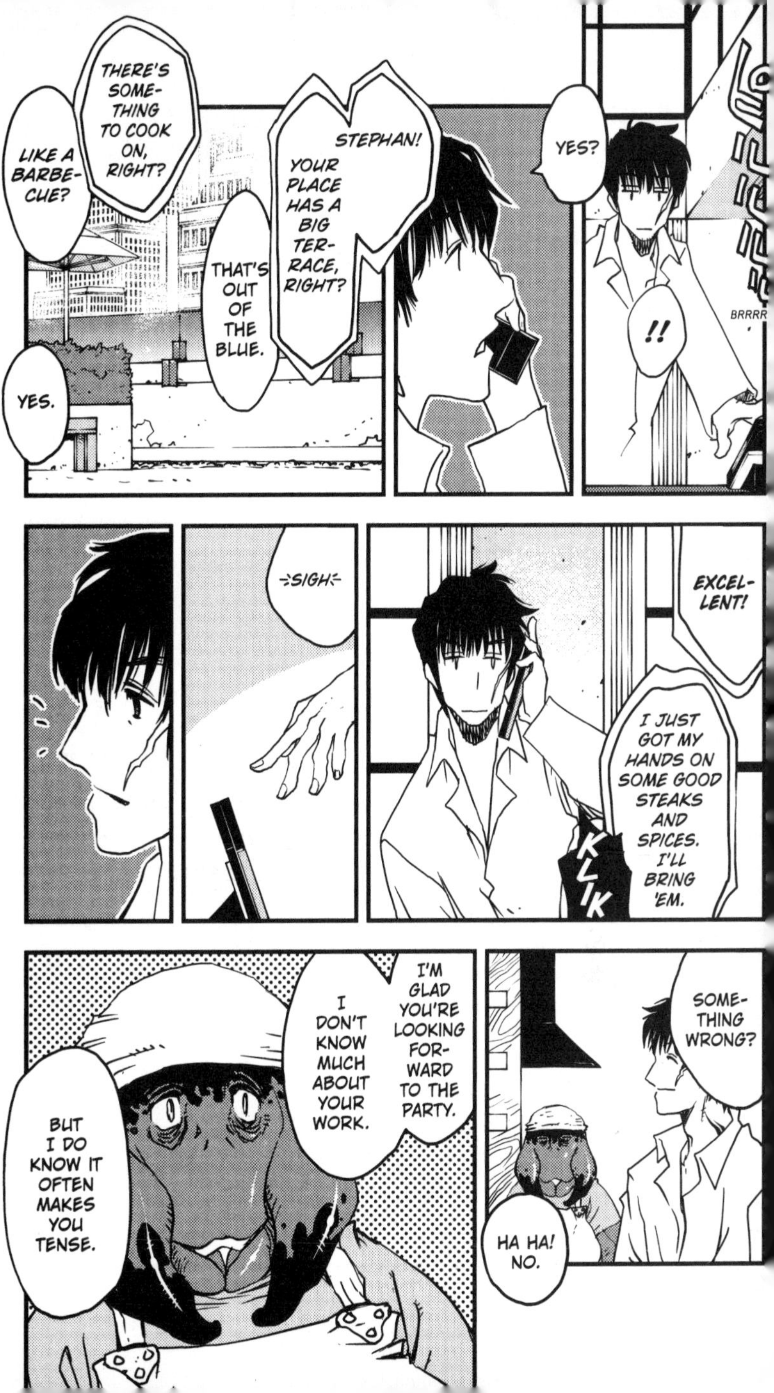
BRRRR
!!
YES?
STEPHAN!
YOUR PLACE HAS A BIG TERRACE, RIGHT?
THAT'S OUT OF THE BLUE.
THERE'S SOMETHING TO COOK ON, RIGHT?
LIKE A BARBECUE?
YES.
EXCELLENT!
I JUST GOT MY HANDS ON SOME GOOD STEAKS AND SPICES. I'LL BRING 'EM.
KLIK
SIGH
SOMETHING WRONG?
HA HA! NO.
I'M GLAD YOU'RE LOOKING FORWARD TO THE PARTY.
I DON'T KNOW MUCH ABOUT YOUR WORK.
BUT I DO KNOW IT OFTEN MAKES YOU TENSE.

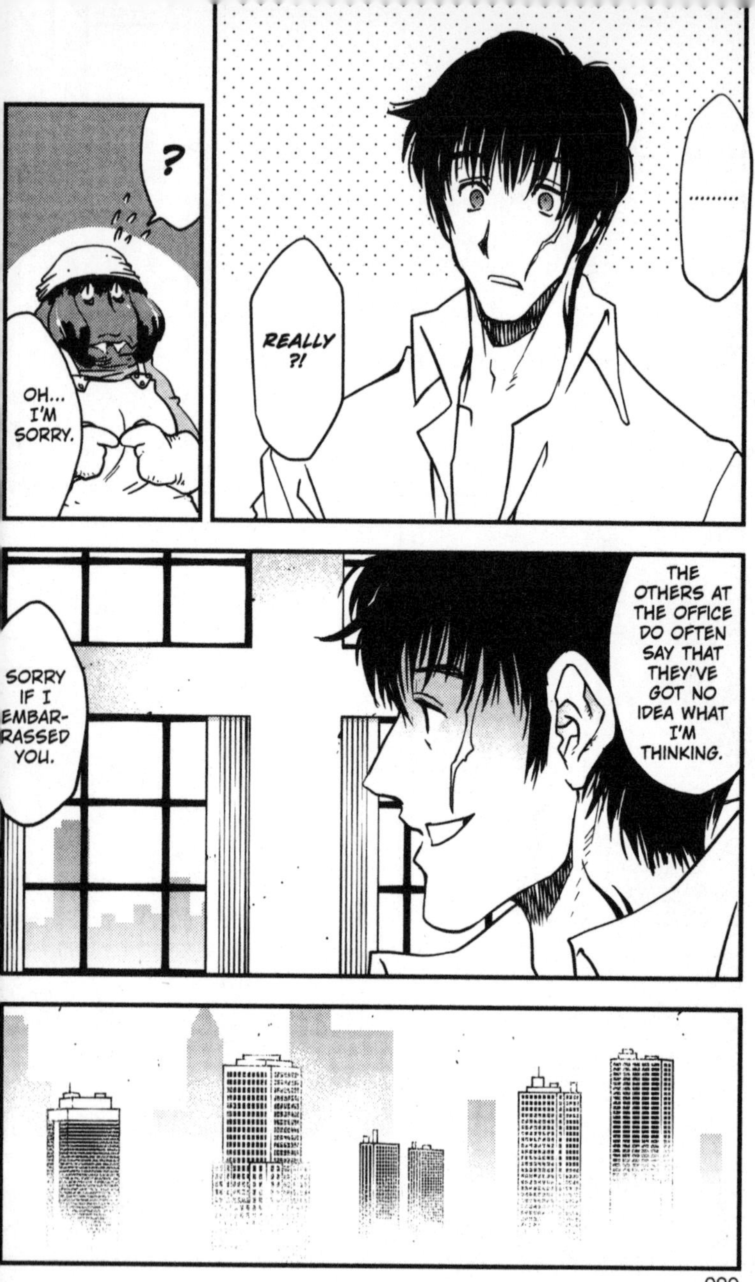
....
REALLY ?!
?
OH... I'M SORRY.
THE OTHERS AT THE OFFICE DO OFTEN SAY THAT THEY'VE GOT NO IDEA WHAT I'M THINKING.
SORRY IF I EMBARRASSED YOU.

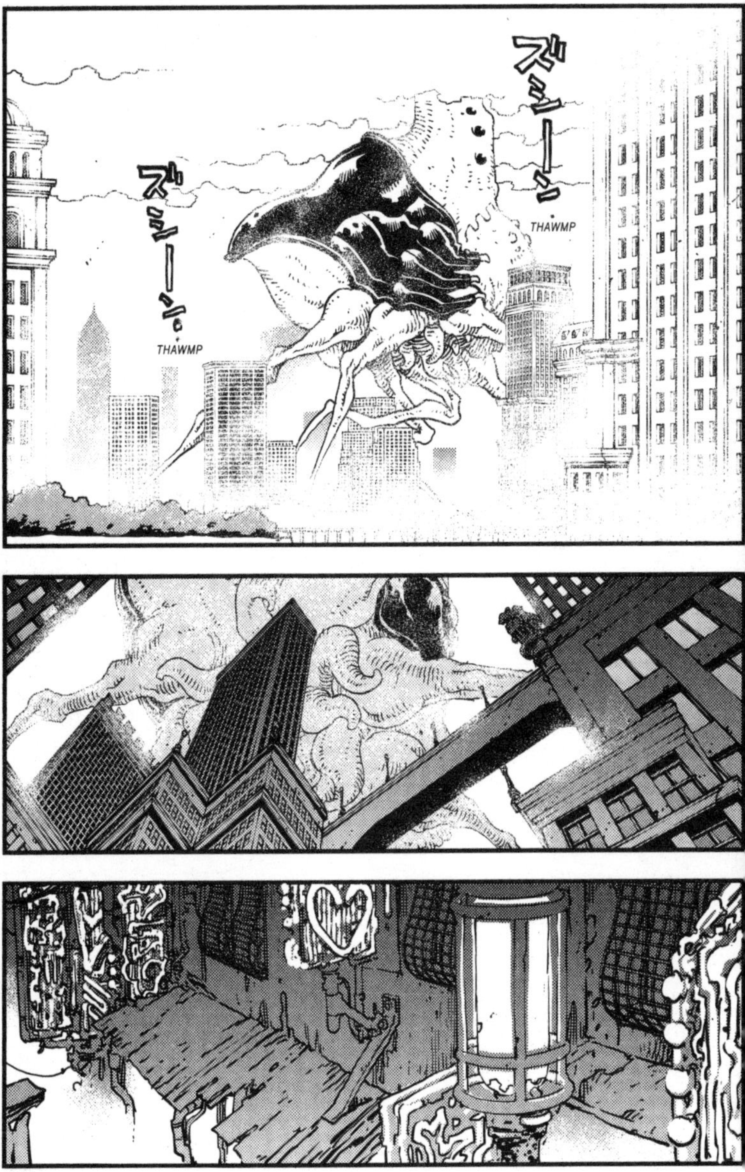
ズシーーン
THAWMP
ズシーーン
THAWMP

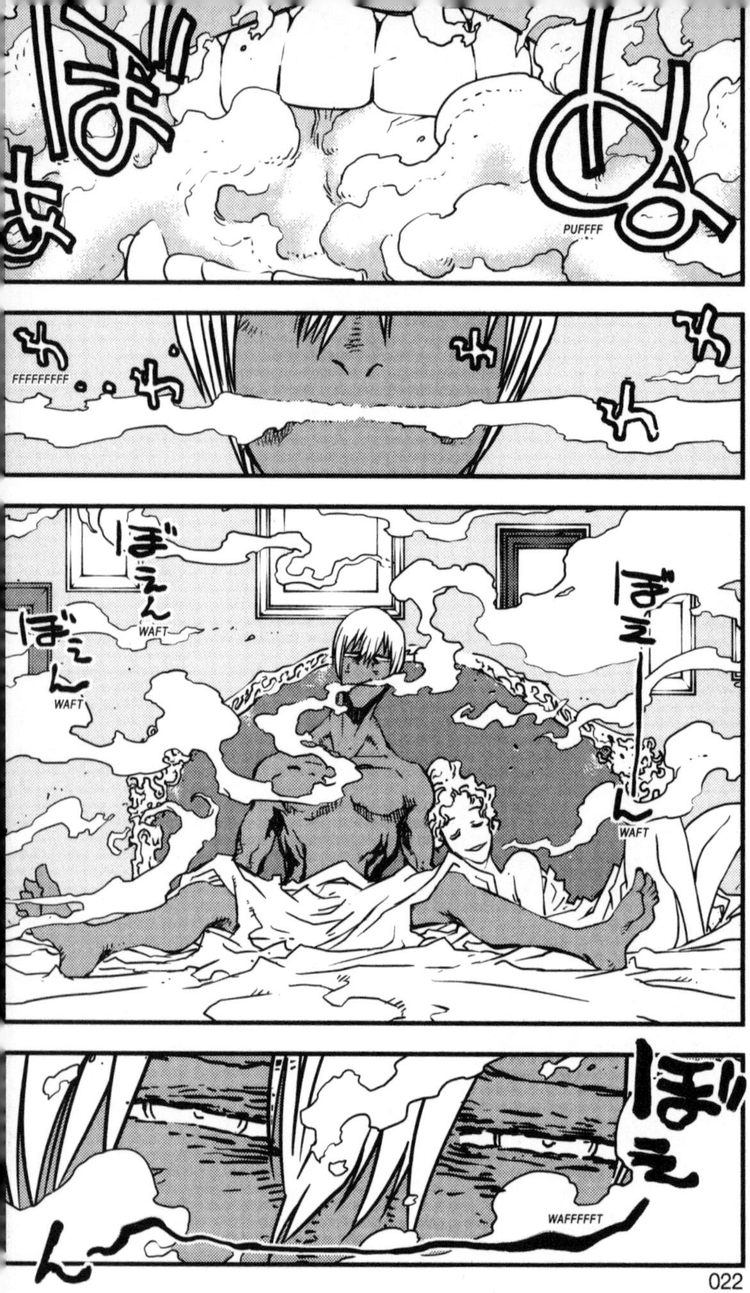
PUFFFF
FFFFFFFFF
ぼえーん
WAFT
ぼえん
WAFT
ぼえん
WAFT
WAFFFFFT

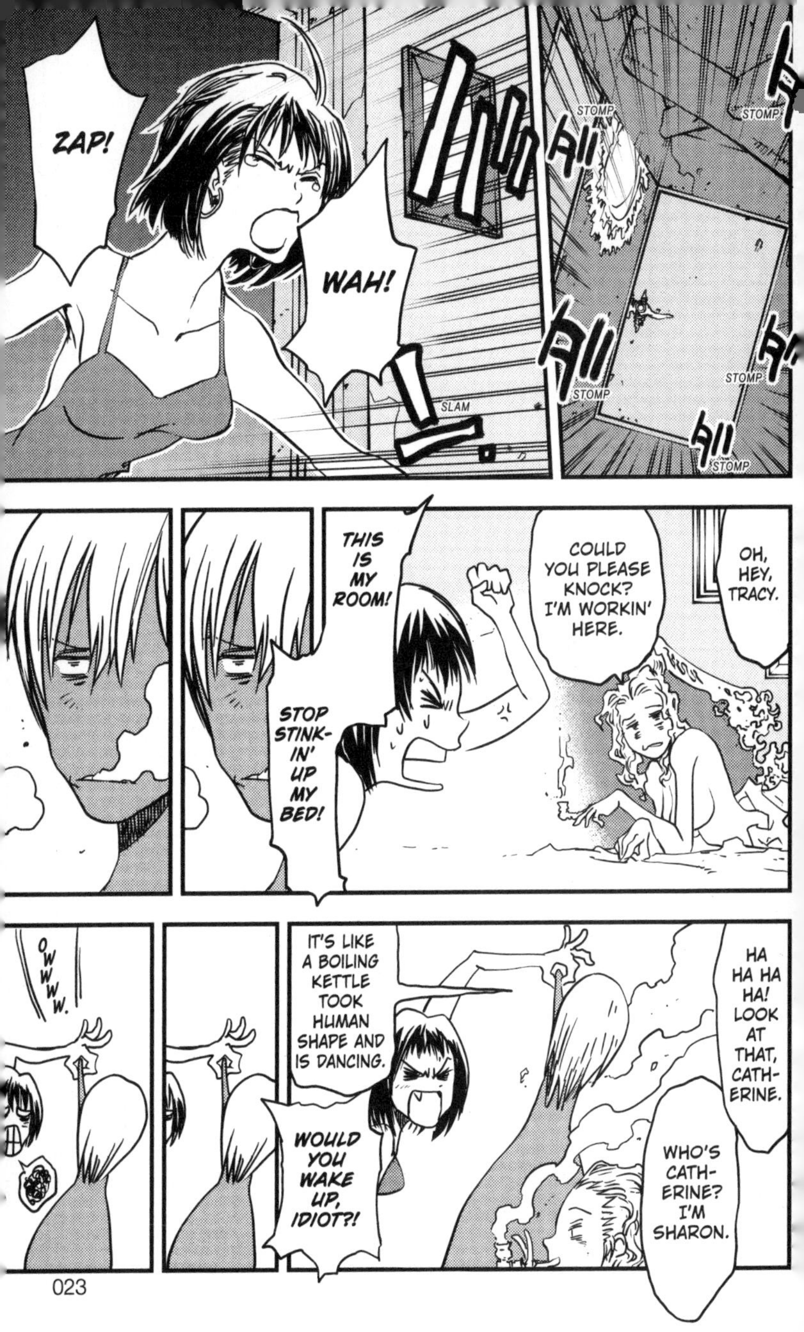
STOMP
STOMP
STOMP
STOMP
STOMP
WAH!
ZAP!
SLAM
OH, HEY, TRACY.
COULD YOU PLEASE KNOCK? I'M WORKIN' HERE.
THIS IS MY ROOM!
STOP STINKIN' UP MY BED!
HA HA HA HA! LOOK AT THAT, CATHERINE.
WHO'S CATHERINE? I'M SHARON.
IT'S LIKE A BOILING KETTLE TOOK HUMAN SHAPE AND IS DANCING.
WOULD YOU WAKE UP, IDIOT?!
OWWWW.

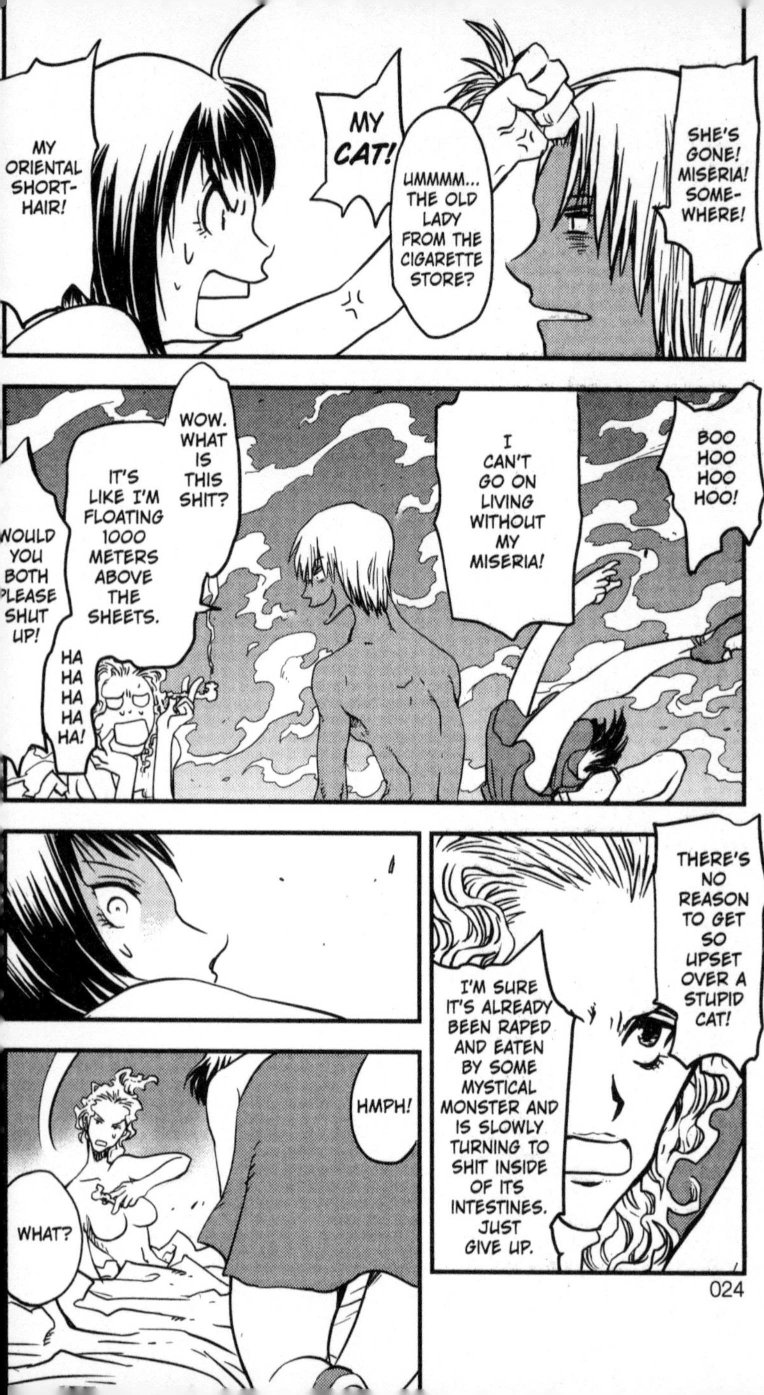
SHE'S GONE! MISERIA! SOME-WHERE!
UMMMM... THE OLD LADY FROM THE CIGARETTE STORE?
MY CAT!
MY ORIENTAL SHORT-HAIR!
BOO HOO HOO HOO!
I CAN'T GO ON LIVING WITHOUT MY MISERIA!
WOW. WHAT IS THIS SHIT?
IT'S LIKE I'M FLOATING 1000 METERS ABOVE THE SHEETS.
HA HA HA HA HA HA!
WOULD YOU BOTH PLEASE SHUT UP!
THERE'S NO REASON TO GET SO UPSET OVER A STUPID CAT!
I'M SURE IT'S ALREADY BEEN RAPED AND EATEN BY SOME MYSTICAL MONSTER AND IS SLOWLY TURNING TO SHIT INSIDE OF ITS INTESTINES. JUST GIVE UP.
HMPH!
WHAT?

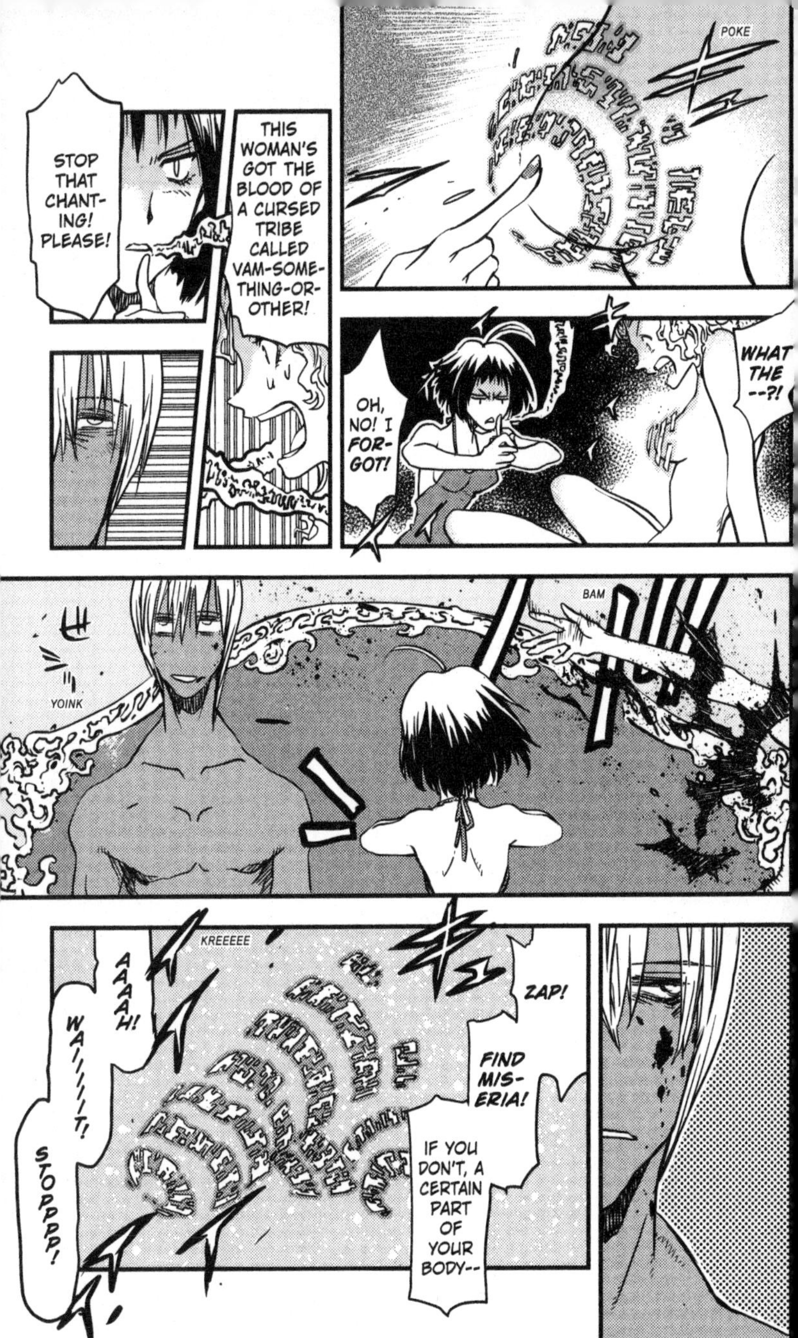

POKE
WHAT THE --?!
OH, NO! I FORGOT!
THIS WOMAN'S GOT THE BLOOD OF A CURSED TRIBE CALLED VAM-SOMETHING-OR-OTHER!
STOP THAT CHANTING! PLEASE!
BAM
YOINK
ZAP!
KREEEEE
FIND MISERIA!
IF YOU DON'T, A CERTAIN PART OF YOUR BODY--
AAAAH!
WAIIIIIT!
STOPPPP!

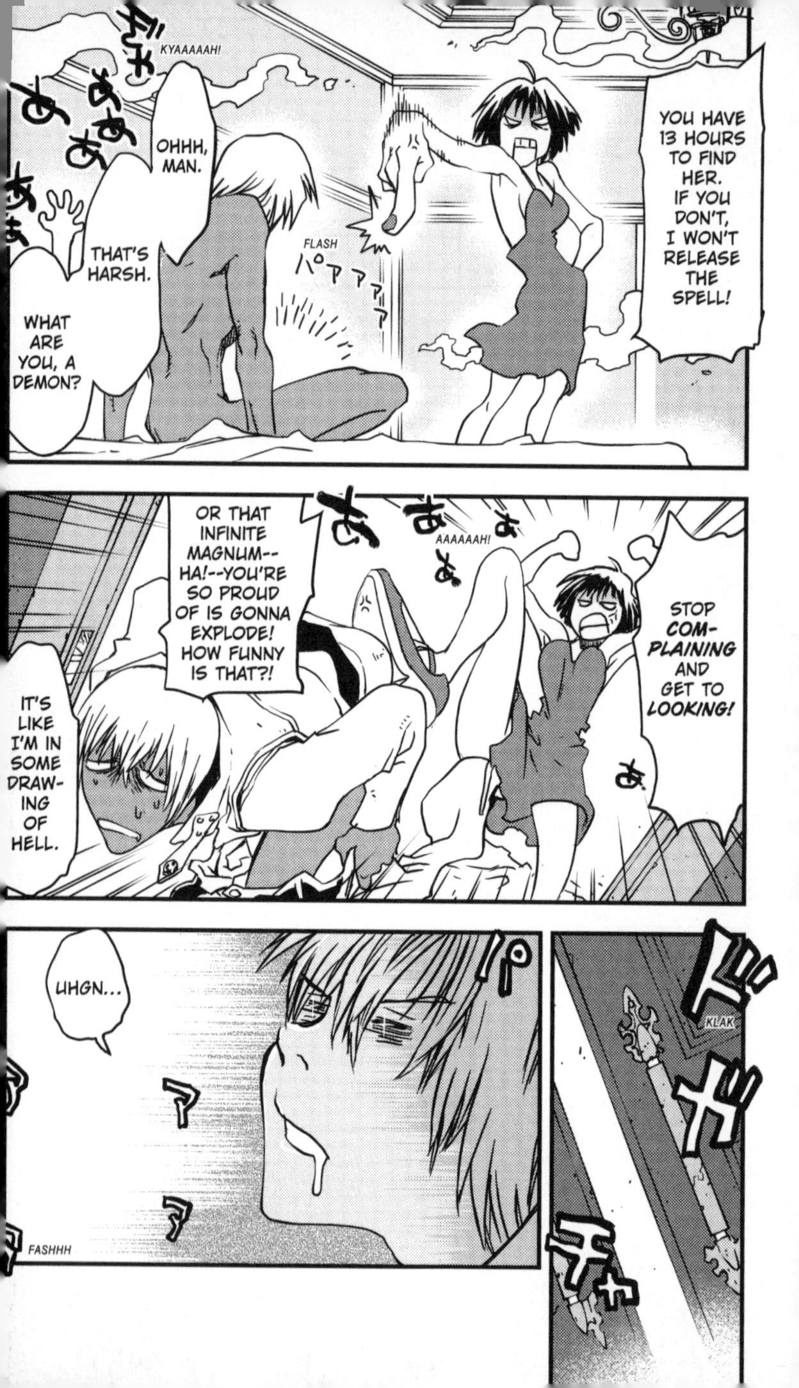
YOU HAVE 13 HOURS TO FIND HER. IF YOU DON'T, I WON'T RELEASE THE SPELL!
FLASH
OHHH, MAN.
THAT'S HARSH.
KYAAAAAH!
WHAT ARE YOU, A DEMON?
STOP COMPLAINING AND GET TO LOOKING!
AAAAAAH!
OR THAT INFINITE MAGNUM--HA!--YOU'RE SO PROUD OF IS GONNA EXPLODE! HOW FUNNY IS THAT?!
IT'S LIKE I'M IN SOME DRAWING OF HELL.
KLAK
UHGN...
FASHHH

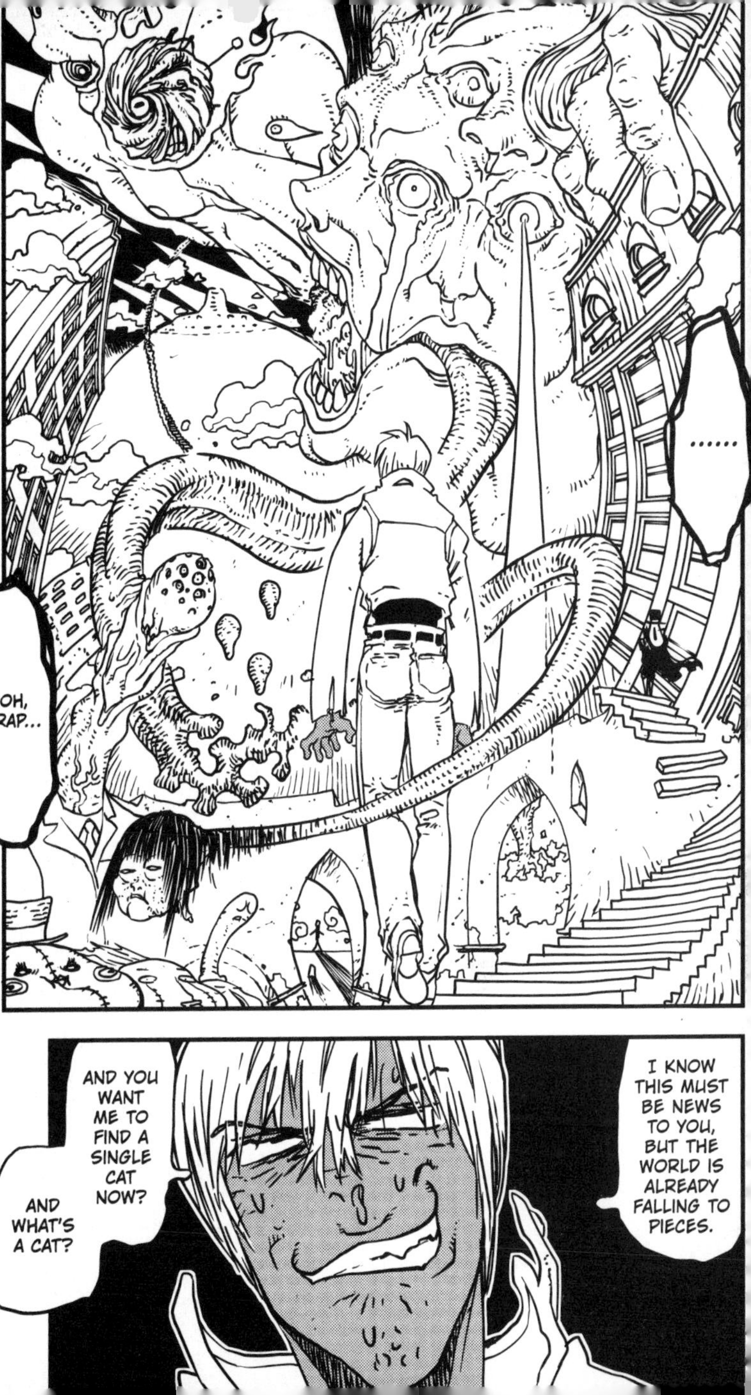
......
OH, CRAP...
I KNOW THIS MUST BE NEWS TO YOU, BUT THE WORLD IS ALREADY FALLING TO PIECES.
AND YOU WANT ME TO FIND A SINGLE CAT NOW?
AND WHAT'S A CAT?

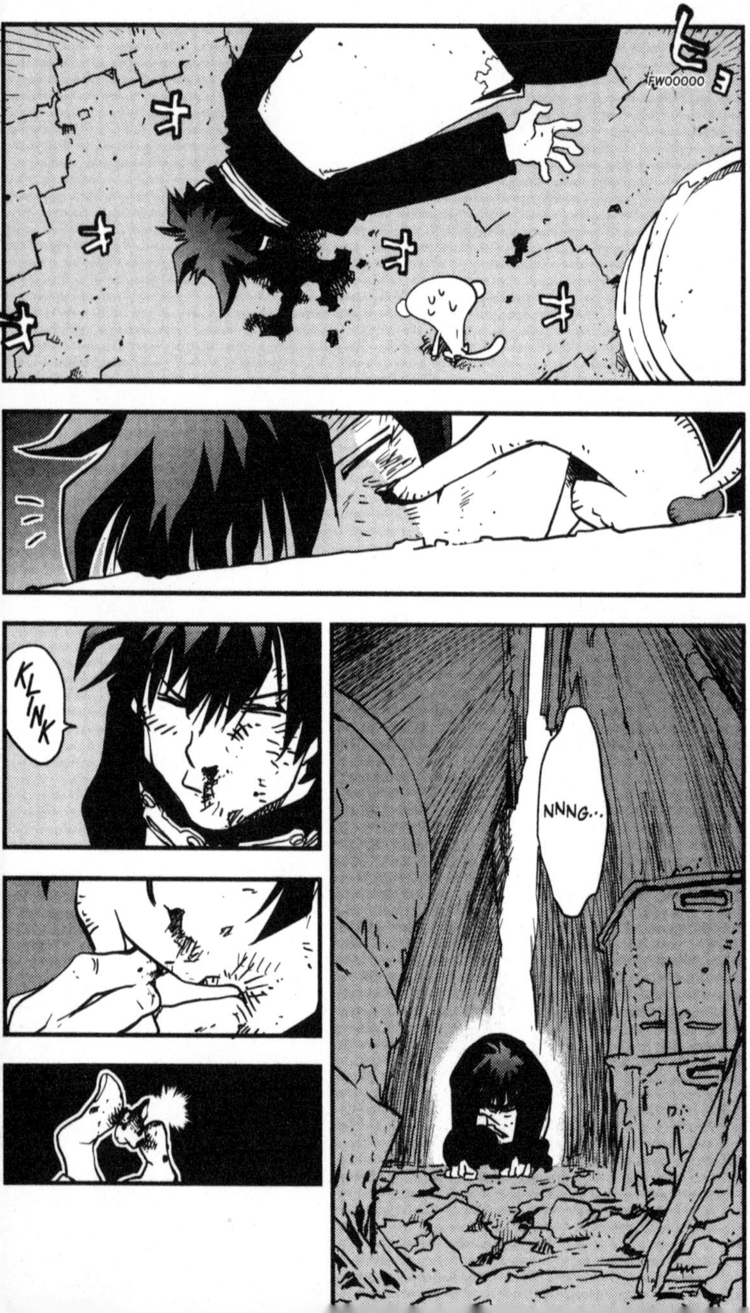
ヒョ
FWOOOOO
オ
オ
オ
オ
NNNG...
KLINK

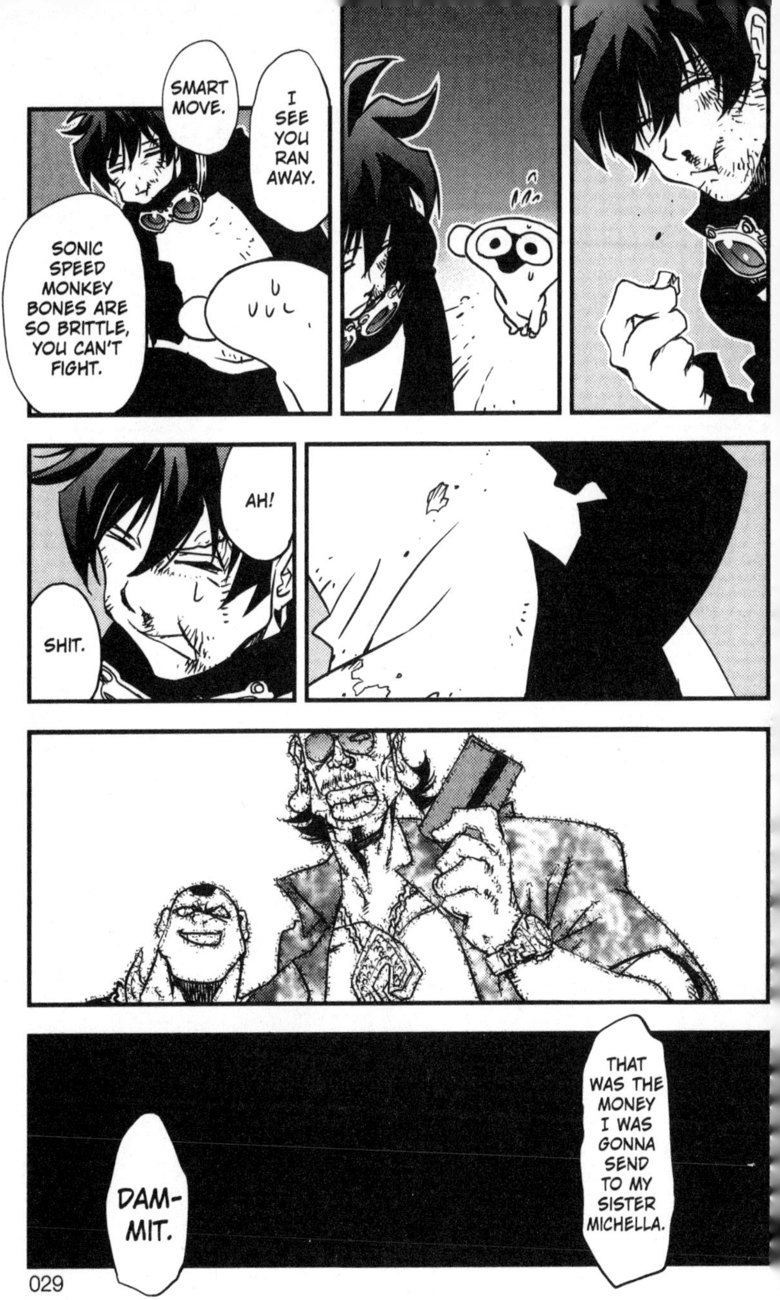
I SEE YOU RAN AWAY.
SMART MOVE.
SONIC SPEED MONKEY BONES ARE SO BRITTLE, YOU CAN'T FIGHT.
AH!
SHIT.
THAT WAS THE MONEY I WAS GONNA SEND TO MY SISTER MICHELLA.
DAM-MIT.

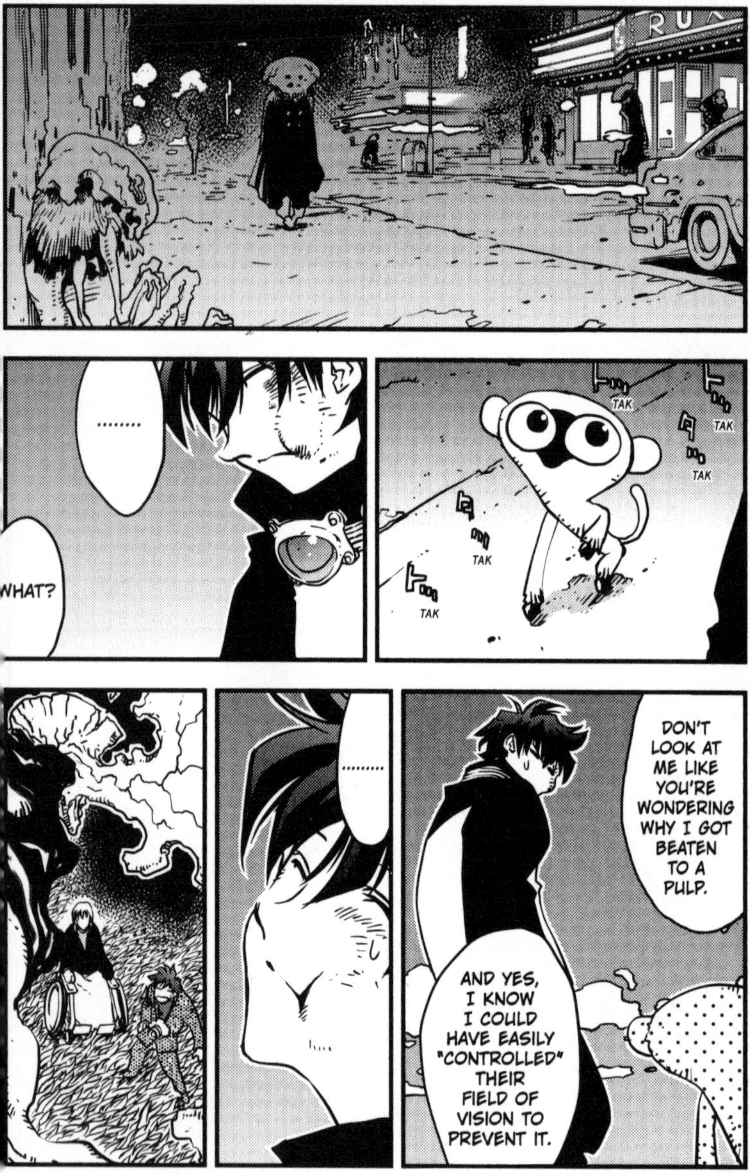
TAK
TAK
TAK
TAK
TAK
....
WHAT?
DON'T LOOK AT ME LIKE YOU'RE WONDERING WHY I GOT BEATEN TO A PULP.
AND YES, I KNOW I COULD HAVE EASILY "CONTROLLED" THEIR FIELD OF VISION TO PREVENT IT.
....

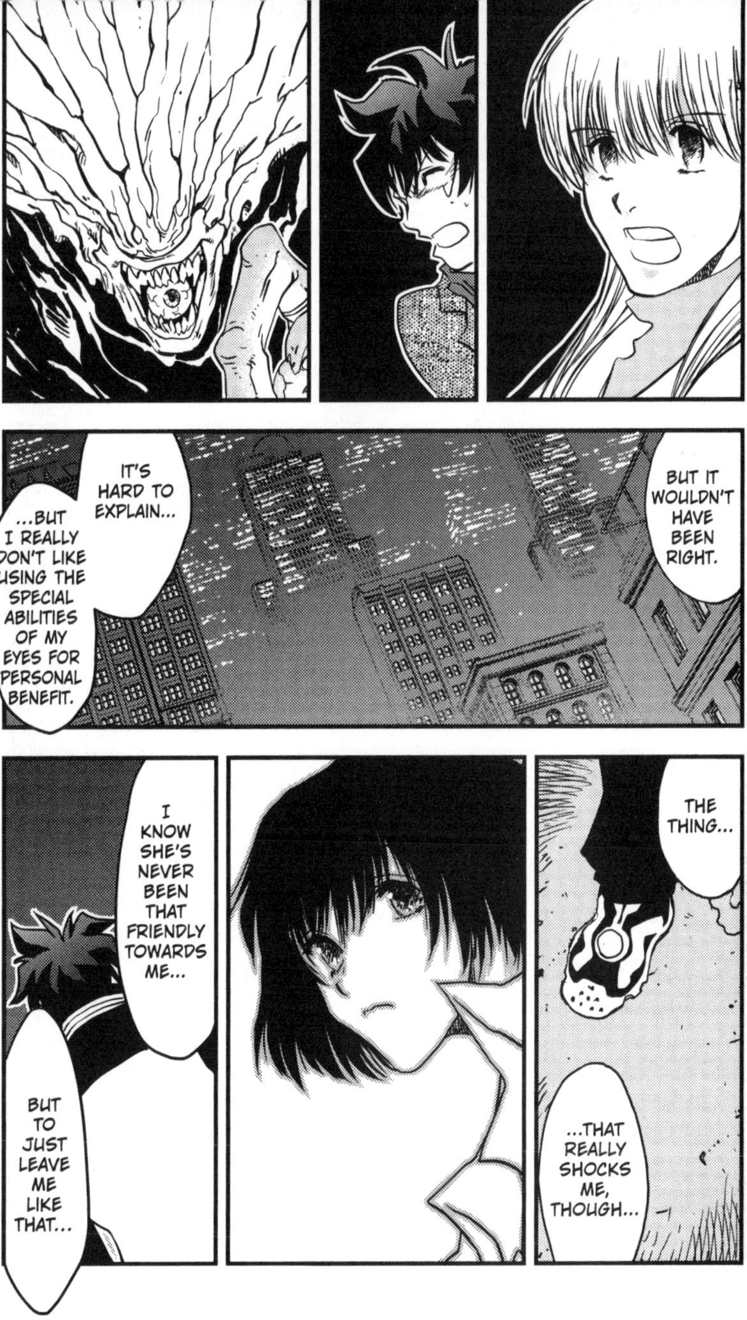
BUT IT WOULDN'T HAVE BEEN RIGHT.
IT'S HARD TO EXPLAIN...
...BUT I REALLY DON'T LIKE USING THE SPECIAL ABILITIES OF MY EYES FOR PERSONAL BENEFIT.
THE THING...
...THAT REALLY SHOCKS ME, THOUGH...
I KNOW SHE'S NEVER BEEN THAT FRIENDLY TOWARDS ME...
BUT TO JUST LEAVE ME LIKE THAT...

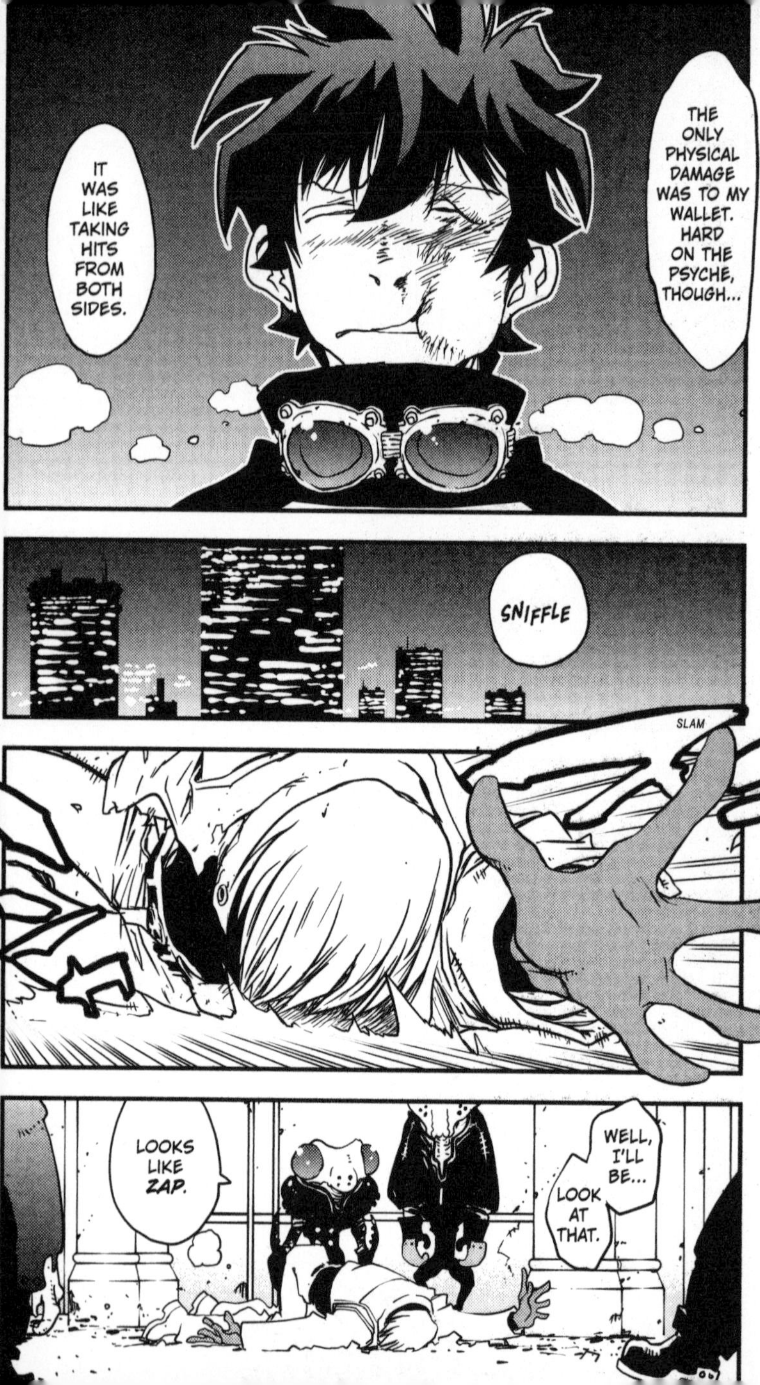
THE ONLY PHYSICAL DAMAGE WAS TO MY WALLET. HARD ON THE PSYCHE, THOUGH...
IT WAS LIKE TAKING HITS FROM BOTH SIDES.
SNIFFLE
SLAM
WELL, I'LL BE...
LOOK AT THAT.
LOOKS LIKE ZAP.

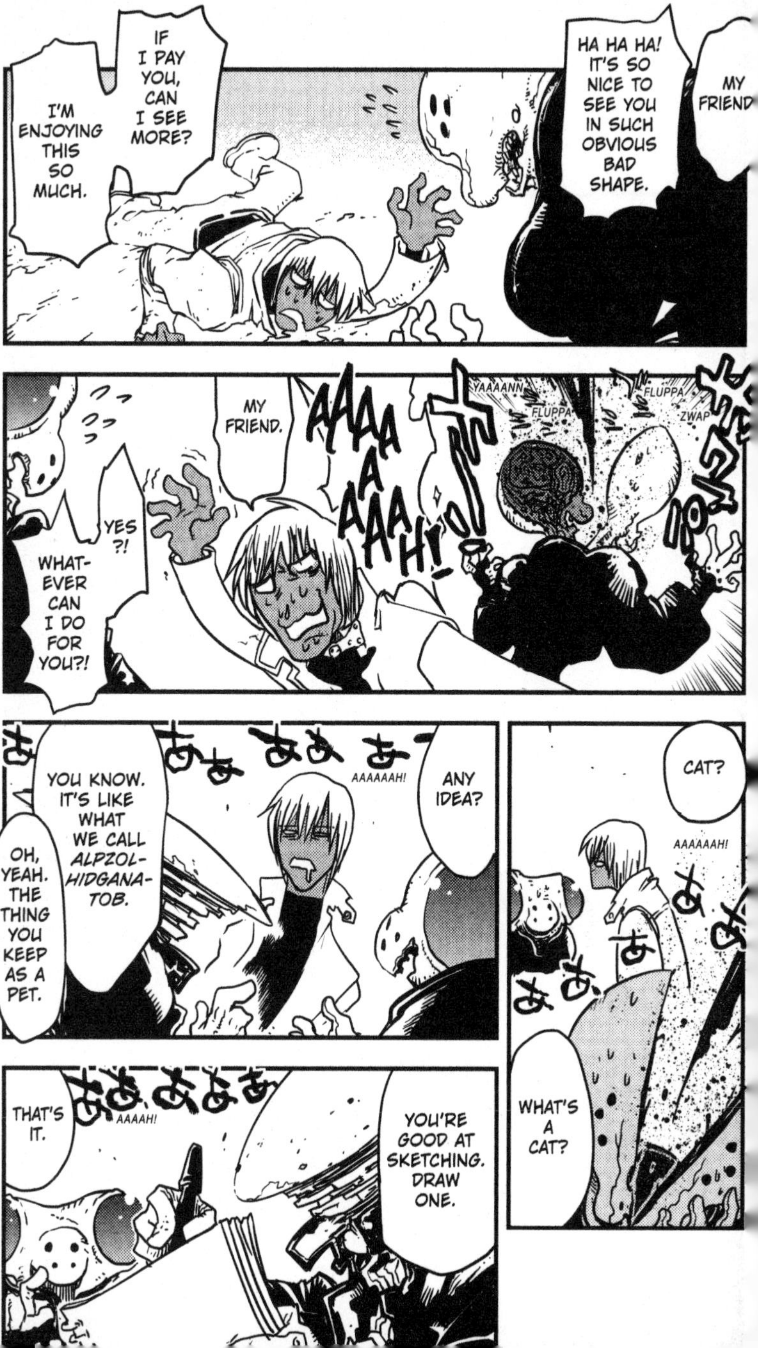
MY FRIEND
HA HA HA! IT'S SO NICE TO SEE YOU IN SUCH OBVIOUS BAD SHAPE.
IF I PAY YOU, CAN I SEE MORE?
I'M ENJOYING THIS SO MUCH.
ZWAP
FLUPPA
FLUPPA
YAAAANN
AAAAAAAAAH!
MY FRIEND.
YES?!
WHAT-EVER CAN I DO FOR YOU?!
CAT?
AAAAAAH!
WHAT'S A CAT?
ANY IDEA?
AAAAAAH!
YOU KNOW. IT'S LIKE WHAT WE CALL ALPZOL-HIDGANA-TOB.
OH, YEAH. THE THING YOU KEEP AS A PET.
YOU'RE GOOD AT SKETCHING. DRAW ONE.
AAAAH!
THAT'S IT.

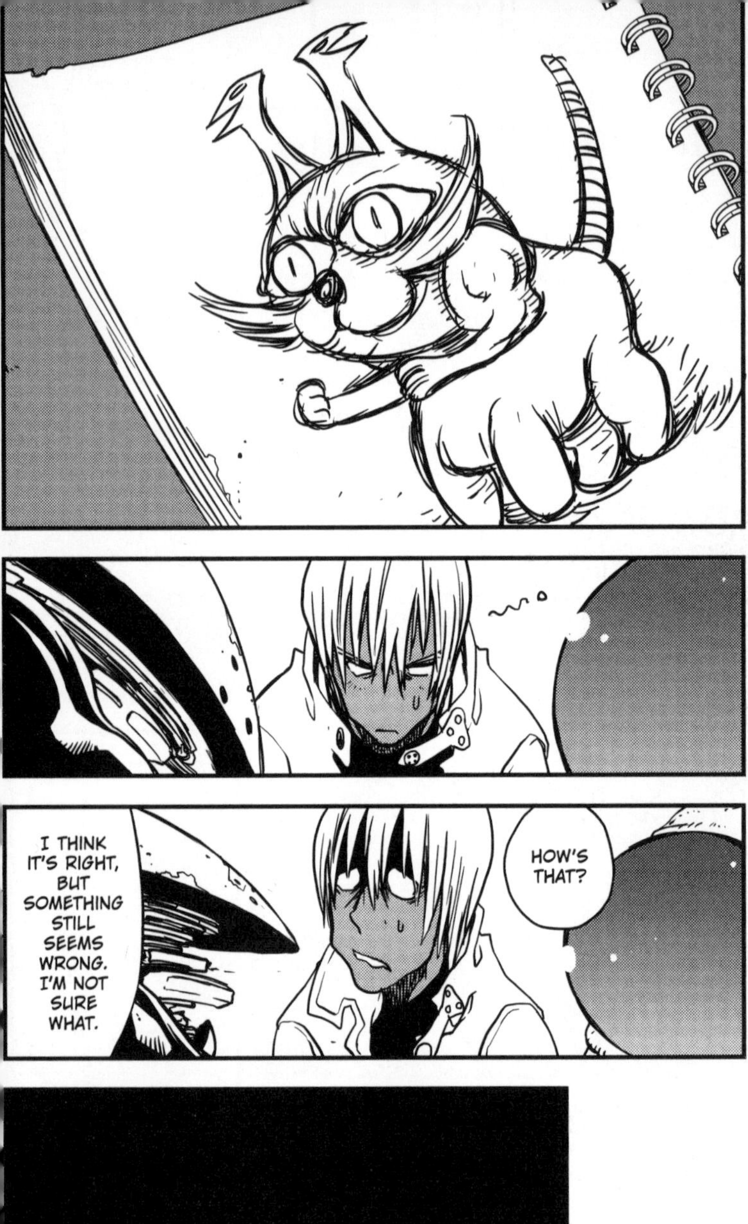
HOW'S THAT?
I THINK IT'S RIGHT, BUT SOMETHING STILL SEEMS WRONG. I'M NOT SURE WHAT.

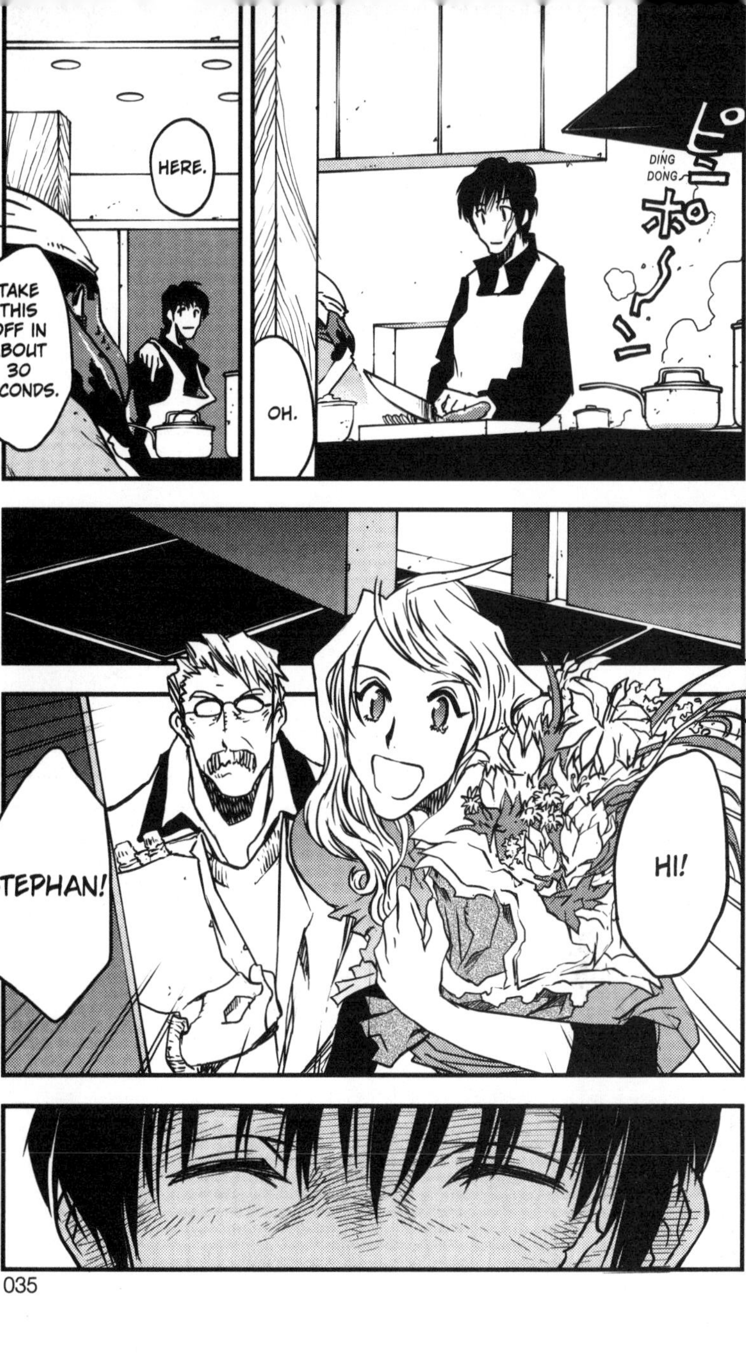
ピンポーン
DING DONG
OH.
HERE.
TAKE THIS OFF IN ABOUT 30 SECONDS.
HI!
STEPHAN!

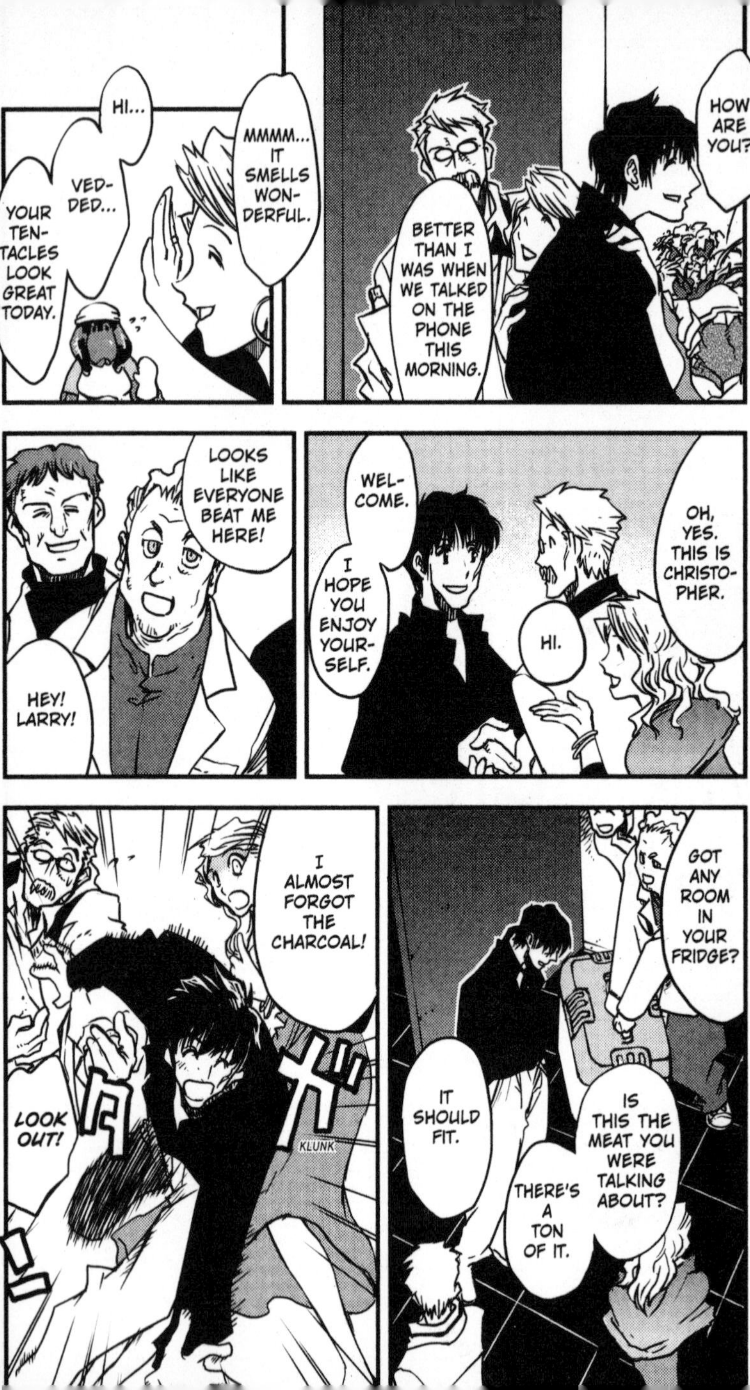
HOW ARE YOU?
BETTER THAN I WAS WHEN WE TALKED ON THE PHONE THIS MORNING.
MMMM... IT SMELLS WONDERFUL.
HI...
VED-DED...
YOUR TEN-TACLES LOOK GREAT TODAY.
OH, YES. THIS IS CHRISTOPHER.
WEL-COME.
HI.
I HOPE YOU ENJOY YOUR-SELF.
LOOKS LIKE EVERYONE BEAT ME HERE!
HEY! LARRY!
GOT ANY ROOM IN YOUR FRIDGE?
IS THIS THE MEAT YOU WERE TALKING ABOUT?
IT SHOULD FIT.
THERE'S A TON OF IT.
I ALMOST FORGOT THE CHARCOAL!
KLUNK
LOOK OUT!

[redacted]

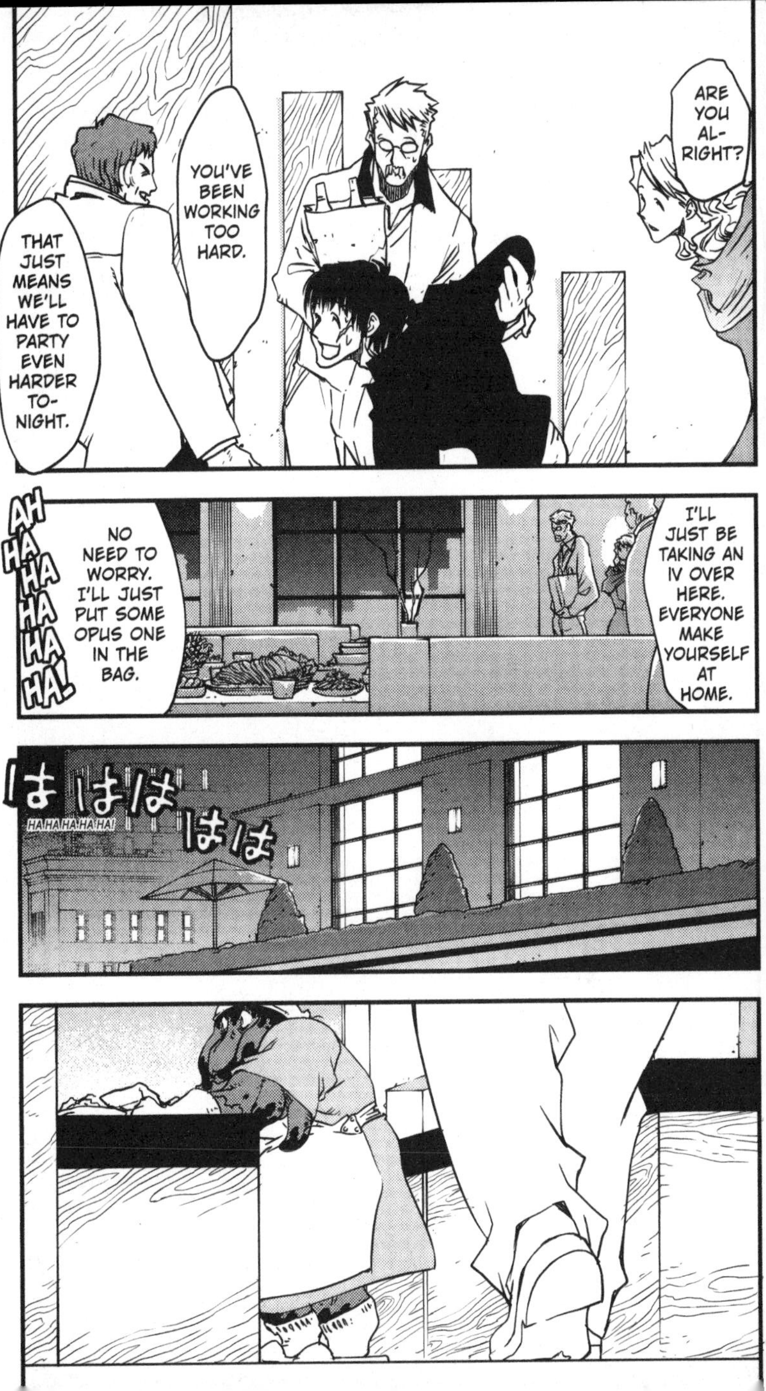
ARE YOU ALRIGHT?
YOU'VE BEEN WORKING TOO HARD.
THAT JUST MEANS WE'LL HAVE TO PARTY EVEN HARDER TONIGHT.
I'LL JUST BE TAKING AN IV OVER HERE. EVERYONE MAKE YOURSELF AT HOME.
NO NEED TO WORRY. I'LL JUST PUT SOME OPUS ONE IN THE BAG.
AH HA HA HA HA HA!
ははははは
HA HA HA HA HA!

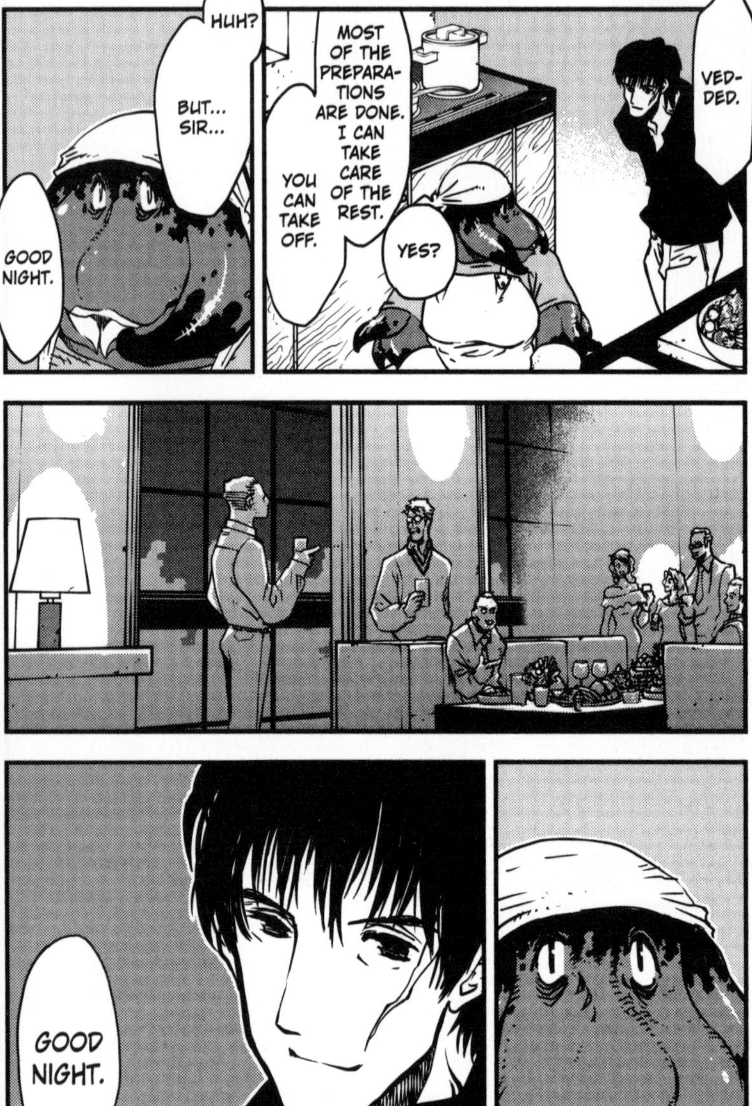
VED-DED.
YES?
MOST OF THE PREPARATIONS ARE DONE. I CAN TAKE CARE OF THE REST.
YOU CAN TAKE OFF.
HUH?
BUT... SIR...
GOOD NIGHT.
GOOD NIGHT.

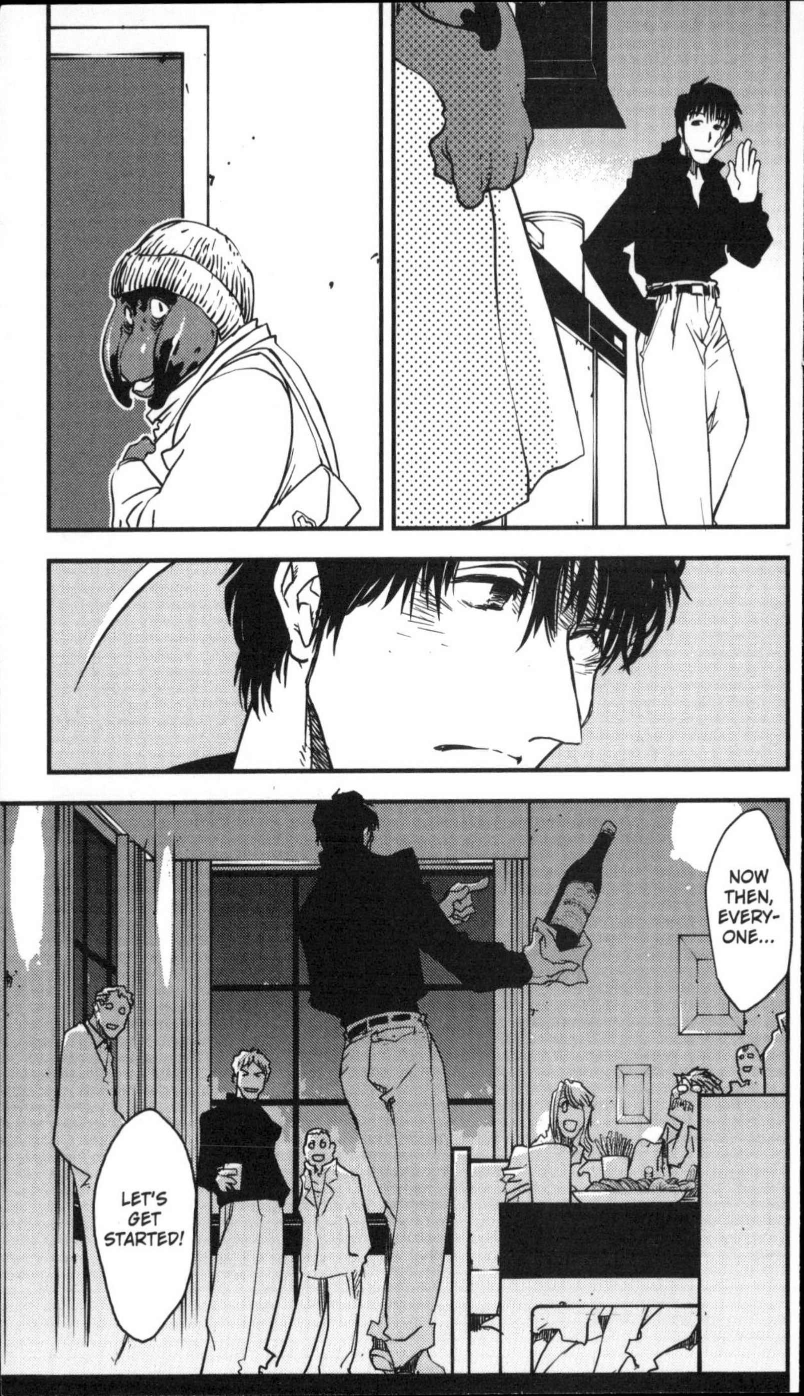
NOW THEN, EVERY-ONE...
LET'S GET STARTED!

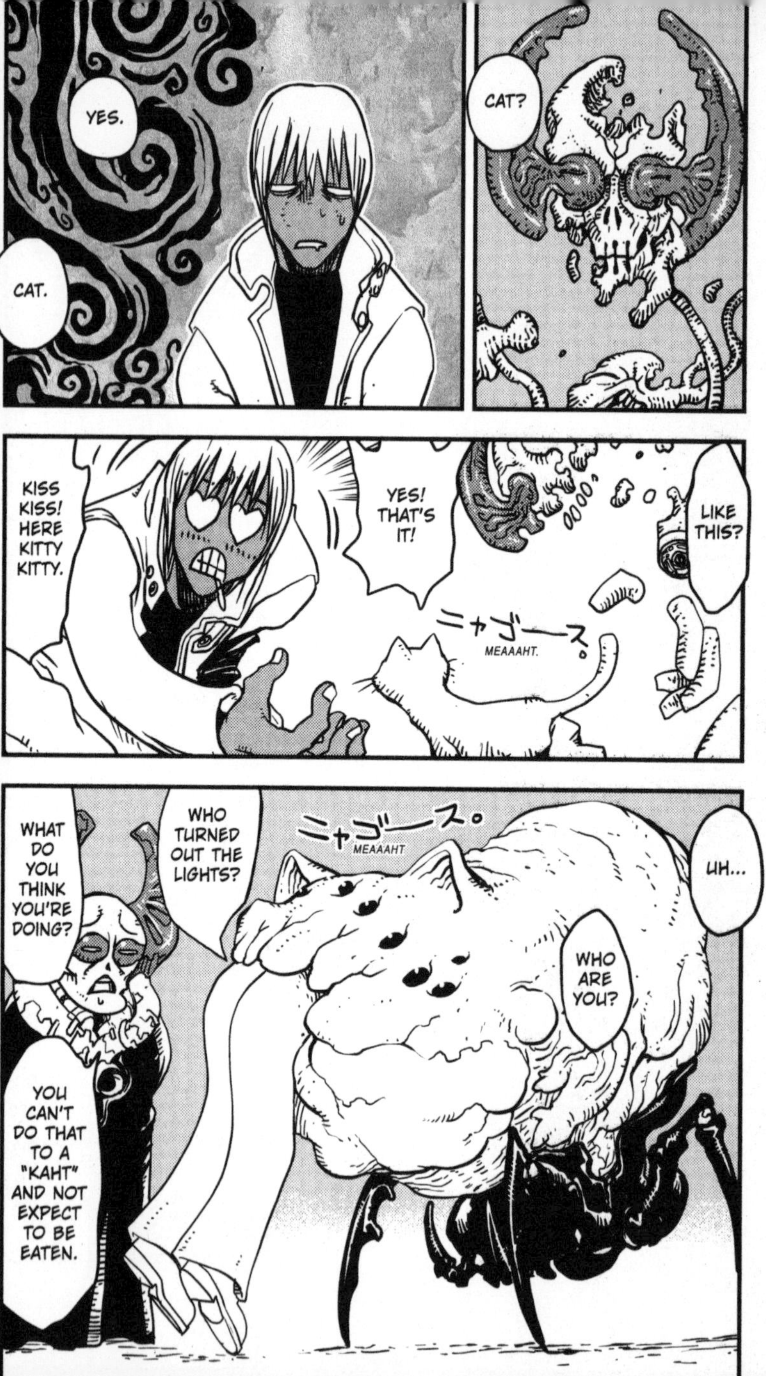
CAT?
YES.
CAT.
LIKE THIS?
YES! THAT'S IT!
KISS KISS! HERE KITTY KITTY.
ニャゴーース。
MEAAAHT.
UH...
WHO ARE YOU?
ニャゴーース。
MEAAAHT
WHO TURNED OUT THE LIGHTS?
WHAT DO YOU THINK YOU'RE DOING?
YOU CAN'T DO THAT TO A "KAHT" AND NOT EXPECT TO BE EATEN.

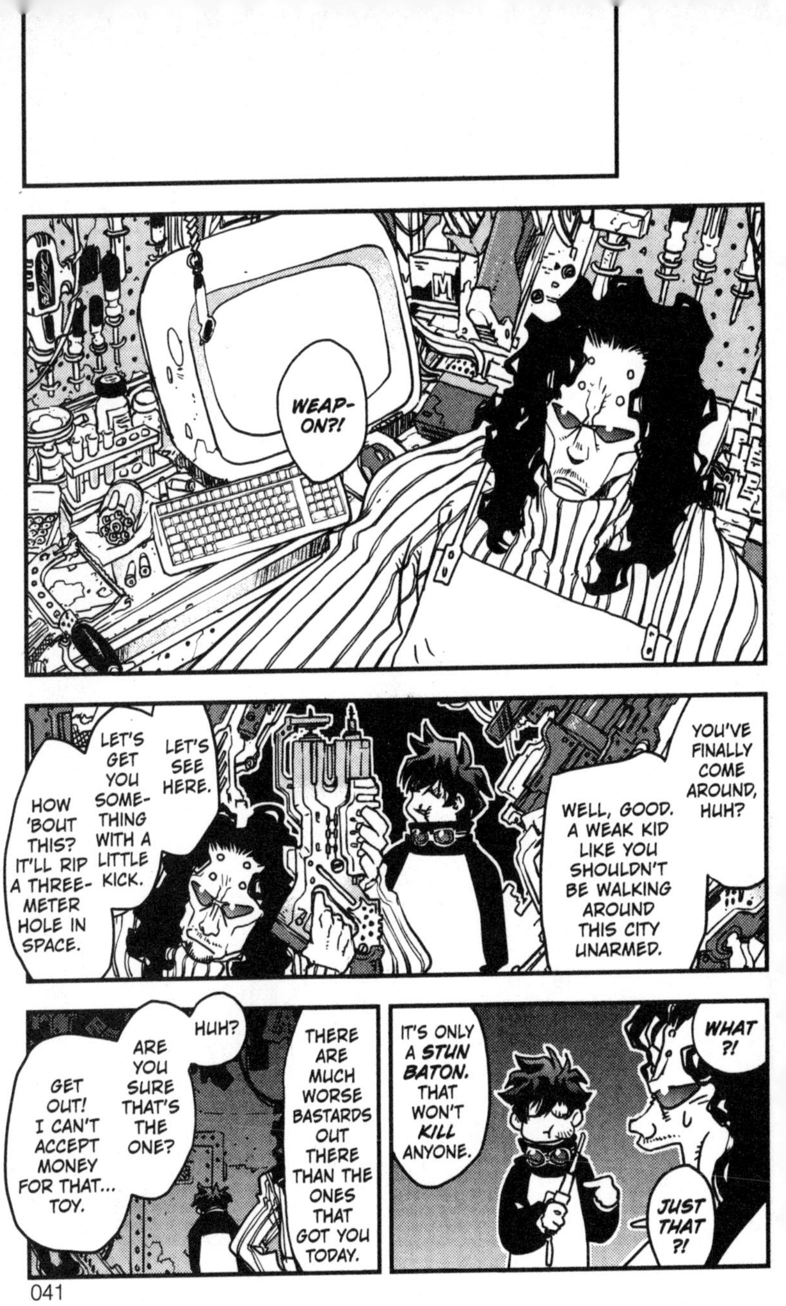
WEAP-ON?!
YOU'VE FINALLY COME AROUND, HUH?
WELL, GOOD. A WEAK KID LIKE YOU SHOULDN'T BE WALKING AROUND THIS CITY UNARMED.
LET'S SEE HERE.
LET'S GET YOU SOMETHING WITH A LITTLE KICK.
HOW 'BOUT THIS? IT'LL RIP A THREE-METER HOLE IN SPACE.
WHAT ?!
IT'S ONLY A **STUN BATON.** THAT WON'T ***KILL*** ANYONE.
JUST THAT ?!
THERE ARE MUCH WORSE BASTARDS OUT THERE THAN THE ONES THAT GOT YOU TODAY.
HUH?
ARE YOU SURE THAT'S THE ONE?
GET OUT! I CAN'T ACCEPT MONEY FOR THAT... TOY.

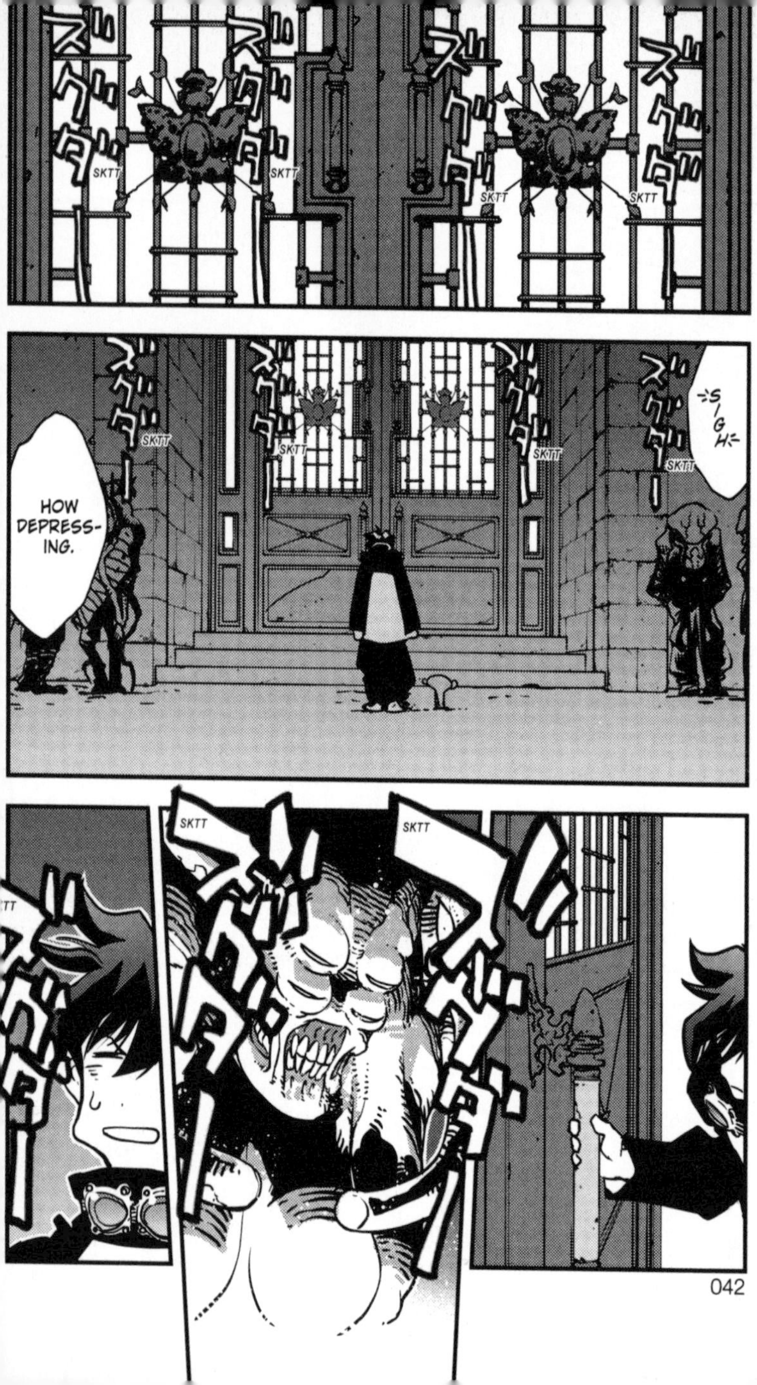
SKTT
SKTT
SKTT
SKTT
SIGH
SKTT
SKTT
SKTT
SKTT
HOW DEPRESSING.
SKTT
SKTT
SKTT

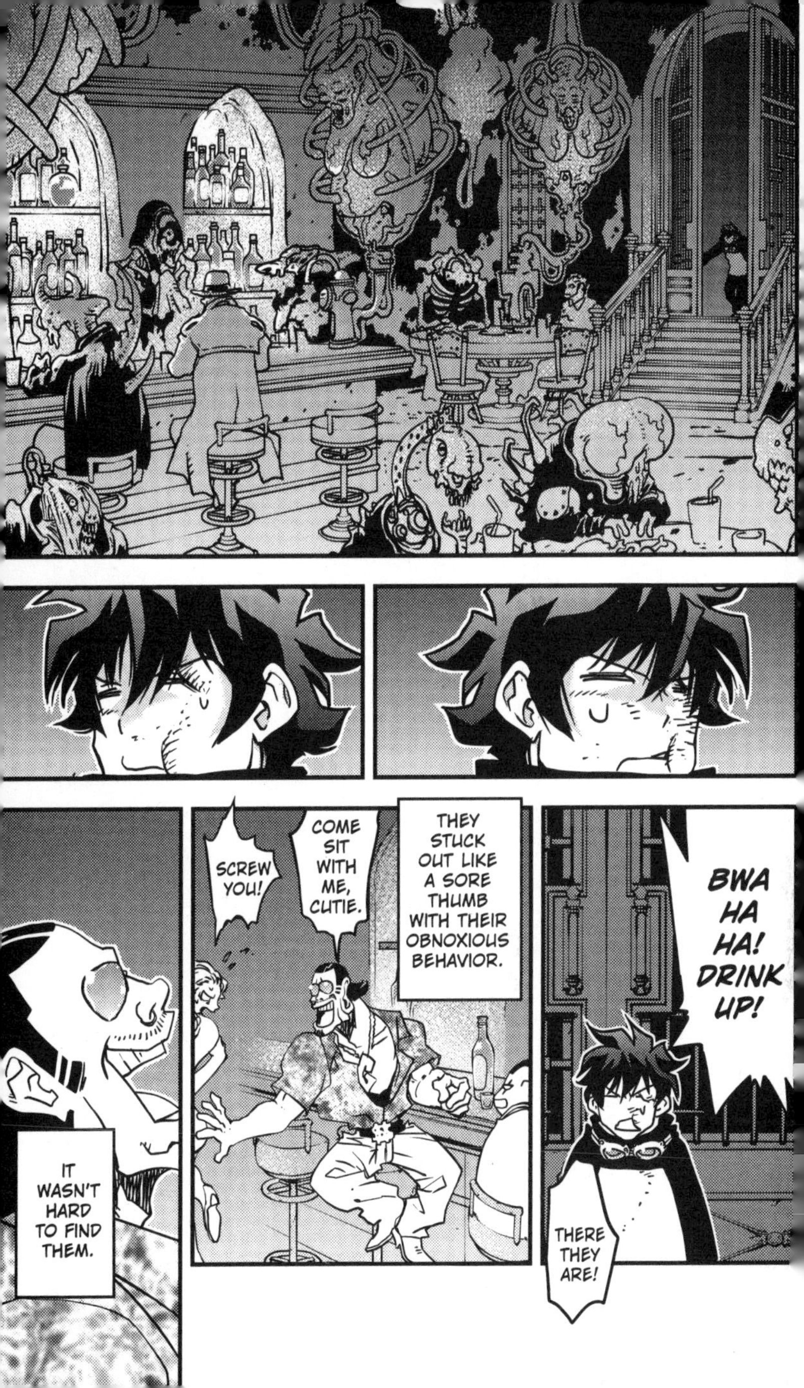
BWA HA HA! DRINK UP!
THERE THEY ARE!
THEY STUCK OUT LIKE A SORE THUMB WITH THEIR OBNOXIOUS BEHAVIOR.
COME SIT WITH ME, CUTIE.
SCREW YOU!
IT WASN'T HARD TO FIND THEM.

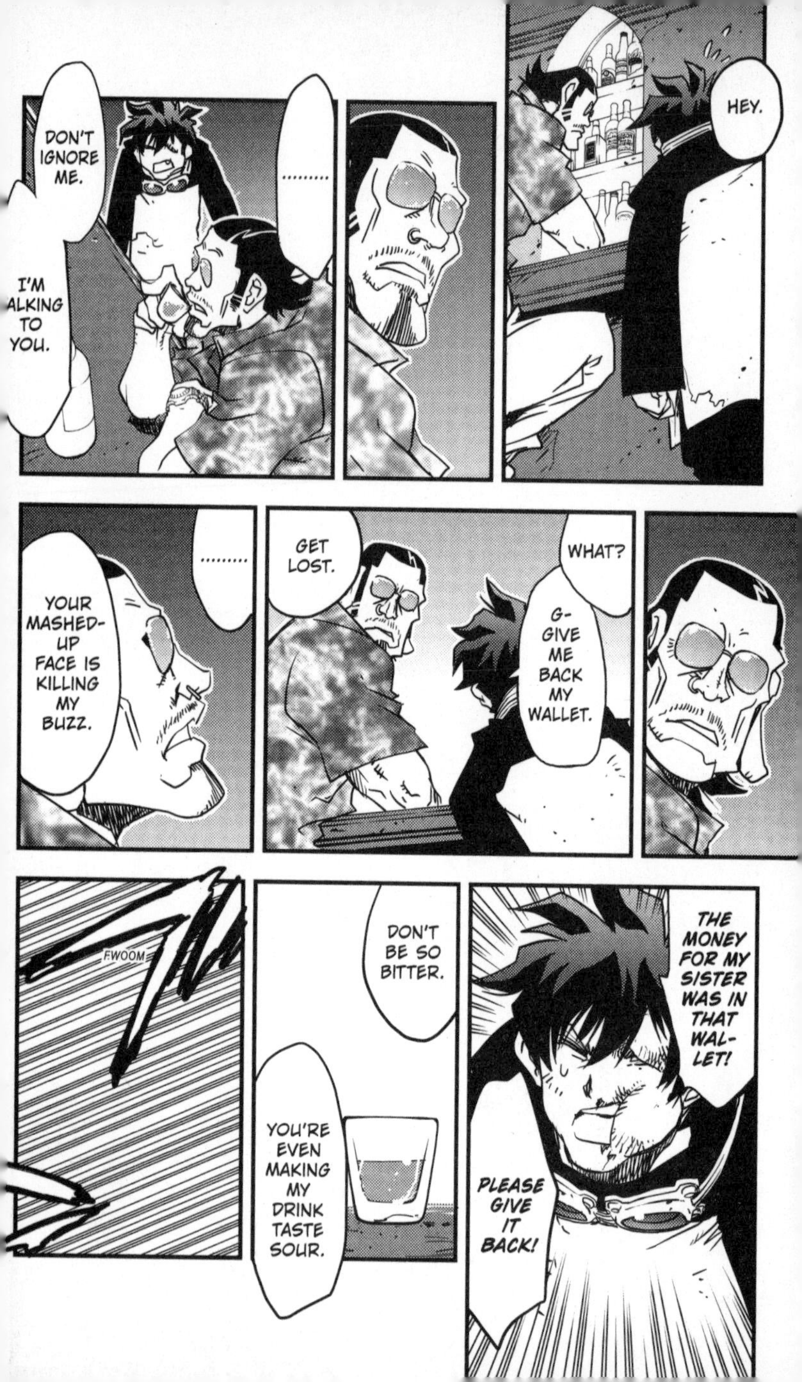
HEY.
....
DON'T IGNORE ME.
I'M ALKING TO YOU.
WHAT?
G-GIVE ME BACK MY WALLET.
GET LOST.
....
YOUR MASHED-UP FACE IS KILLING MY BUZZ.
THE MONEY FOR MY SISTER WAS IN THAT WAL-LET!
PLEASE GIVE IT BACK!
DON'T BE SO BITTER.
YOU'RE EVEN MAKING MY DRINK TASTE SOUR.
FWOOM

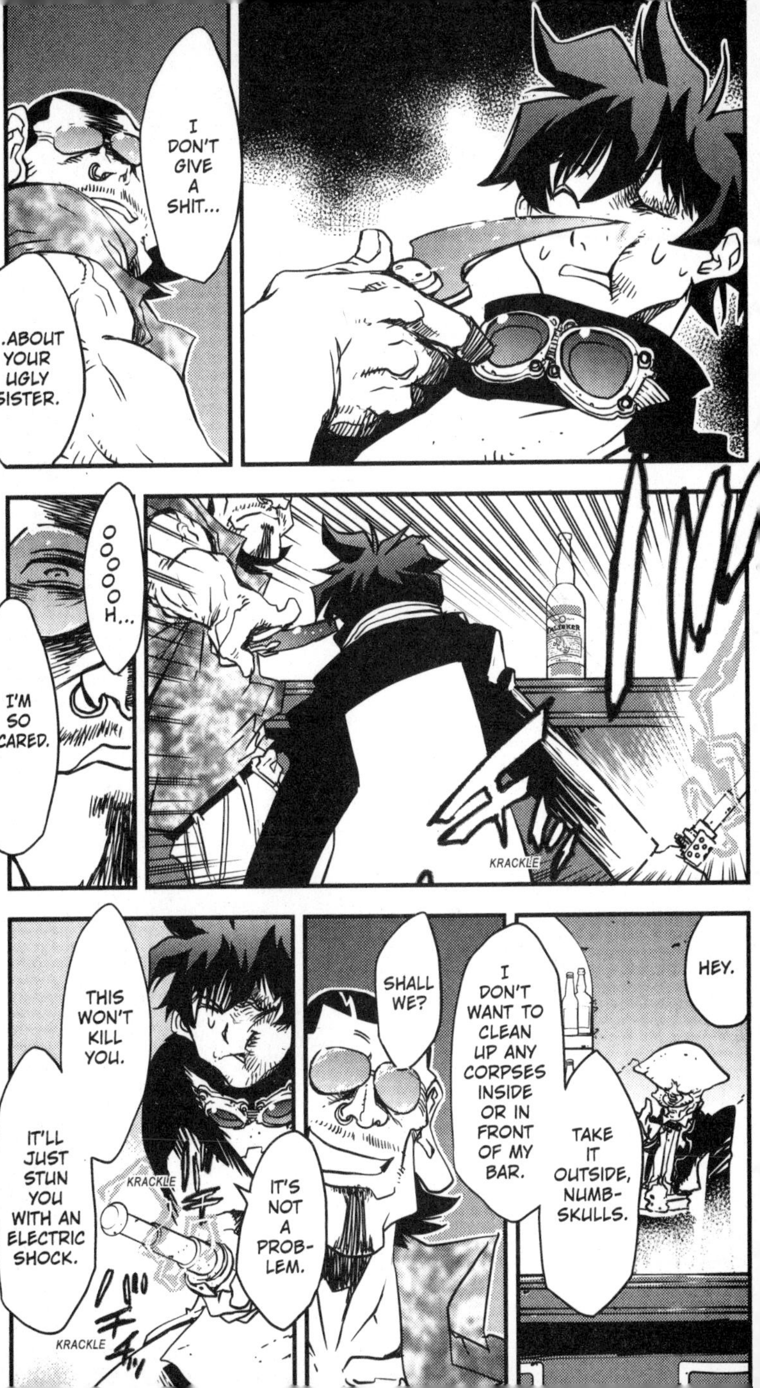
I DON'T GIVE A SHIT...
...ABOUT YOUR UGLY SISTER.
KRACKLE
OOOOOH...
I'M SO SCARED.
HEY.
I DON'T WANT TO CLEAN UP ANY CORPSES INSIDE OR IN FRONT OF MY BAR.
TAKE IT OUTSIDE, NUMB-SKULLS.
SHALL WE?
IT'S NOT A PROB-LEM.
THIS WON'T KILL YOU.
IT'LL JUST STUN YOU WITH AN ELECTRIC SHOCK.
KRACKLE
KRACKLE

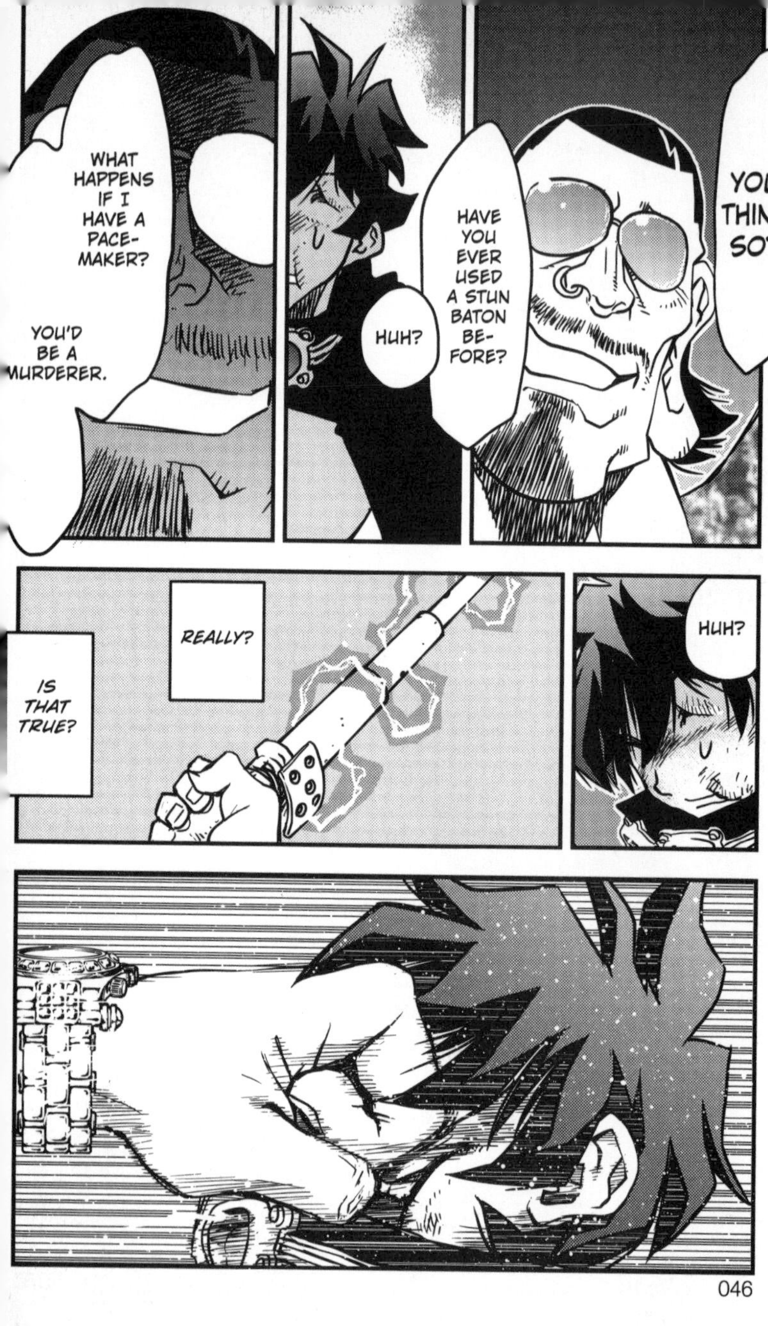
YOU THINK SO?
HAVE YOU EVER USED A STUN BATON BE-FORE?
HUH?
WHAT HAPPENS IF I HAVE A PACE-MAKER?
YOU'D BE A MURDERER.
HUH?
REALLY?
IS THAT TRUE?

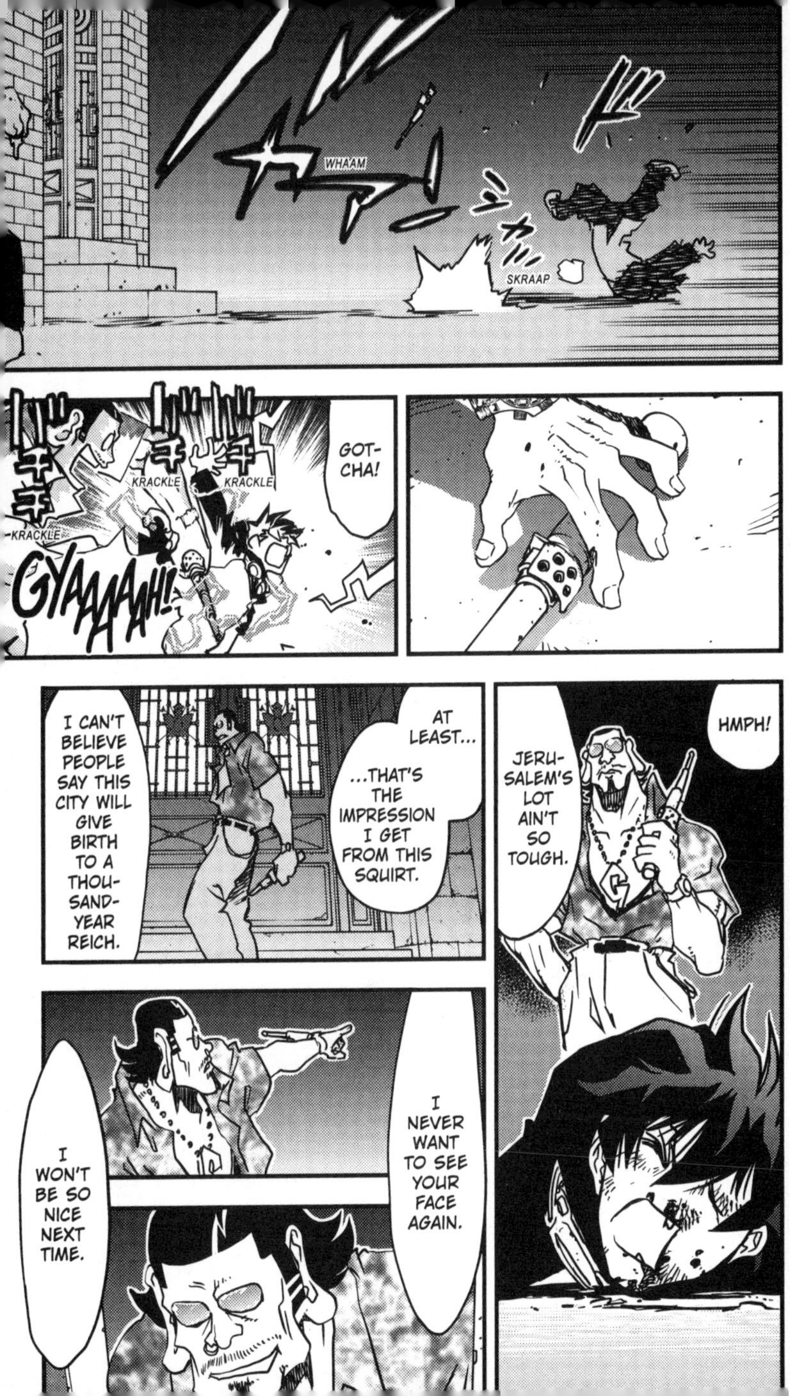
WHAAM
SKRAAP
GOT-CHA!
KRACKLE
KRACKLE
KRACKLE
GYAAAAAH!
HMPH!
JERU-SALEM'S LOT AIN'T SO TOUGH.
AT LEAST...
...THAT'S THE IMPRESSION I GET FROM THIS SQUIRT.
I CAN'T BELIEVE PEOPLE SAY THIS CITY WILL GIVE BIRTH TO A THOUSAND-YEAR REICH.
I NEVER WANT TO SEE YOUR FACE AGAIN.
I WON'T BE SO NICE NEXT TIME.

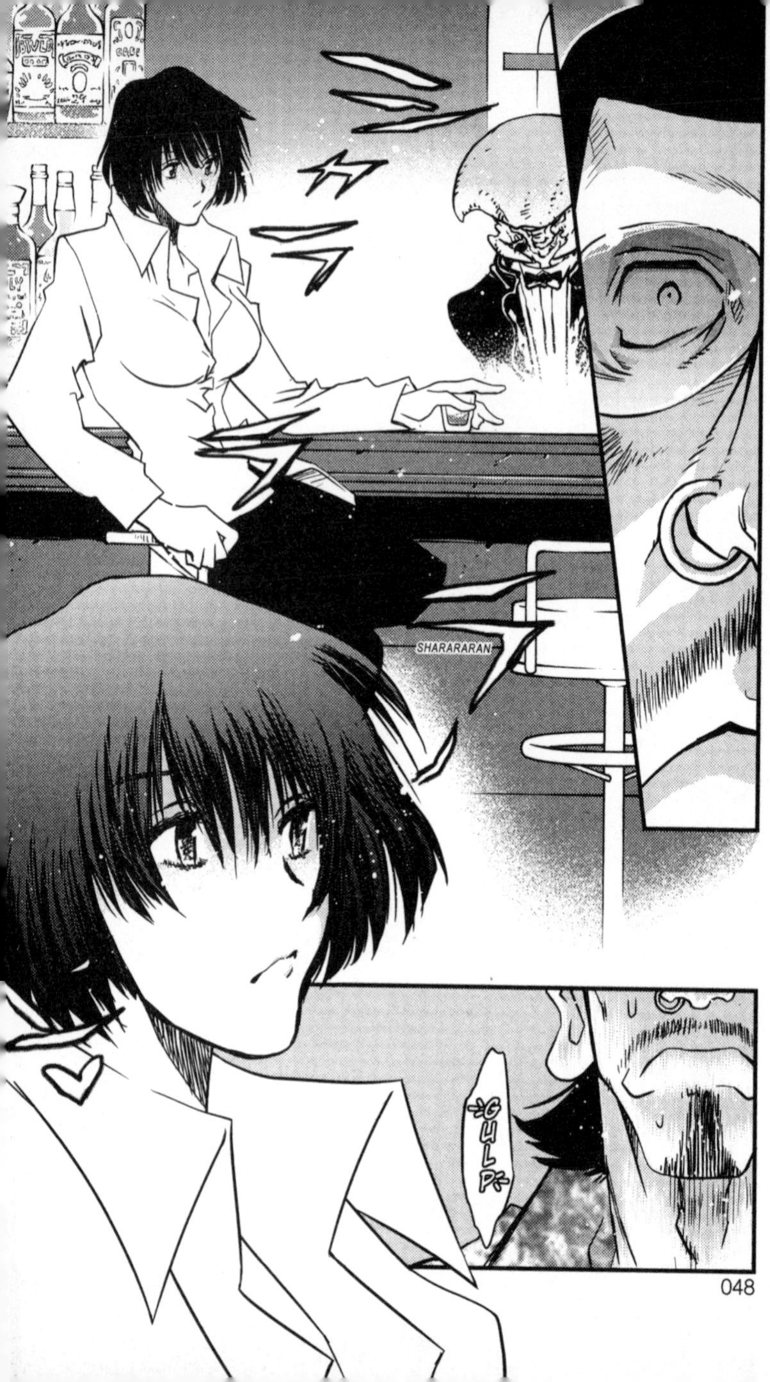
SHARARARAN
GULP

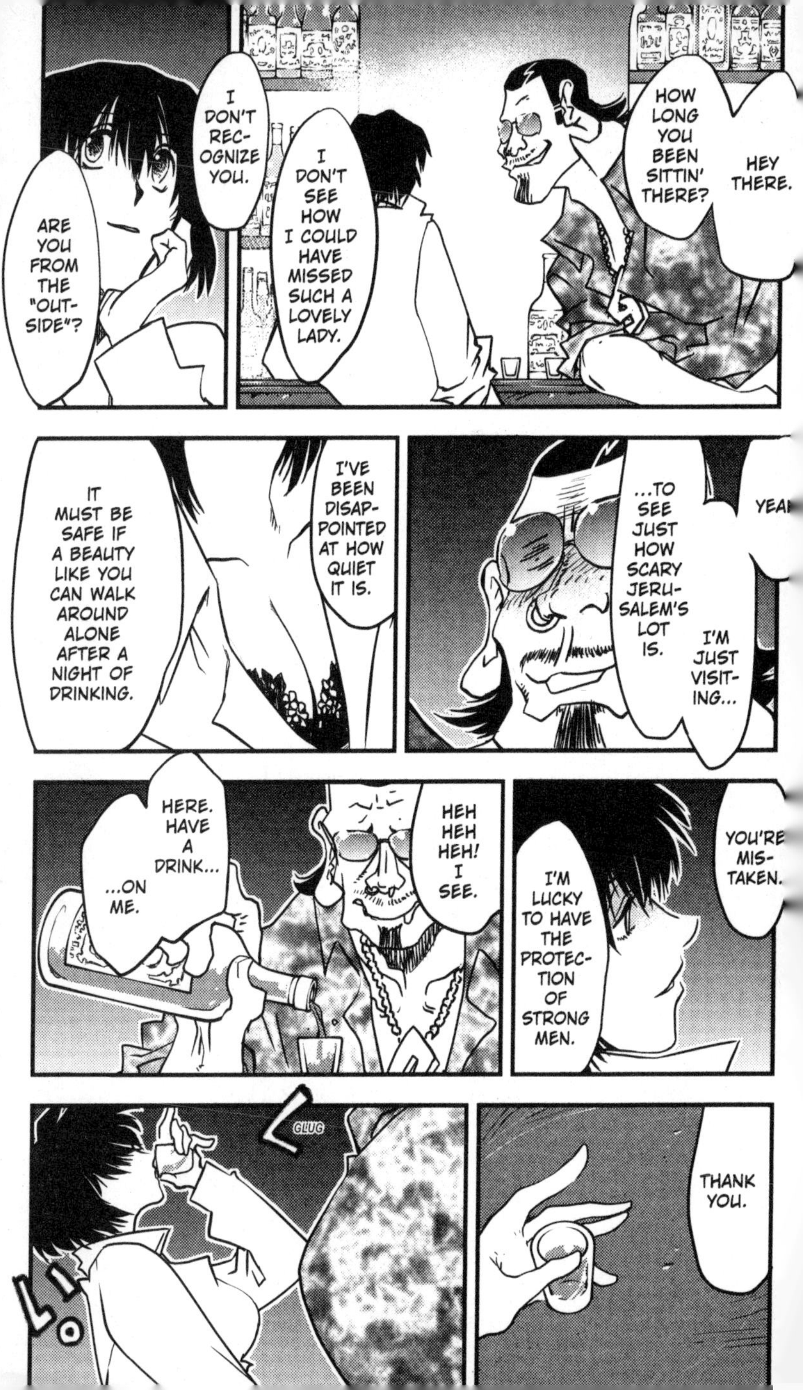
HEY THERE.
HOW LONG YOU BEEN SITTIN' THERE?
I DON'T SEE HOW I COULD HAVE MISSED SUCH A LOVELY LADY.
I DON'T RECOGNIZE YOU.
ARE YOU FROM THE "OUTSIDE"?
YEA
I'M JUST VISITING...
...TO SEE JUST HOW SCARY JERUSALEM'S LOT IS.
I'VE BEEN DISAPPOINTED AT HOW QUIET IT IS.
IT MUST BE SAFE IF A BEAUTY LIKE YOU CAN WALK AROUND ALONE AFTER A NIGHT OF DRINKING.
YOU'RE MISTAKEN.
I'M LUCKY TO HAVE THE PROTECTION OF STRONG MEN.
HEH HEH HEH! I SEE.
HERE. HAVE A DRINK...
...ON ME.
THANK YOU.
GLUG

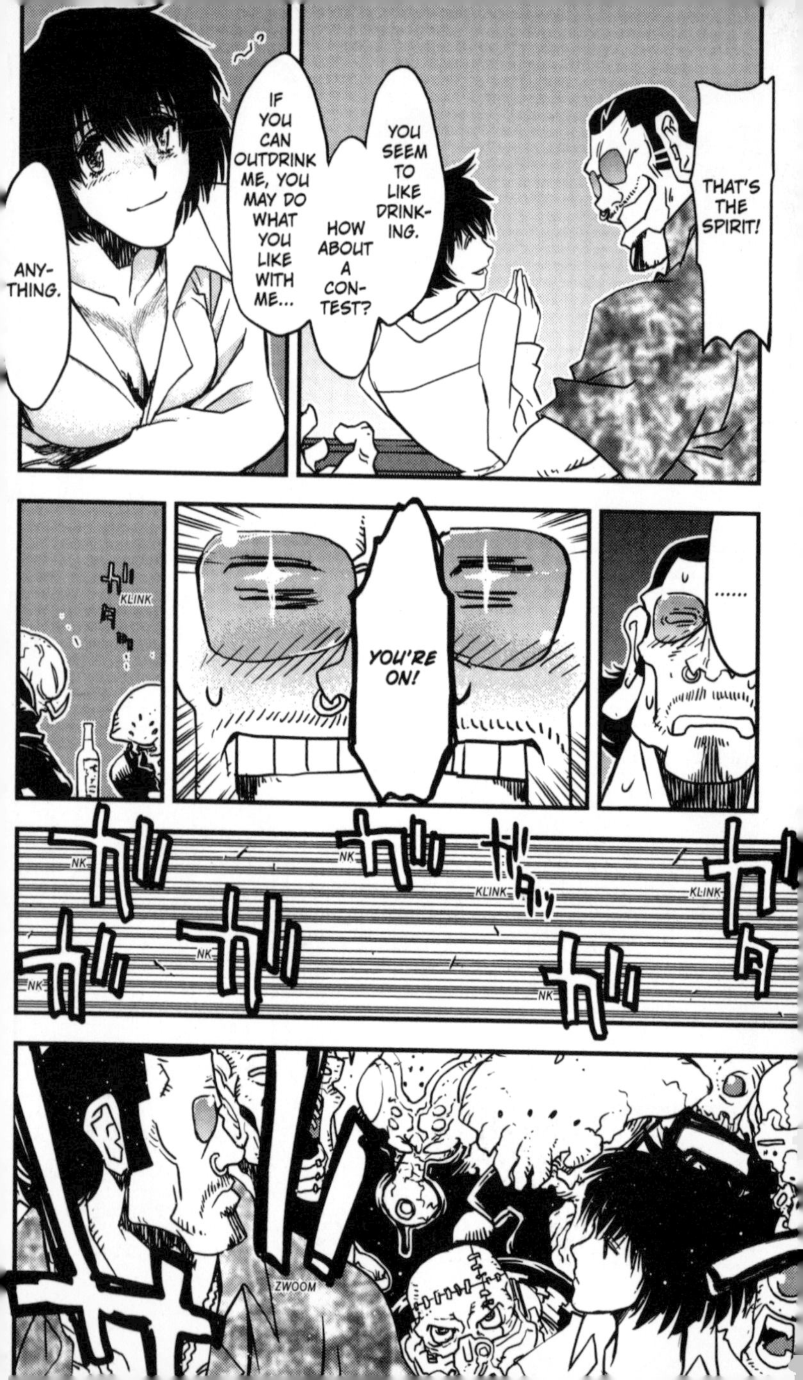
THAT'S THE SPIRIT!
YOU SEEM TO LIKE DRINKING.
HOW ABOUT A CONTEST?
IF YOU CAN OUTDRINK ME, YOU MAY DO WHAT YOU LIKE WITH ME...
ANYTHING.
......
YOU'RE ON!
KLINK
KLINK
NK
KLINK
NK
NK
NK
NK
ZWOOM

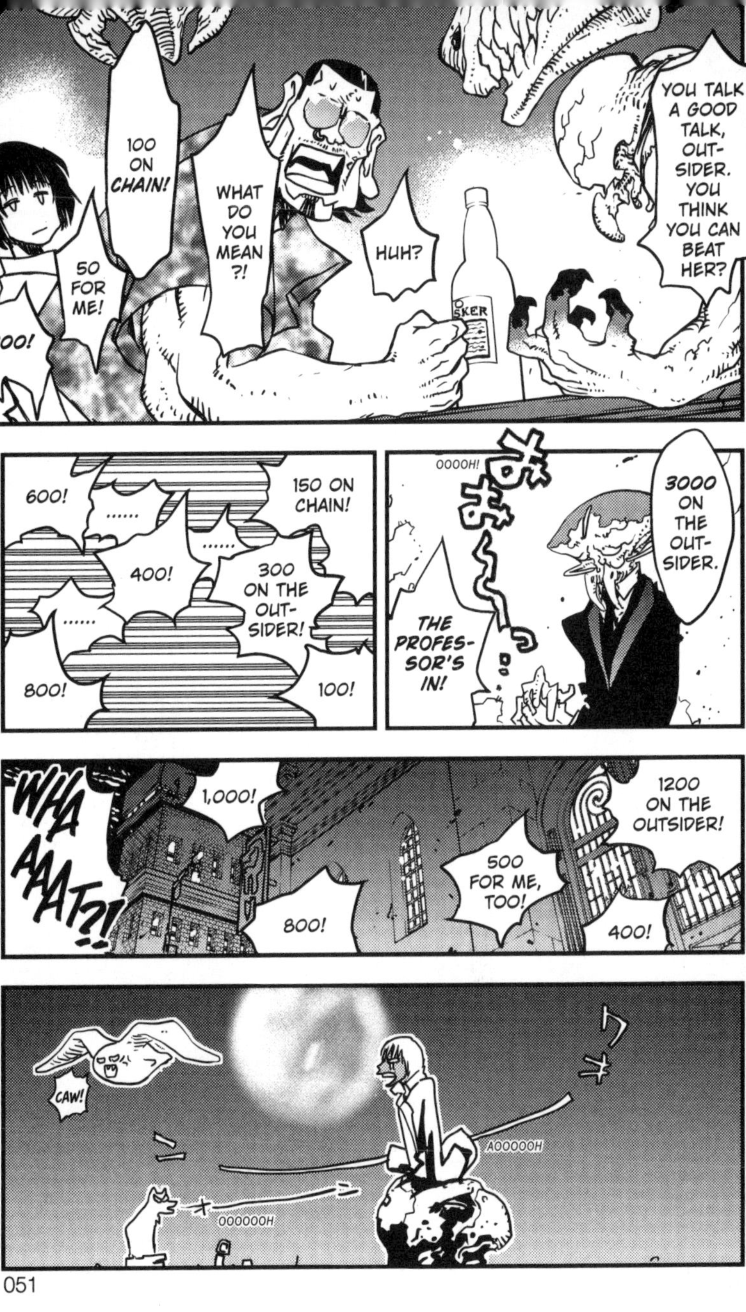

YOU TALK A GOOD TALK, OUT-SIDER. YOU THINK YOU CAN BEAT HER?
HUH?
WHAT DO YOU MEAN ?!
100 ON CHAIN!
50 FOR ME!
200!
3000 ON THE OUT-SIDER.
OOOOH!
THE PROFES-SOR'S IN!
150 ON CHAIN!
600!
......
......
400!
300 ON THE OUT-SIDER!
......
800!
100!
1200 ON THE OUTSIDER!
500 FOR ME, TOO!
1,000!
800!
400!
WHAAAAT?!
AOOOOOH
CAW!
OOOOOOH

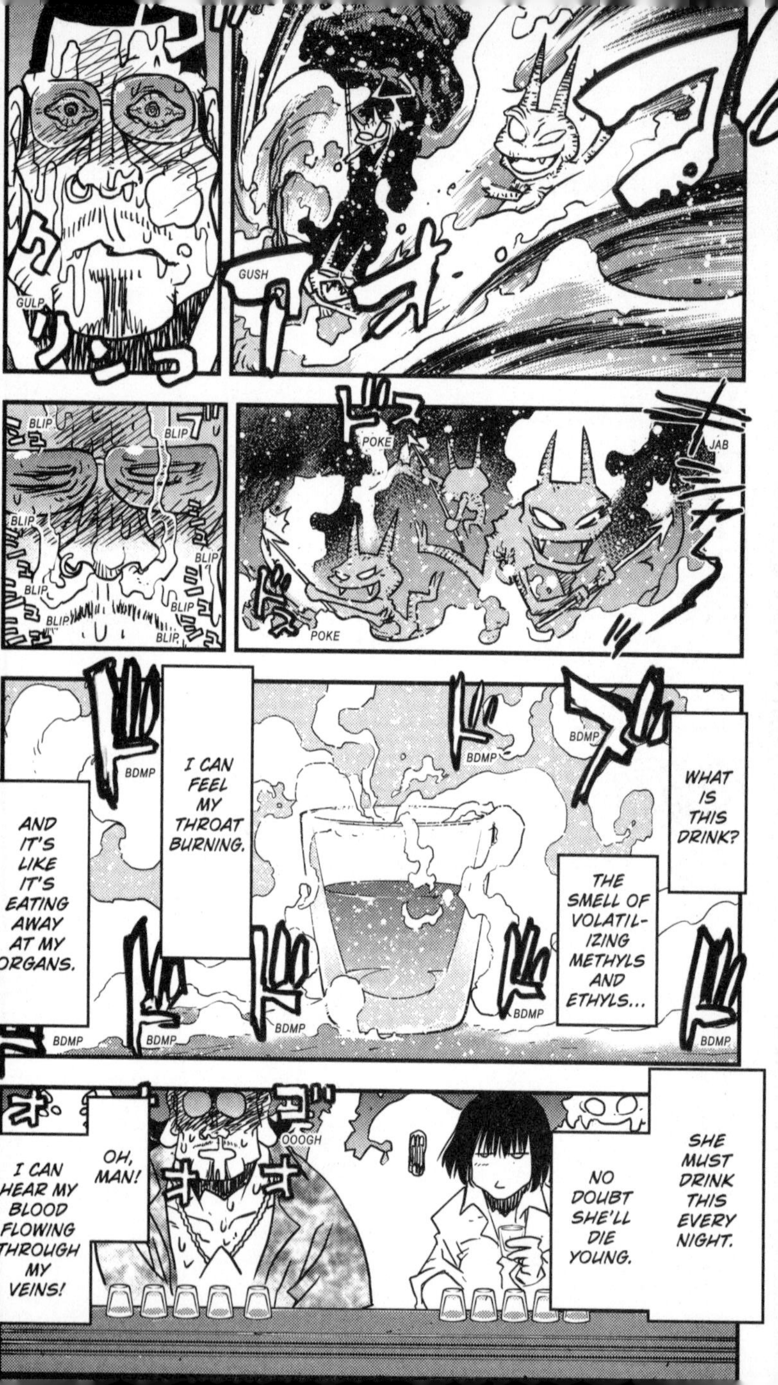
GUSH
GULP
JAB
POKE
POKE
BLIP
BLIP
BLIP
BLIP
BLIP
BLIP
BLIP
BLIP
BDMP
WHAT IS THIS DRINK?
THE SMELL OF VOLATIL-IZING METHYLS AND ETHYLS...
BDMP
BDMP
BDMP
I CAN FEEL MY THROAT BURNING.
BDMP
BDMP
BDMP
AND IT'S LIKE IT'S EATING AWAY AT MY ORGANS.
BDMP
SHE MUST DRINK THIS EVERY NIGHT.
NO DOUBT SHE'LL DIE YOUNG.
OOOGH
OH, MAN!
I CAN HEAR MY BLOOD FLOWING THROUGH MY VEINS!

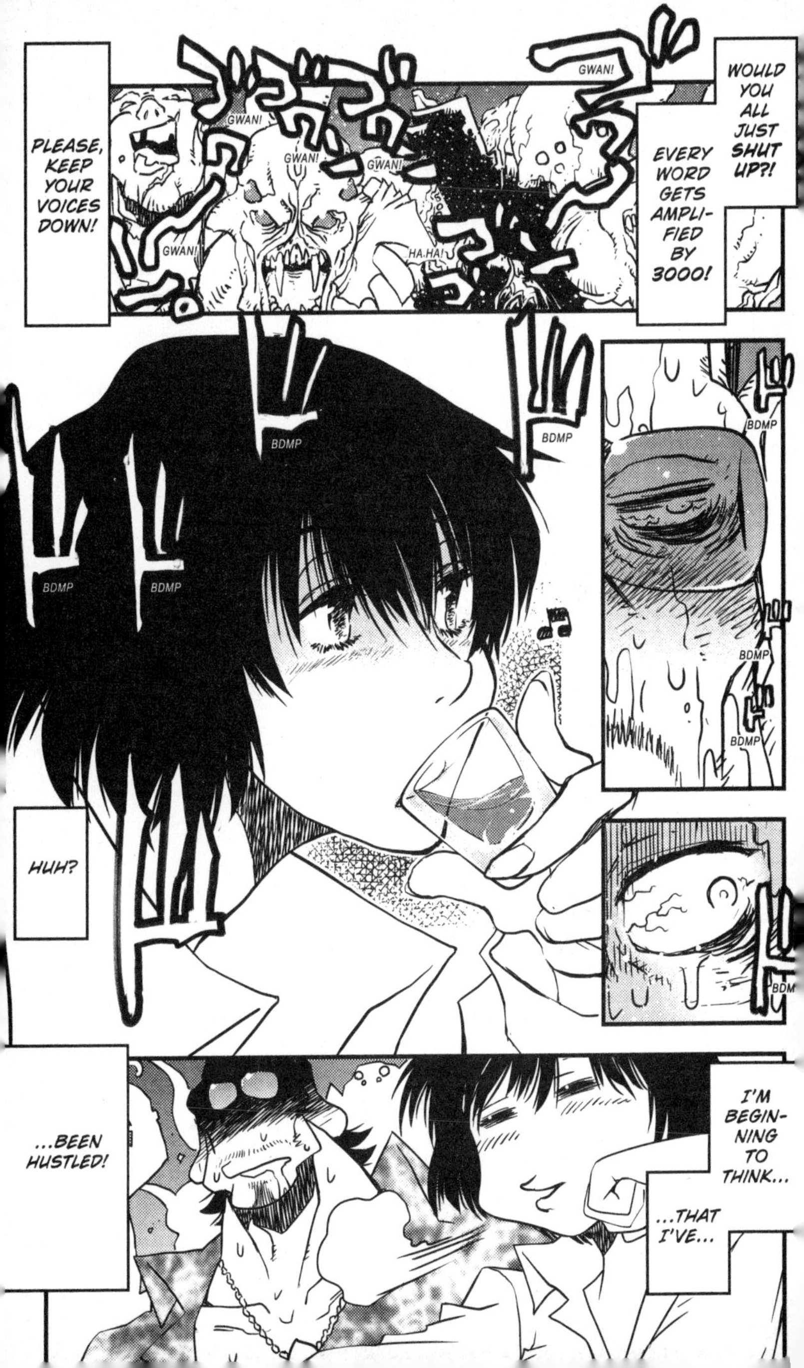
WOULD YOU ALL JUST SHUT UP?!
EVERY WORD GETS AMPLIFIED BY 3000!
GWAN!
HA HA!
GWAN!
GWAN!
GWAN!
GWAN!
PLEASE, KEEP YOUR VOICES DOWN!
BDMP
BDMP
BDMP
BDMP
BDMP
BDMP
BDMP
BDMP
BDM
HUH?
I'M BEGINNING TO THINK...
...THAT I'VE...
...BEEN HUSTLED!

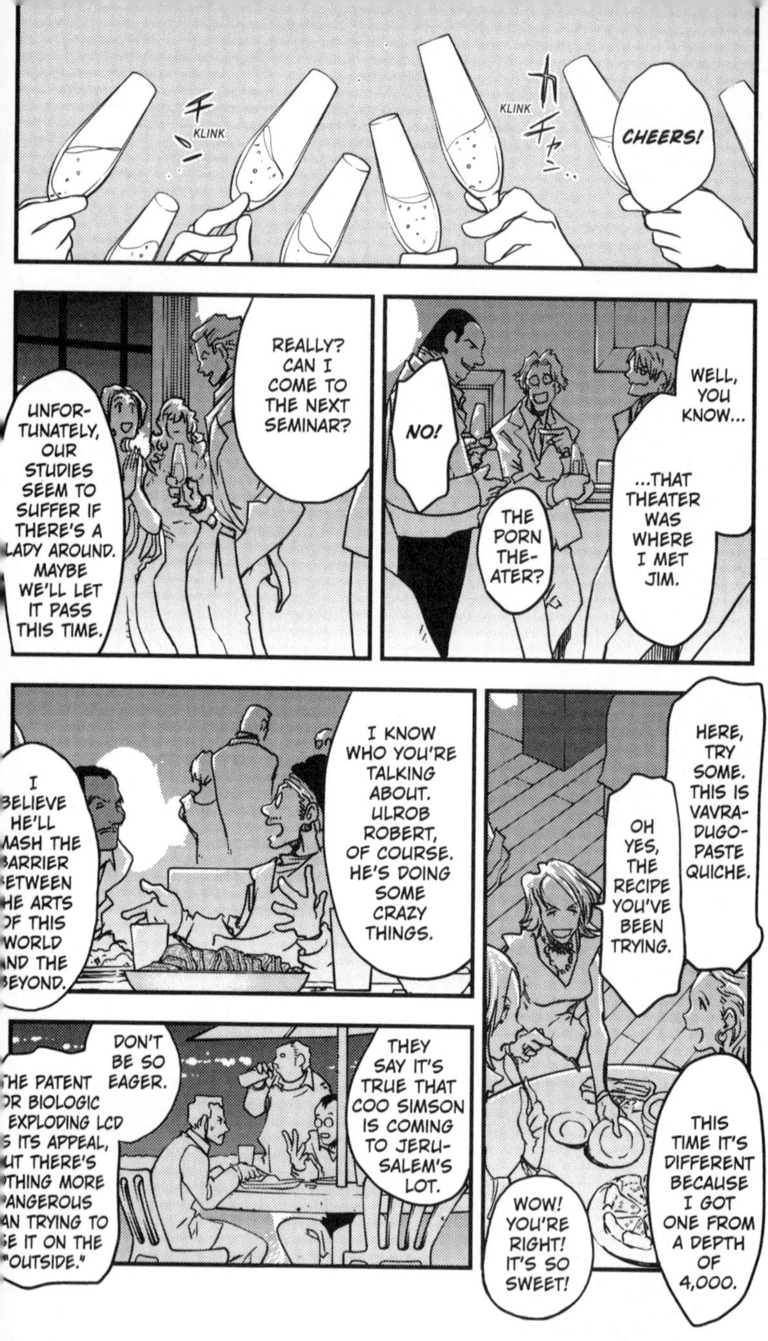

CHEERS!
KLINK
カチャ
KLINK
チ
WELL, YOU KNOW...
...THAT THEATER WAS WHERE I MET JIM.
THE PORN THE-ATER?
NO!
REALLY? CAN I COME TO THE NEXT SEMINAR?
UNFOR-TUNATELY, OUR STUDIES SEEM TO SUFFER IF THERE'S A LADY AROUND. MAYBE WE'LL LET IT PASS THIS TIME.
HERE, TRY SOME. THIS IS VAVRA-DUGO-PASTE QUICHE.
OH YES, THE RECIPE YOU'VE BEEN TRYING.
THIS TIME IT'S DIFFERENT BECAUSE I GOT ONE FROM A DEPTH OF 4,000.
WOW! YOU'RE RIGHT! IT'S SO SWEET!
I KNOW WHO YOU'RE TALKING ABOUT. ULROB ROBERT, OF COURSE. HE'S DOING SOME CRAZY THINGS.
I BELIEVE HE'LL MASH THE BARRIER BETWEEN THE ARTS OF THIS WORLD AND THE BEYOND.
THEY SAY IT'S TRUE THAT COO SIMSON IS COMING TO JERU-SALEM'S LOT.
DON'T BE SO EAGER.
THE PATENT OR BIOLOGIC EXPLODING LCD IS ITS APPEAL, BUT THERE'S NOTHING MORE DANGEROUS THAN TRYING TO USE IT ON THE "OUTSIDE."

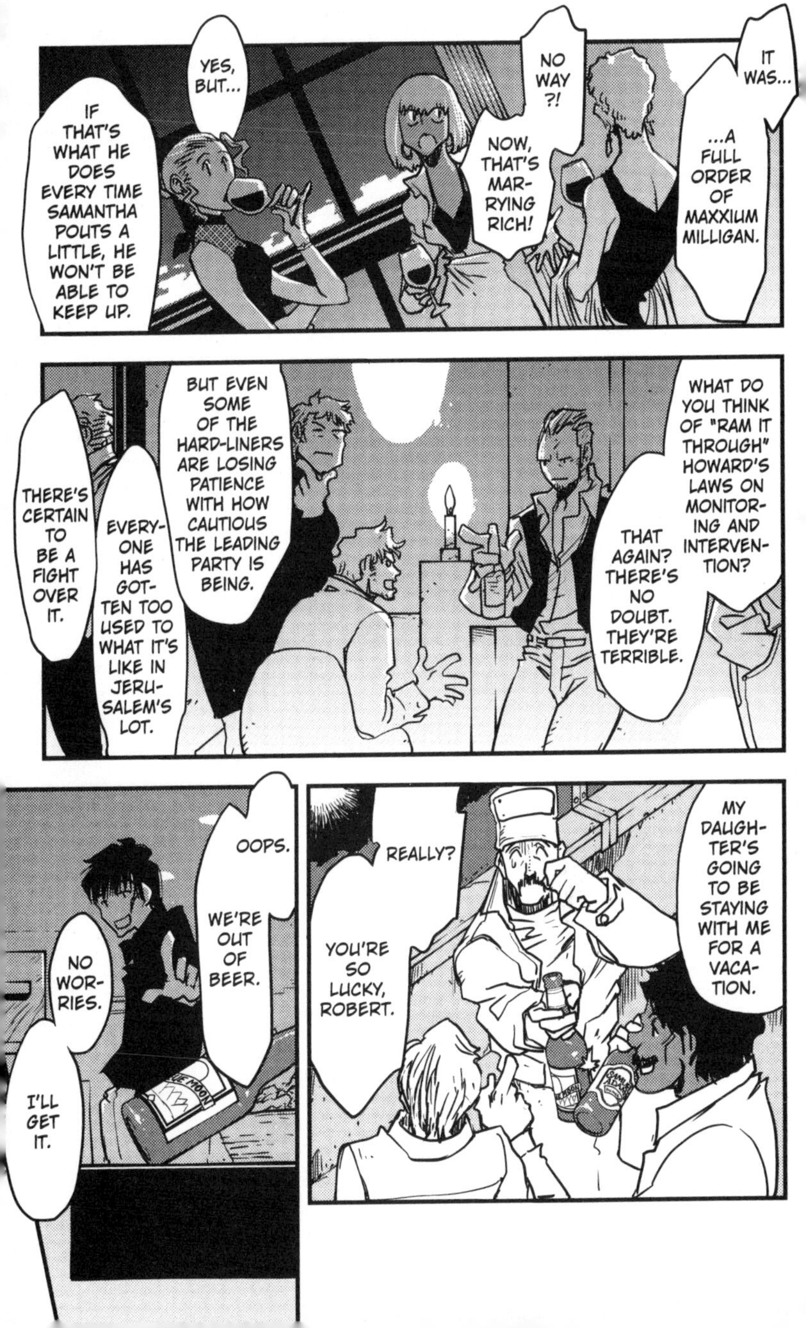
IT WAS...
...A FULL ORDER OF MAXXIUM MILLIGAN.
NO WAY?!
NOW, THAT'S MAR-RYING RICH!
YES, BUT...
IF THAT'S WHAT HE DOES EVERY TIME SAMANTHA POUTS A LITTLE, HE WON'T BE ABLE TO KEEP UP.
WHAT DO YOU THINK OF "RAM IT THROUGH" HOWARD'S LAWS ON MONITOR-ING AND INTERVEN-TION?
THAT AGAIN? THERE'S NO DOUBT. THEY'RE TERRIBLE.
BUT EVEN SOME OF THE HARD-LINERS ARE LOSING PATIENCE WITH HOW CAUTIOUS THE LEADING PARTY IS BEING.
EVERY-ONE HAS GOT-TEN TOO USED TO WHAT IT'S LIKE IN JERU-SALEM'S LOT.
THERE'S CERTAIN TO BE A FIGHT OVER IT.
MY DAUGH-TER'S GOING TO BE STAYING WITH ME FOR A VACA-TION.
REALLY?
YOU'RE SO LUCKY, ROBERT.
OOPS.
WE'RE OUT OF BEER.
NO WOR-RIES.
I'LL GET IT.

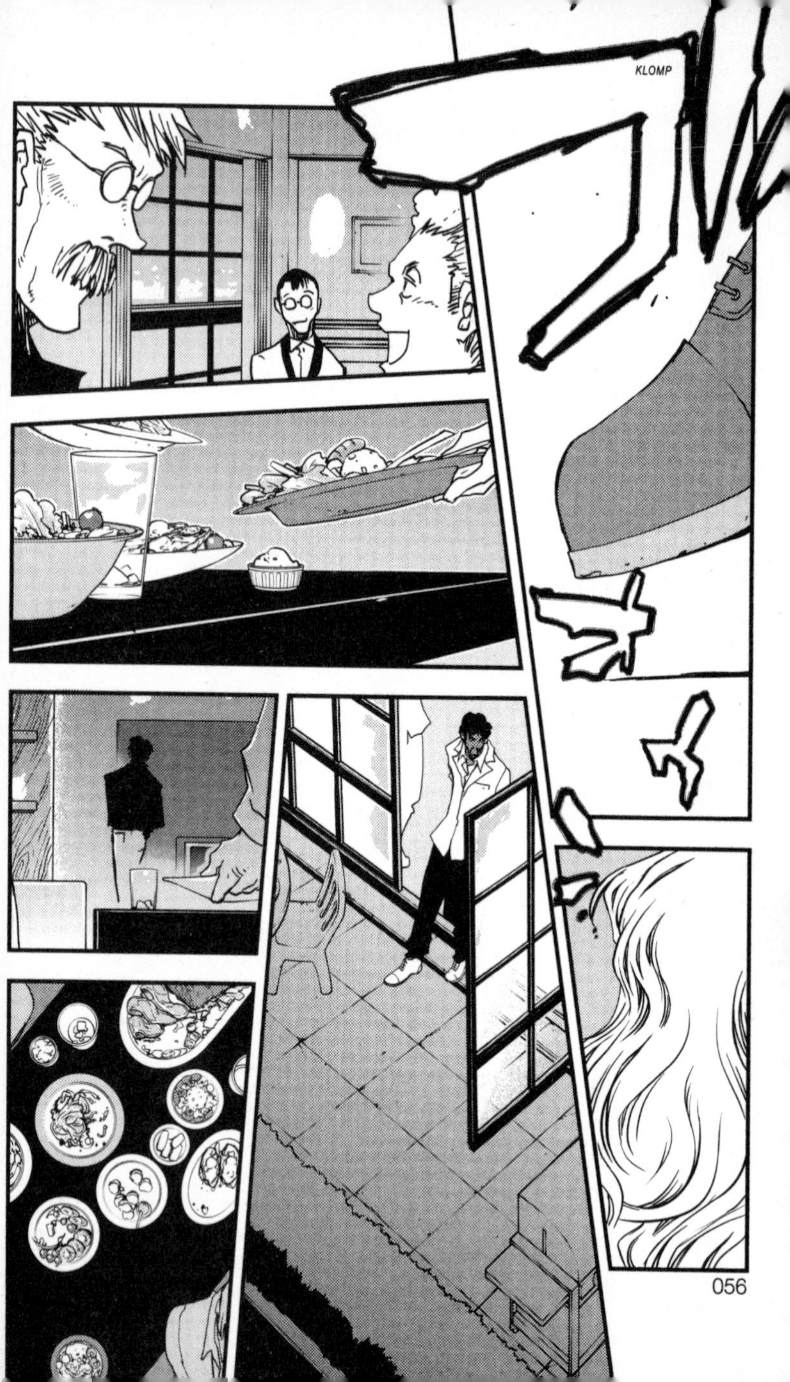
KLOMP

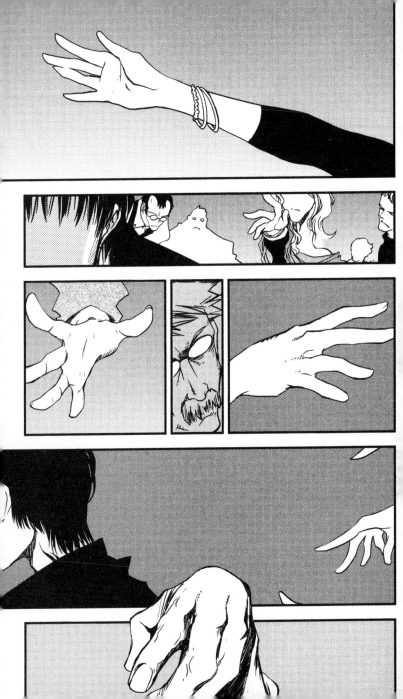

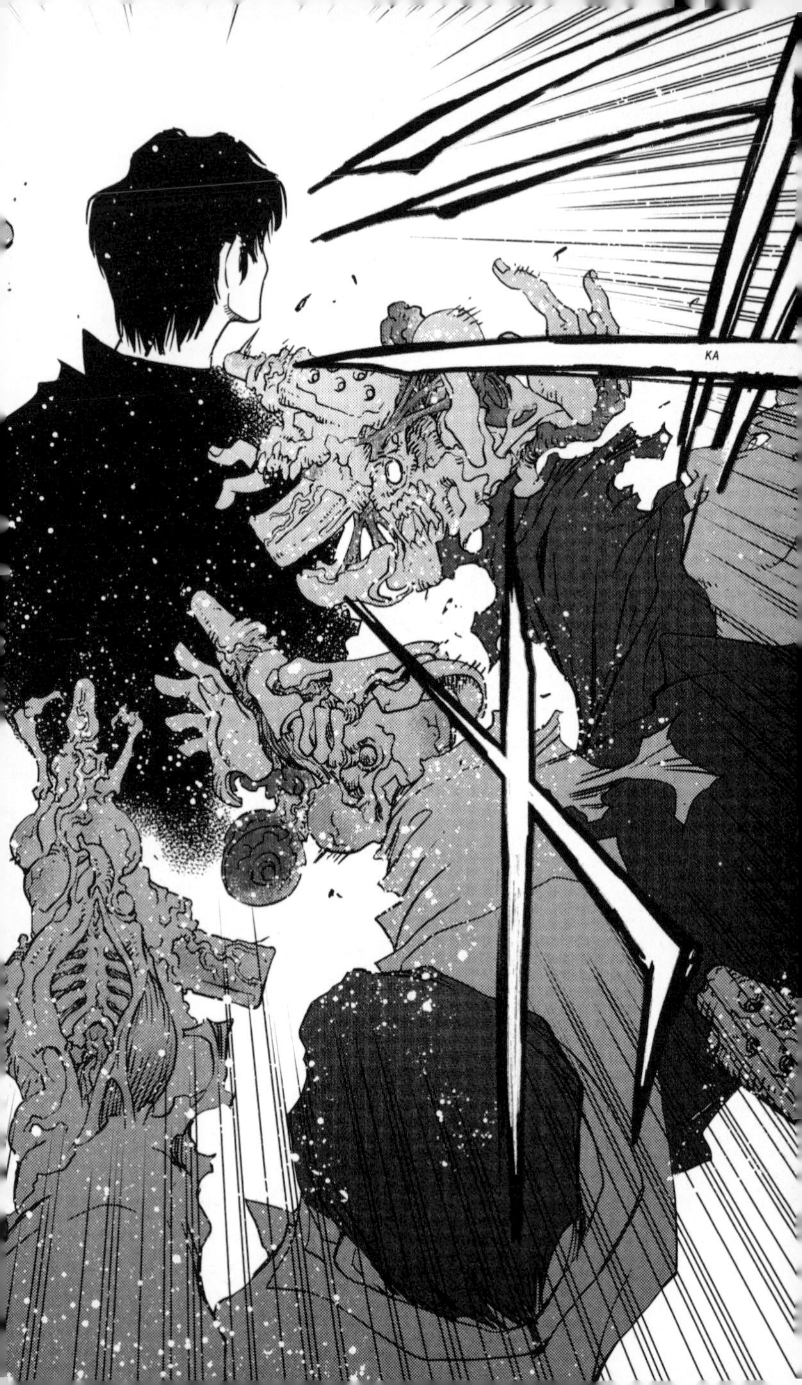
KA

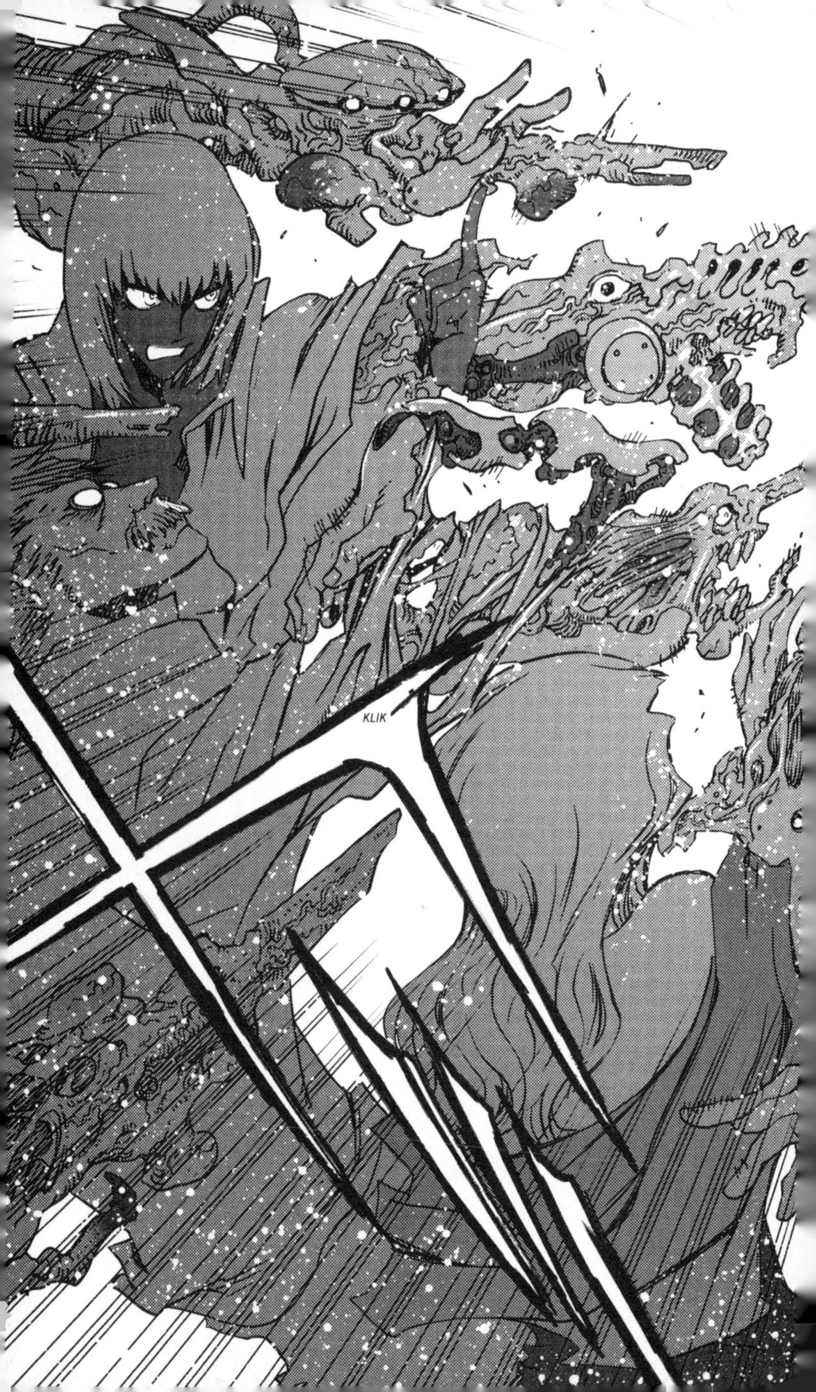
KLIK

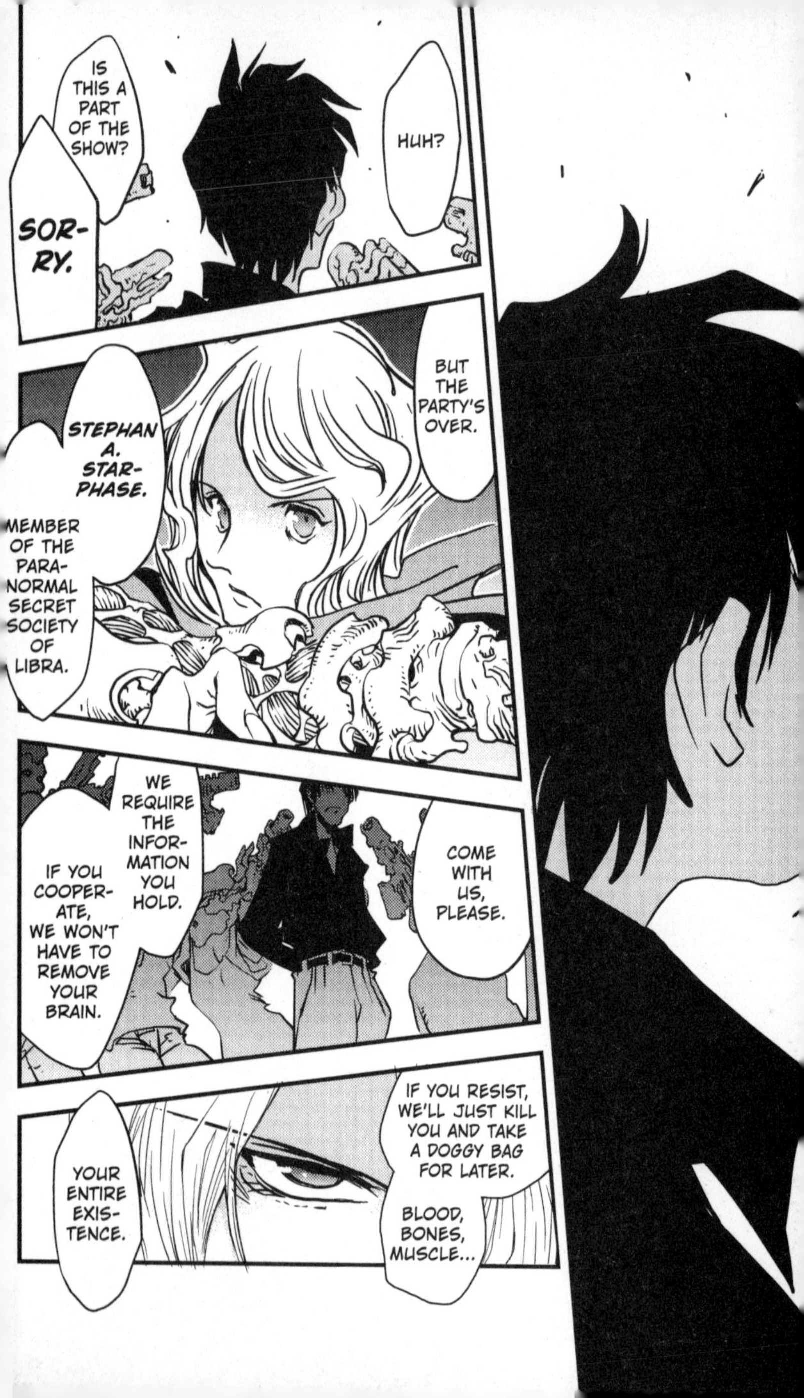
HUH?
IS THIS A PART OF THE SHOW?
SORRY.
BUT THE PARTY'S OVER.
STEPHAN A. STARPHASE.
MEMBER OF THE PARANORMAL SECRET SOCIETY OF LIBRA.
COME WITH US, PLEASE.
WE REQUIRE THE INFORMATION YOU HOLD.
IF YOU COOPERATE, WE WON'T HAVE TO REMOVE YOUR BRAIN.
IF YOU RESIST, WE'LL JUST KILL YOU AND TAKE A DOGGY BAG FOR LATER.
BLOOD, BONES, MUSCLE...
YOUR ENTIRE EXISTENCE.

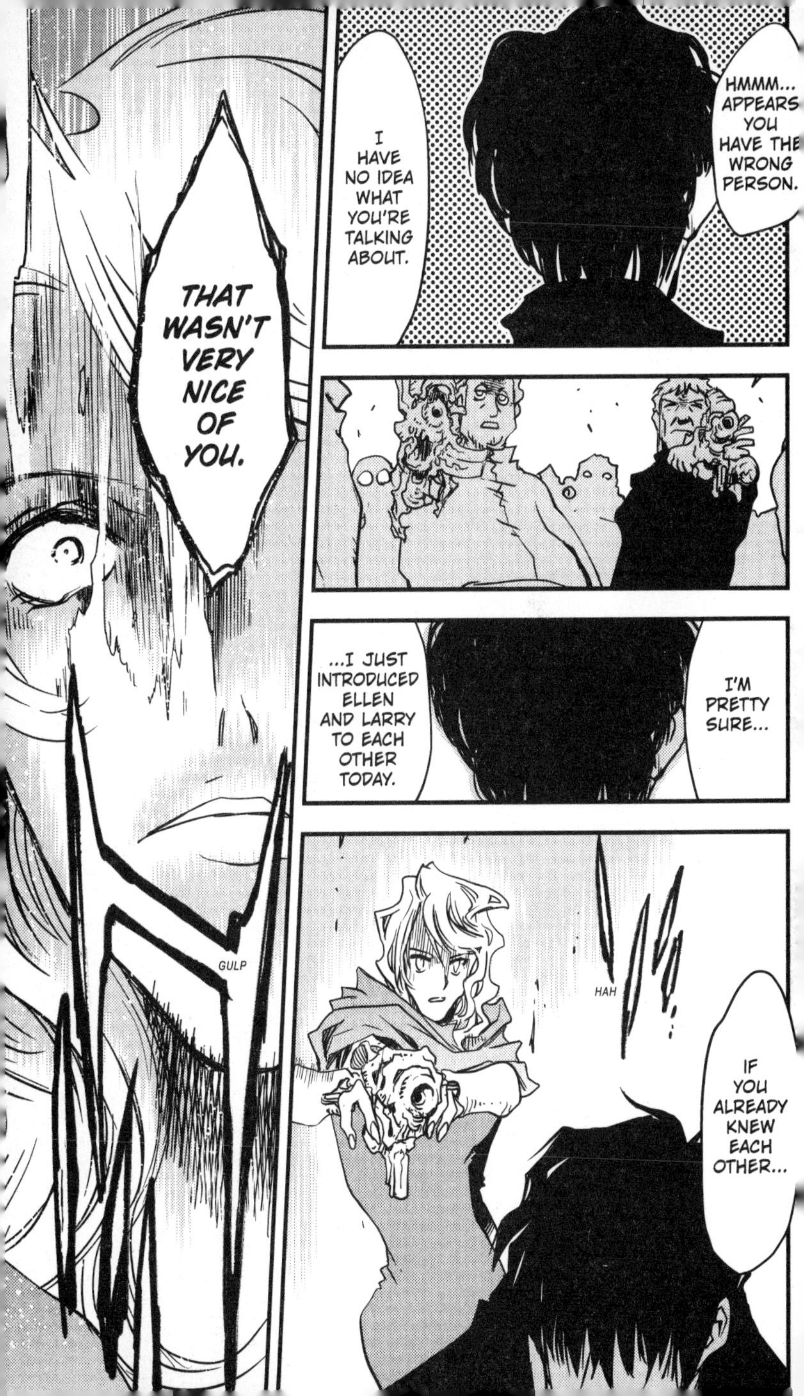
HMMMM... APPEARS YOU HAVE THE WRONG PERSON.
I HAVE NO IDEA WHAT YOU'RE TALKING ABOUT.
I'M PRETTY SURE...
...I JUST INTRODUCED ELLEN AND LARRY TO EACH OTHER TODAY.
IF YOU ALREADY KNEW EACH OTHER...
HAH
THAT WASN'T VERY NICE OF YOU.
GULP

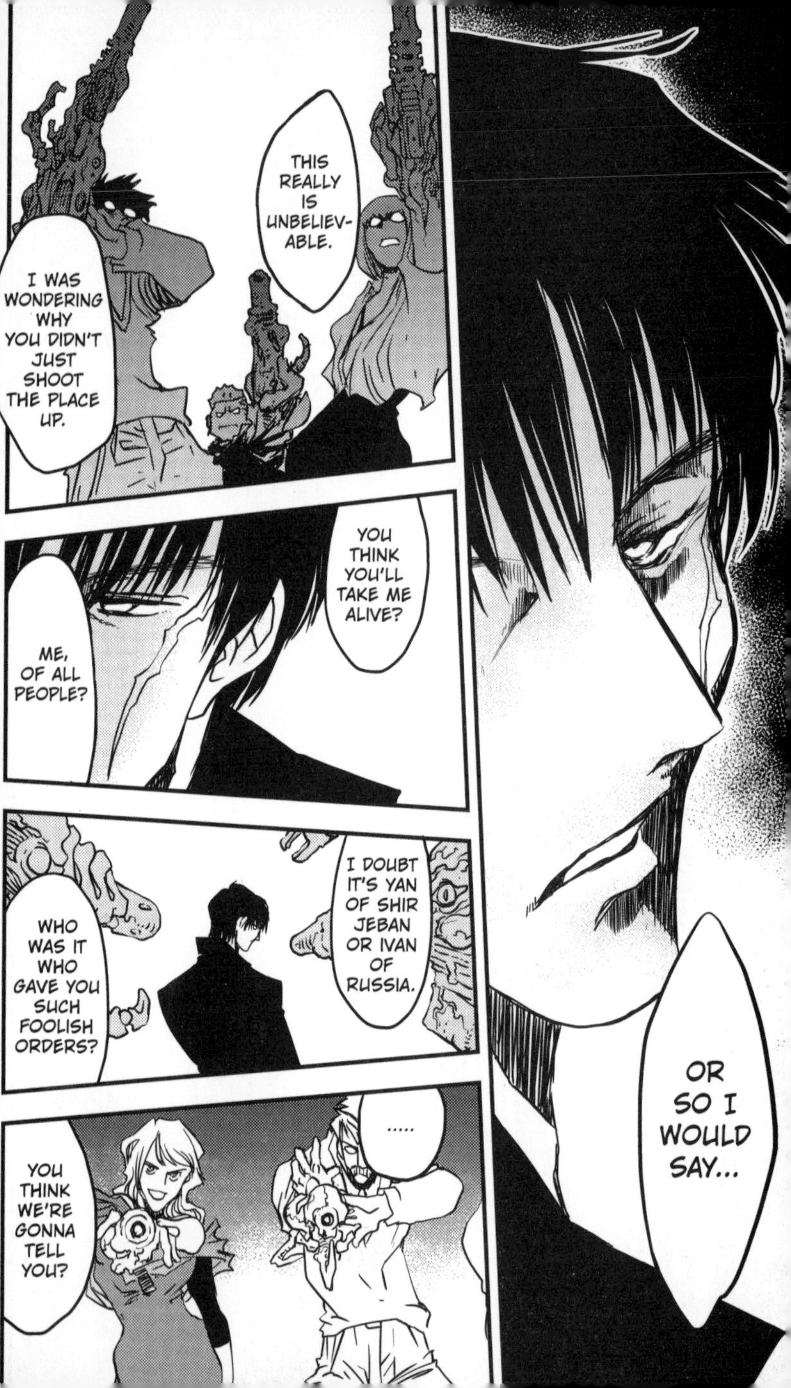
THIS REALLY IS UNBELIEVABLE.
I WAS WONDERING WHY YOU DIDN'T JUST SHOOT THE PLACE UP.
YOU THINK YOU'LL TAKE ME ALIVE?
ME, OF ALL PEOPLE?
I DOUBT IT'S YAN OF SHIR JEBAN OR IVAN OF RUSSIA.
WHO WAS IT WHO GAVE YOU SUCH FOOLISH ORDERS?
.....
YOU THINK WE'RE GONNA TELL YOU?
OR SO I WOULD SAY...

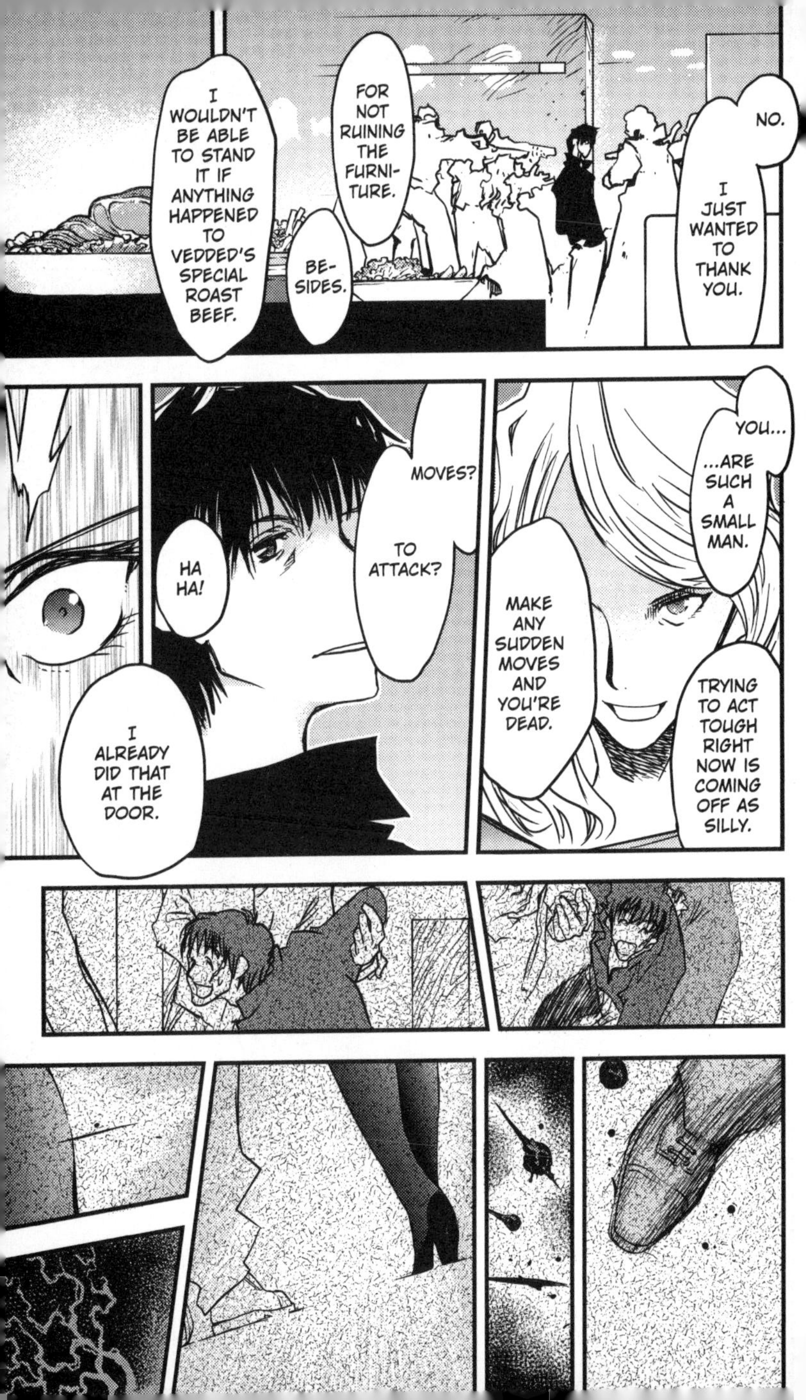
NO.
I JUST WANTED TO THANK YOU.
FOR NOT RUINING THE FURNI-TURE.
BE-SIDES.
I WOULDN'T BE ABLE TO STAND IT IF ANYTHING HAPPENED TO VEDDED'S SPECIAL ROAST BEEF.
YOU...
...ARE SUCH A SMALL MAN.
TRYING TO ACT TOUGH RIGHT NOW IS COMING OFF AS SILLY.
MAKE ANY SUDDEN MOVES AND YOU'RE DEAD.
MOVES?
TO ATTACK?
HA HA!
I ALREADY DID THAT AT THE DOOR.

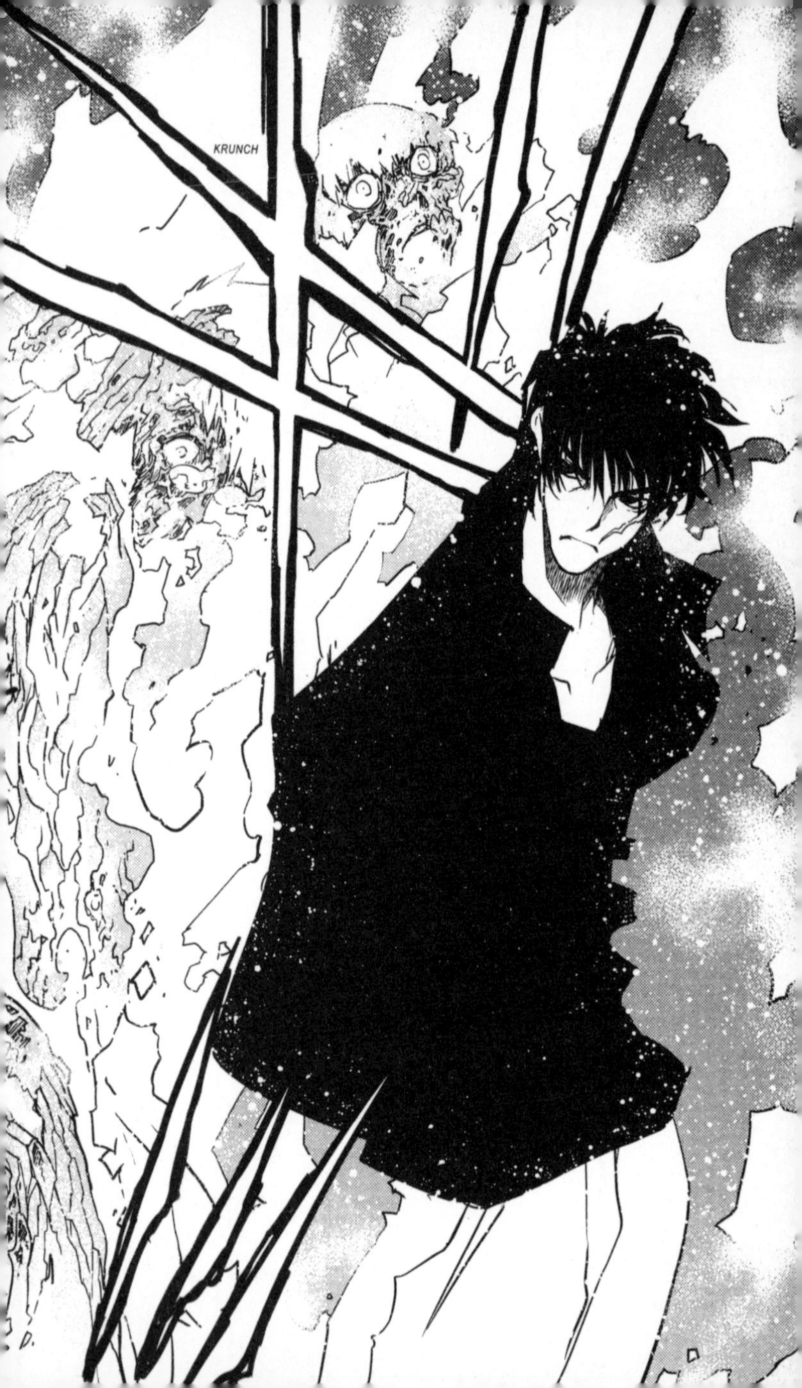
KRUNCH

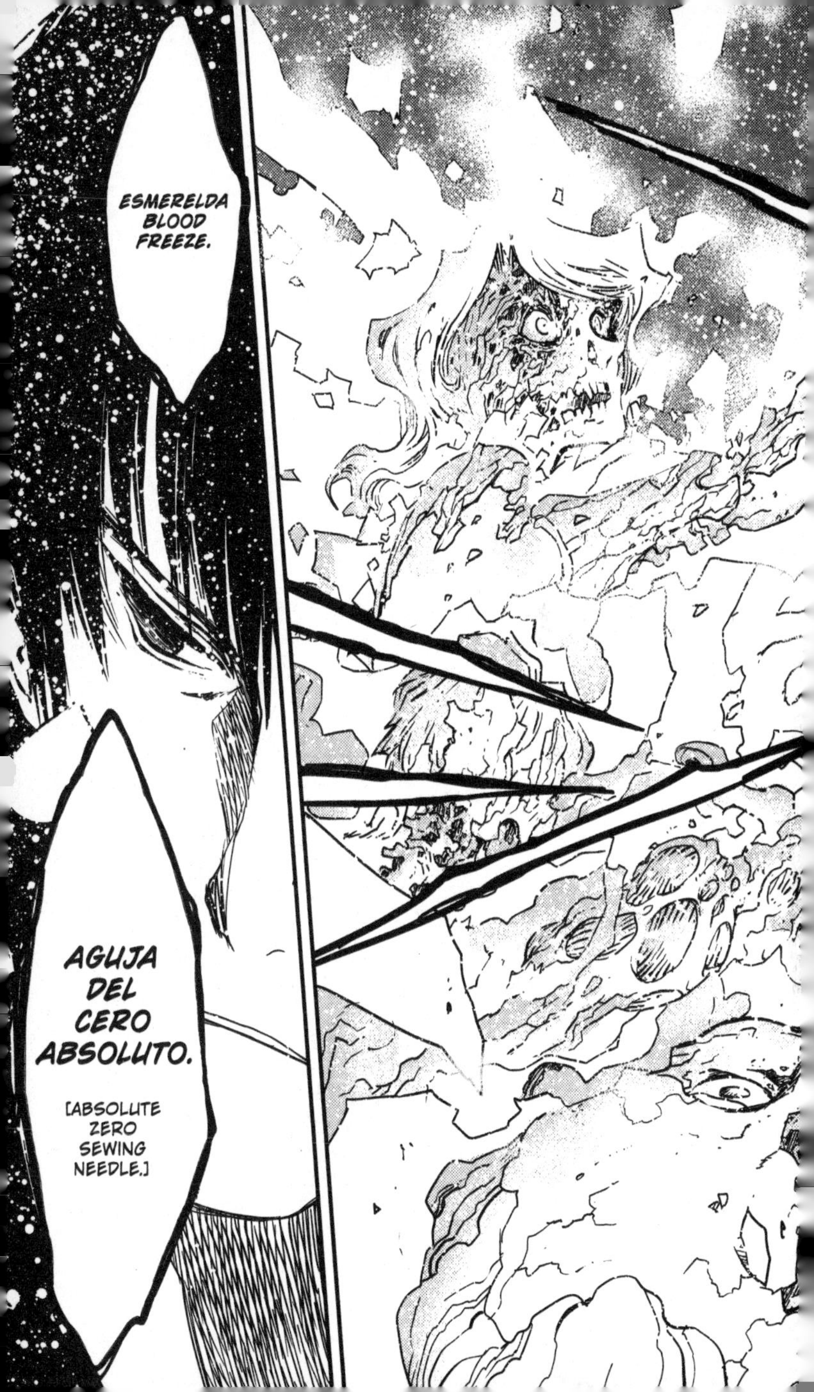

ESMERELDA BLOOD FREEZE.
AGUJA DEL CERO ABSOLUTO.
[ABSOLUTE ZERO SEWING NEEDLE.]

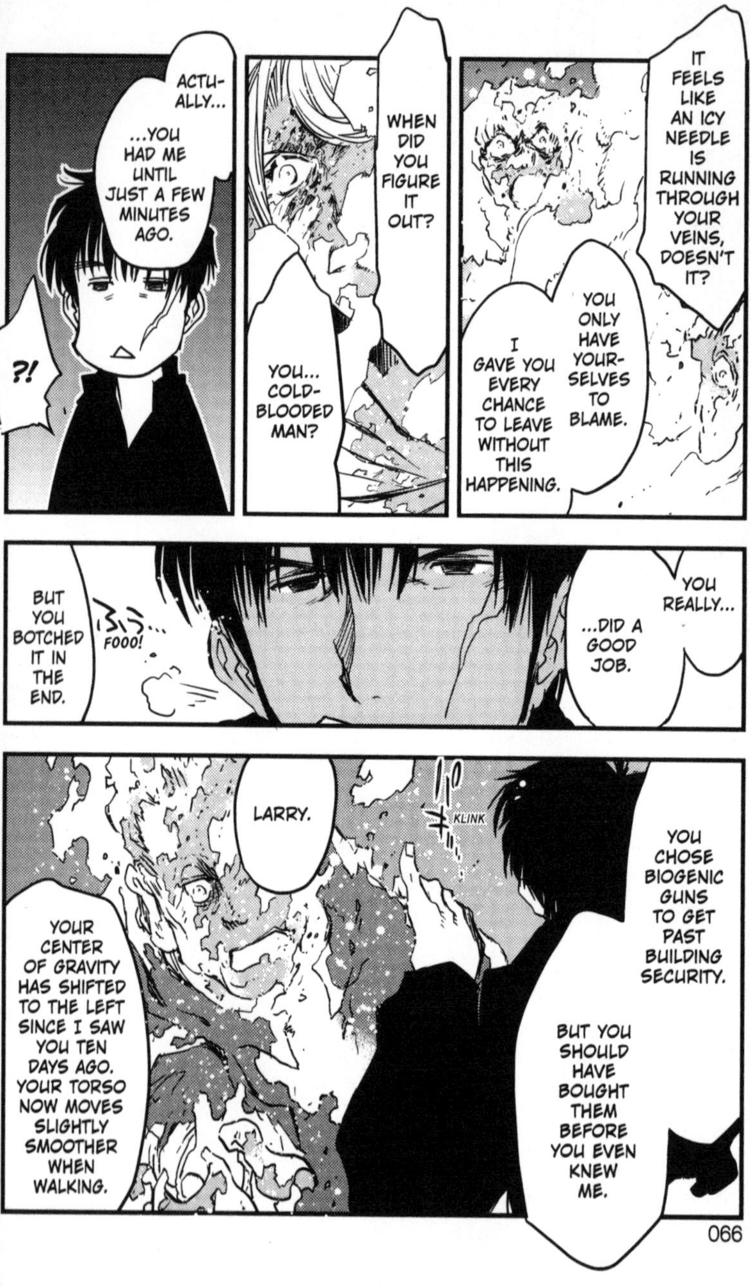
IT FEELS LIKE AN ICY NEEDLE IS RUNNING THROUGH YOUR VEINS, DOESN'T IT?
YOU ONLY HAVE YOURSELVES TO BLAME.
I GAVE YOU EVERY CHANCE TO LEAVE WITHOUT THIS HAPPENING.
WHEN DID YOU FIGURE IT OUT?
YOU... COLD-BLOODED MAN?
ACTUALLY...
...YOU HAD ME UNTIL JUST A FEW MINUTES AGO.
?!
YOU REALLY...
...DID A GOOD JOB.
ふう... FOOO!
BUT YOU BOTCHED IT IN THE END.
KLINK
YOU CHOSE BIOGENIC GUNS TO GET PAST BUILDING SECURITY.
BUT YOU SHOULD HAVE BOUGHT THEM BEFORE YOU EVEN KNEW ME.
LARRY.
YOUR CENTER OF GRAVITY HAS SHIFTED TO THE LEFT SINCE I SAW YOU TEN DAYS AGO. YOUR TORSO NOW MOVES SLIGHTLY SMOOTHER WHEN WALKING.

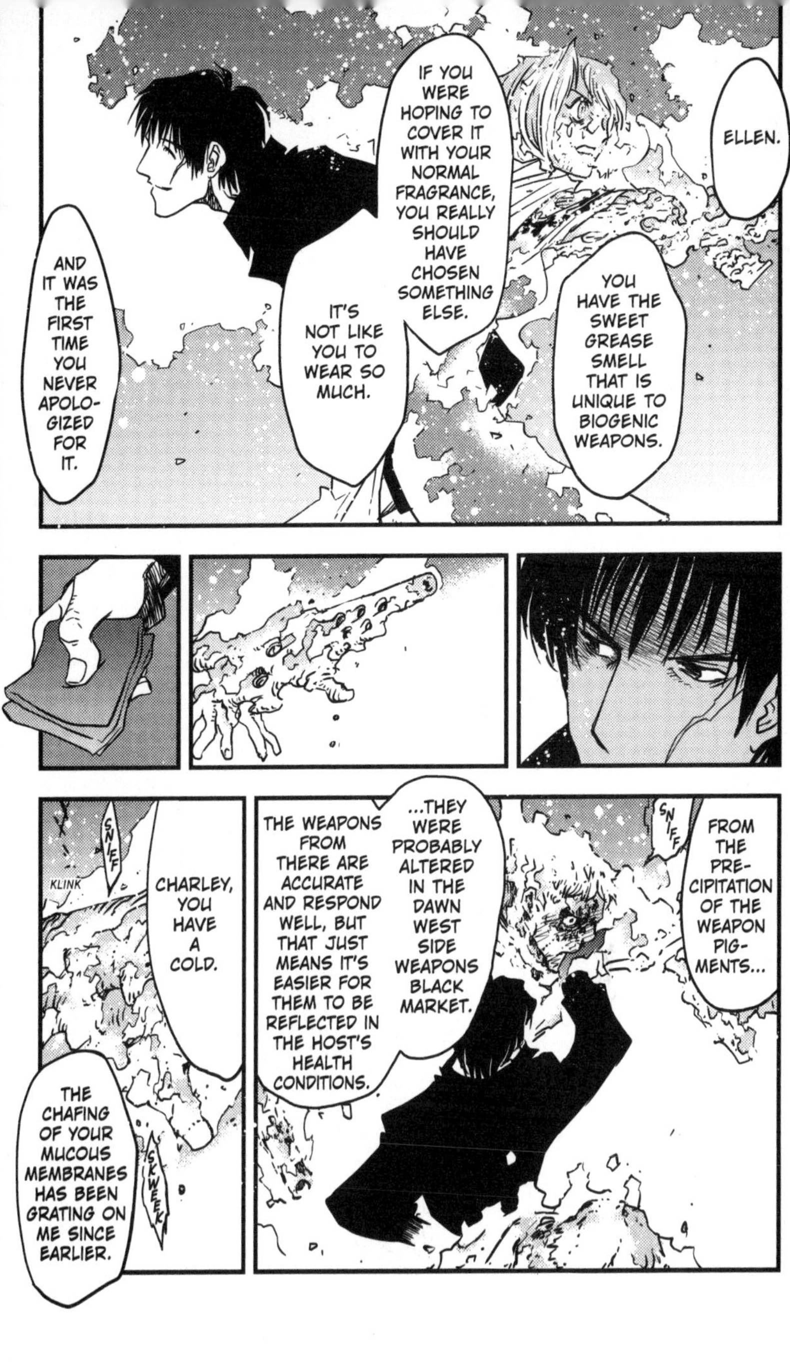

ELLEN.
YOU HAVE THE SWEET GREASE SMELL THAT IS UNIQUE TO BIOGENIC WEAPONS.
IF YOU WERE HOPING TO COVER IT WITH YOUR NORMAL FRAGRANCE, YOU REALLY SHOULD HAVE CHOSEN SOMETHING ELSE.
IT'S NOT LIKE YOU TO WEAR SO MUCH.
AND IT WAS THE FIRST TIME YOU NEVER APOLOGIZED FOR IT.
SNIFF
FROM THE PRECIPITATION OF THE WEAPON PIGMENTS...
...THEY WERE PROBABLY ALTERED IN THE DAWN WEST SIDE WEAPONS BLACK MARKET.
THE WEAPONS FROM THERE ARE ACCURATE AND RESPOND WELL, BUT THAT JUST MEANS IT'S EASIER FOR THEM TO BE REFLECTED IN THE HOST'S HEALTH CONDITIONS.
CHARLEY, YOU HAVE A COLD.
SNIFF
KLINK
THE CHAFING OF YOUR MUCOUS MEMBRANES HAS BEEN GRATING ON ME SINCE EARLIER.
SKWEEK

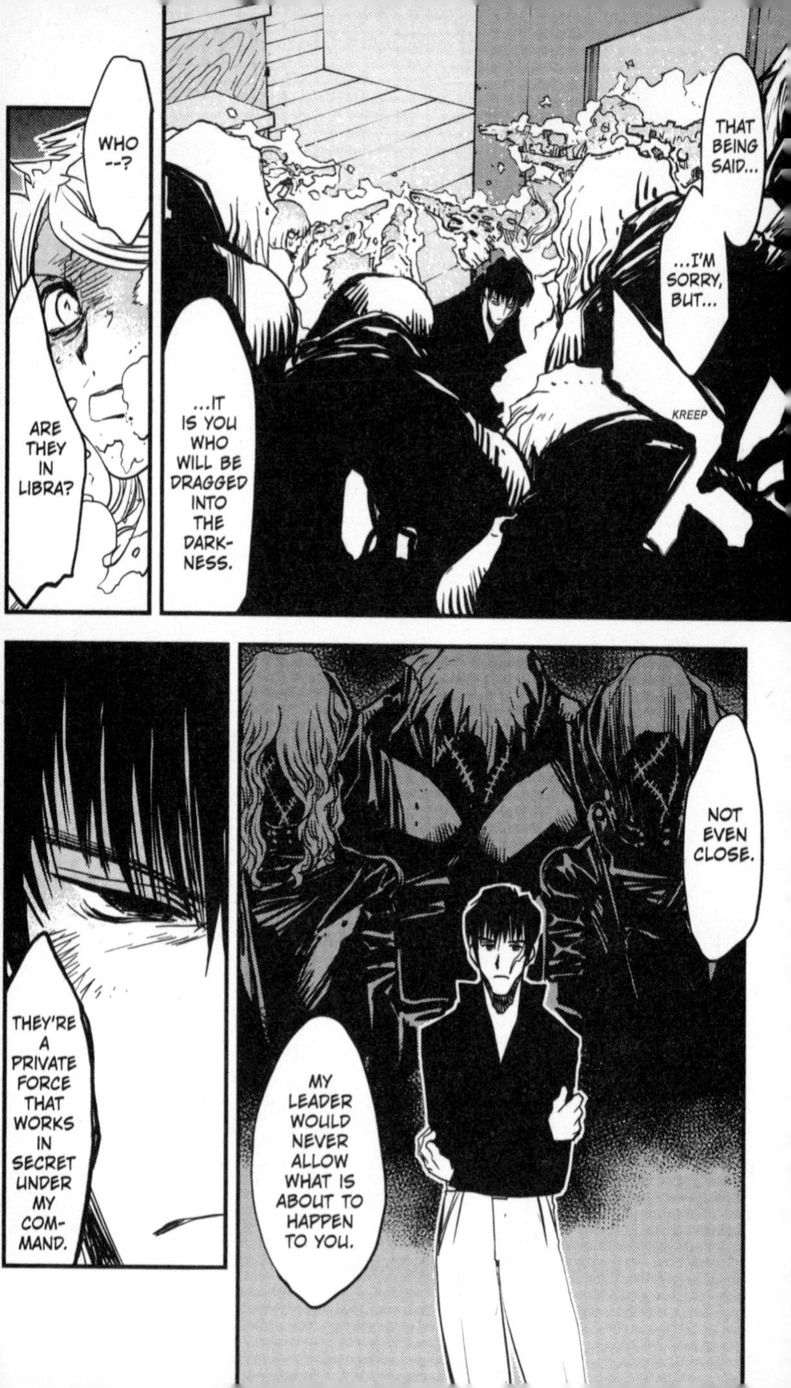
THAT BEING SAID...
...I'M SORRY, BUT...
KREEP
...IT IS YOU WHO WILL BE DRAGGED INTO THE DARKNESS.
WHO --?
ARE THEY IN LIBRA?
NOT EVEN CLOSE.
MY LEADER WOULD NEVER ALLOW WHAT IS ABOUT TO HAPPEN TO YOU.
THEY'RE A PRIVATE FORCE THAT WORKS IN SECRET UNDER MY COMMAND.

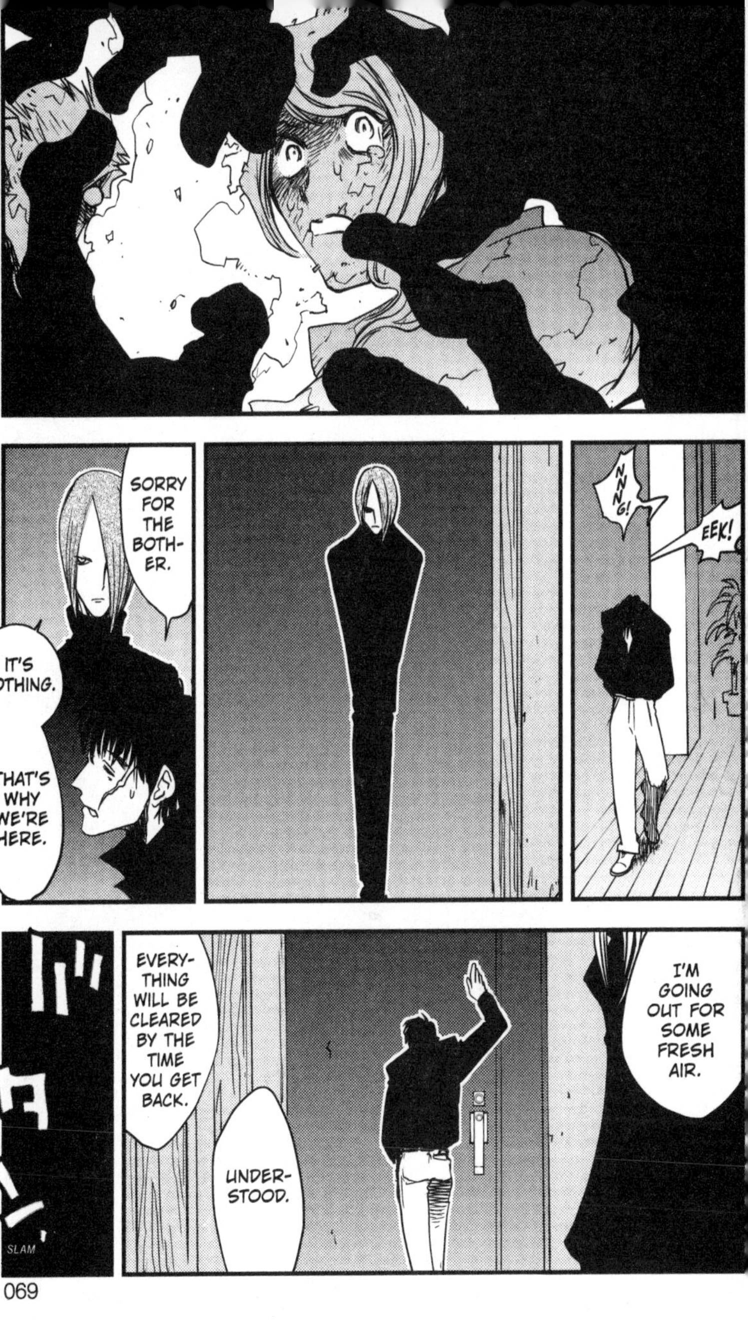
NNNG!
EEK!
SORRY FOR THE BOTHER.
IT'S NOTHING.
THAT'S WHY WE'RE HERE.
I'M GOING OUT FOR SOME FRESH AIR.
EVERYTHING WILL BE CLEARED BY THE TIME YOU GET BACK.
UNDERSTOOD.
SLAM

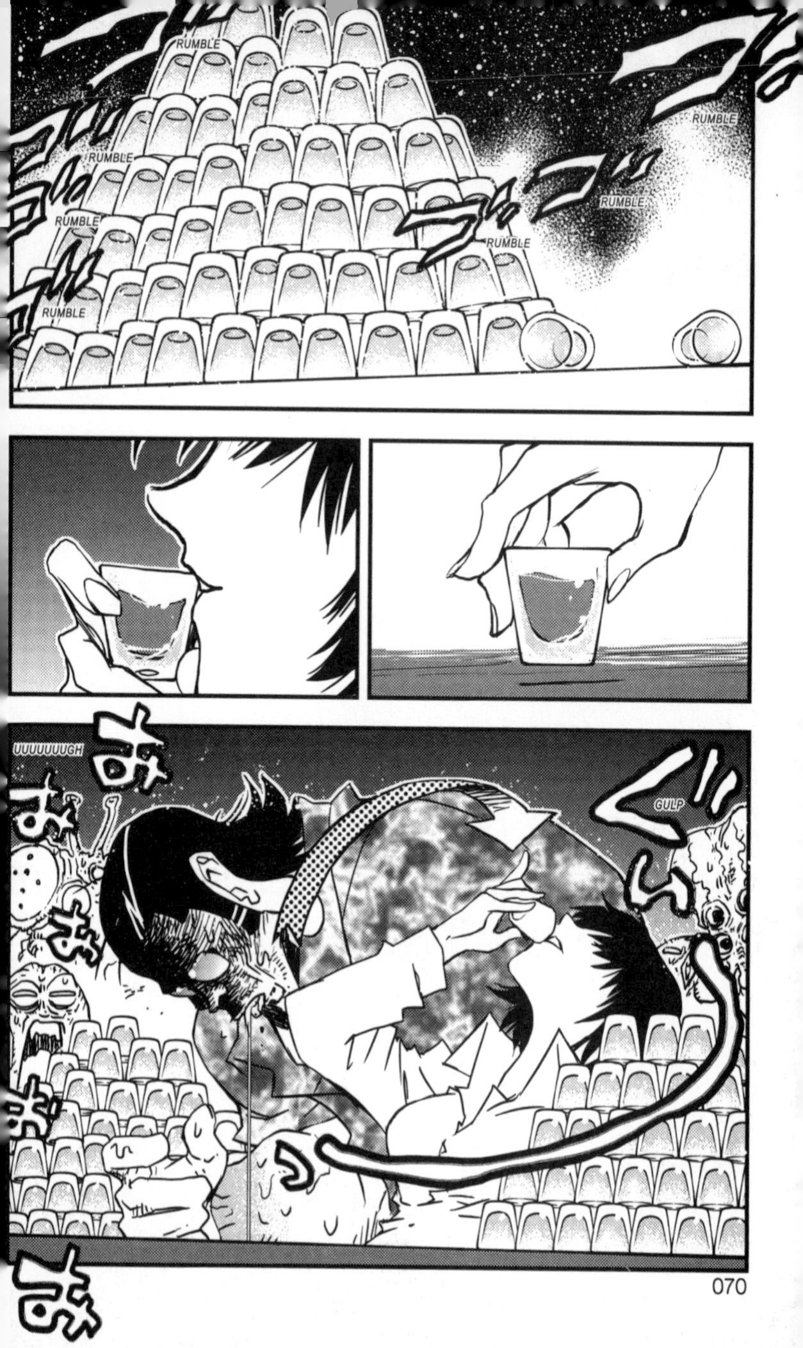

RUMBLE
RUMBLE
RUMBLE
RUMBLE
RUMBLE
RUMBLE
RUMBLE
GULP
UUUUUUUGH

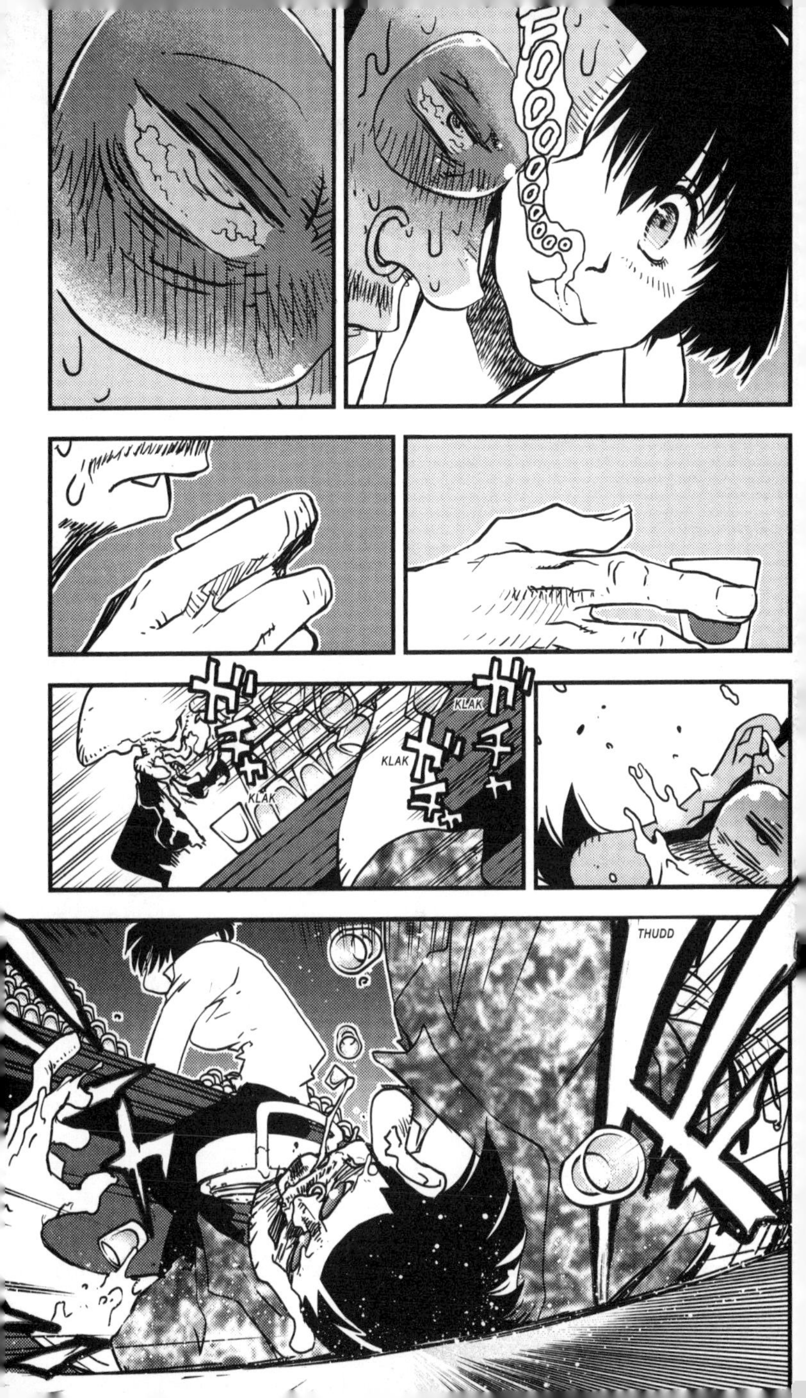
FOOOOOOOOOO
ガチャ
KLAK
ガチャ
KLAK
ガチャ
KLAK
THUDD

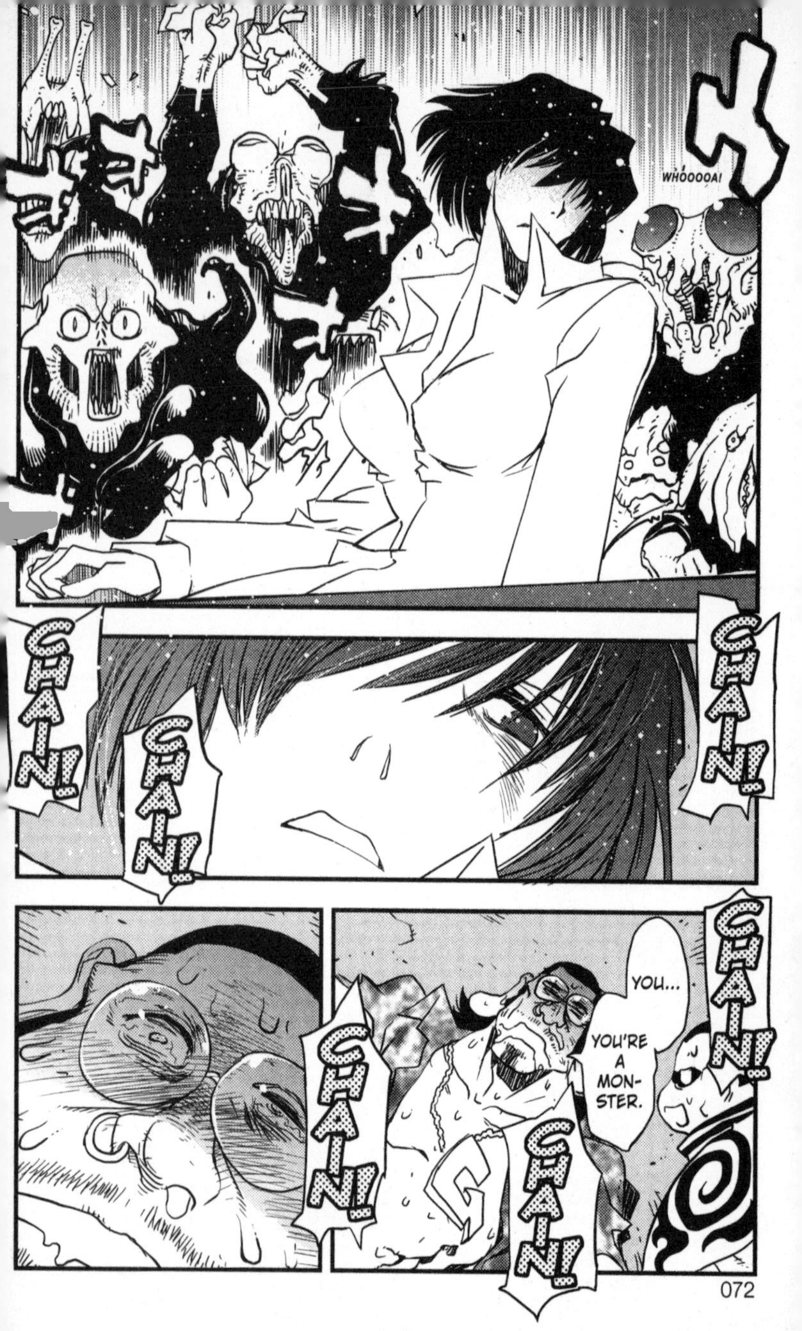
WHOOOOA!
CHAIN!
CHAIN!
CHAIN!
CHAIN!
YOU...
YOU'RE A MON-STER.
CHAIN!
CHAIN!

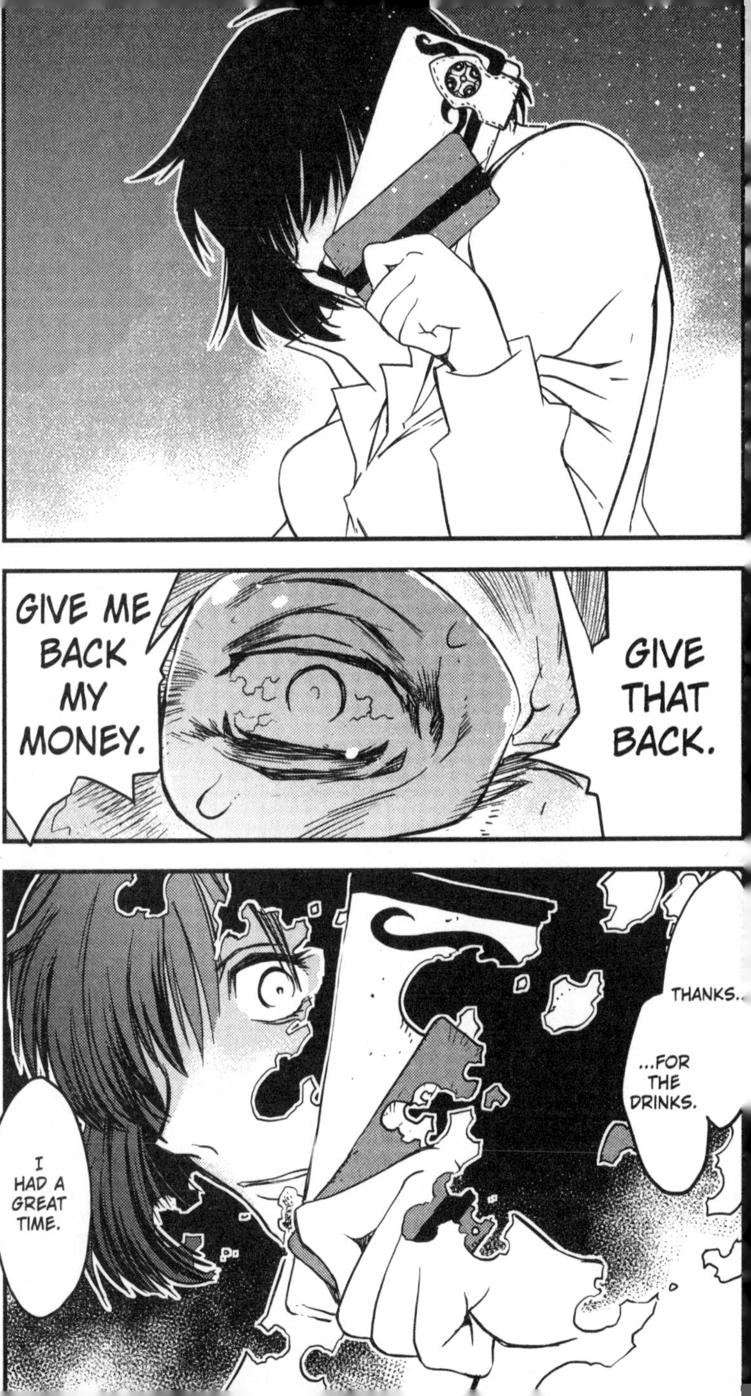
GIVE THAT BACK.
GIVE ME BACK MY MONEY.
THANKS...
...FOR THE DRINKS.
I HAD A GREAT TIME.

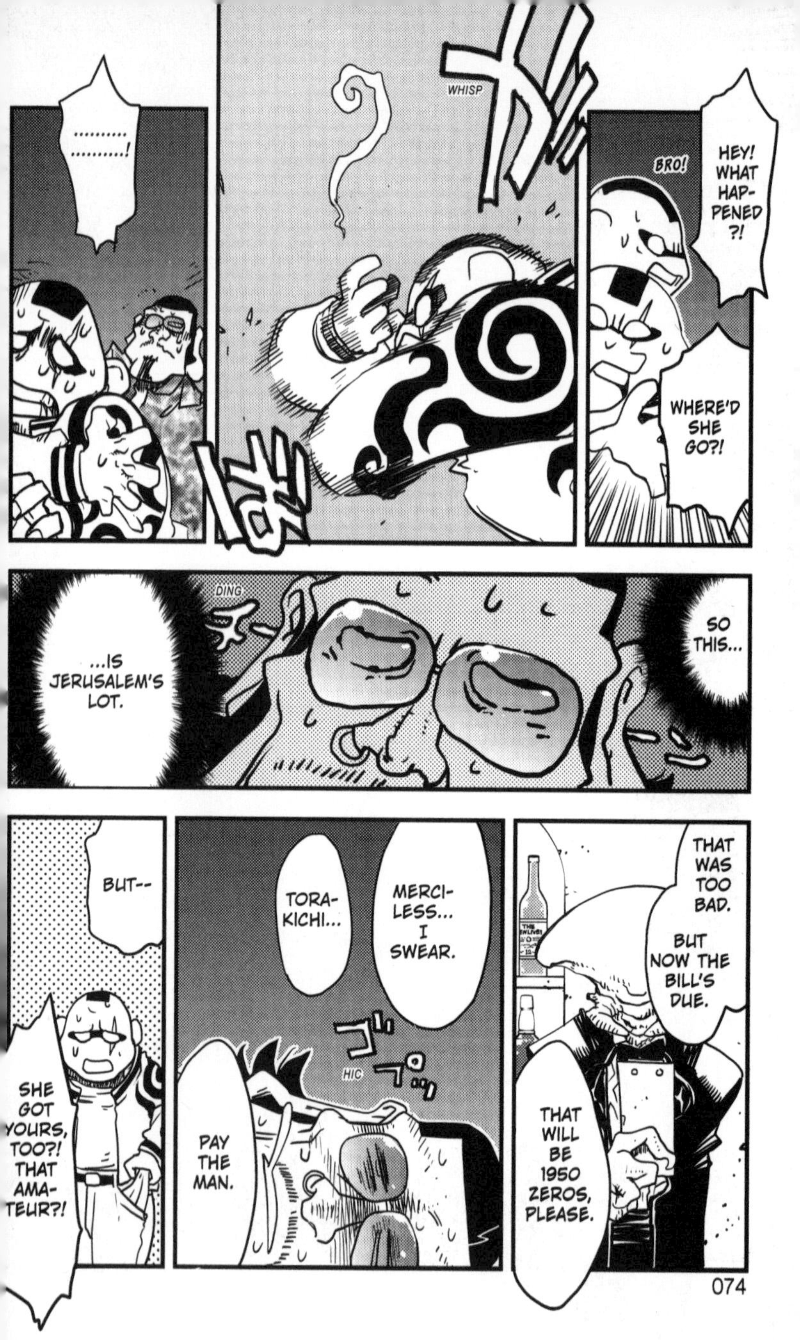
HEY! WHAT HAP-PENED ?!
BRO!
WHERE'D SHE GO?!
WHISP
....
...........!
SO THIS...
DING
...IS JERUSALEM'S LOT.
THAT WAS TOO BAD.
BUT NOW THE BILL'S DUE.
THAT WILL BE 1950 ZEROS, PLEASE.
MERCI-LESS... I SWEAR.
TORA-KICHI...
HIC
PAY THE MAN.
BUT--
SHE GOT YOURS, TOO?! THAT AMA-TEUR?!

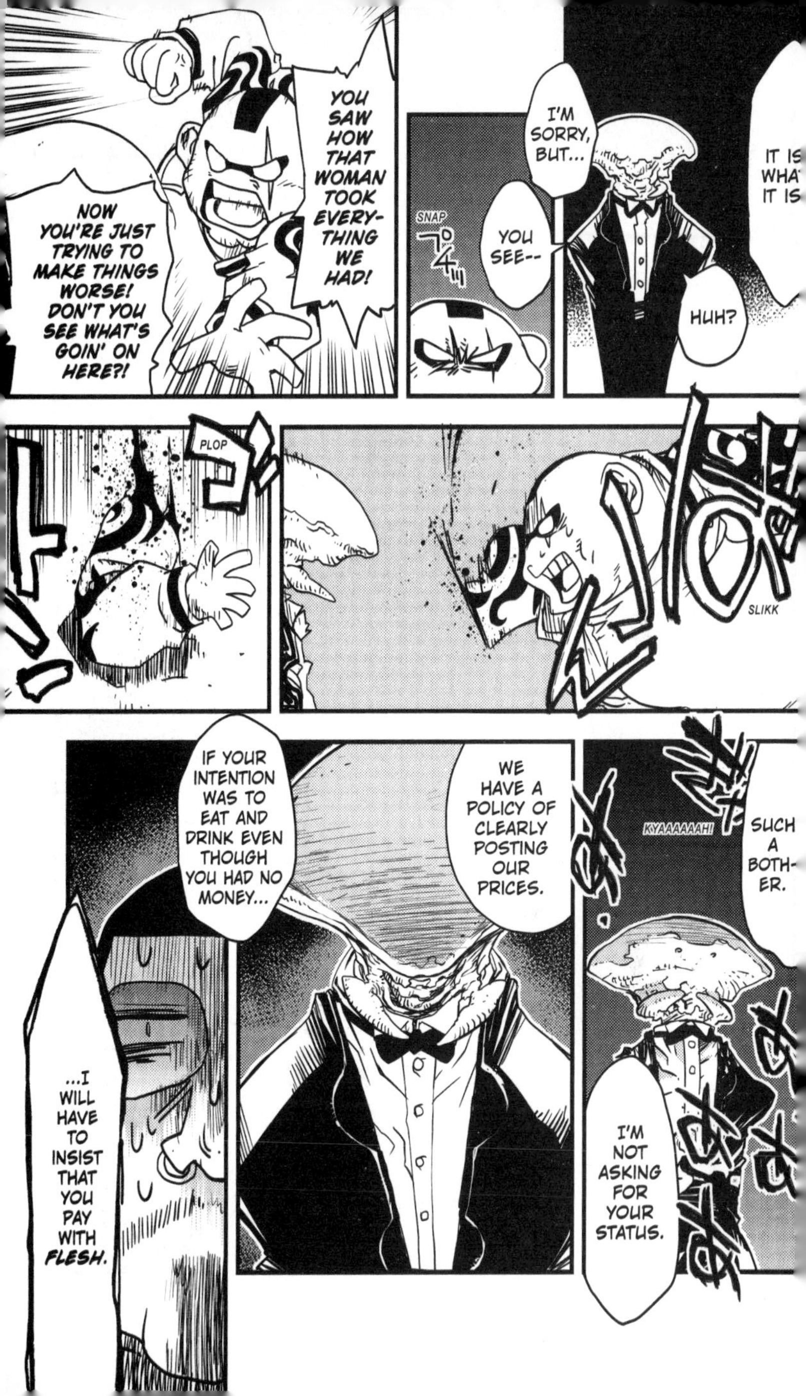
IT IS WHAT IT IS
I'M SORRY, BUT...
YOU SEE--
HUH?
SNAP
YOU SAW HOW THAT WOMAN TOOK EVERYTHING WE HAD!
NOW YOU'RE JUST TRYING TO MAKE THINGS WORSE! DON'T YOU SEE WHAT'S GOIN' ON HERE?!
SLIKK
PLOP
SUCH A BOTHER.
KYAAAAAAH!
I'M NOT ASKING FOR YOUR STATUS.
WE HAVE A POLICY OF CLEARLY POSTING OUR PRICES.
IF YOUR INTENTION WAS TO EAT AND DRINK EVEN THOUGH YOU HAD NO MONEY...
...I WILL HAVE TO INSIST THAT YOU PAY WITH *FLESH*.

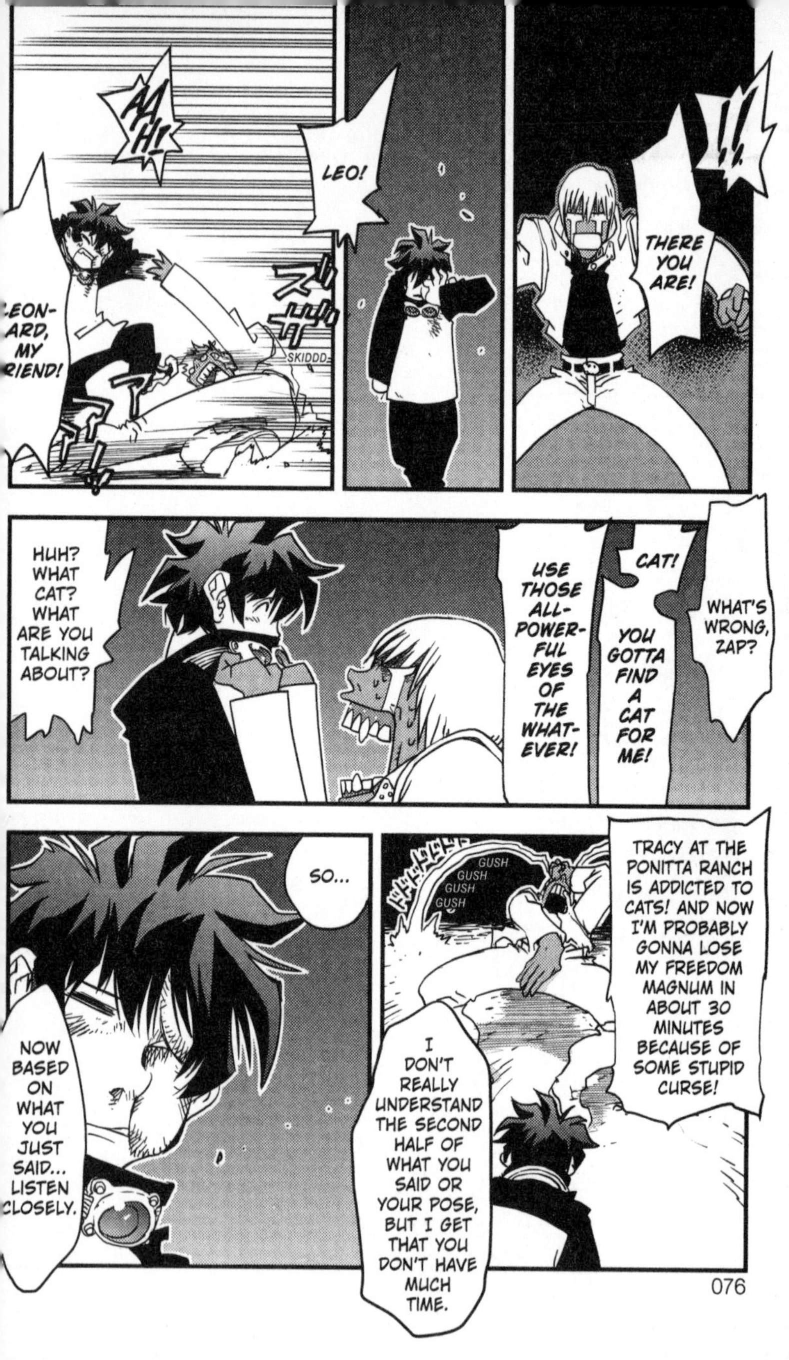
!!
THERE YOU ARE!
LEO!
AAH!
SKIDDD
LEON-ARD, MY FRIEND!
WHAT'S WRONG, ZAP?
CAT!
YOU GOTTA FIND A CAT FOR ME!
USE THOSE ALL-POWERFUL EYES OF THE WHATEVER!
HUH? WHAT CAT? WHAT ARE YOU TALKING ABOUT?
TRACY AT THE PONITTA RANCH IS ADDICTED TO CATS! AND NOW I'M PROBABLY GONNA LOSE MY FREEDOM MAGNUM IN ABOUT 30 MINUTES BECAUSE OF SOME STUPID CURSE!
GUSH
GUSH
GUSH
GUSH
I DON'T REALLY UNDERSTAND THE SECOND HALF OF WHAT YOU SAID OR YOUR POSE, BUT I GET THAT YOU DON'T HAVE MUCH TIME.
SO...
NOW BASED ON WHAT YOU JUST SAID... LISTEN CLOSELY.

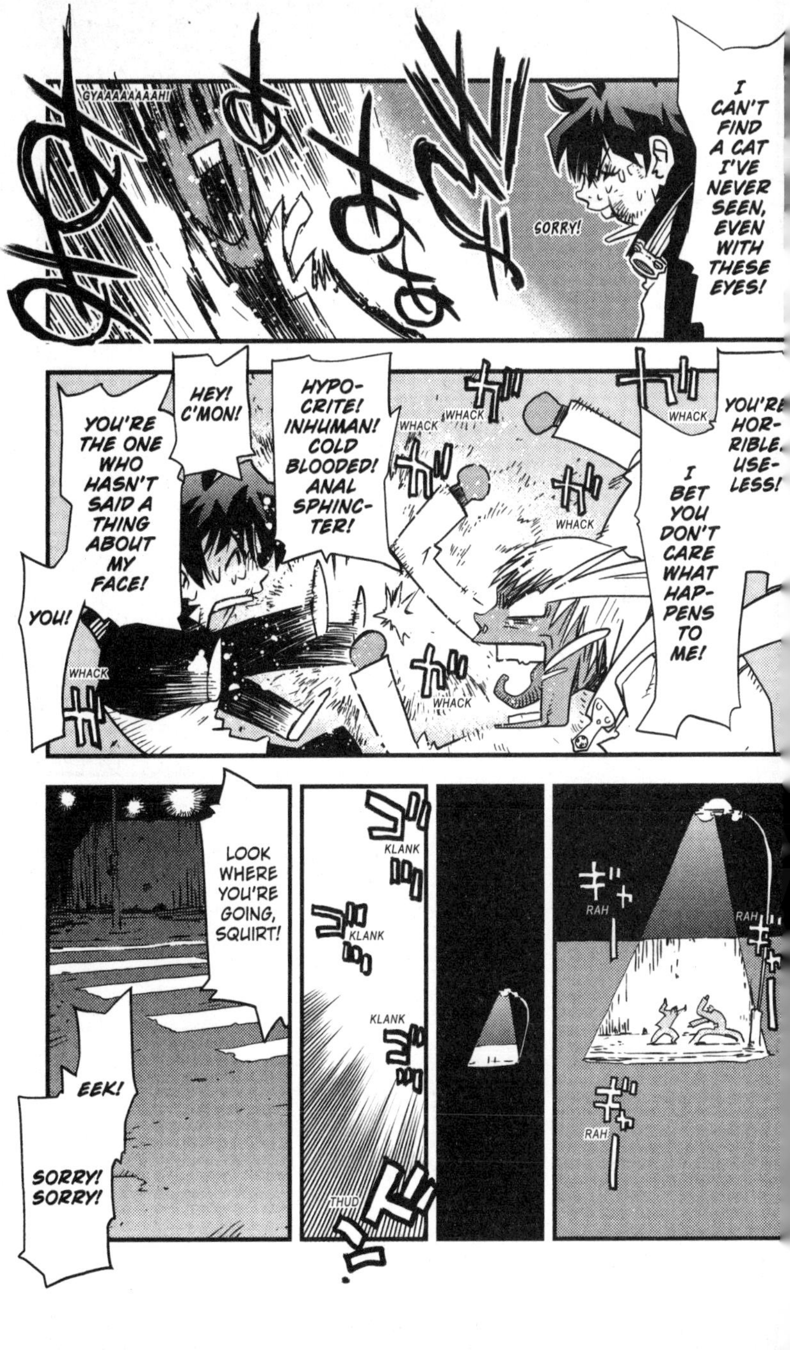
I CAN'T FIND A CAT I'VE NEVER SEEN, EVEN WITH THESE EYES!
SORRY!
GYAAAAAAAAH!
YOU'RE HORRIBLE. USELESS!
WHACK
I BET YOU DON'T CARE WHAT HAPPENS TO ME!
WHACK
WHACK
WHACK
WHACK
HYPOCRITE! INHUMAN! COLD BLOODED! ANAL SPHINCTER!
HEY! C'MON!
YOU'RE THE ONE WHO HASN'T SAID A THING ABOUT MY FACE!
YOU!
WHACK
RAH
RAH
RAH
KLANK
KLANK
KLANK
THUD
LOOK WHERE YOU'RE GOING, SQUIRT!
EEK!
SORRY! SORRY!

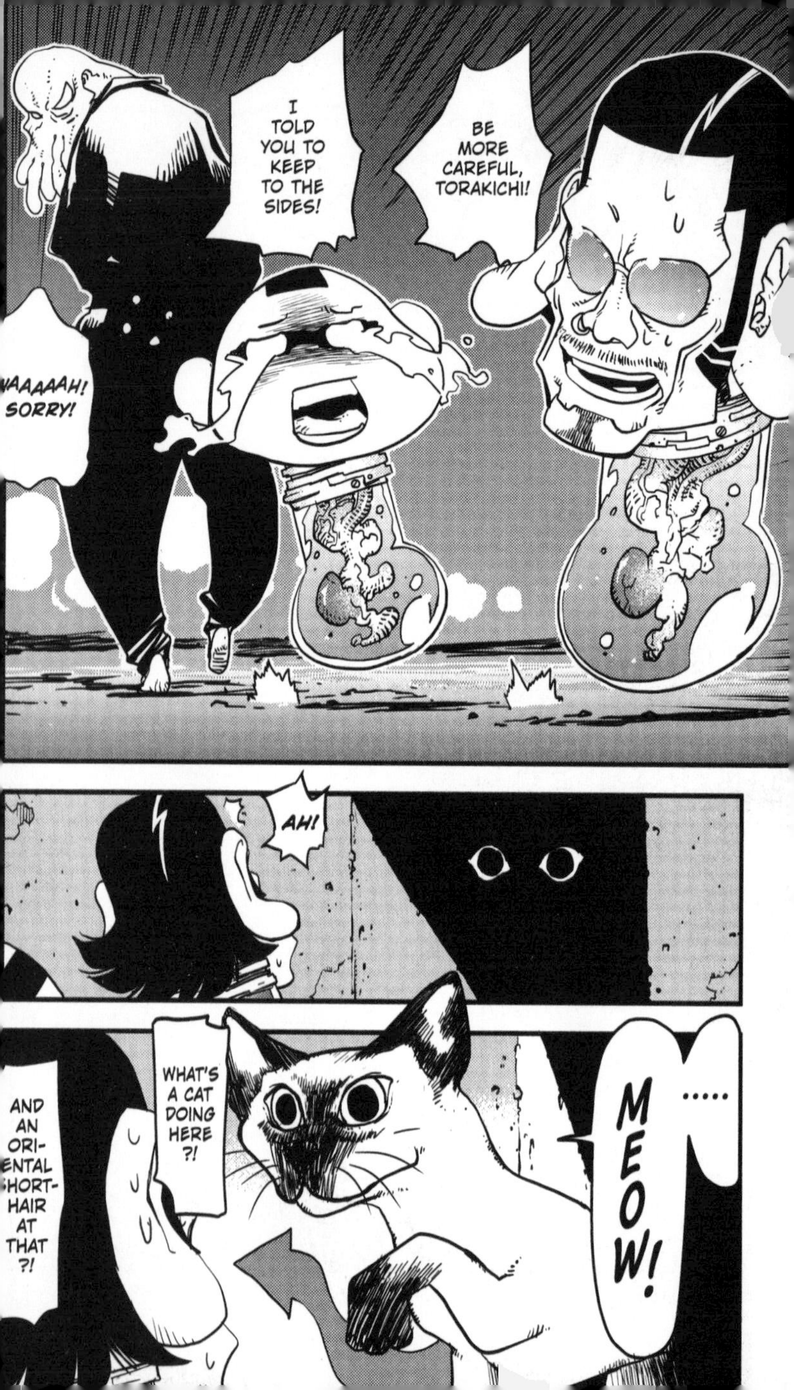
BE MORE CAREFUL, TORAKICHI!
I TOLD YOU TO KEEP TO THE SIDES!
AAAAAH! SORRY!
AH!
.....
MEOW!
WHAT'S A CAT DOING HERE ?!
AND AN ORI-ENTAL HORT-HAIR AT THAT ?!

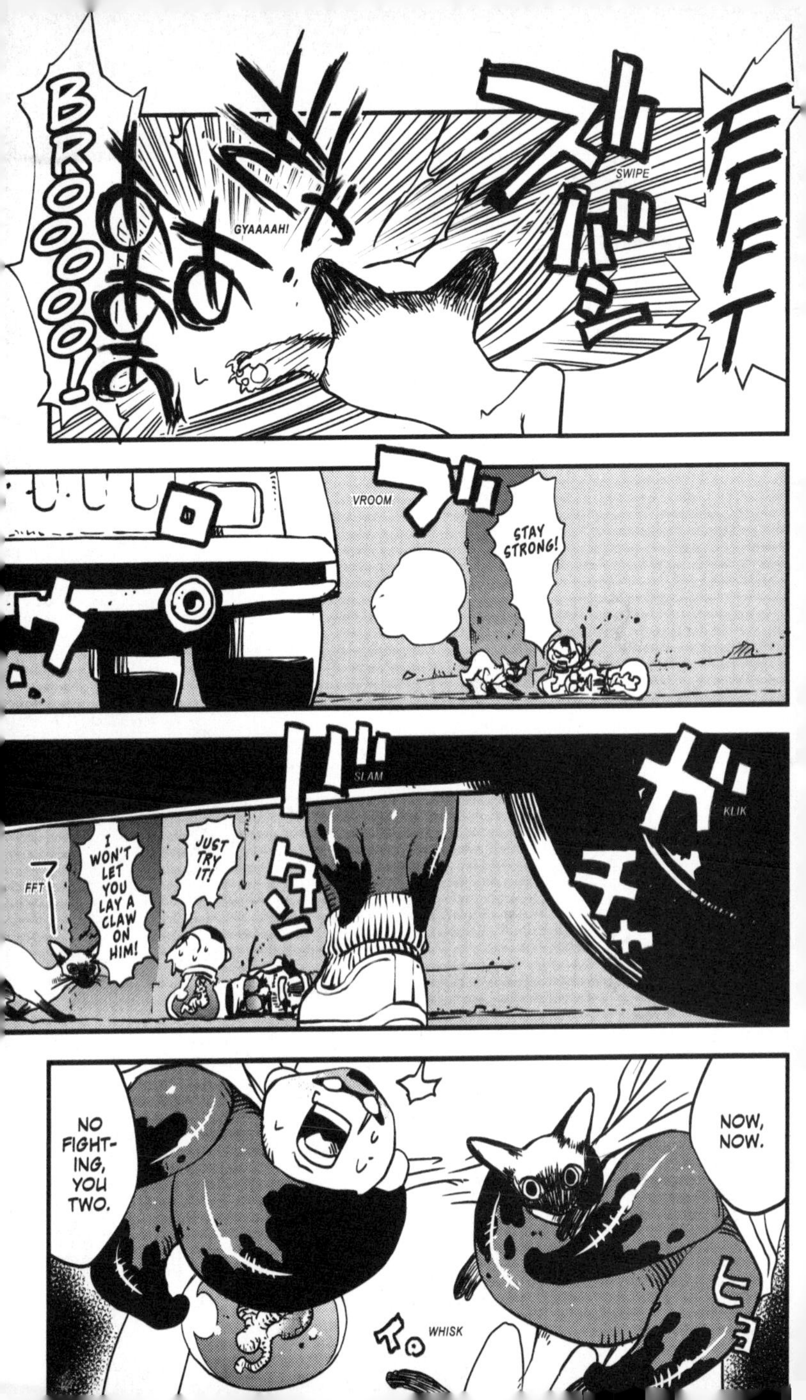
FFFFT
SWIPE
GYAAAAH!
BROOOOOO!
VROOM
STAY STRONG!
KLIK
SLAM
JUST TRY IT!
I WON'T LET YOU LAY A CLAW ON HIM!
FFT
NOW, NOW.
NO FIGHTING, YOU TWO.
WHISK

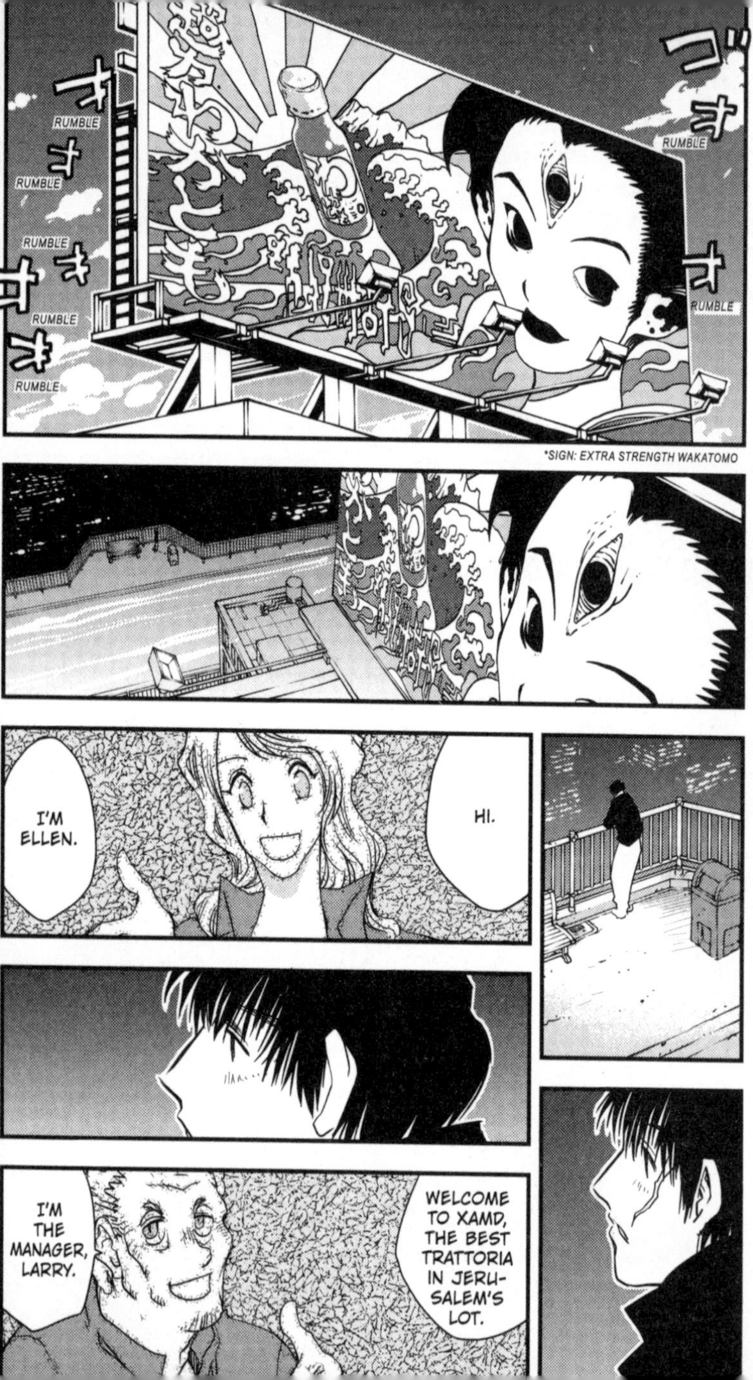
RUMBLE
RUMBLE
RUMBLE
RUMBLE
RUMBLE
RUMBLE
RUMBLE
*SIGN: EXTRA STRENGTH WAKATOMO
HI.
I'M ELLEN.
HAA...
WELCOME TO XAMD, THE BEST TRATTORIA IN JERU-SALEM'S LOT.
I'M THE MANAGER, LARRY.

I GUESS...

...I ALLOWED MYSELF TO FROLIC AROUND TOO MUCH.

....
....

YEAH.

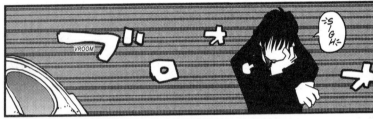

VROOM

-SIGH-

OOOOM

SKREECH

SIR?

SLAM

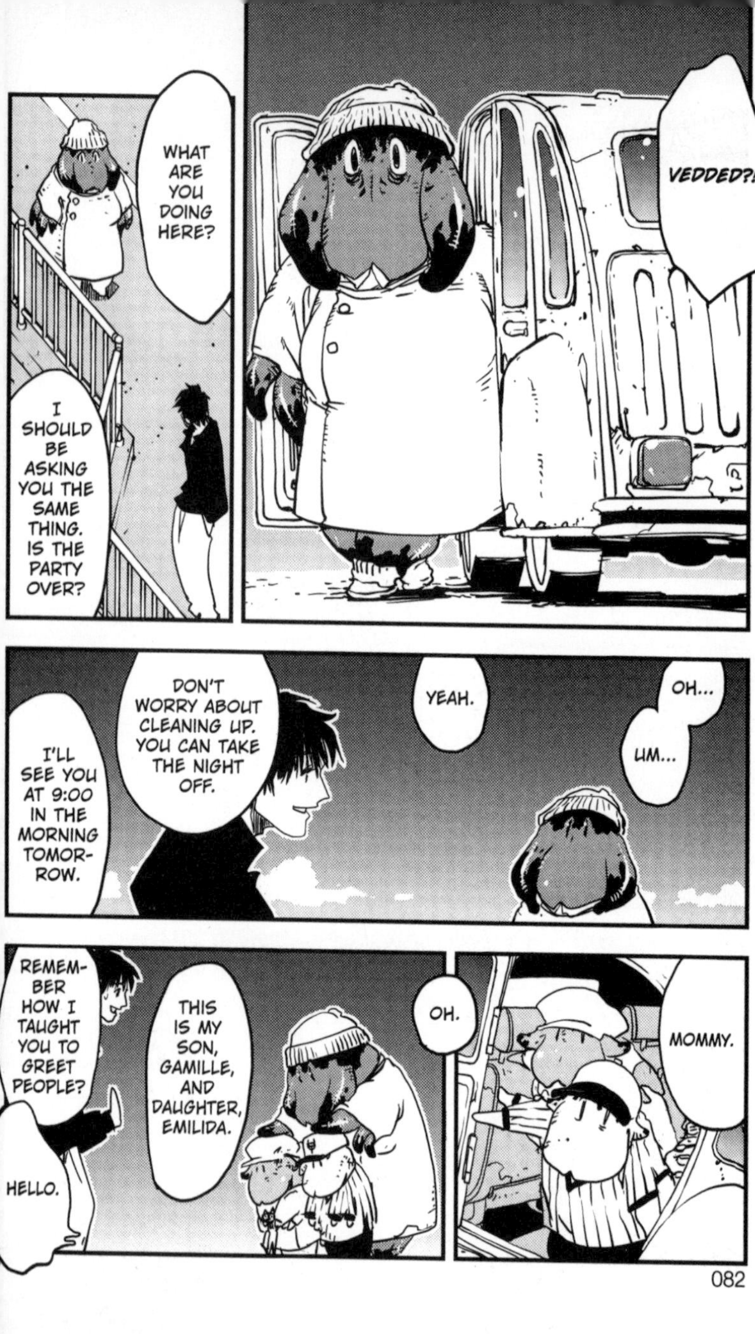
VEDDED?!
WHAT ARE YOU DOING HERE?
I SHOULD BE ASKING YOU THE SAME THING. IS THE PARTY OVER?
OH...
UM...
YEAH.
DON'T WORRY ABOUT CLEANING UP. YOU CAN TAKE THE NIGHT OFF.
I'LL SEE YOU AT 9:00 IN THE MORNING TOMORROW.
MOMMY.
OH.
THIS IS MY SON, GAMILLE, AND DAUGHTER, EMILIDA.
REMEMBER HOW I TAUGHT YOU TO GREET PEOPLE?
HELLO.

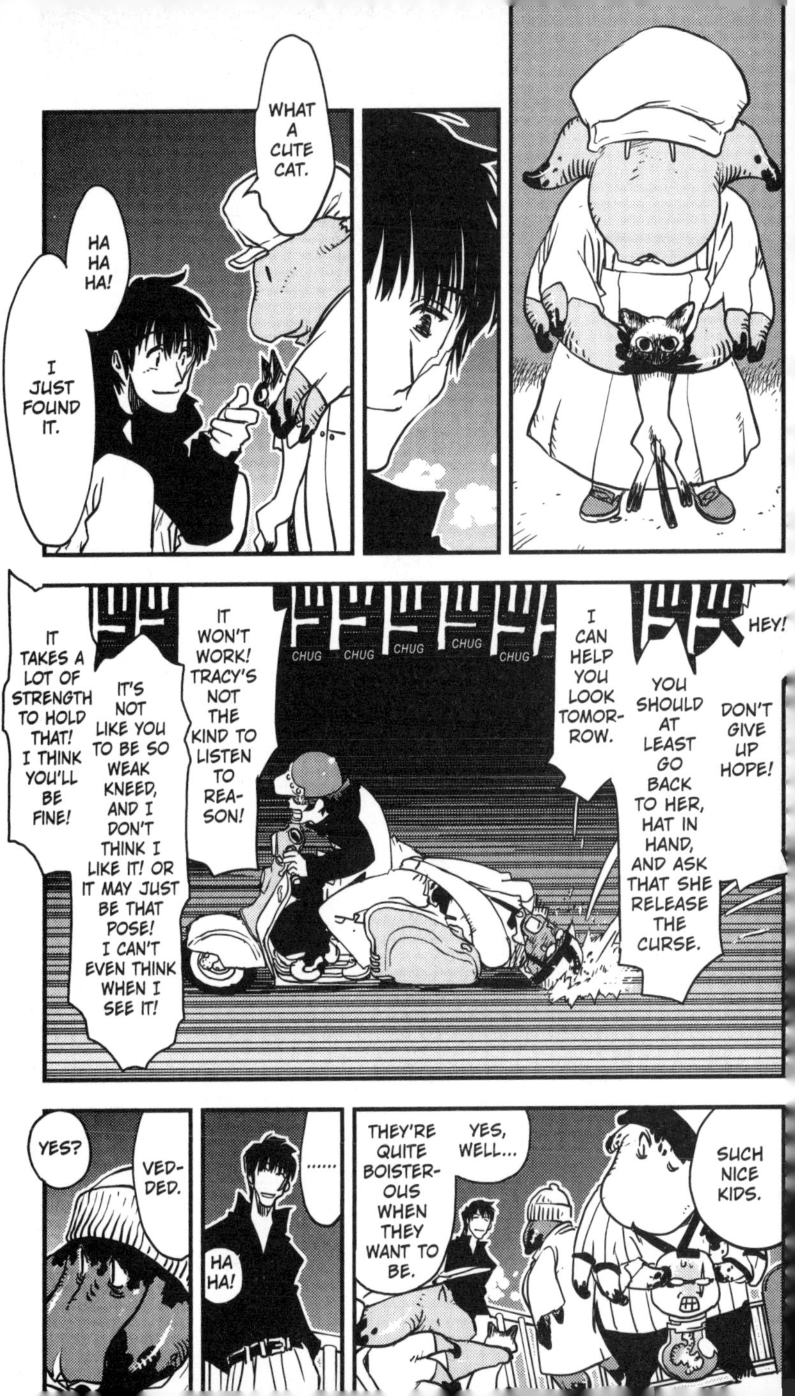
WHAT A CUTE CAT.
HA HA HA!
I JUST FOUND IT.
HEY!
DON'T GIVE UP HOPE!
YOU SHOULD AT LEAST GO BACK TO HER, HAT IN HAND, AND ASK THAT SHE RELEASE THE CURSE.
I CAN HELP YOU LOOK TOMOR-ROW.
CHUG CHUG CHUG CHUG CHUG
IT WON'T WORK! TRACY'S NOT THE KIND TO LISTEN TO REA-SON!
IT'S NOT LIKE YOU TO BE SO WEAK KNEED, AND I DON'T THINK I LIKE IT! OR IT MAY JUST BE THAT POSE! I CAN'T EVEN THINK WHEN I SEE IT!
IT TAKES A LOT OF STRENGTH TO HOLD THAT! I THINK YOU'LL BE FINE!
SUCH NICE KIDS.
YES, WELL...
THEY'RE QUITE BOISTER-OUS WHEN THEY WANT TO BE.
......
HA HA!
VED-DED.
YES?

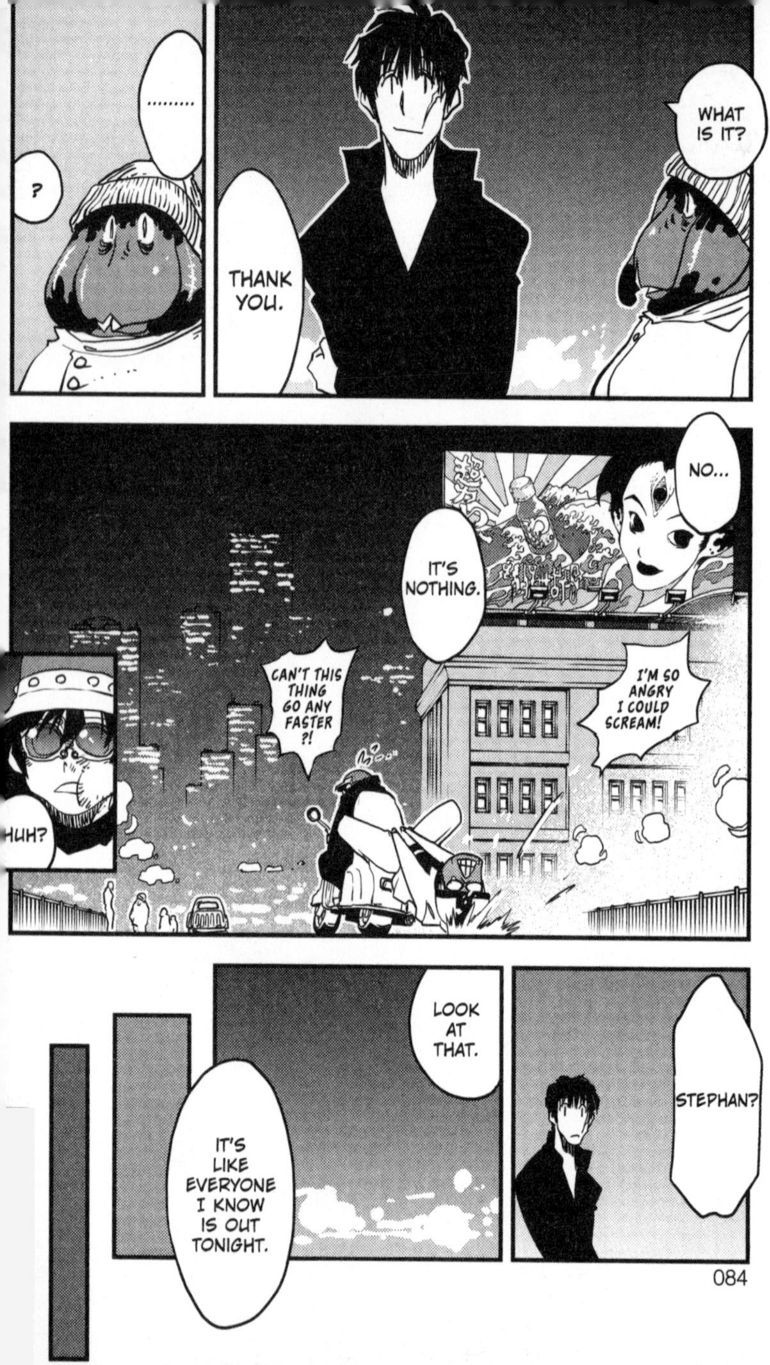
WHAT IS IT?
THANK YOU.
....
?
NO...
IT'S NOTHING.
I'M SO ANGRY I COULD SCREAM!
CAN'T THIS THING GO ANY FASTER ?!
HUH?
STEPHAN?
LOOK AT THAT.
IT'S LIKE EVERYONE I KNOW IS OUT TONIGHT.

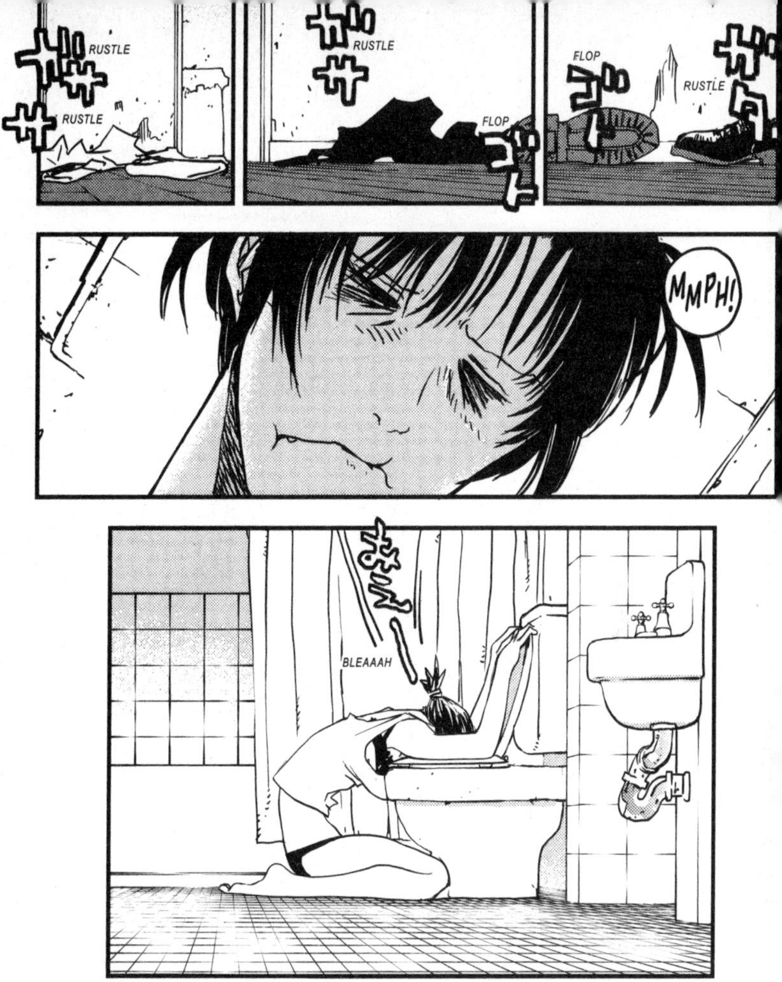
RUSTLE
FLOP
RUSTLE
FLOP
RUSTLE
RUSTLE
MMPH!
BLEAAAH

BLOOD BLOCKADE BATTLEFRONT

DAY IN DAY OUT

END

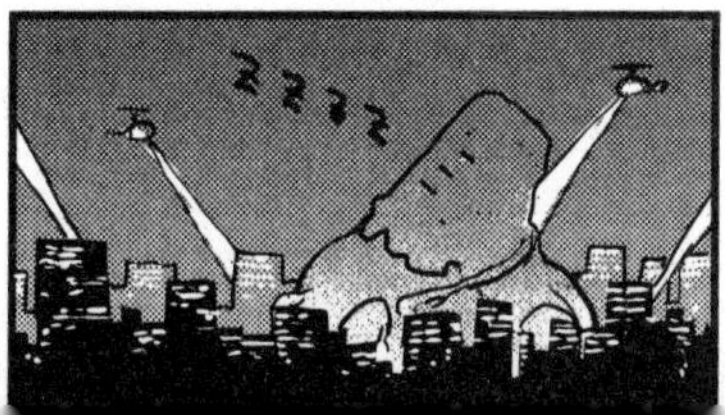

BLOOD·BLOCKADE BATTLEFRONT

BLOOD BLOCKADE BATTLEFRONT

血界戰線 **3**

THE TREMOROUS
BLOOD HAMMER

—震撃の血槌—

THE TREMOROUS BLOOD HAMMER

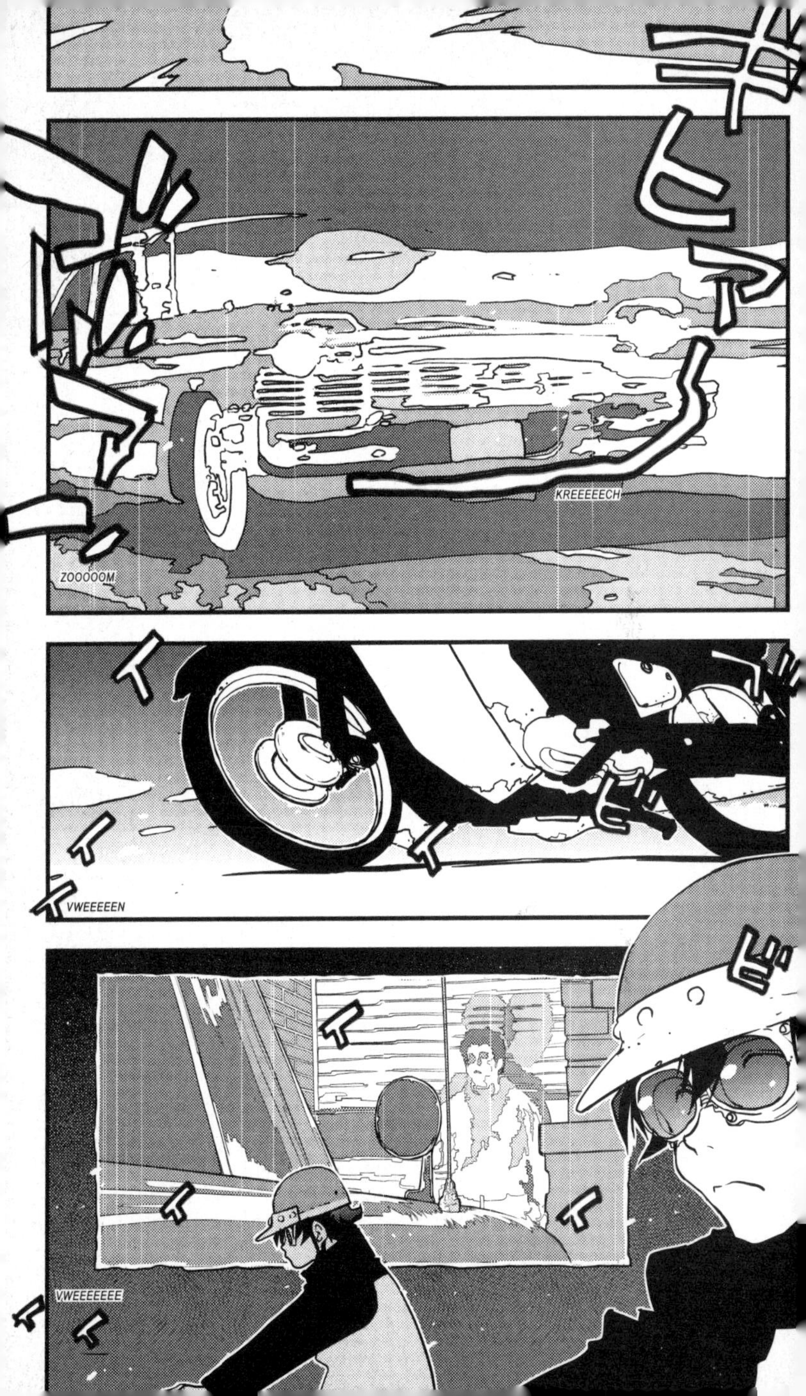
KREEEEECH
ZOOOOOM
VWEEEEEN
VWEEEEEEE

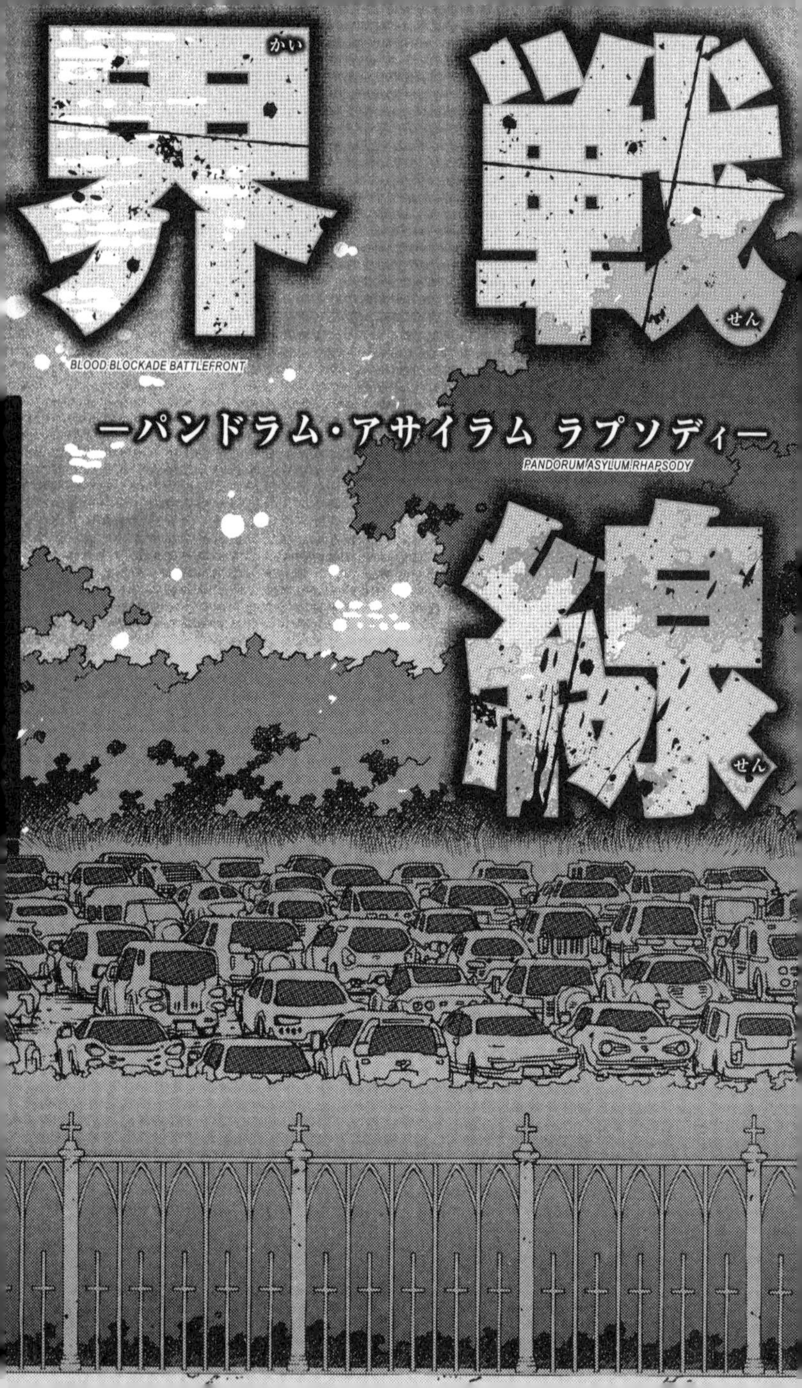

界戦線
かい
せん
せん
BLOOD BLOCKADE BATTLEFRONT
ーパンドラム・アサイラム ラプソディー
PANDORUM ASYLUM RHAPSODY

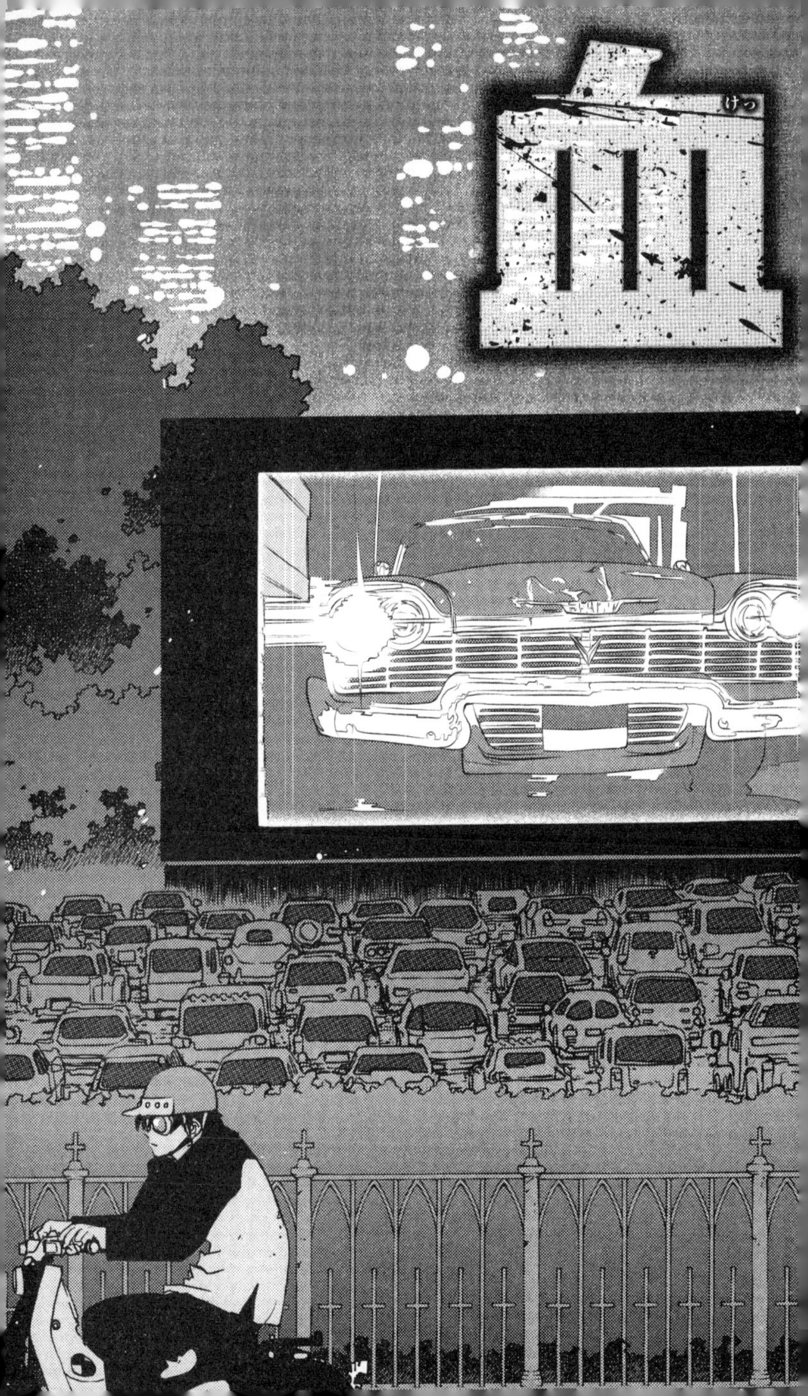
血
けつ

KYAAAH
WHAM
BAM
WHAM
THUD
SMASH
KACHUNK

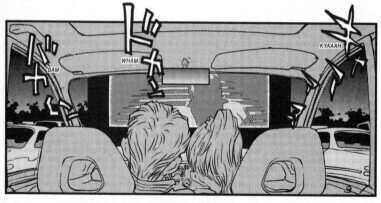

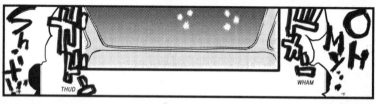

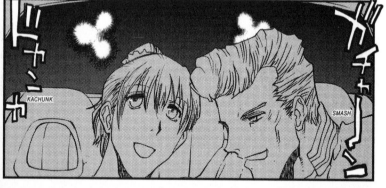

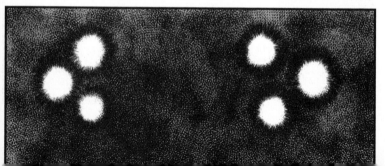

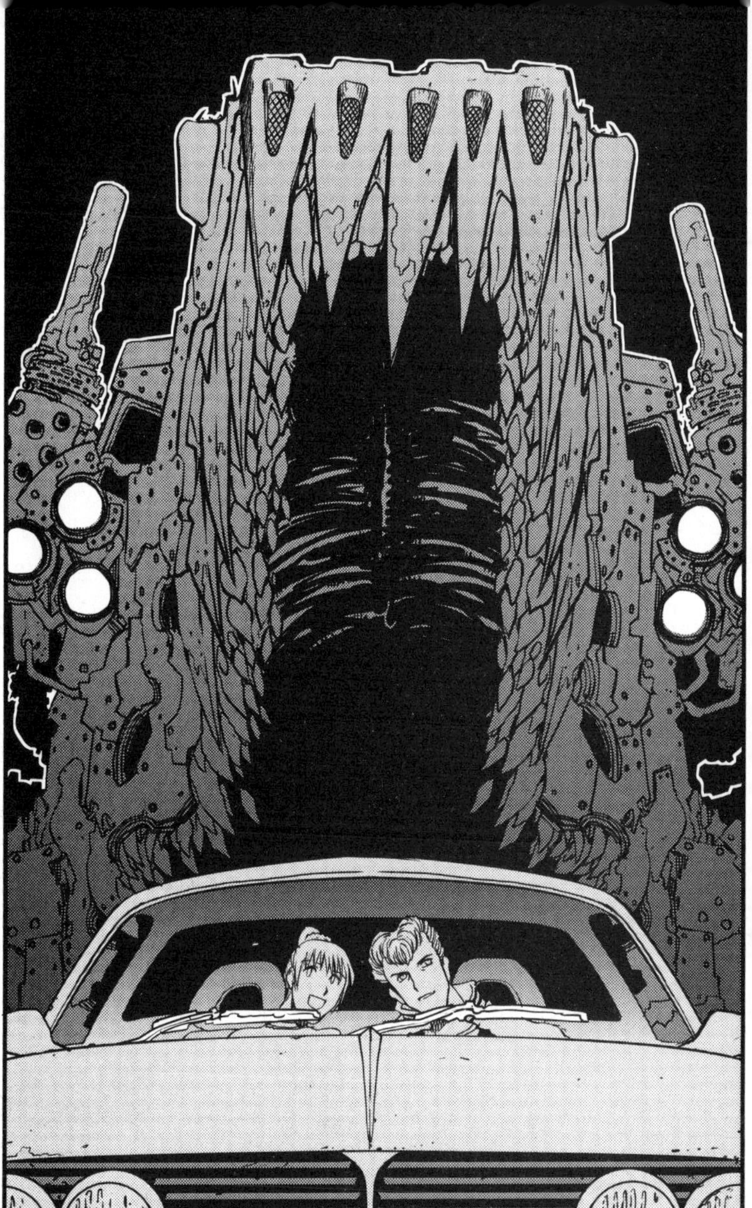

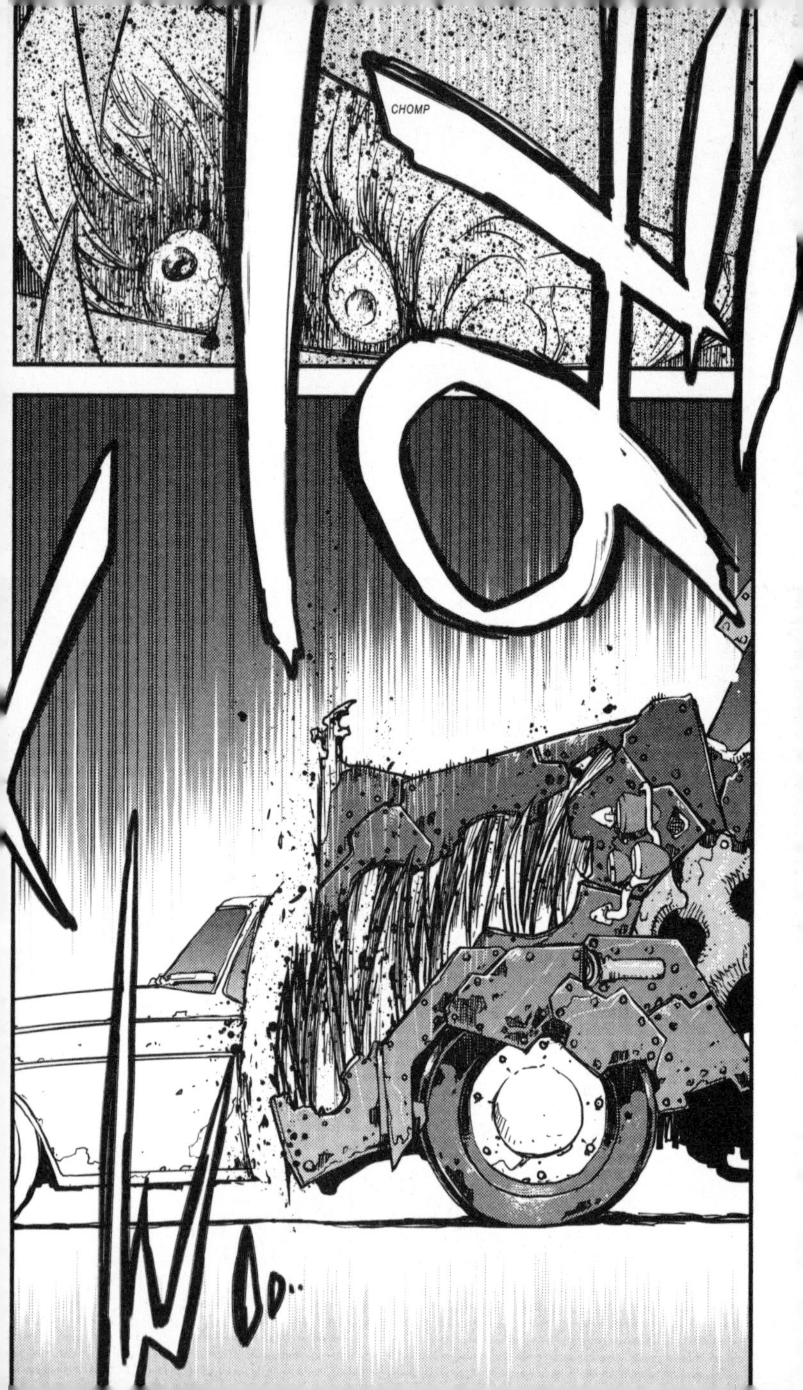
CHOMP

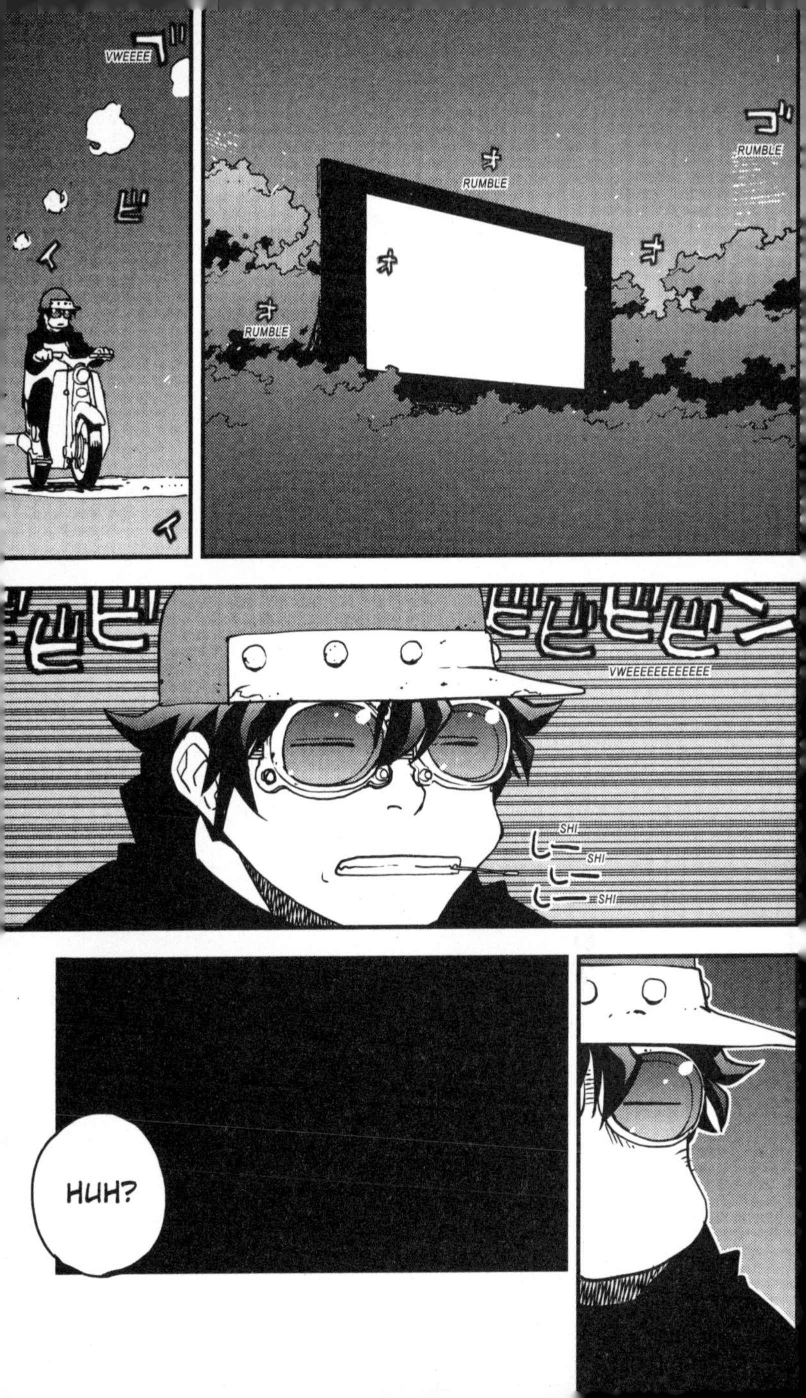
RUMBLE
RUMBLE
RUMBLE
VWEEEE
VWEEEEEEEEEEEE
SHI
SHI
SHI
HUH?

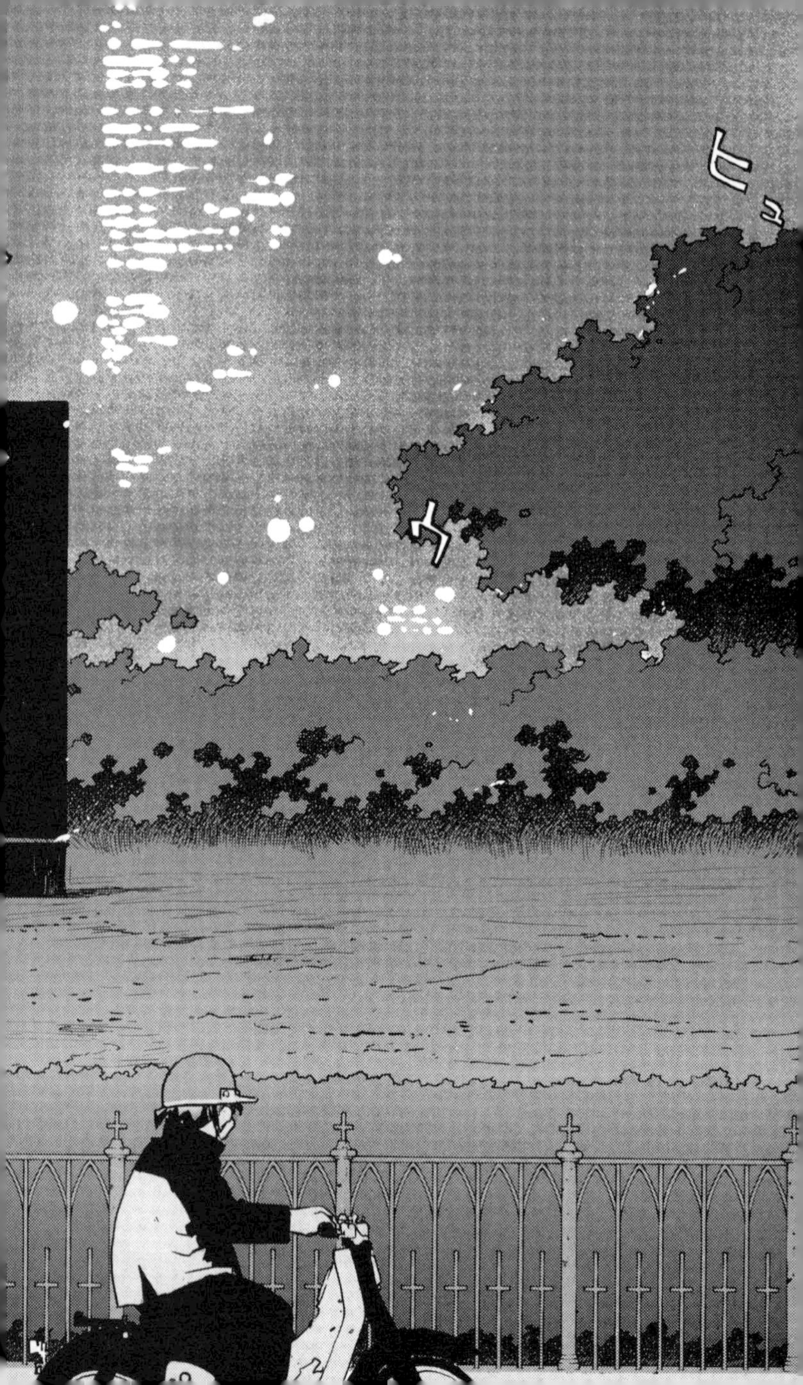
ヒュ
ウ

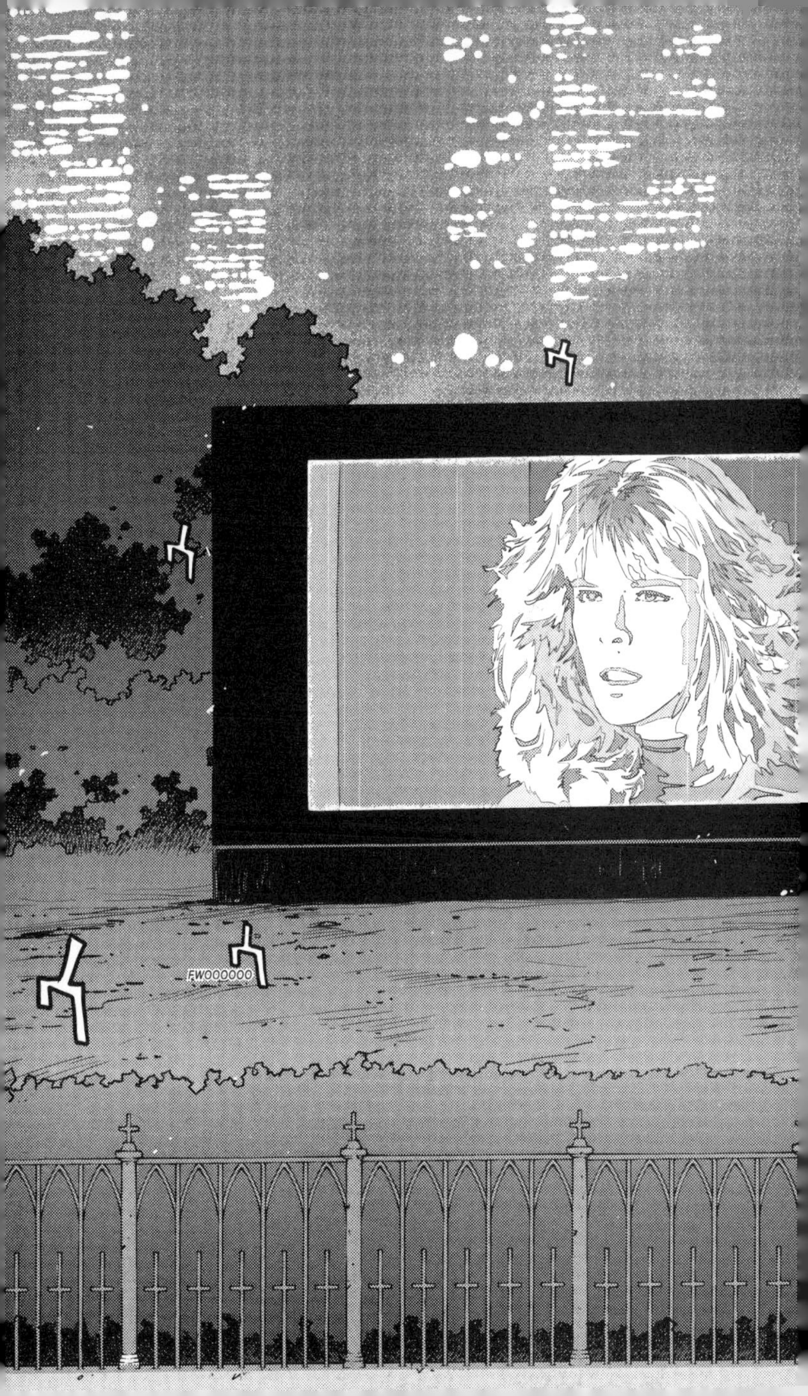
FWOOOOOO

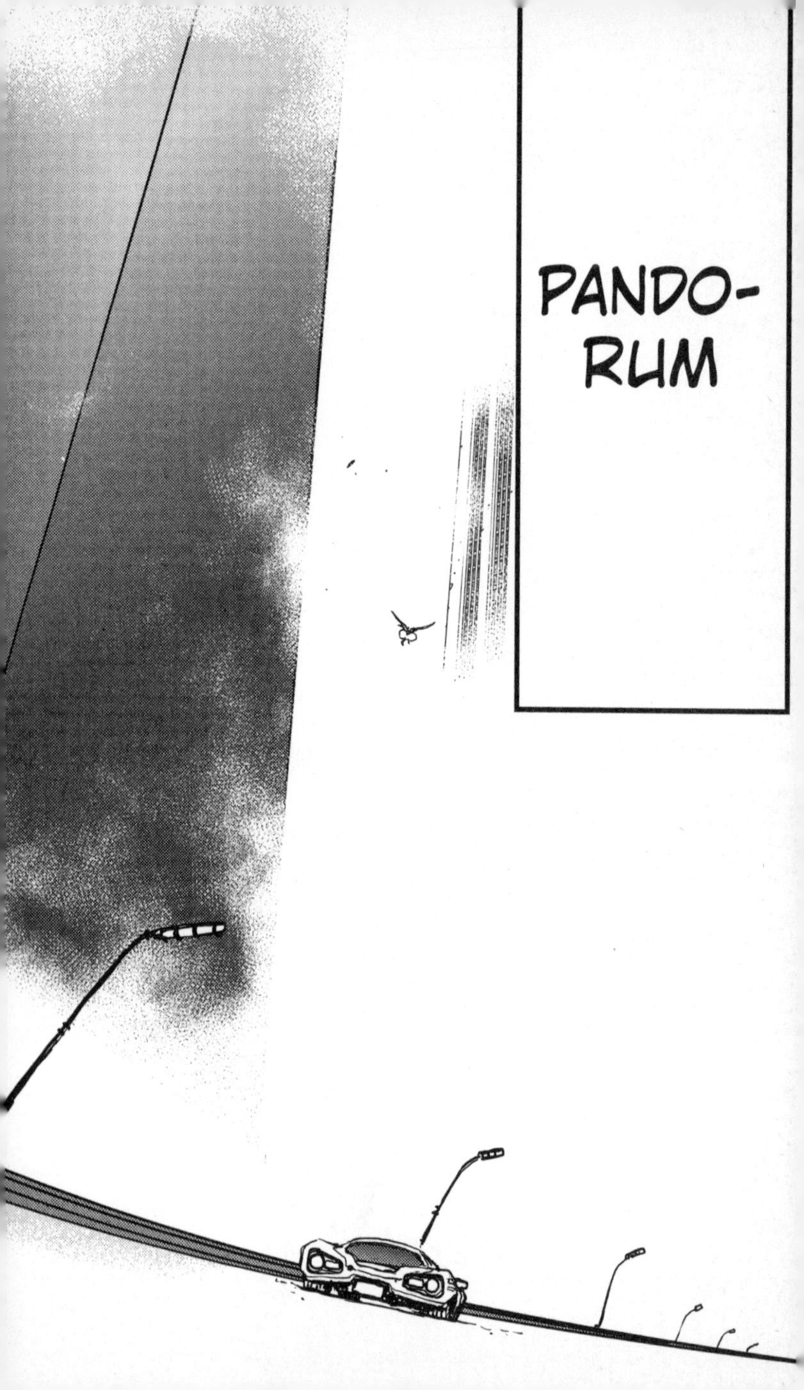
PANDO-
RUM

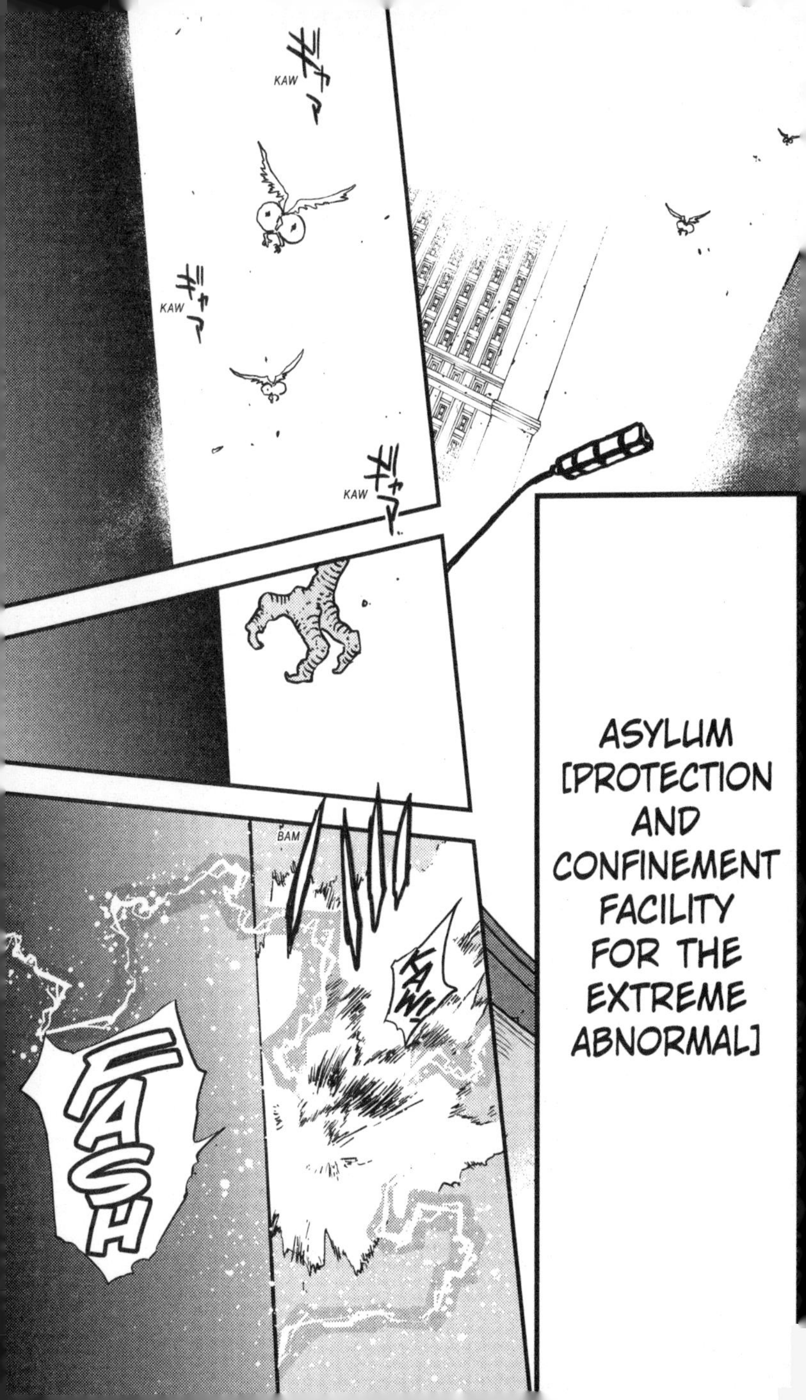
KAW
KAW
KAW
ASYLUM [PROTECTION AND CONFINEMENT FACILITY FOR THE EXTREME ABNORMAL]
BAM
KAW!!
FASH

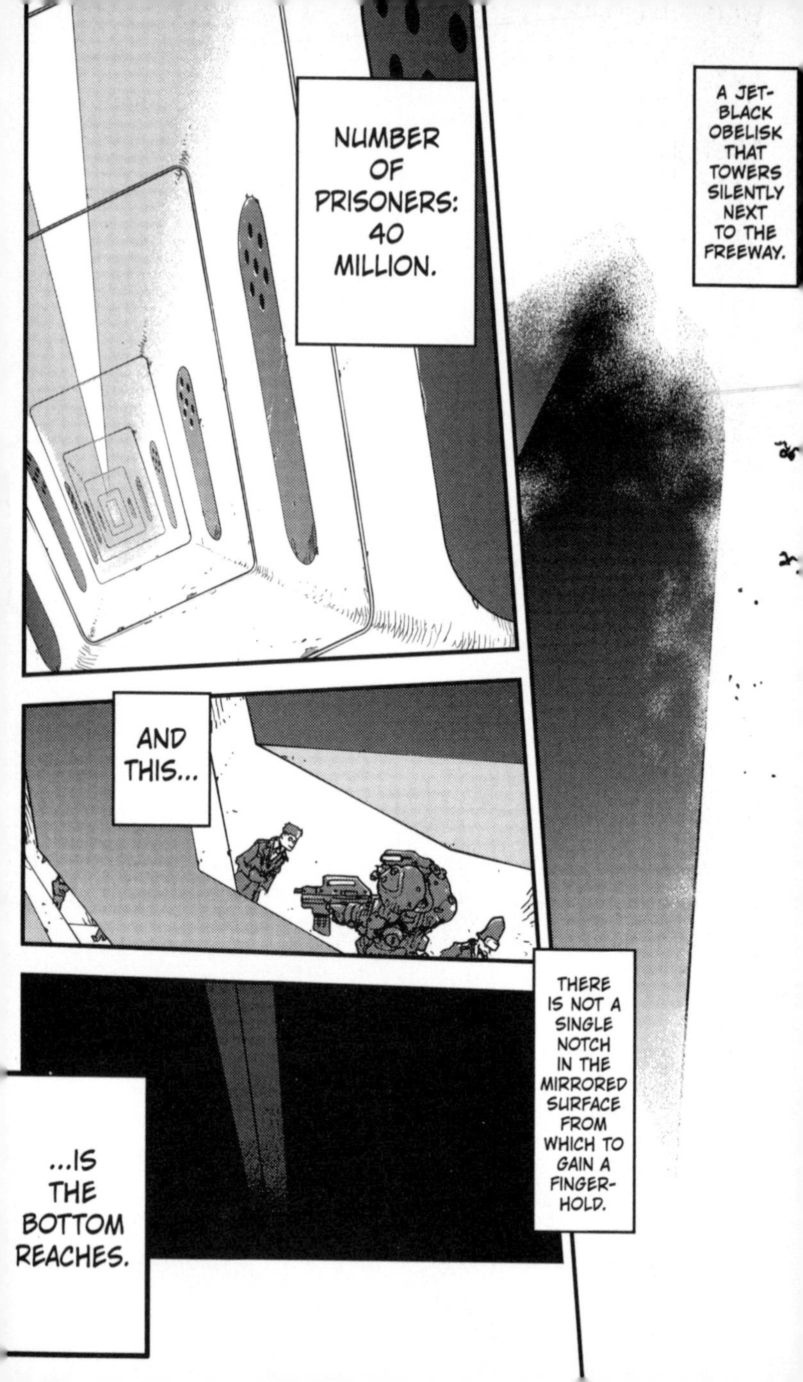
A JET-BLACK OBELISK THAT TOWERS SILENTLY NEXT TO THE FREEWAY.
THERE IS NOT A SINGLE NOTCH IN THE MIRRORED SURFACE FROM WHICH TO GAIN A FINGER-HOLD.
NUMBER OF PRISONERS: 40 MILLION.
AND THIS...
...IS THE BOTTOM REACHES.

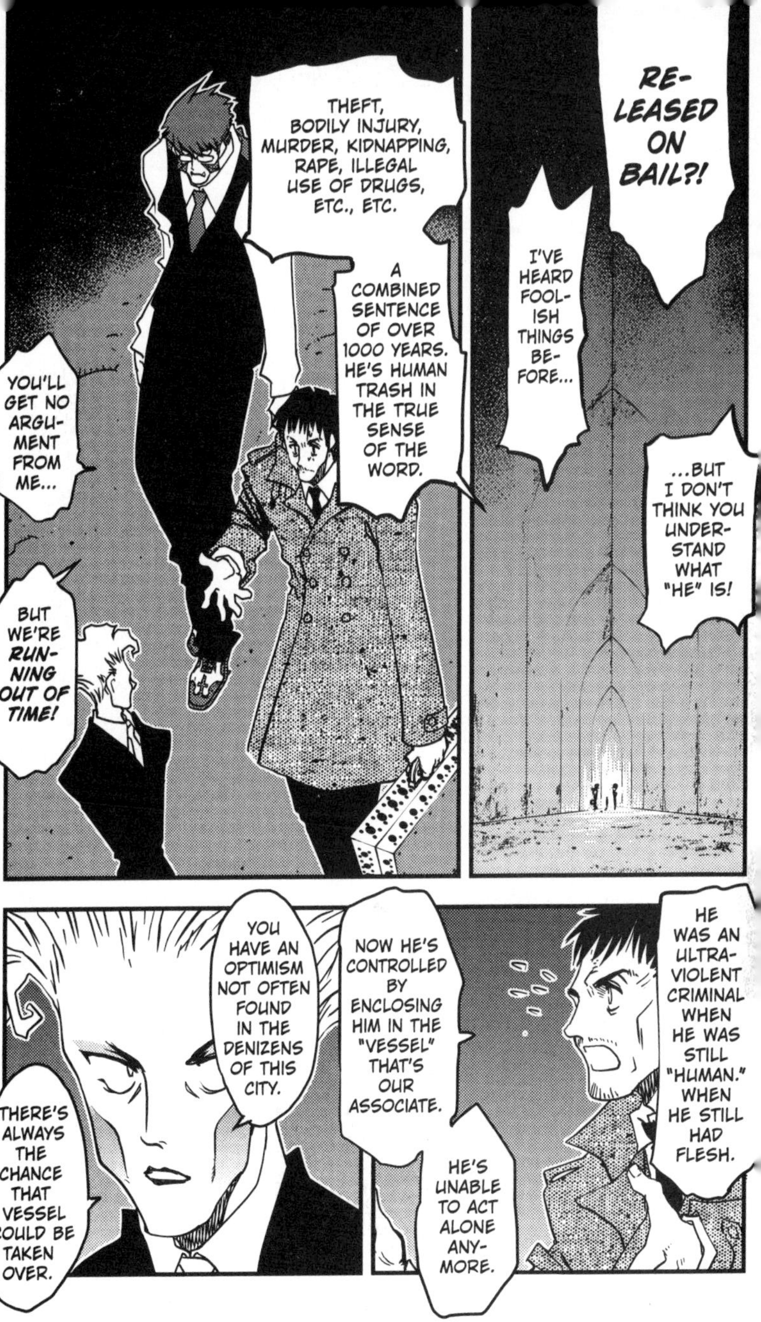
RE-LEASED ON BAIL?!
I'VE HEARD FOOLISH THINGS BEFORE...
...BUT I DON'T THINK YOU UNDERSTAND WHAT "HE" IS!
THEFT, BODILY INJURY, MURDER, KIDNAPPING, RAPE, ILLEGAL USE OF DRUGS, ETC., ETC.
A COMBINED SENTENCE OF OVER 1000 YEARS. HE'S HUMAN TRASH IN THE TRUE SENSE OF THE WORD.
YOU'LL GET NO ARGUMENT FROM ME...
BUT WE'RE *RUNNING OUT OF TIME!*
HE WAS AN ULTRA-VIOLENT CRIMINAL WHEN HE WAS STILL "HUMAN." WHEN HE STILL HAD FLESH.
NOW HE'S CONTROLLED BY ENCLOSING HIM IN THE "VESSEL" THAT'S OUR ASSOCIATE.
HE'S UNABLE TO ACT ALONE ANYMORE.
YOU HAVE AN OPTIMISM NOT OFTEN FOUND IN THE DENIZENS OF THIS CITY.
THERE'S ALWAYS THE CHANCE THAT VESSEL COULD BE TAKEN OVER.

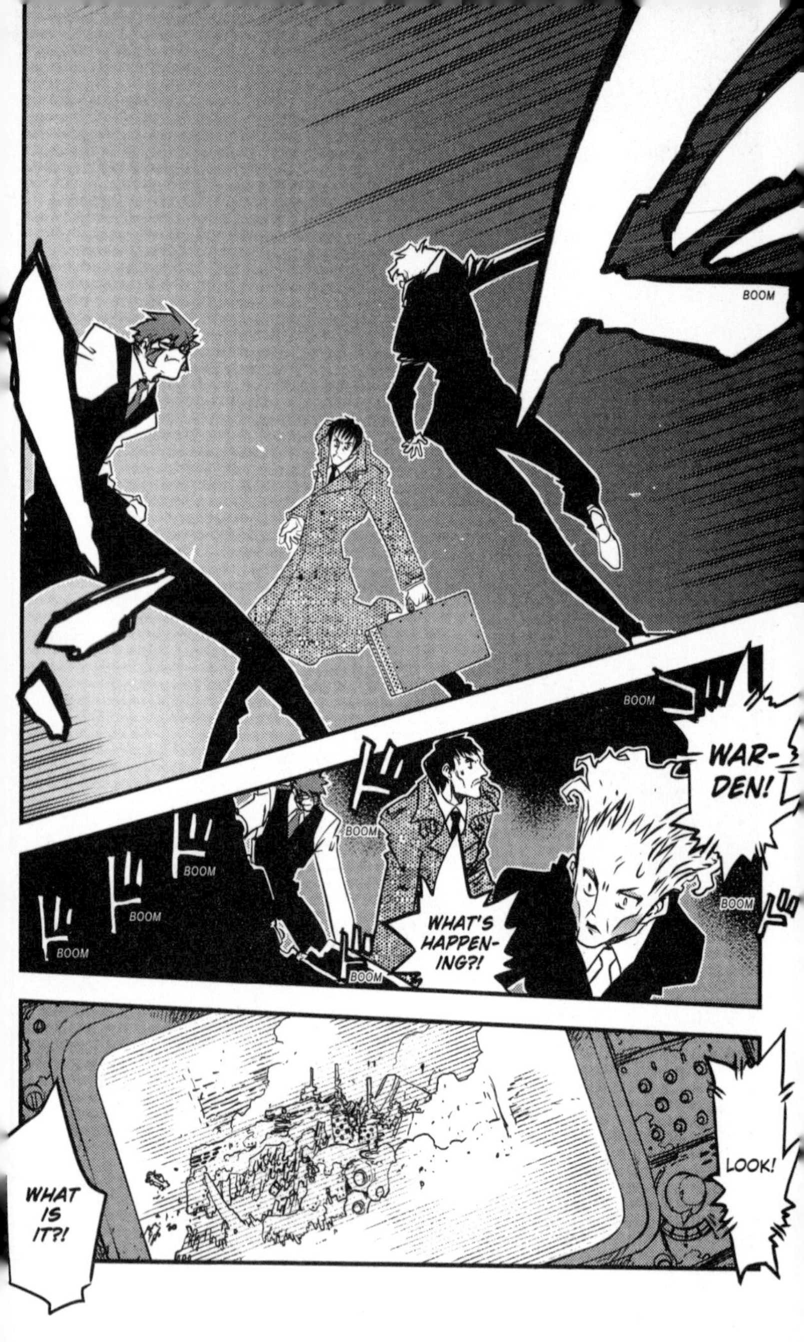
BOOM
BOOM
WAR-DEN!
BOOM
WHAT'S HAPPEN-ING?!
BOOM
BOOM
BOOM
BOOM
BOOM
LOOK!
WHAT IS IT?!

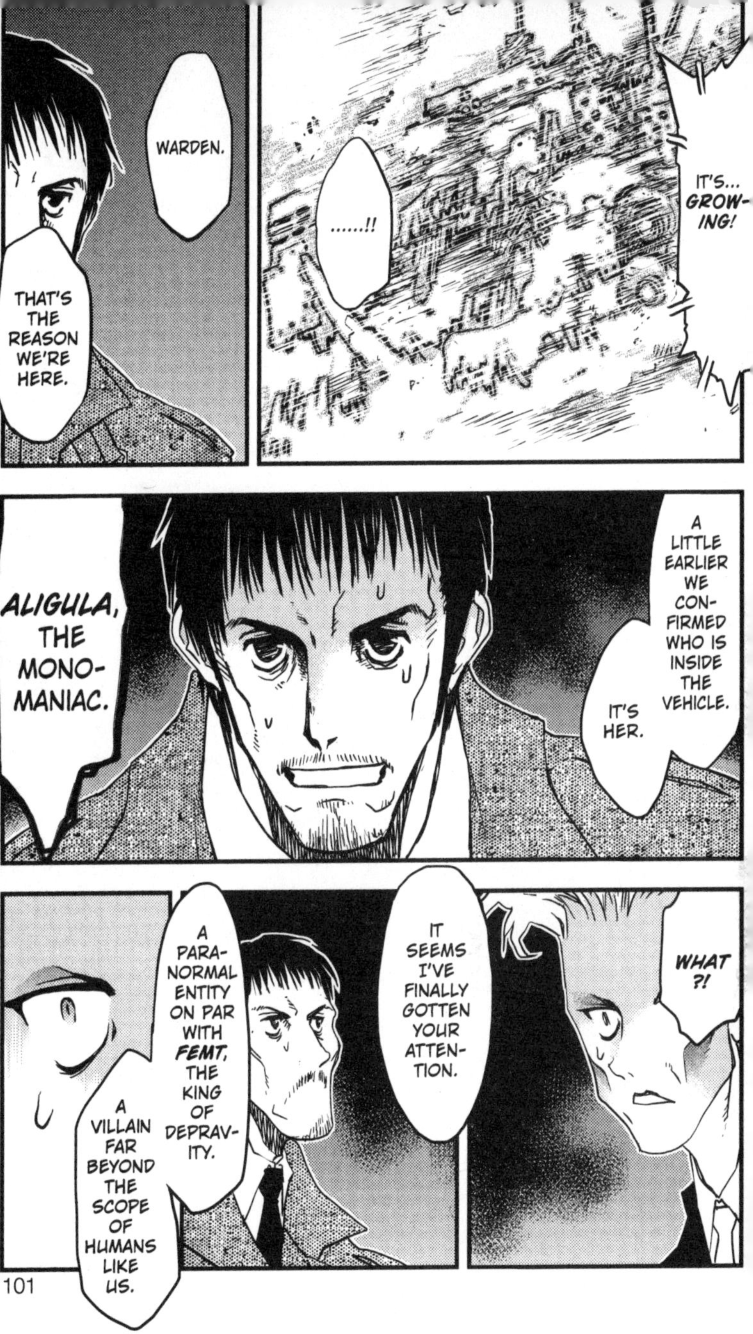
IT'S... GROWING!
......!!
WARDEN.
THAT'S THE REASON WE'RE HERE.
A LITTLE EARLIER WE CONFIRMED WHO IS INSIDE THE VEHICLE.
IT'S HER.
ALIGULA, THE MONOMANIAC.
WHAT?!
IT SEEMS I'VE FINALLY GOTTEN YOUR ATTENTION.
A PARANORMAL ENTITY ON PAR WITH FEMT, THE KING OF DEPRAVITY.
A VILLAIN FAR BEYOND THE SCOPE OF HUMANS LIKE US.

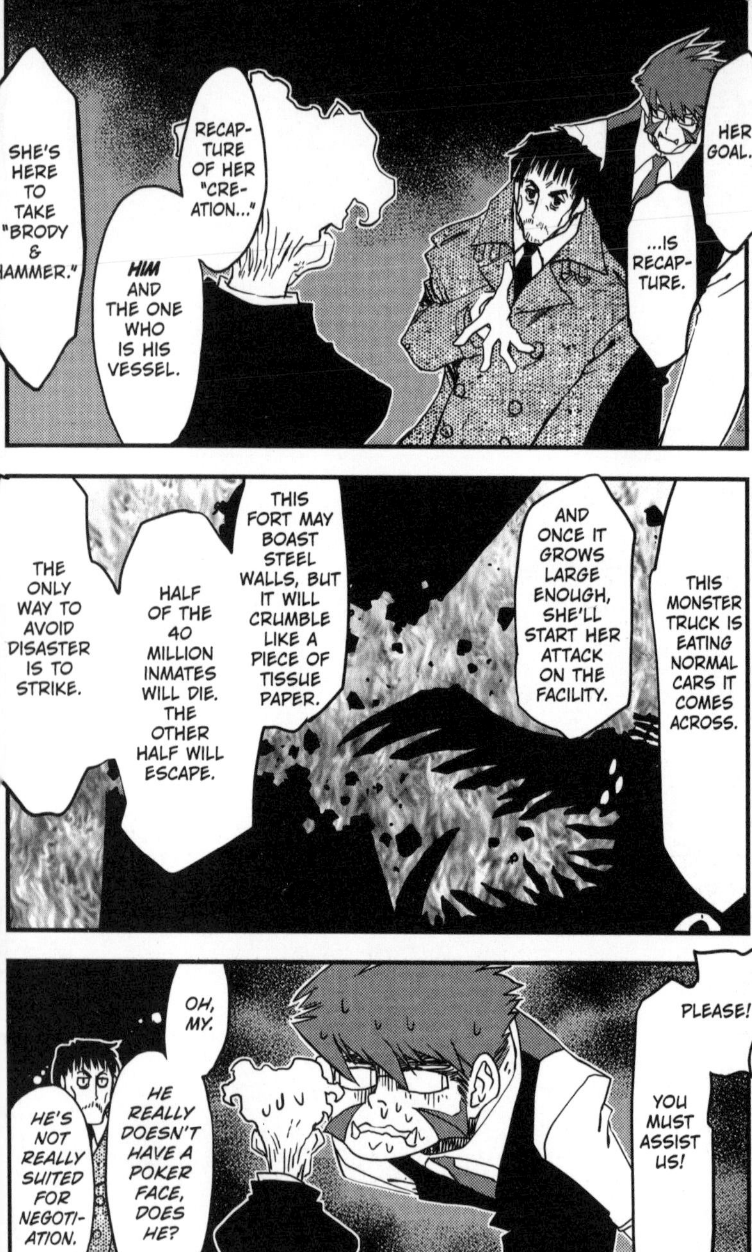
HER GOAL...
...IS RECAPTURE.
RECAPTURE OF HER "CREATION..."
HIM AND THE ONE WHO IS HIS VESSEL.
SHE'S HERE TO TAKE "BRODY & HAMMER."
THIS MONSTER TRUCK IS EATING NORMAL CARS IT COMES ACROSS.
AND ONCE IT GROWS LARGE ENOUGH, SHE'LL START HER ATTACK ON THE FACILITY.
THIS FORT MAY BOAST STEEL WALLS, BUT IT WILL CRUMBLE LIKE A PIECE OF TISSUE PAPER.
HALF OF THE 40 MILLION INMATES WILL DIE. THE OTHER HALF WILL ESCAPE.
THE ONLY WAY TO AVOID DISASTER IS TO STRIKE.
PLEASE!
YOU MUST ASSIST US!
OH, MY.
HE REALLY DOESN'T HAVE A POKER FACE, DOES HE?
HE'S NOT REALLY SUITED FOR NEGOTIATION.

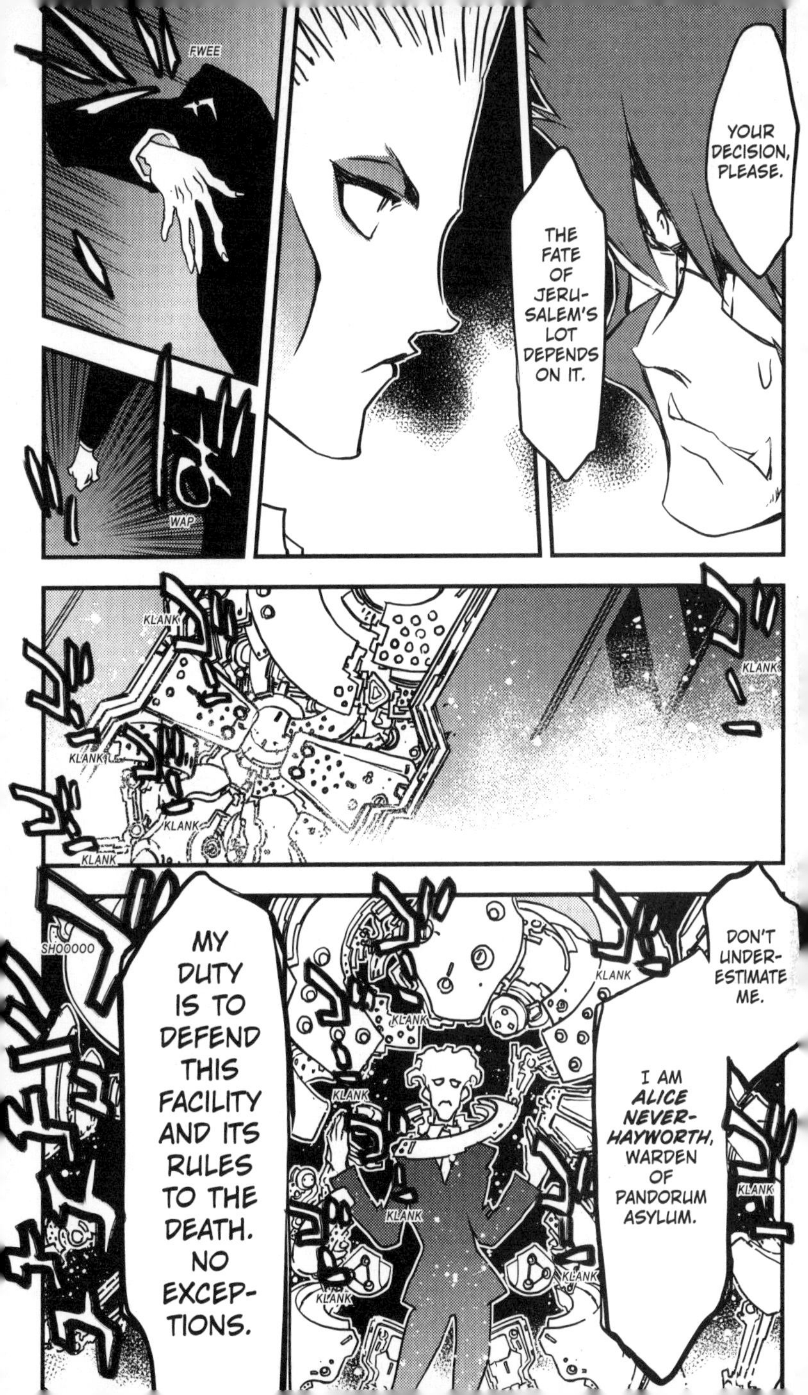
YOUR DECISION, PLEASE.
THE FATE OF JERU-SALEM'S LOT DEPENDS ON IT.
FWEE
WAP
KLANK
KLANK
KLANK
KLANK
KLANK
DON'T UNDER-ESTIMATE ME.
I AM *ALICE NEVER-HAYWORTH*, WARDEN OF PANDORUM ASYLUM.
KLANK
KLANK
KLANK
KLANK
KLANK
KLANK
KLANK
MY DUTY IS TO DEFEND THIS FACILITY AND ITS RULES TO THE DEATH. NO EXCEP-TIONS.
SHOOOOO

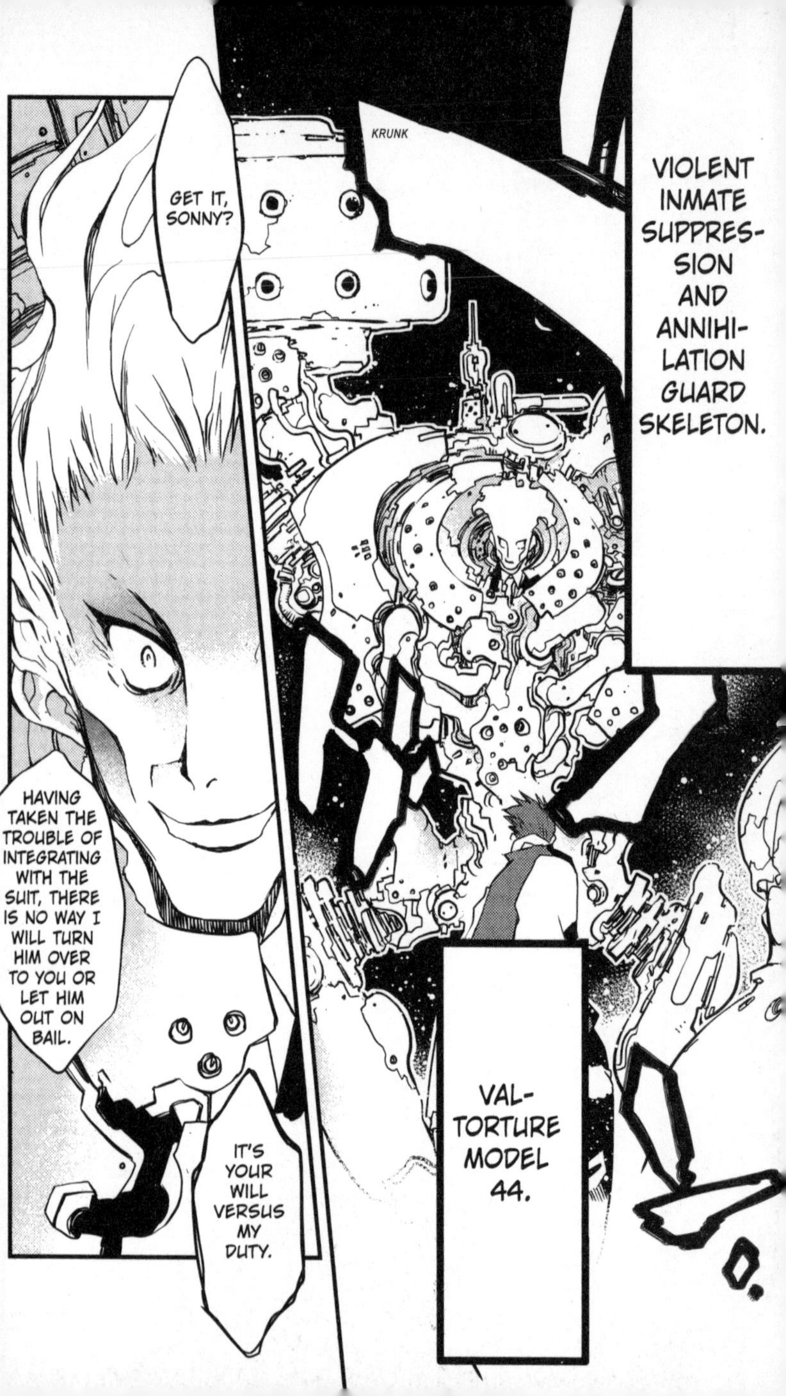
VIOLENT INMATE SUPPRES-SION AND ANNIHI-LATION GUARD SKELETON.
KRUNK
VAL-TORTURE MODEL 44.
O.
GET IT, SONNY?
HAVING TAKEN THE TROUBLE OF INTEGRATING WITH THE SUIT, THERE IS NO WAY I WILL TURN HIM OVER TO YOU OR LET HIM OUT ON BAIL.
IT'S YOUR WILL VERSUS MY DUTY.

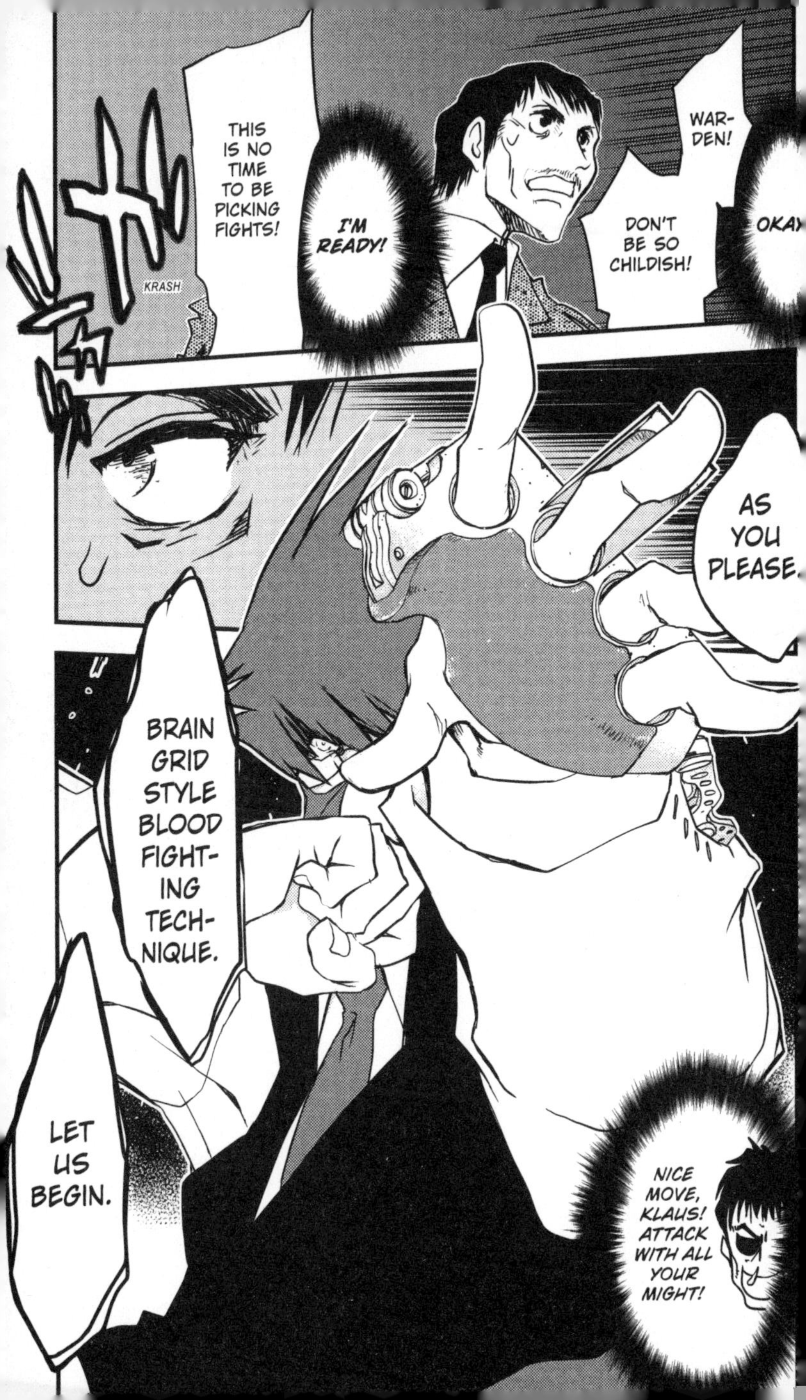
OKAY
WAR-DEN!
DON'T BE SO CHILDISH!
I'M READY!
THIS IS NO TIME TO BE PICKING FIGHTS!
KRASH
AS YOU PLEASE.
BRAIN GRID STYLE BLOOD FIGHT-ING TECH-NIQUE.
LET US BEGIN.
NICE MOVE, KLAUS! ATTACK WITH ALL YOUR MIGHT!

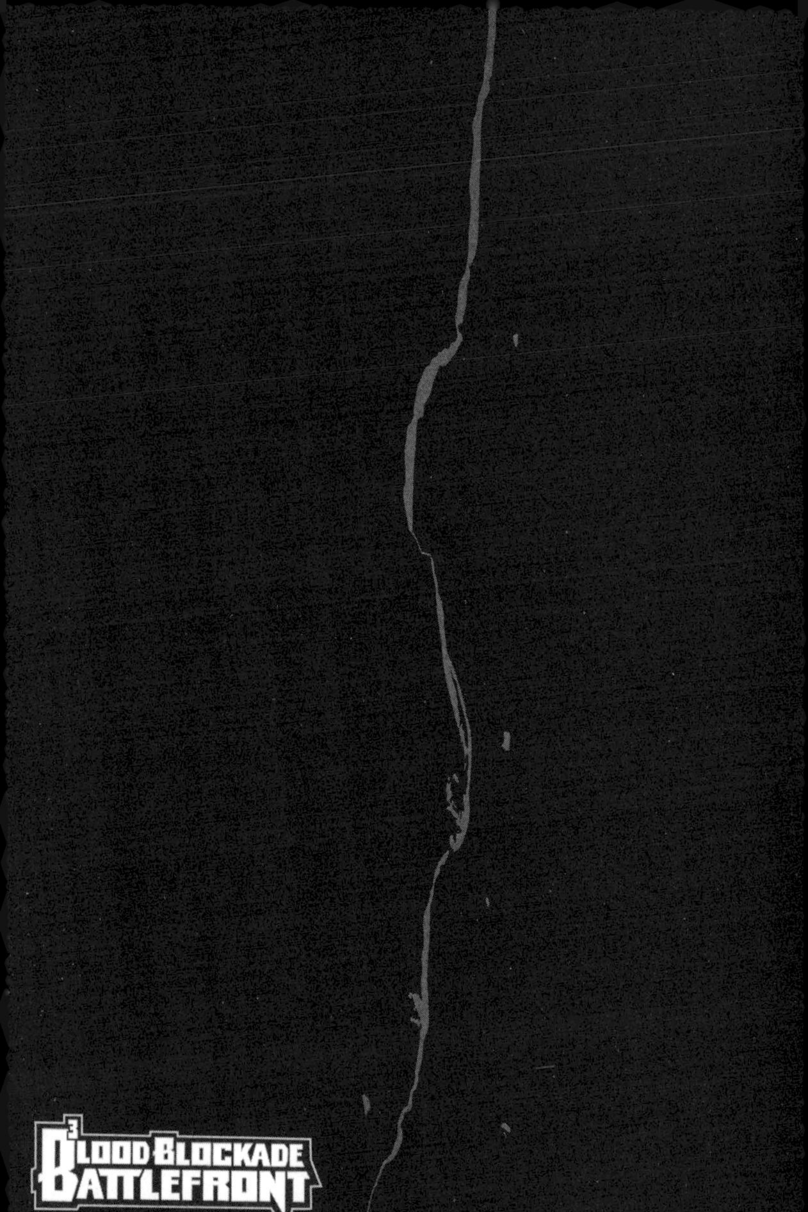

BLOOD BLOCKADE BATTLEFRONT

BLOOD BLOCKADE BATTLEFRONT

血界戦線 3

THE TREMOROUS BLOOD HAMMER

—震撃の血槌—

THE TREMOROUS BLOOD HAMMER

RUMBLE
RUMBLE
RUMBLE
LEO!
CHUG
CHUG
CHUG
CHUG
WHAT?!
CHUG
YOU HUNGRY?!
NO WAY!
CHUG CHUG CHUG CHUG
WE'RE ALREADY LATE TO THE MEETING AS IT IS.
C'MON, YOU KILL-JOY!
FIVE SECONDS! THAT'S ALL IT WILL TAKE!
VWEEEE
HE SAYS AS I SKILLFULLY CHANGE LANES AND HEAD IN THE DIRECTION OF GOGO ICHIBAN-KAN.
YOU CAN'T EVEN ORDER IN FIVE SECONDS!
HEY! WHAT ARE YOU --?!

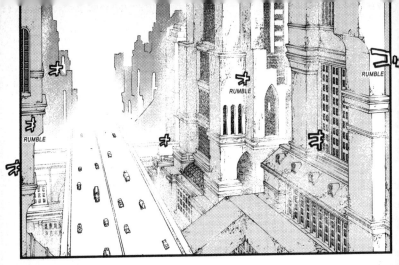

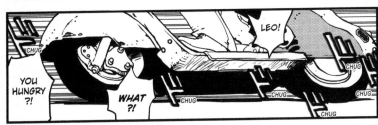

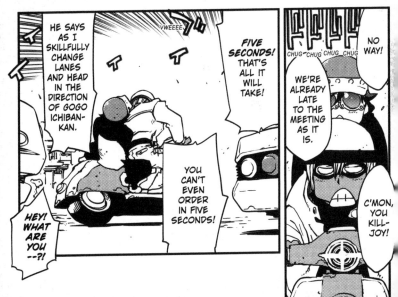

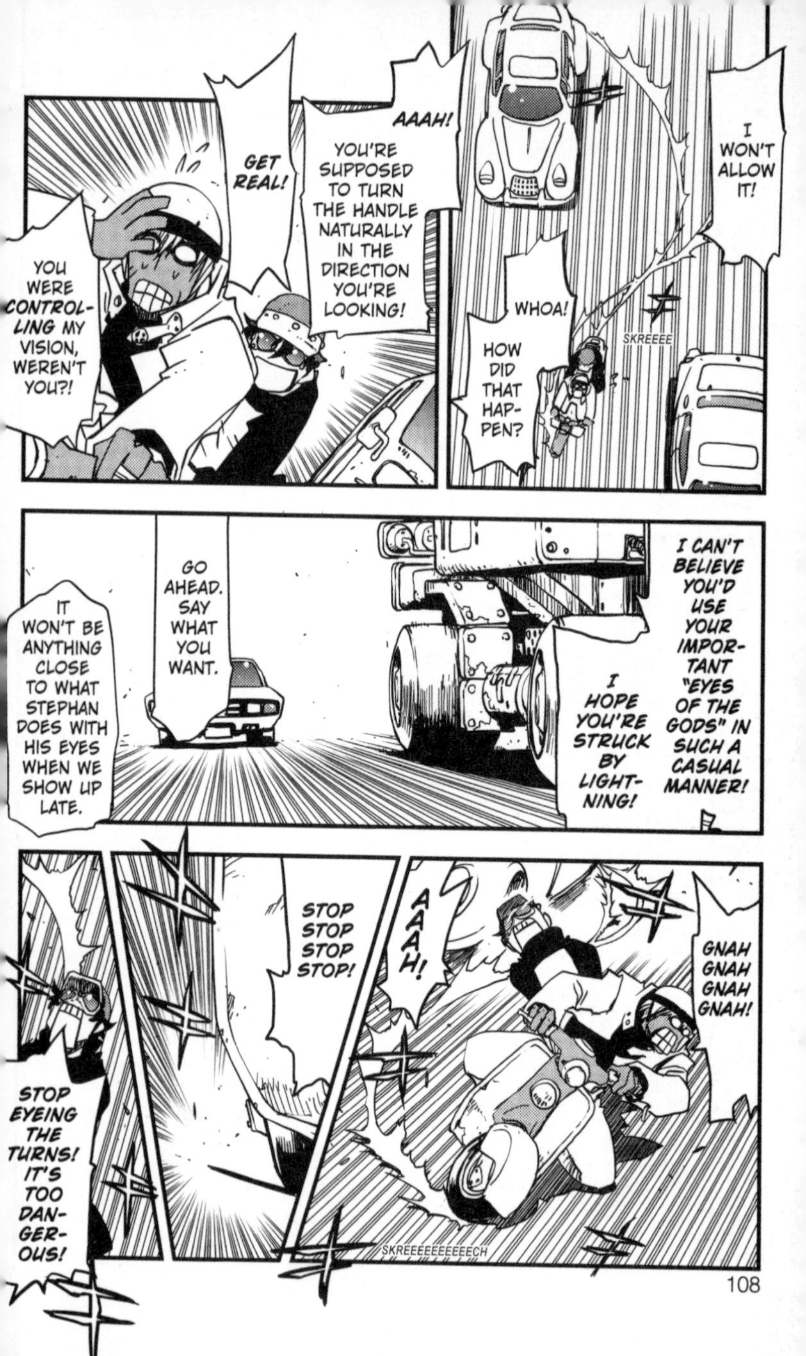
I WON'T ALLOW IT!
WHOA!
HOW DID THAT HAPPEN?
SKREEEE
AAAH!
YOU'RE SUPPOSED TO TURN THE HANDLE NATURALLY IN THE DIRECTION YOU'RE LOOKING!
GET REAL!
YOU WERE CONTROLLING MY VISION, WEREN'T YOU?!
I CAN'T BELIEVE YOU'D USE YOUR IMPORTANT "EYES OF THE GODS" IN SUCH A CASUAL MANNER!
I HOPE YOU'RE STRUCK BY LIGHTNING!
GO AHEAD. SAY WHAT YOU WANT.
IT WON'T BE ANYTHING CLOSE TO WHAT STEPHAN DOES WITH HIS EYES WHEN WE SHOW UP LATE.
GNAH GNAH GNAH GNAH!
AAAH!
SKREEEEEEEEEEECH
STOP STOP STOP STOP!
STOP EYEING THE TURNS! IT'S TOO DANGEROUS!

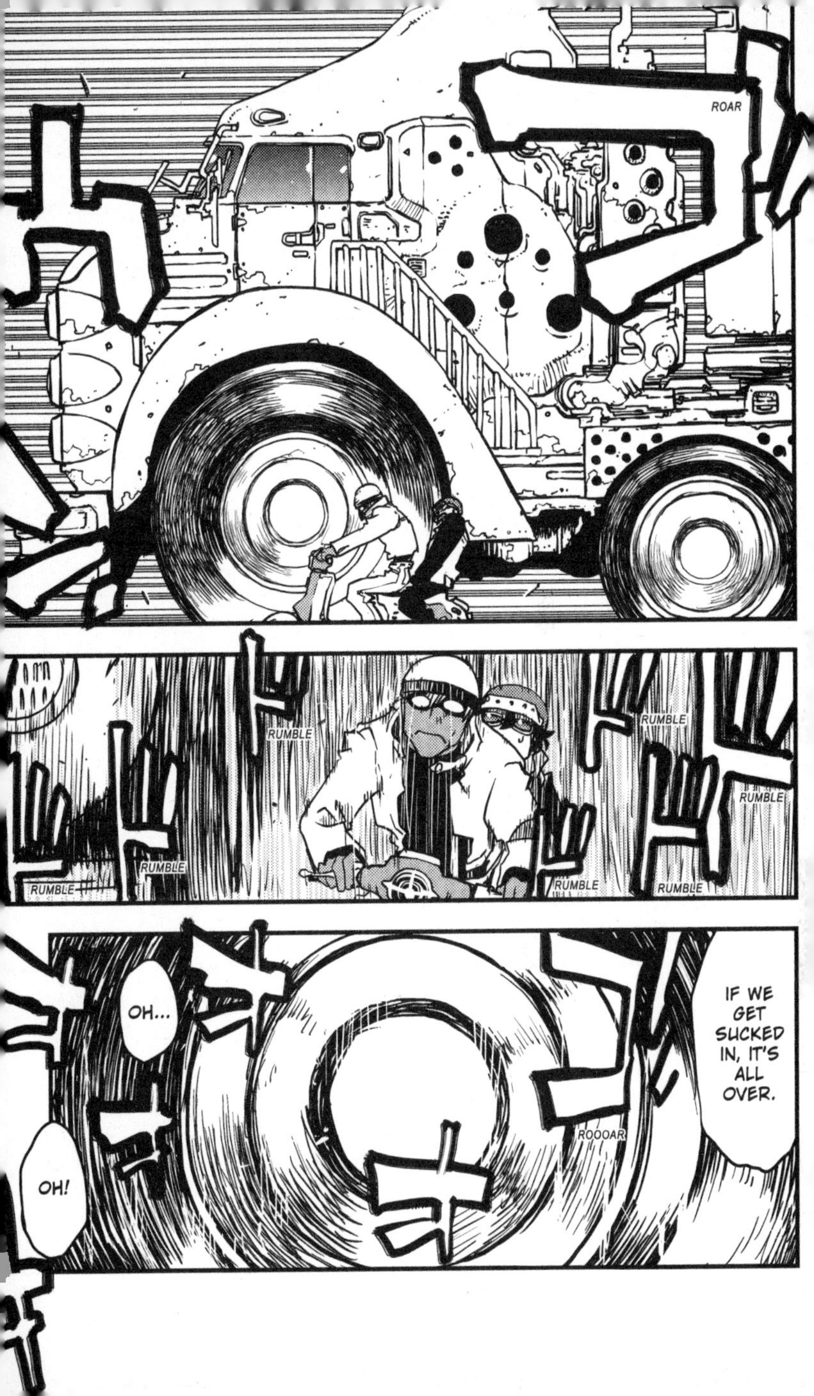
ROAR
RUMBLE
RUMBLE
RUMBLE
RUMBLE
RUMBLE
RUMBLE
RUMBLE
IF WE GET SUCKED IN, IT'S ALL OVER.
ROOOAR
OH...
OH!

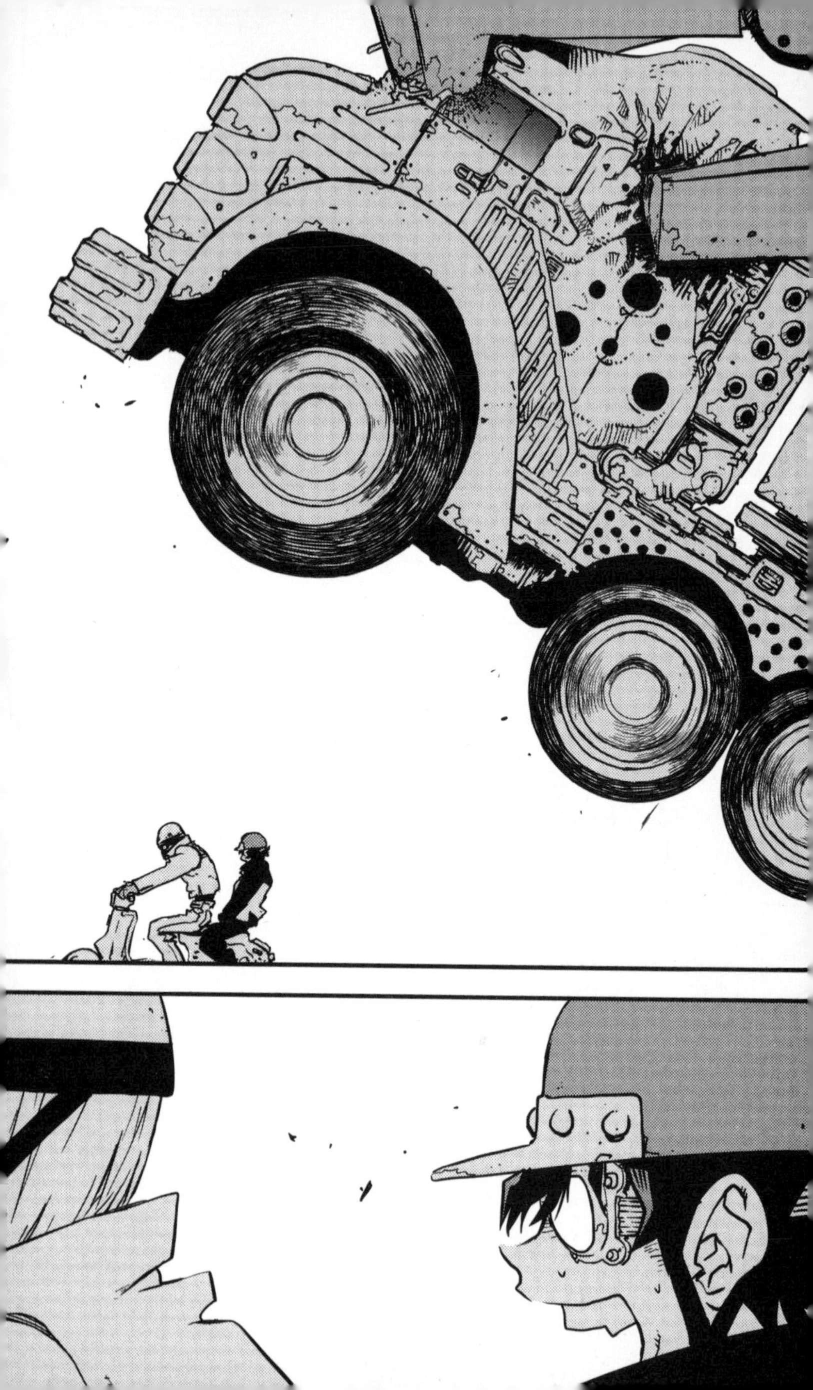

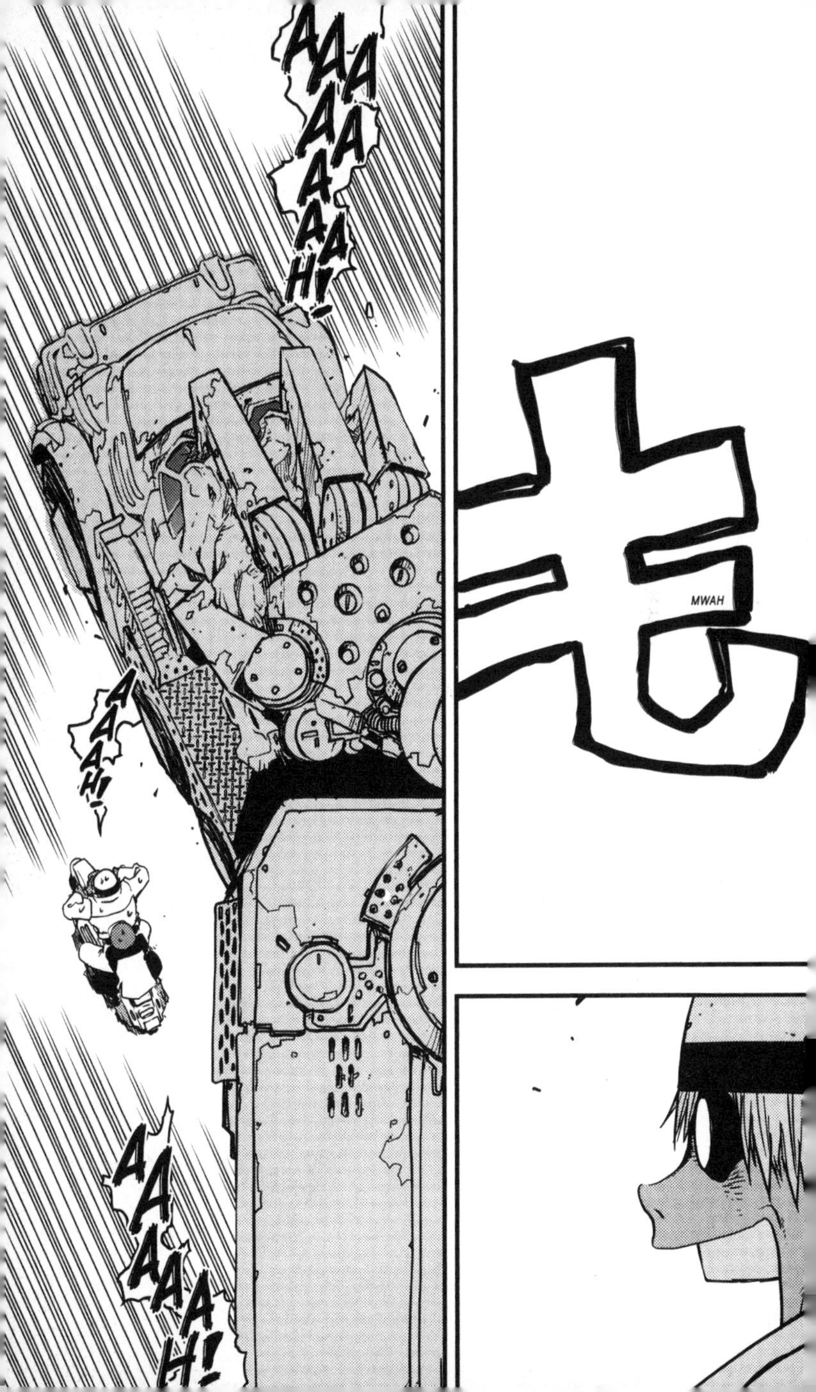
MWAH
AAAAAAAAH!
AAAAH!
AAAAAAH!

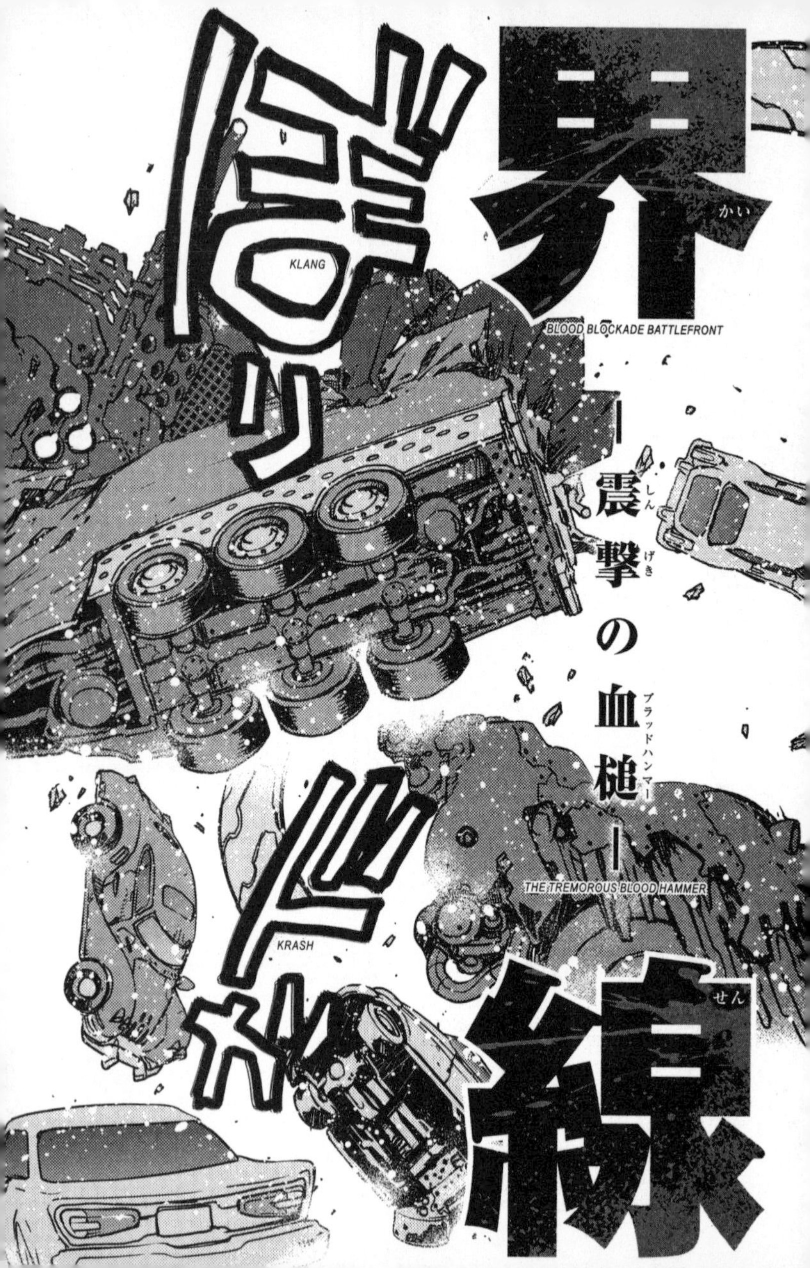
界
BLOOD BLOCKADE BATTLEFRONT
―震撃の血槌―
THE TREMOROUS BLOOD HAMMER
線
KLANG
KRASH

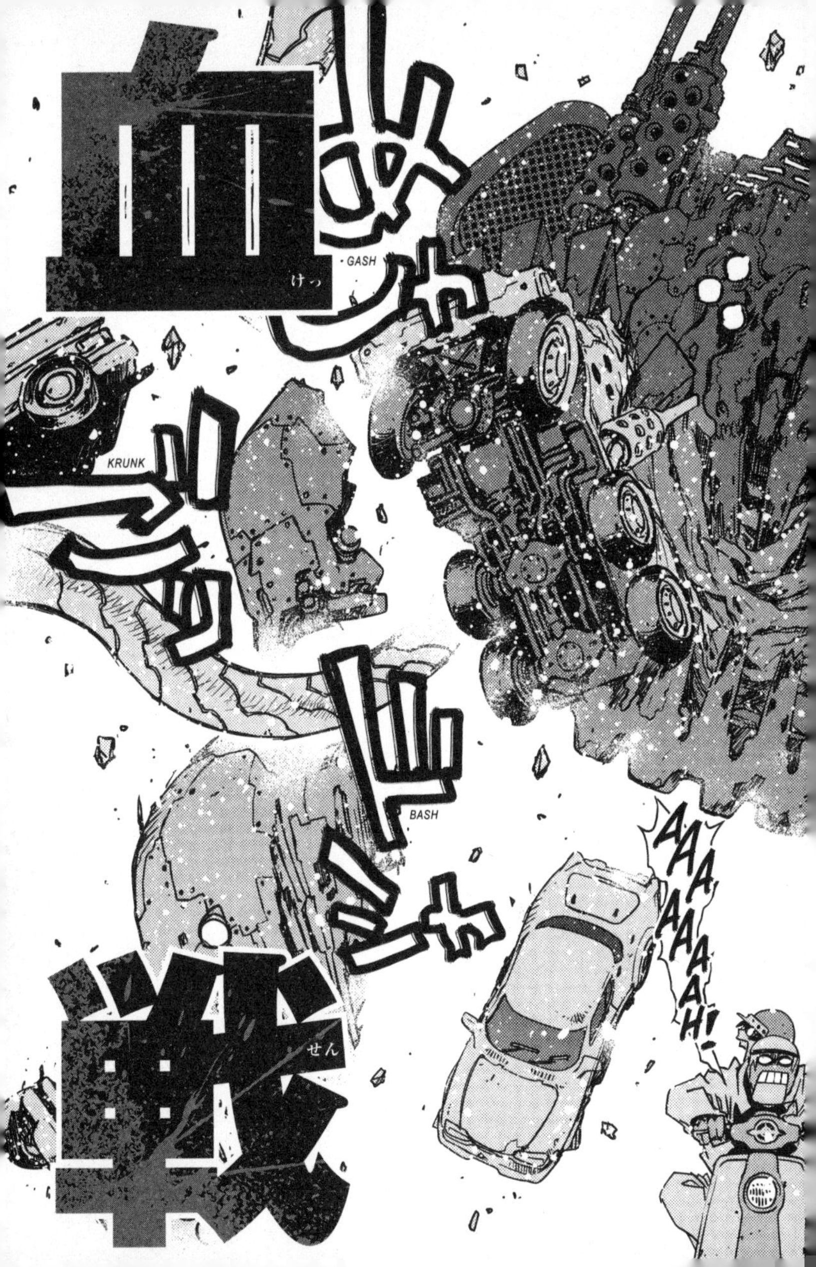

血
けっ
GASH
KRUNK
BASH
戦
せん
AAAAAAAAH!

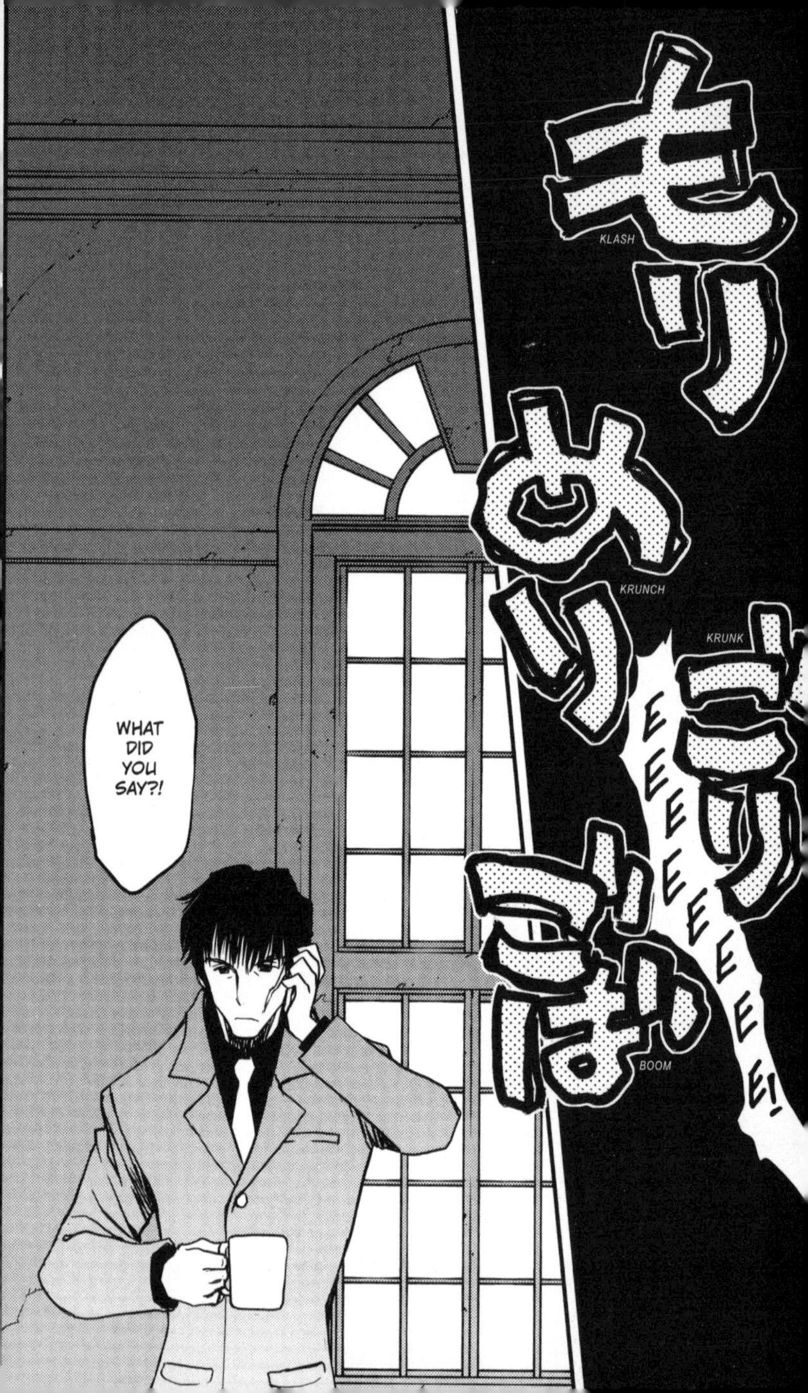
KLASH
KRUNCH
KRUNK
BOOM
EEEEEEEE!
WHAT DID YOU SAY?!

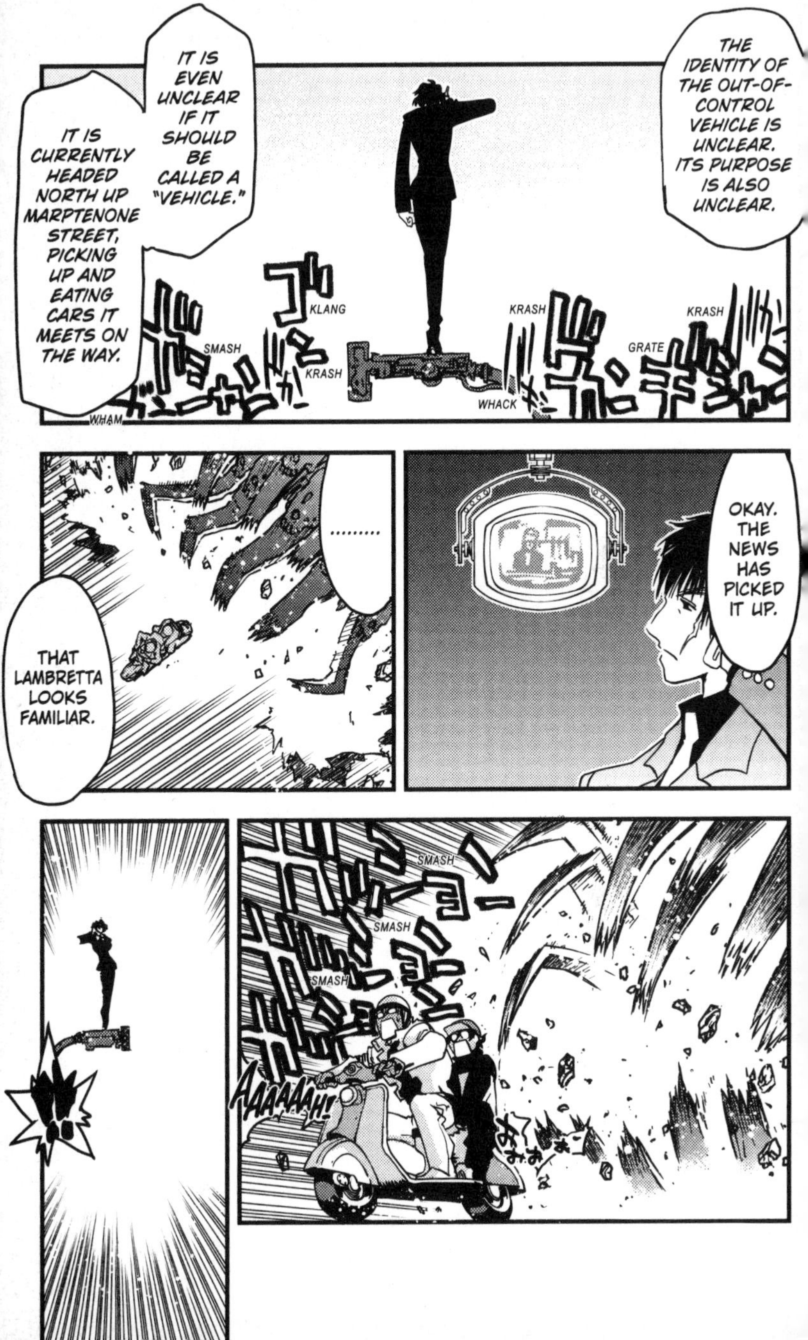
THE IDENTITY OF THE OUT-OF-CONTROL VEHICLE IS UNCLEAR. ITS PURPOSE IS ALSO UNCLEAR.
IT IS EVEN UNCLEAR IF IT SHOULD BE CALLED A "VEHICLE."
IT IS CURRENTLY HEADED NORTH UP MARPTENONE STREET, PICKING UP AND EATING CARS IT MEETS ON THE WAY.
KRASH
GRATE
KRASH
WHACK
KLANG
KRASH
SMASH
WHAM
OKAY. THE NEWS HAS PICKED IT UP.
....
THAT LAMBRETTA LOOKS FAMILIAR.
SMASH
SMASH
SMASH
AAAAAAH!
!!

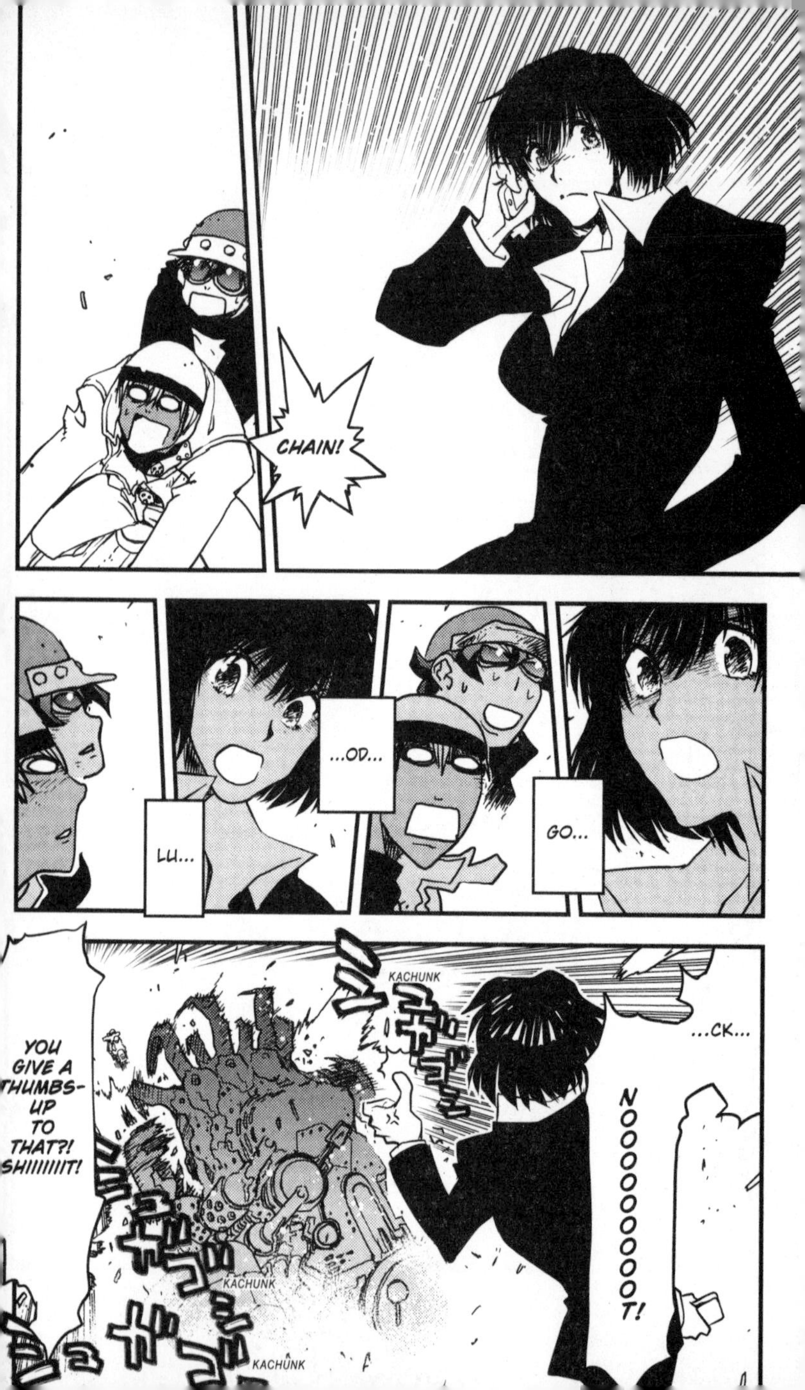
CHAIN!
GO...
...OD...
LU...
...CK...
NOOOOOOOOOOOT!
KACHUNK
YOU GIVE A THUMBS-UP TO THAT?! SHIIIIIIIT!
KACHUNK
KACHUNK

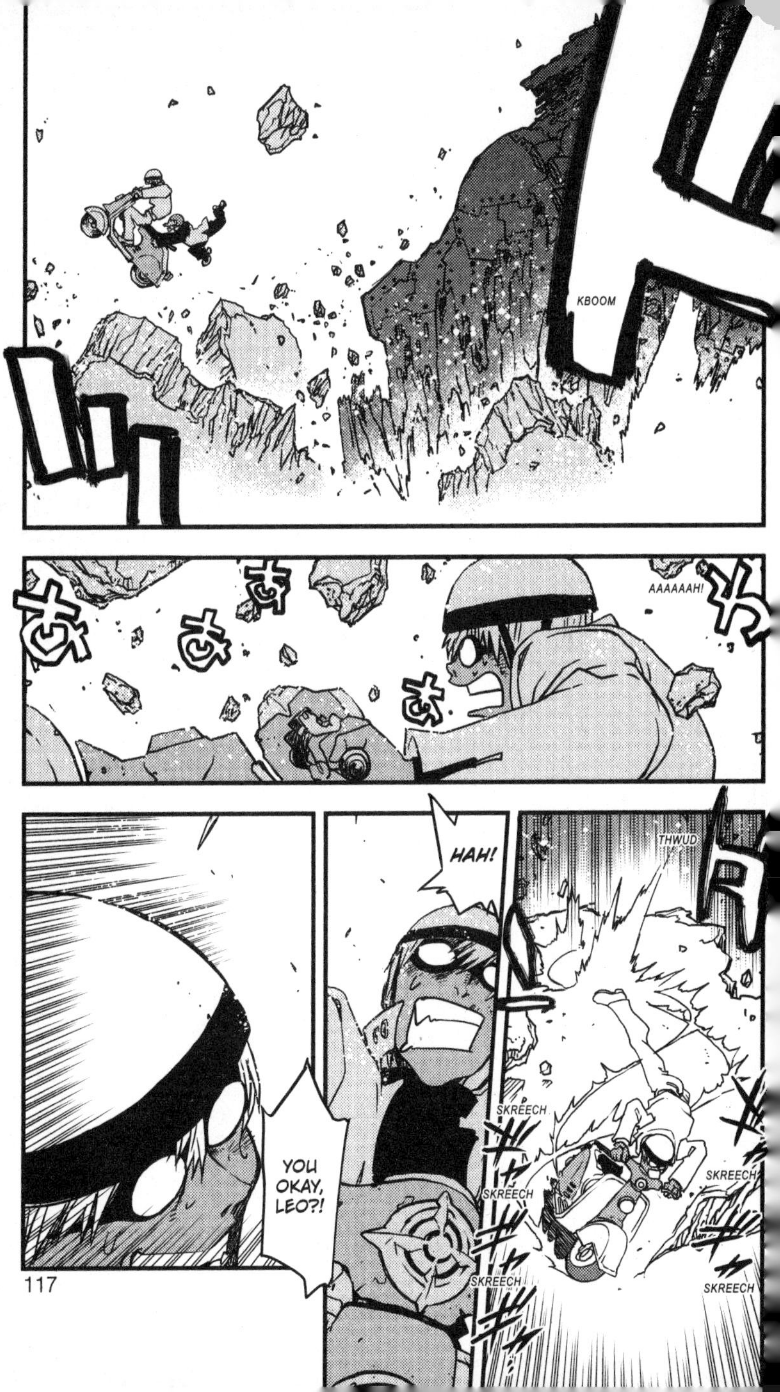
KBOOM
AAAAAAH!
THWUD
SKREECH
SKREECH
SKREECH
SKREECH
SKREECH
HAH!
YOU OKAY, LEO?!

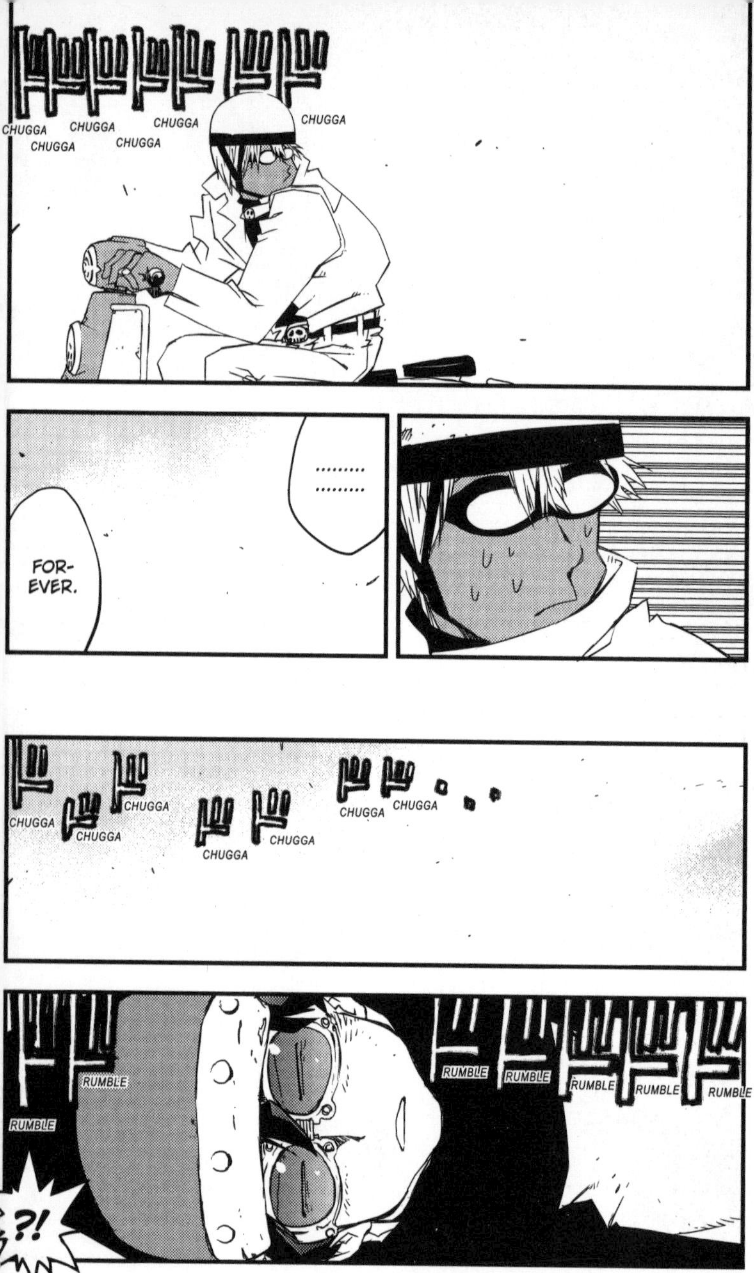
CHUGGA
CHUGGA
CHUGGA
CHUGGA
CHUGGA
CHUGGA
....
....
FOR-EVER.
CHUGGA
CHUGGA
CHUGGA
CHUGGA
CHUGGA
CHUGGA
CHUGGA
RUMBLE
RUMBLE
RUMBLE
RUMBLE
RUMBLE
RUMBLE
RUMBLE
?!

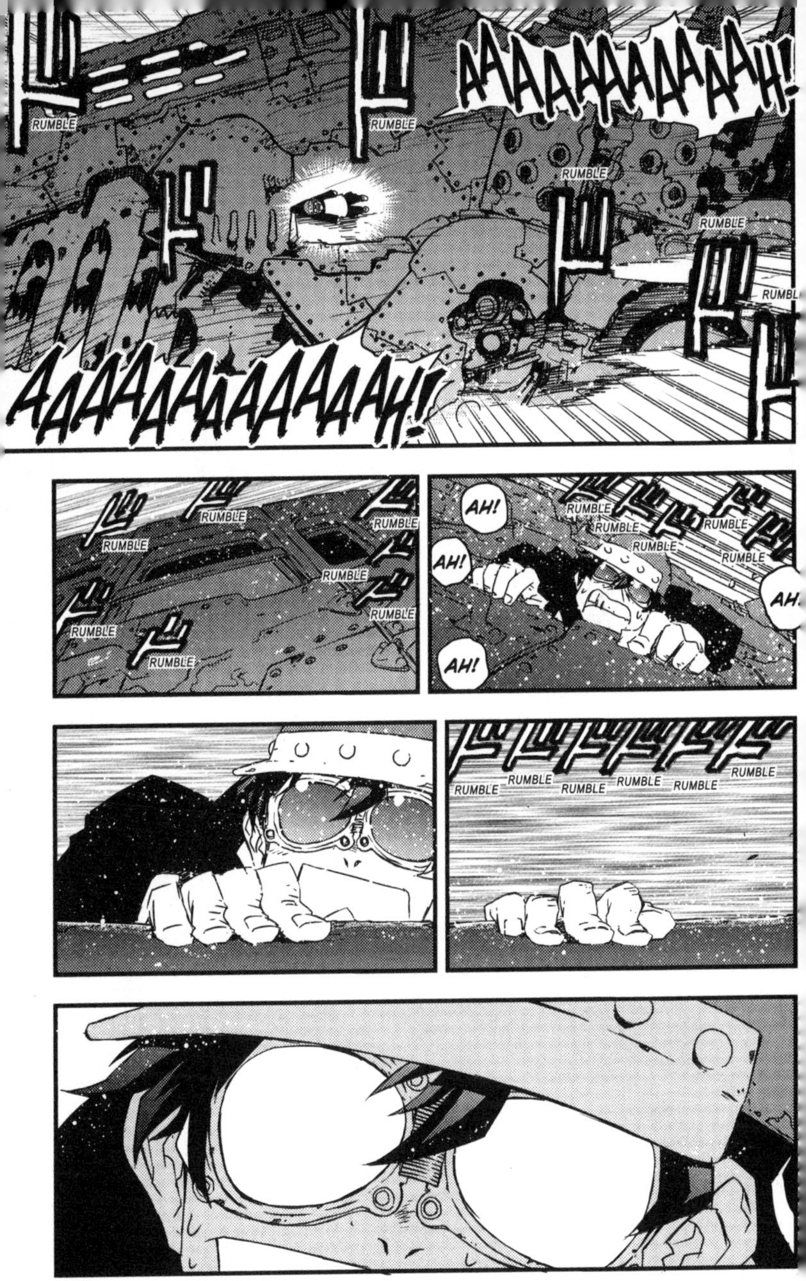
AAAAAAAAAAH!
RUMBLE
RUMBLE
RUMBLE
RUMBLE
RUMBLE
AAAAAAAAAAAAAH!
AH
AH!
AH!
AH!
RUMBLE
RUMBLE
RUMBLE
RUMBLE
RUMBLE
RUMBLE
RUMBLE
RUMBLE
RUMBLE
RUMBLE
RUMBLE
RUMBLE
RUMBLE
RUMBLE
RUMBLE
RUMBLE
RUMBLE
RUMBLE

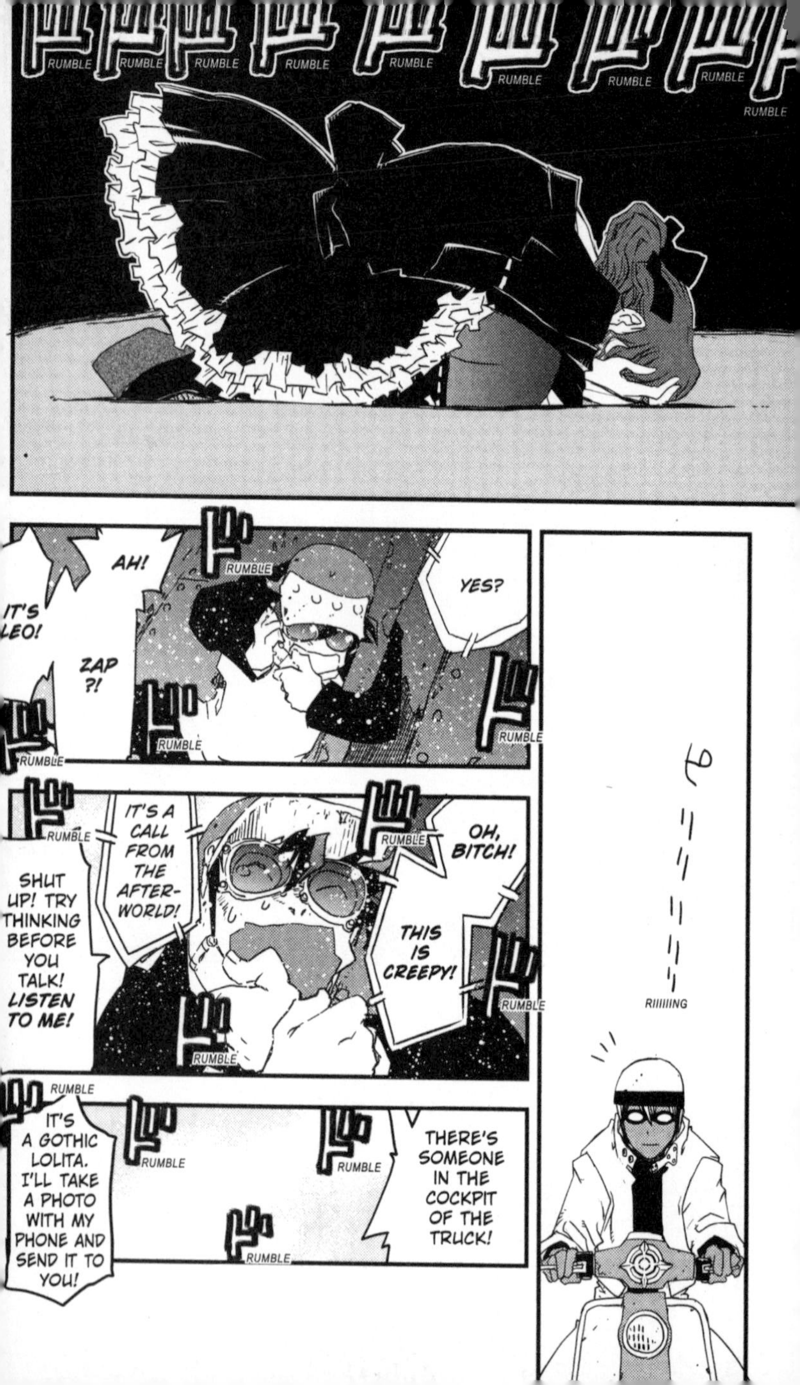
RUMBLE RUMBLE RUMBLE RUMBLE RUMBLE RUMBLE RUMBLE RUMBLE RUMBLE
RIIIIIING
RUMBLE
YES?
AH!
IT'S LEO!
ZAP ?!
RUMBLE RUMBLE RUMBLE
RUMBLE RUMBLE
OH, BITCH!
THIS IS CREEPY!
IT'S A CALL FROM THE AFTER-WORLD!
SHUT UP! TRY THINKING BEFORE YOU TALK! LISTEN TO ME!
RUMBLE RUMBLE
RUMBLE RUMBLE RUMBLE
THERE'S SOMEONE IN THE COCKPIT OF THE TRUCK!
IT'S A GOTHIC LOLITA. I'LL TAKE A PHOTO WITH MY PHONE AND SEND IT TO YOU!
RUMBLE

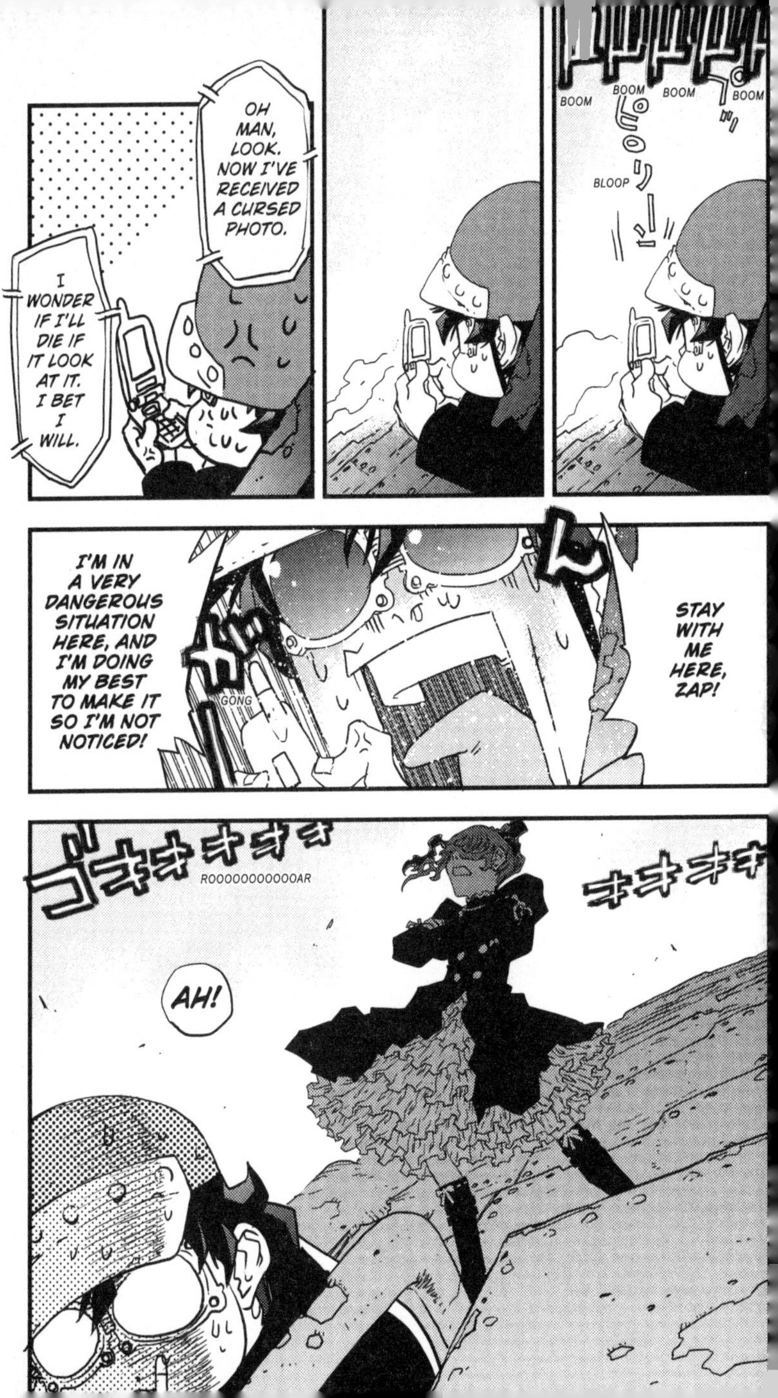
BOOM BOOM BOOM BOOM
BLOOP
OH MAN, LOOK. NOW I'VE RECEIVED A CURSED PHOTO.
I WONDER IF I'LL DIE IF IT LOOK AT IT. I BET I WILL.
STAY WITH ME HERE, ZAP!
I'M IN A VERY DANGEROUS SITUATION HERE, AND I'M DOING MY BEST TO MAKE IT SO I'M NOT NOTICED!
GONG
ROOOOOOOOOOOAR
AH!

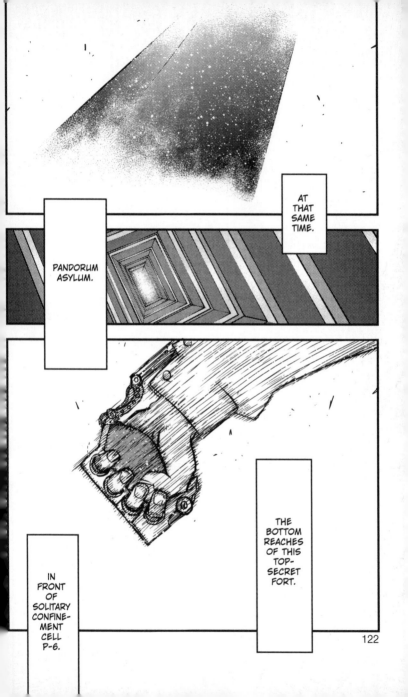

AT THAT SAME TIME.

PANDORUM ASYLUM.

THE BOTTOM REACHES OF THIS TOP-SECRET FORT.

IN FRONT OF SOLITARY CONFINE-MENT CELL P-6.

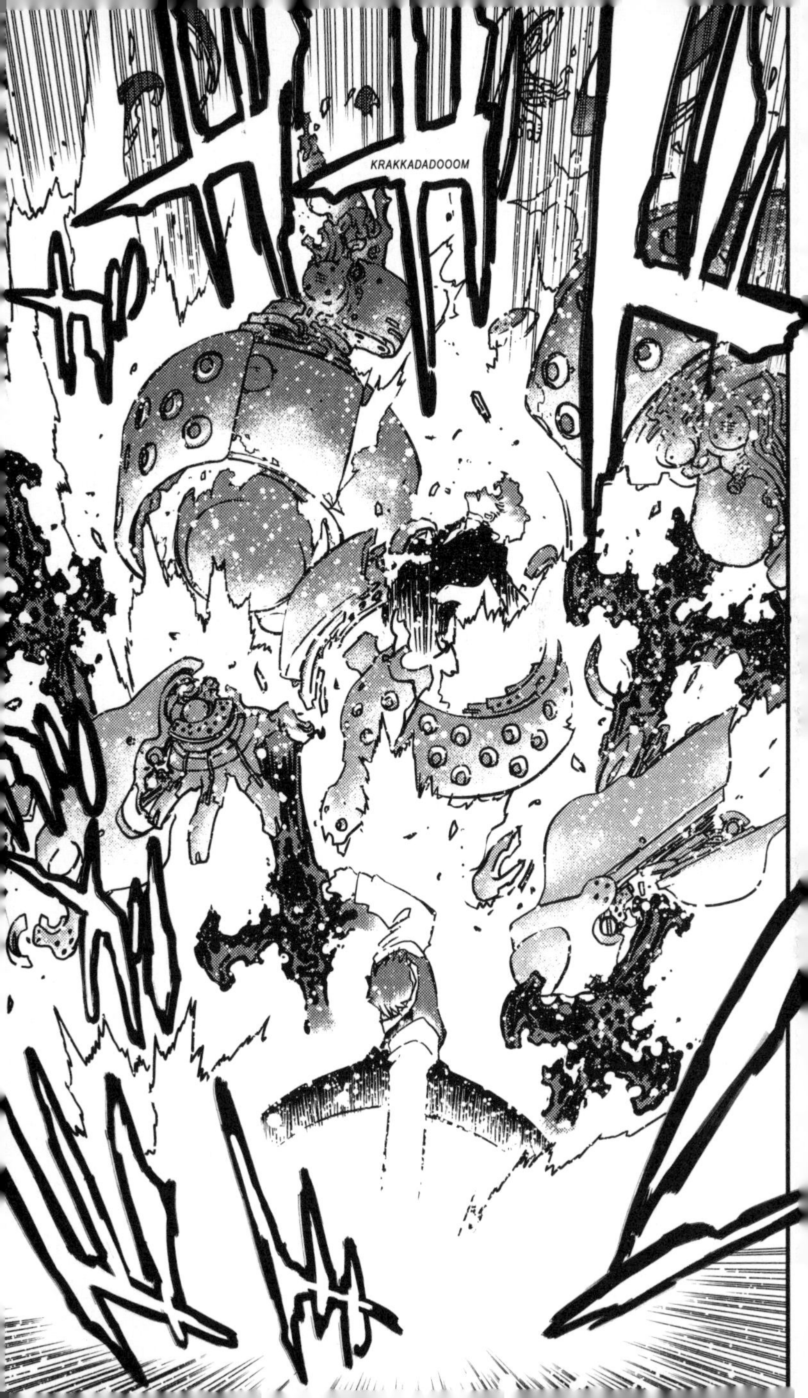
KRAKKADADOOOM

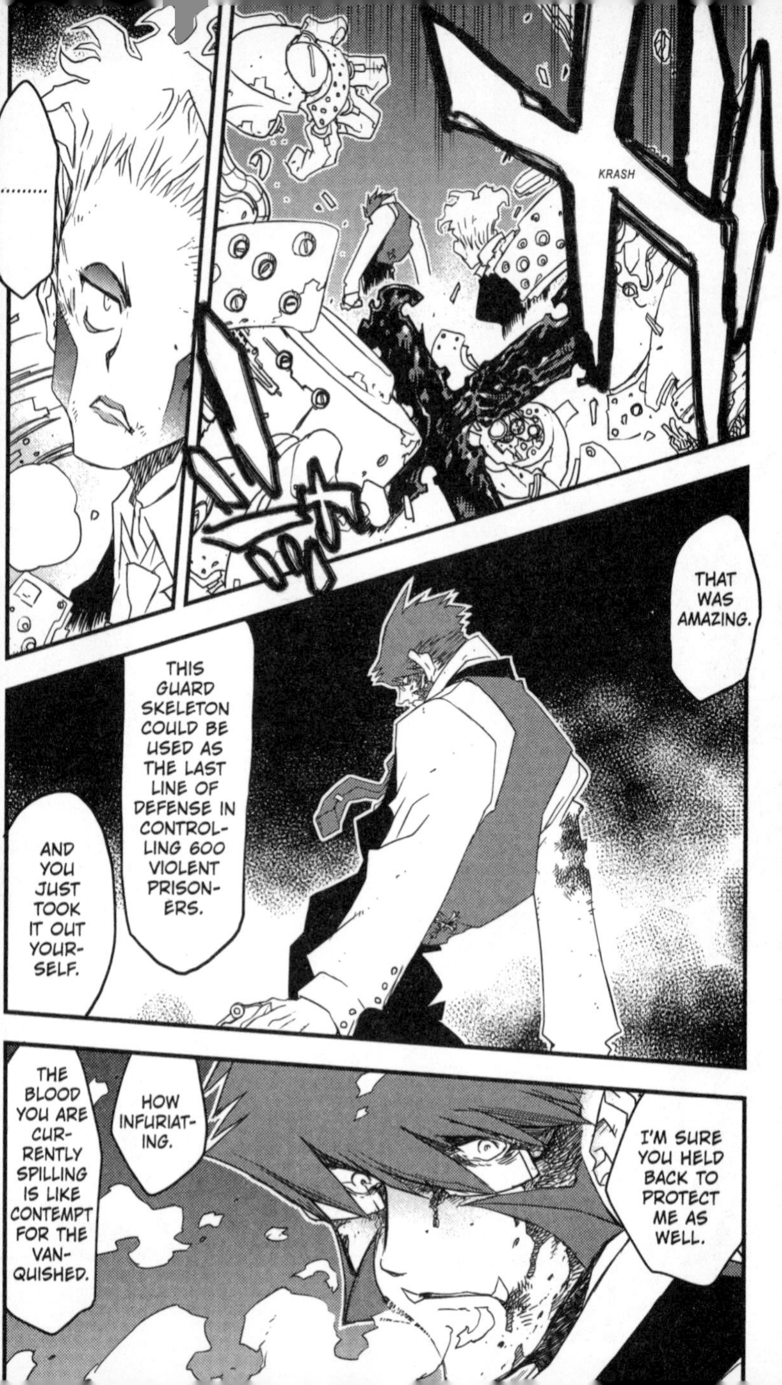
KRASH
....
THAT WAS AMAZING.
THIS GUARD SKELETON COULD BE USED AS THE LAST LINE OF DEFENSE IN CONTROL-LING 600 VIOLENT PRISON-ERS.
AND YOU JUST TOOK IT OUT YOUR-SELF.
I'M SURE YOU HELD BACK TO PROTECT ME AS WELL.
HOW INFURIAT-ING.
THE BLOOD YOU ARE CUR-RENTLY SPILLING IS LIKE CONTEMPT FOR THE VAN-QUISHED.

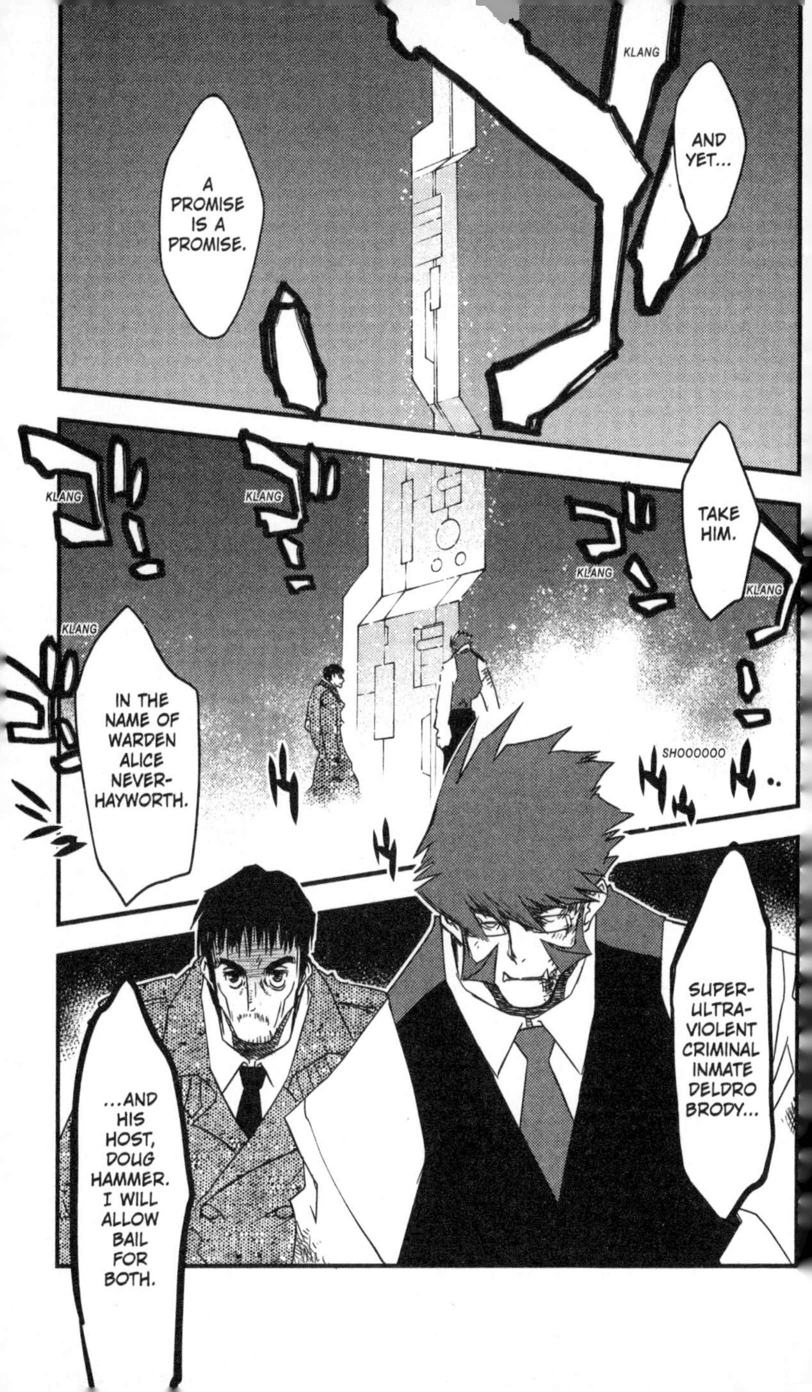
KLANG
AND YET...
A PROMISE IS A PROMISE.
TAKE HIM.
KLANG
KLANG
KLANG
KLANG
KLANG
IN THE NAME OF WARDEN ALICE NEVER-HAYWORTH.
SHOOOOOO
SUPER-ULTRA-VIOLENT CRIMINAL INMATE DELDRO BRODY...
...AND HIS HOST, DOUG HAMMER. I WILL ALLOW BAIL FOR BOTH.

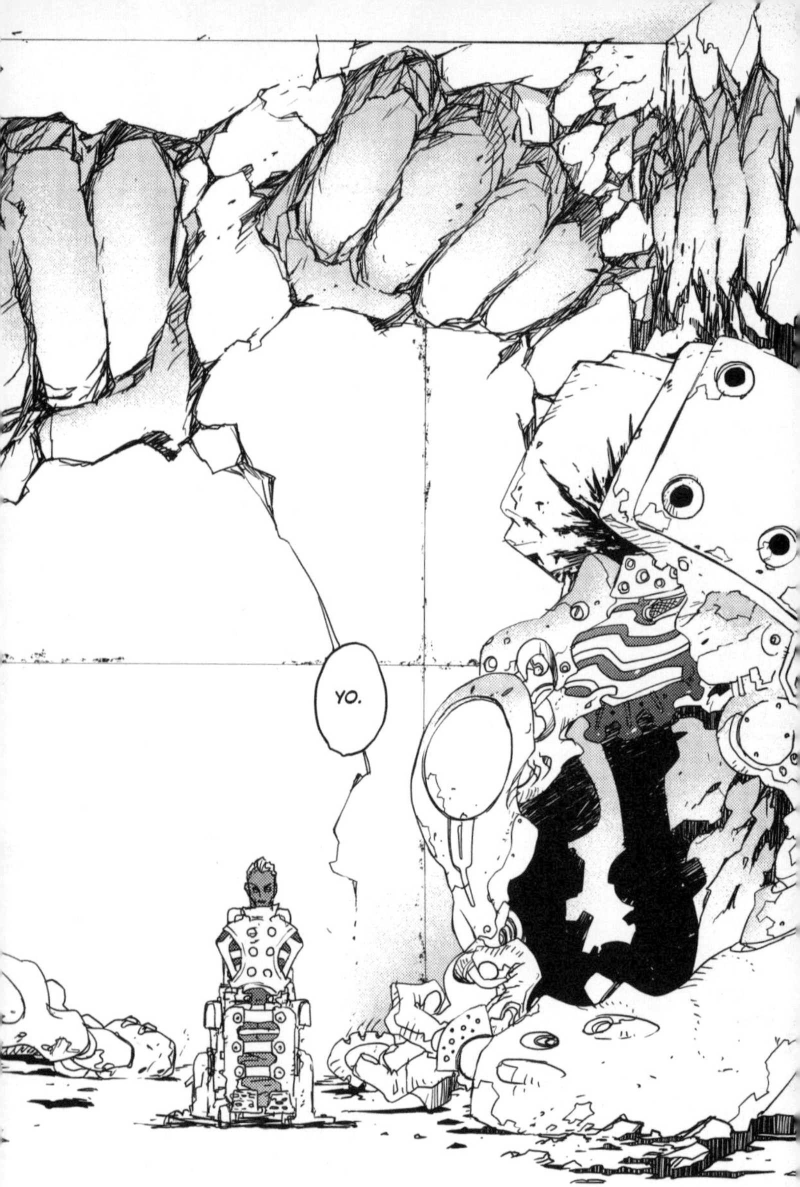
YO.

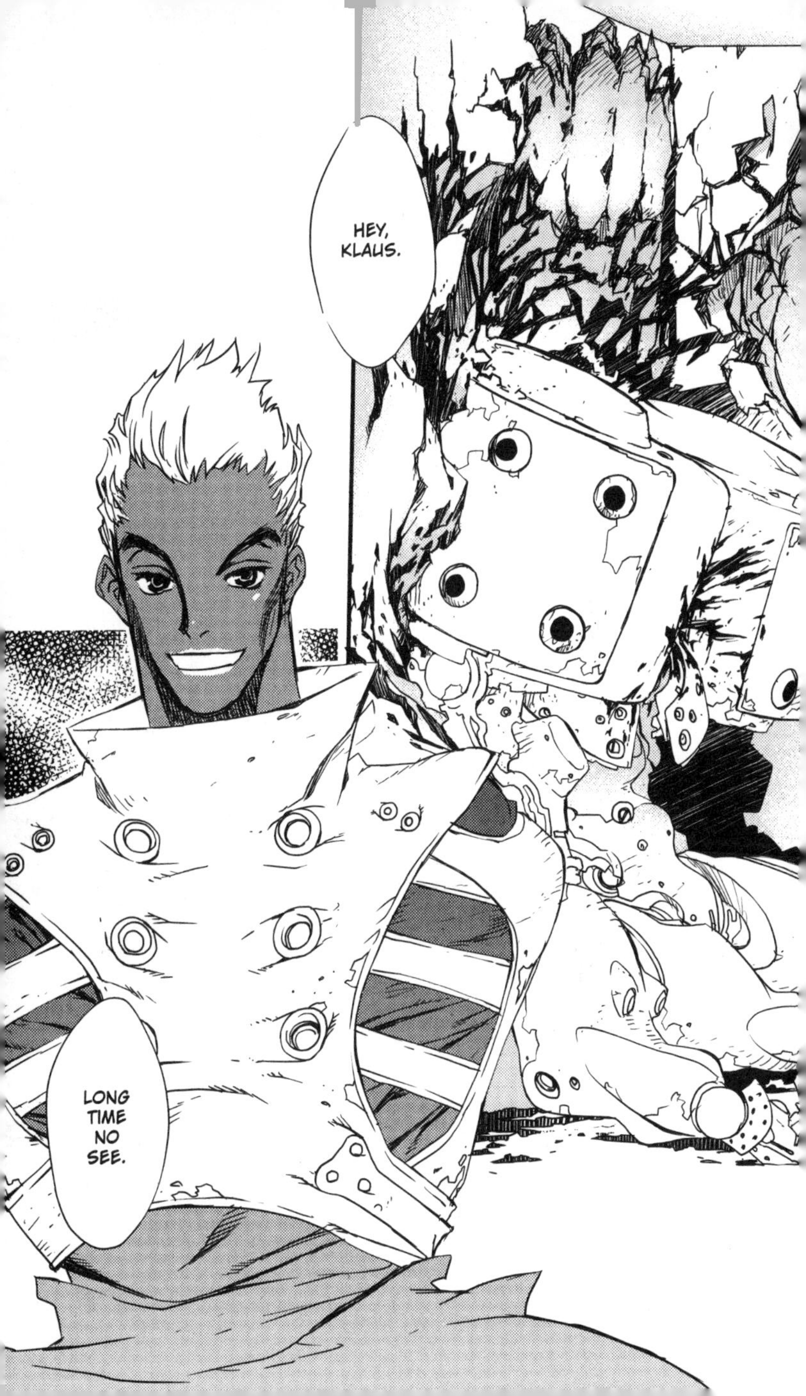
HEY, KLAUS.
LONG TIME NO SEE.

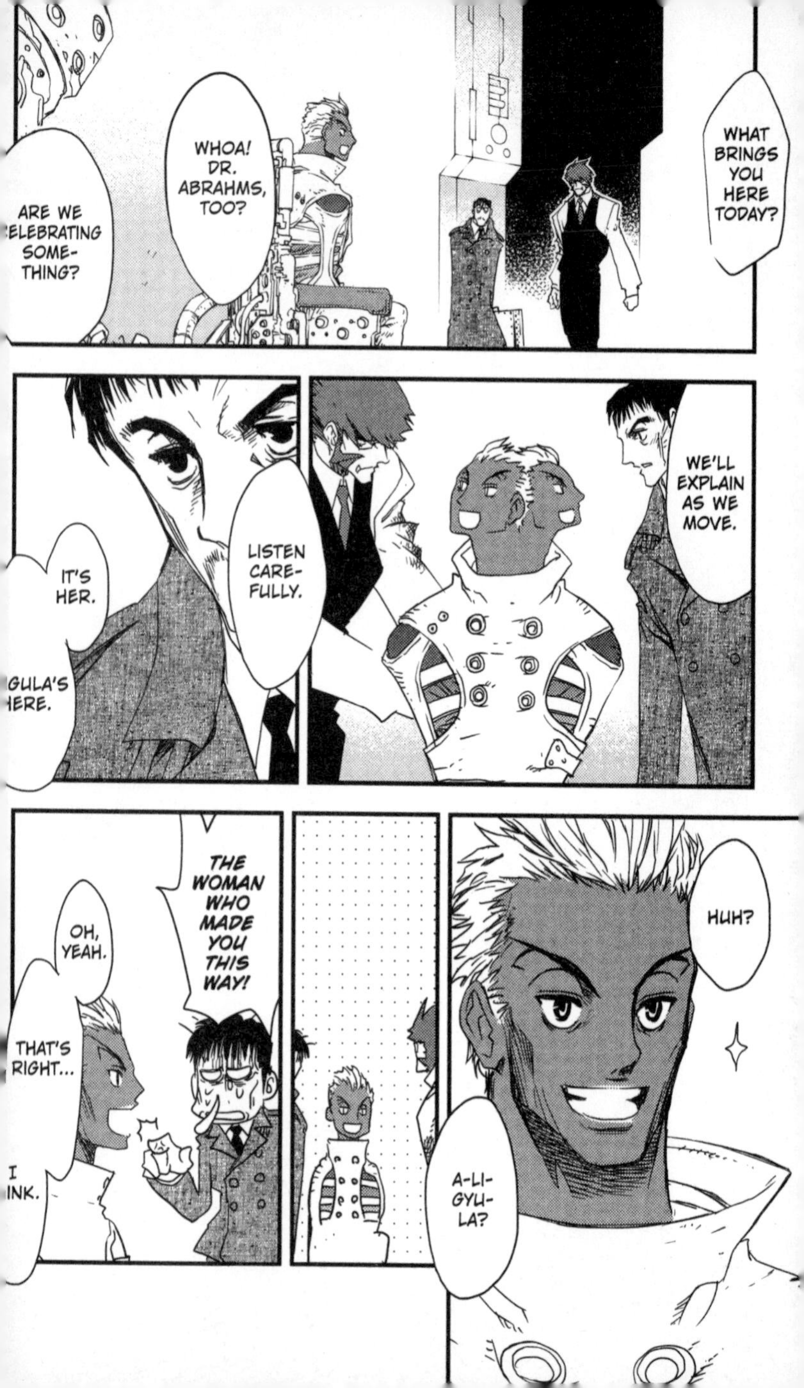
WHAT BRINGS YOU HERE TODAY?
WHOA! DR. ABRAHMS, TOO?
ARE WE ELEBRATING SOME-THING?
WE'LL EXPLAIN AS WE MOVE.
LISTEN CARE-FULLY.
IT'S HER.
GULA'S HERE.
HUH?
A-LI-GYU-LA?
THE WOMAN WHO MADE YOU THIS WAY!
OH, YEAH.
THAT'S RIGHT...
I INK.

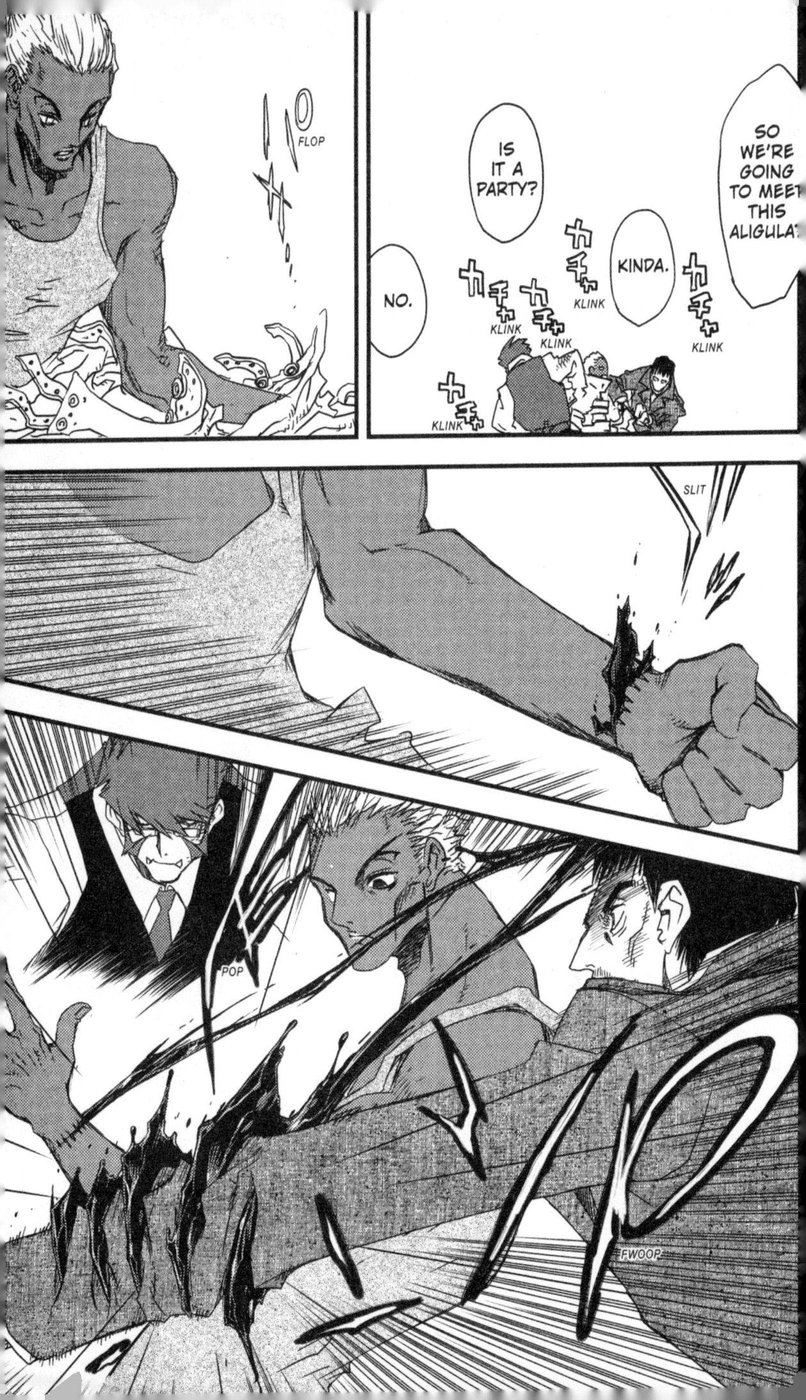

SO WE'RE GOING TO MEET THIS ALIGULA
KLINK
KINDA.
KLINK
IS IT A PARTY?
KLINK
KLINK
NO.
KLINK
FLOP
SLIT
POP
FWOOP

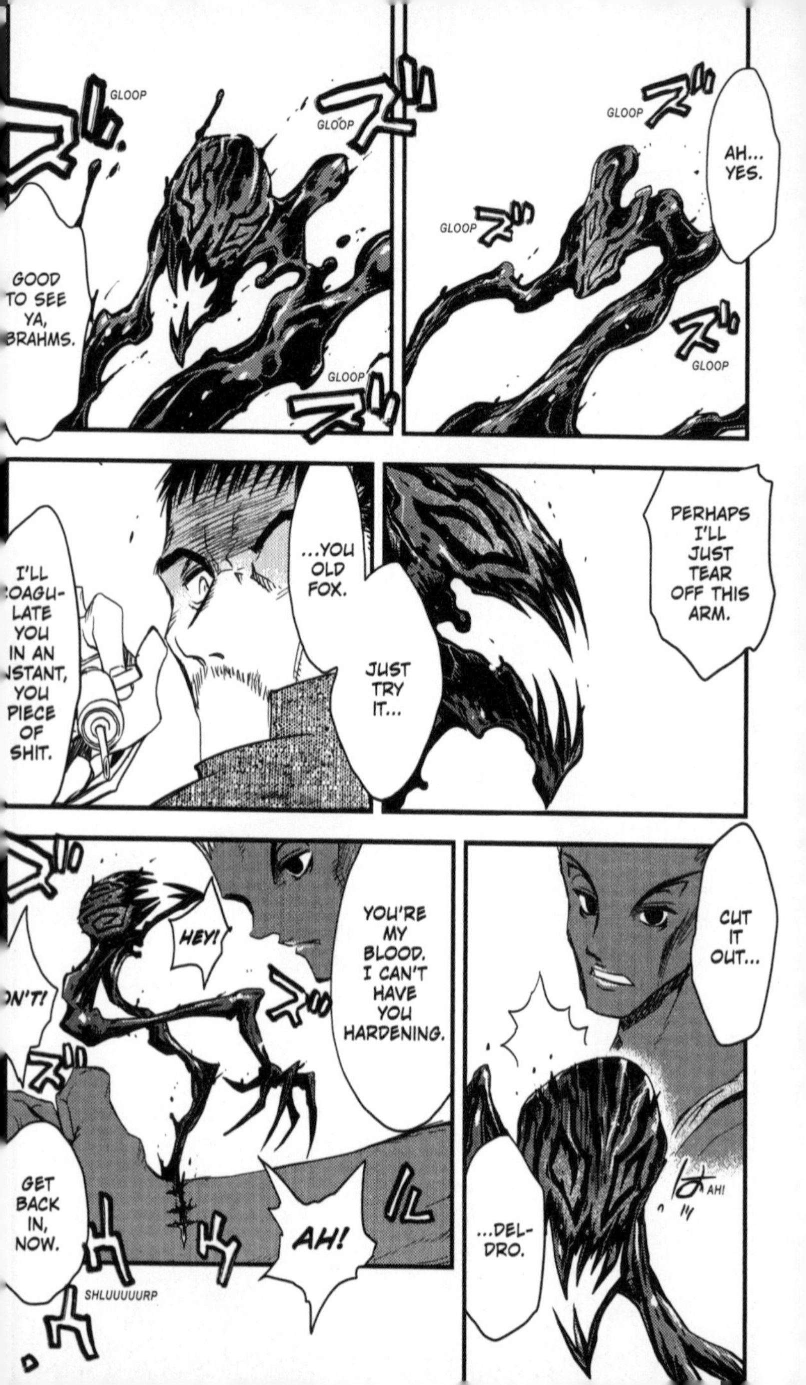
GLOOP
AH... YES.
GLOOP
GLOOP
GLOOP
GLOOP
GOOD TO SEE YA, BRAHMS.
GLOOP
PERHAPS I'LL JUST TEAR OFF THIS ARM.
...YOU OLD FOX.
JUST TRY IT...
I'LL OAGU-LATE YOU IN AN NSTANT, YOU PIECE OF SHIT.
CUT IT OUT...
AH!
...DEL-DRO.
YOU'RE MY BLOOD. I CAN'T HAVE YOU HARDENING.
HEY!
N'T!
AH!
GET BACK IN, NOW.
SHLUUUUURP

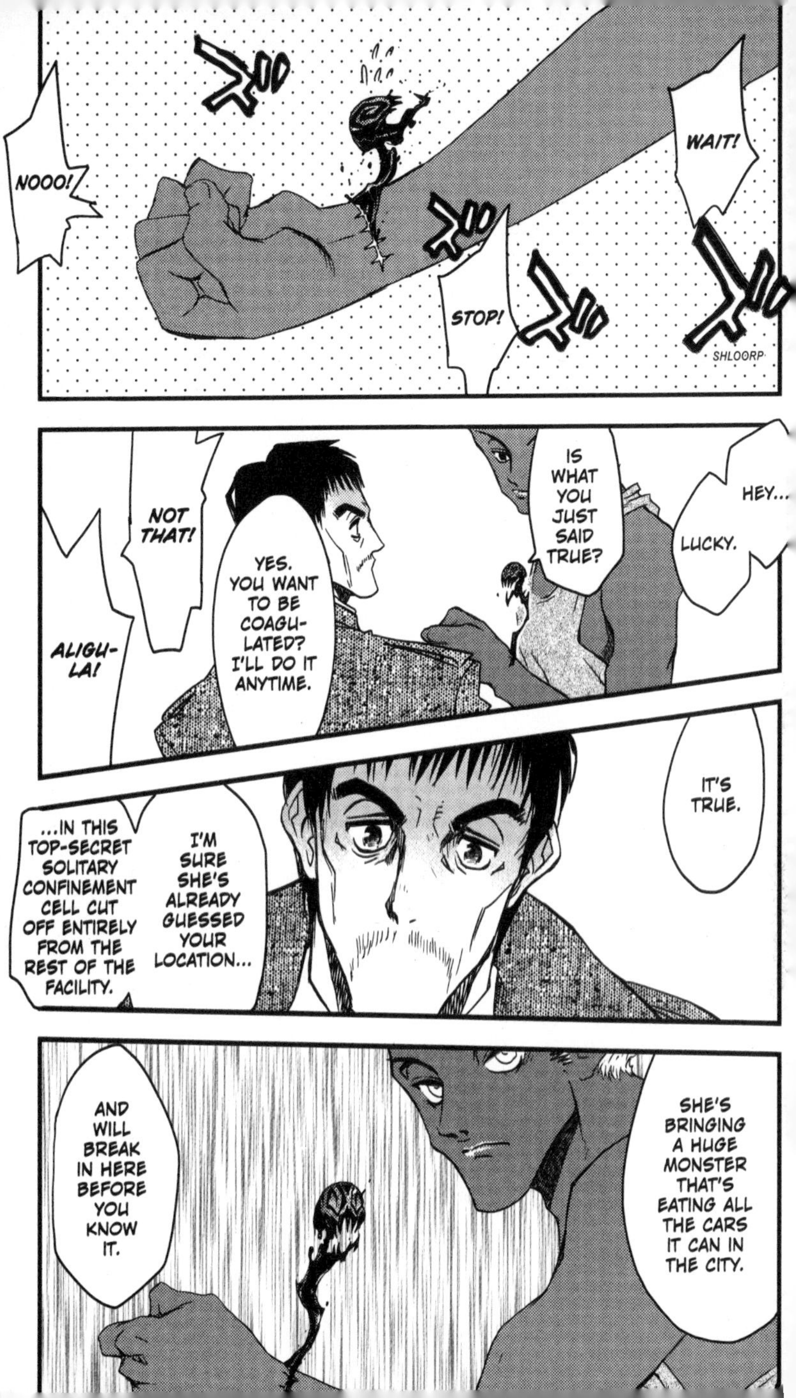
WAIT!
SHLOORP
STOP!
NOOO!
HEY... LUCKY.
IS WHAT YOU JUST SAID TRUE?
YES. YOU WANT TO BE COAGULATED? I'LL DO IT ANYTIME.
NOT THAT!
ALIGULA!
IT'S TRUE.
I'M SURE SHE'S ALREADY GUESSED YOUR LOCATION...
...IN THIS TOP-SECRET SOLITARY CONFINEMENT CELL CUT OFF ENTIRELY FROM THE REST OF THE FACILITY.
SHE'S BRINGING A HUGE MONSTER THAT'S EATING ALL THE CARS IT CAN IN THE CITY.
AND WILL BREAK IN HERE BEFORE YOU KNOW IT.

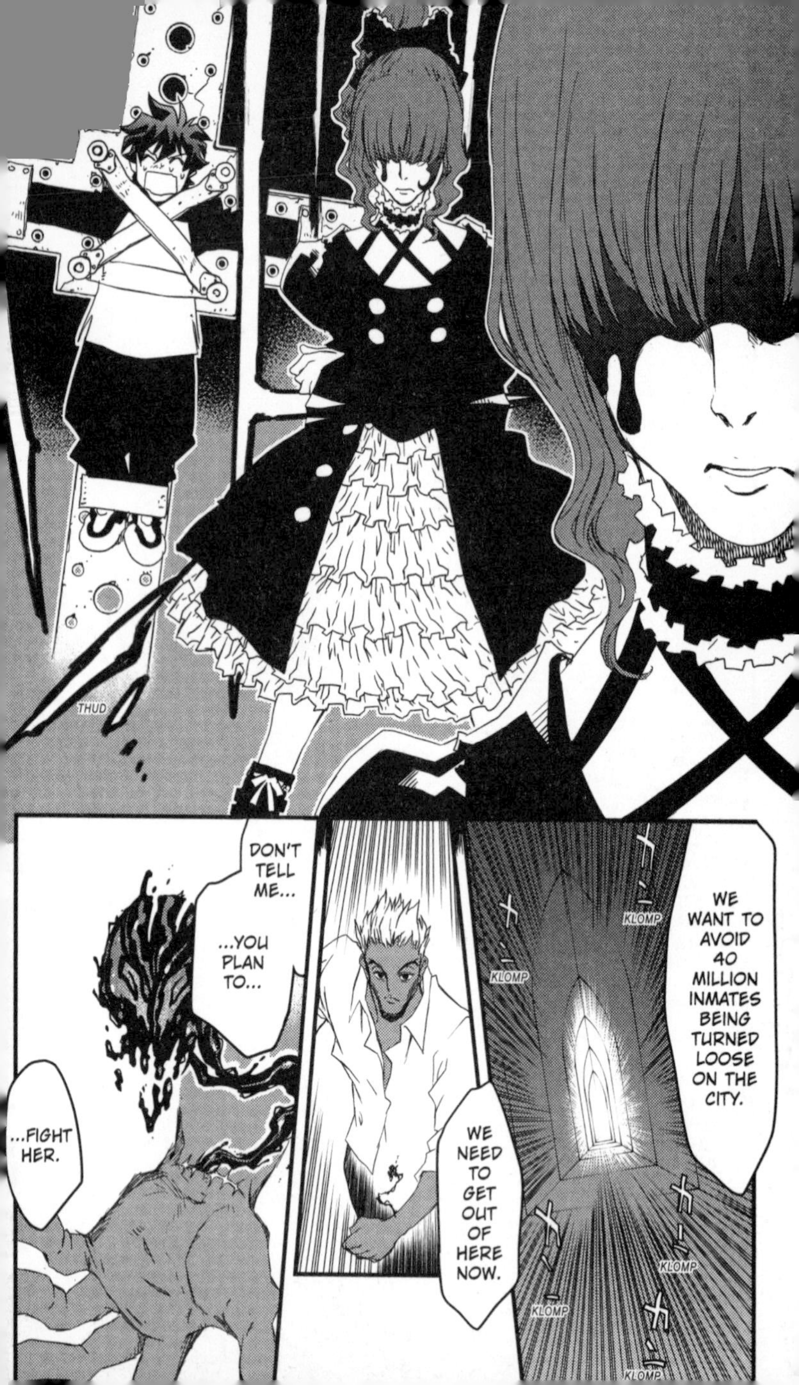
THUD
KLOMP
KLOMP
WE WANT TO AVOID 40 MILLION INMATES BEING TURNED LOOSE ON THE CITY.
KLOMP
KLOMP
KLOMP
WE NEED TO GET OUT OF HERE NOW.
DON'T TELL ME...
...YOU PLAN TO...
...FIGHT HER.

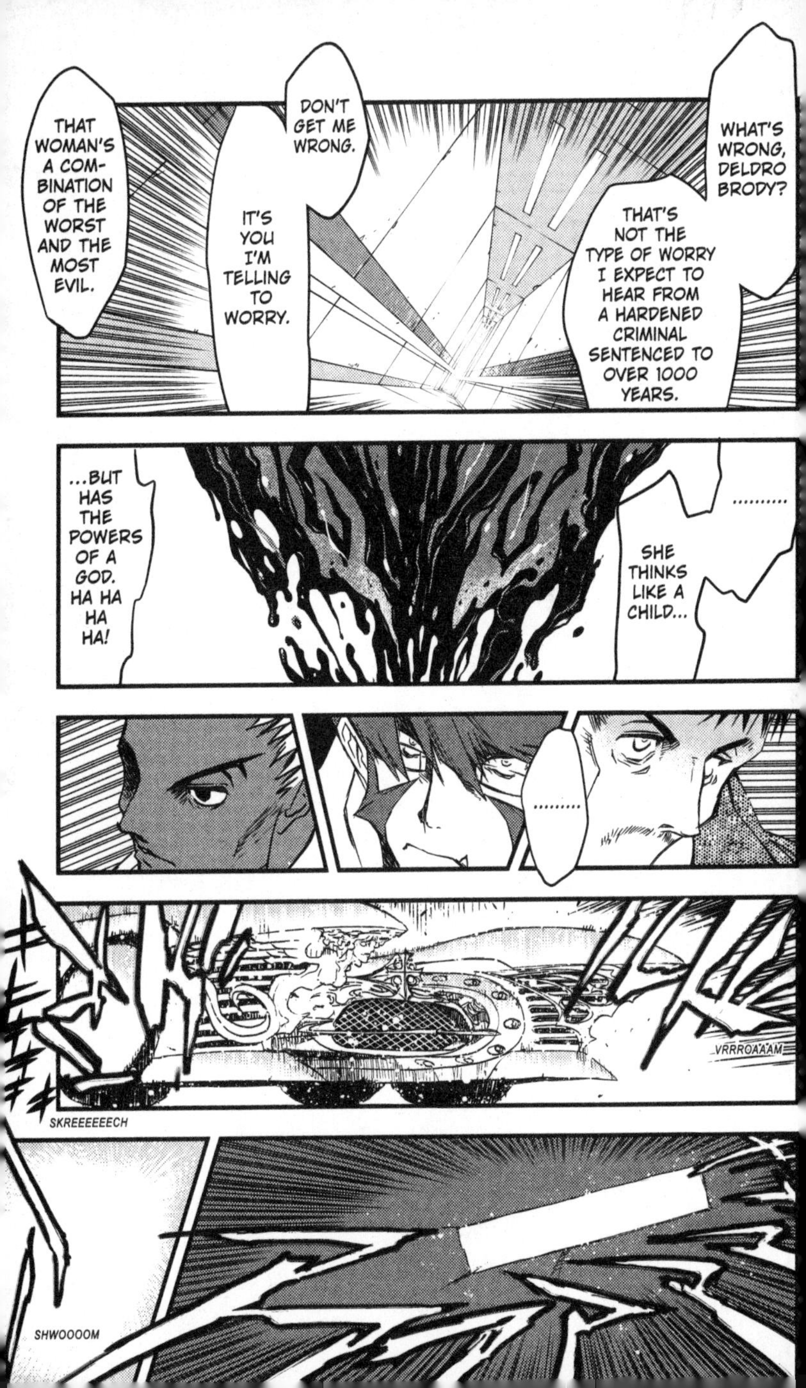
WHAT'S WRONG, DELDRO BRODY?
THAT'S NOT THE TYPE OF WORRY I EXPECT TO HEAR FROM A HARDENED CRIMINAL SENTENCED TO OVER 1000 YEARS.
DON'T GET ME WRONG.
IT'S YOU I'M TELLING TO WORRY.
THAT WOMAN'S A COMBINATION OF THE WORST AND THE MOST EVIL.
....
SHE THINKS LIKE A CHILD...
...BUT HAS THE POWERS OF A GOD. HA HA HA HA!
....
VRRROAAAM
SKREEEEEECH
SHWOOOOM

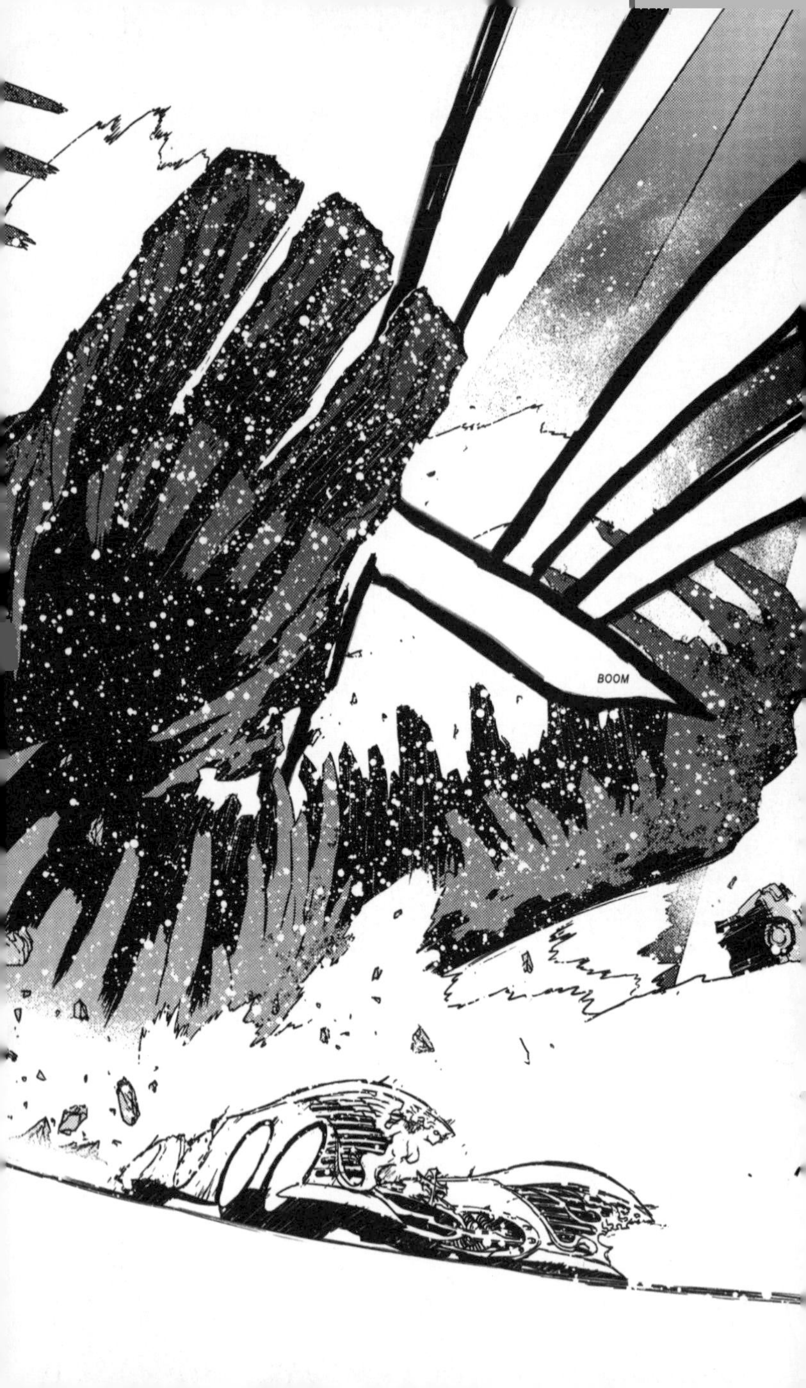
BOOM

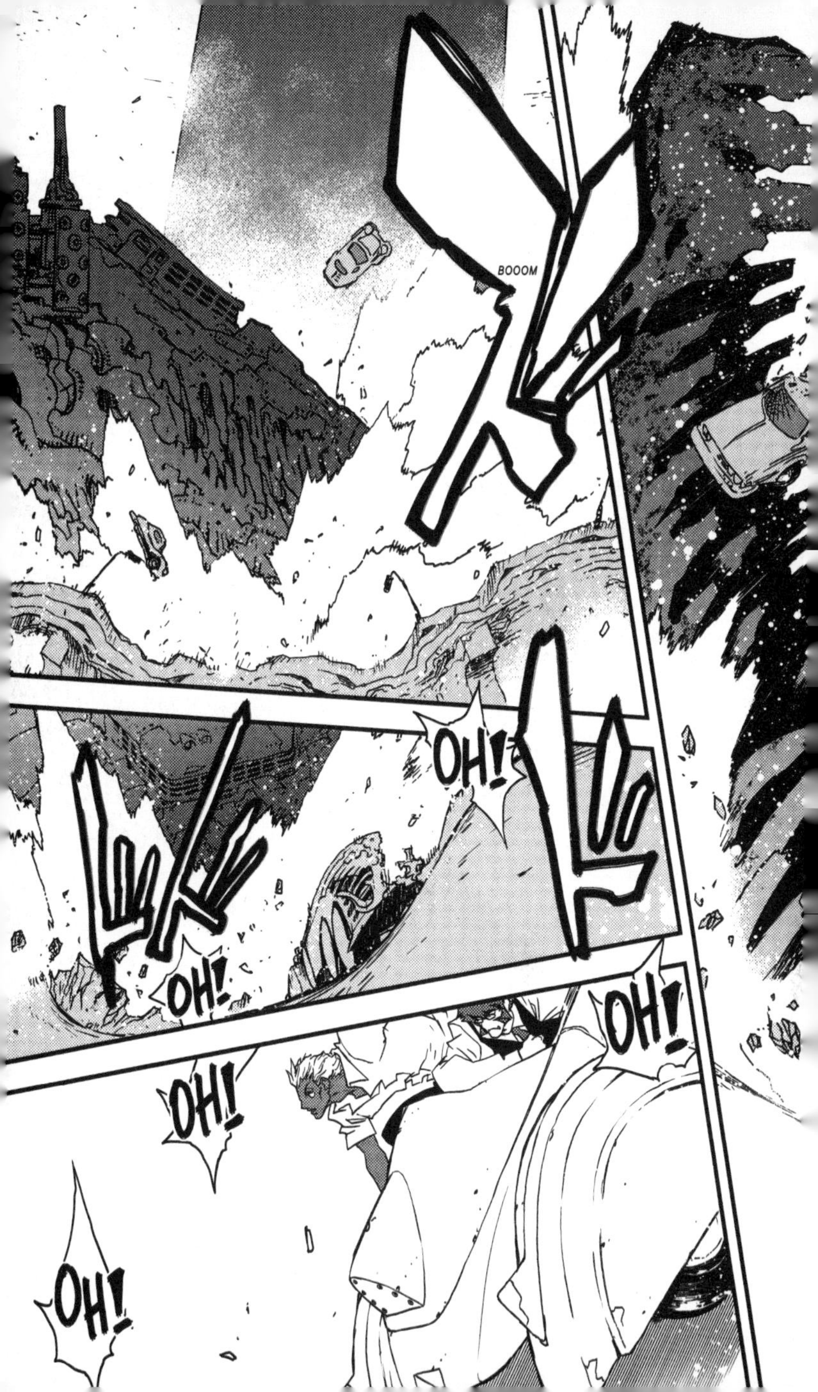
BOOOM
OH!
OH!
OH!
OH!
OH!

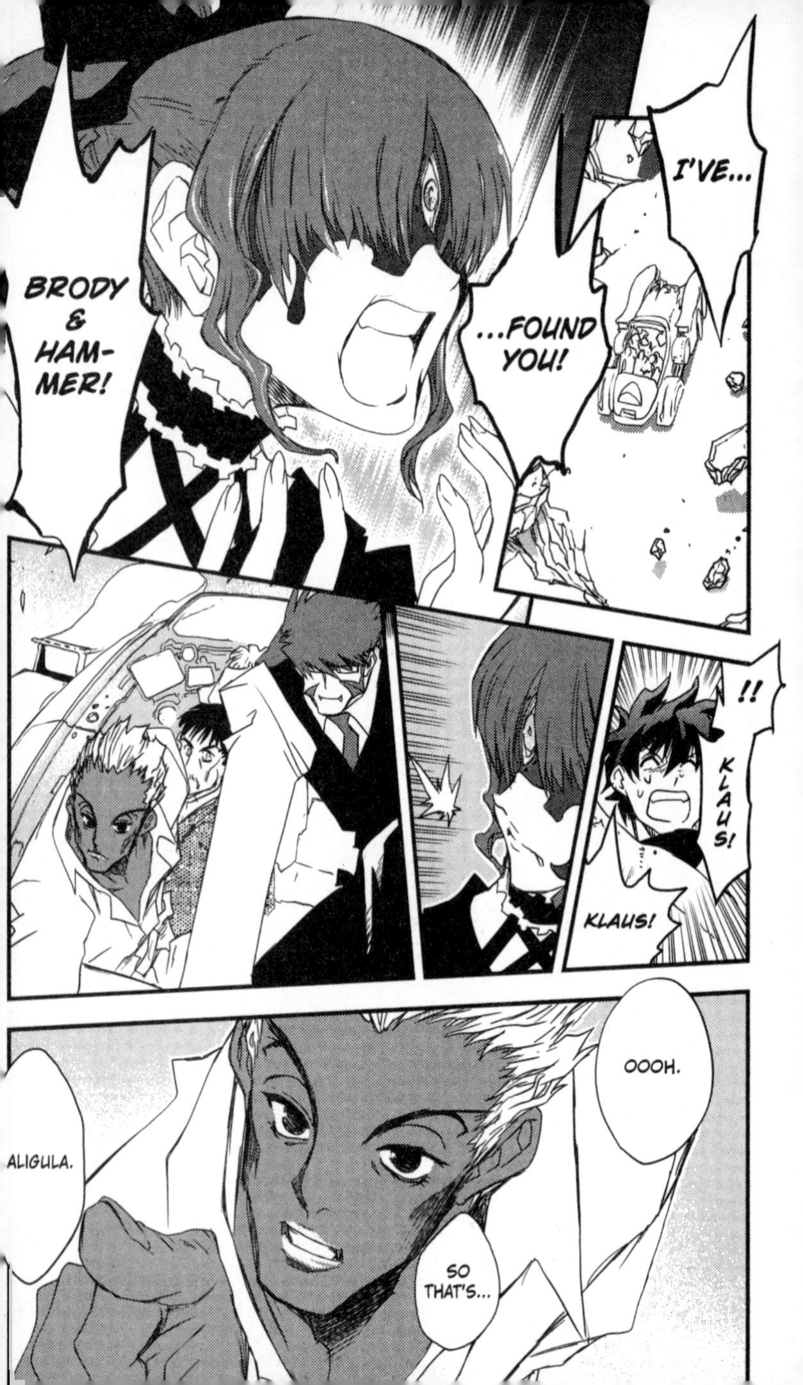
I'VE...
...FOUND YOU!
BRODY & HAM-MER!
!!
KLAUS!
KLAUS!
OOOH.
SO THAT'S...
ALIGULA.

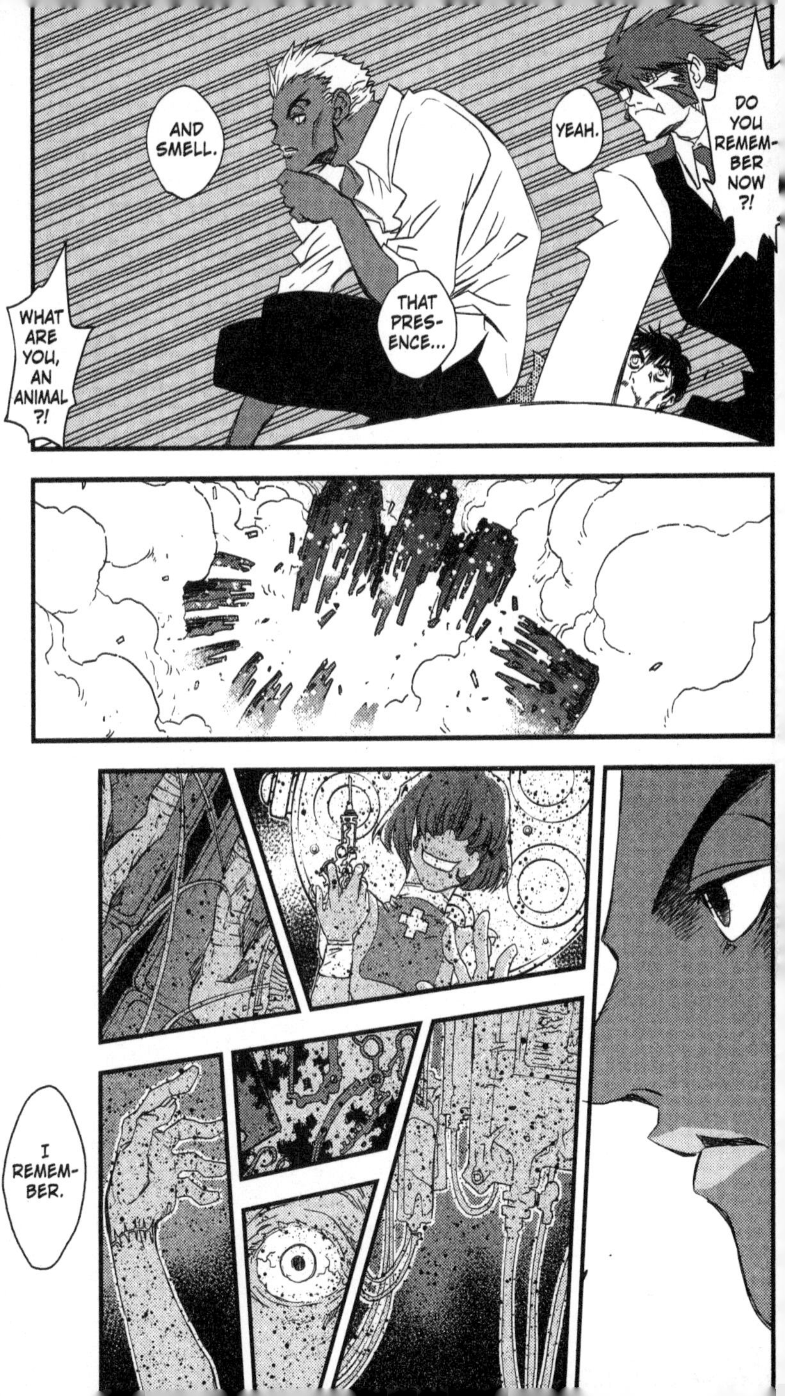
DO YOU REMEM-BER NOW ?!
YEAH.
AND SMELL.
THAT PRES-ENCE...
WHAT ARE YOU, AN ANIMAL ?!
I REMEM-BER.

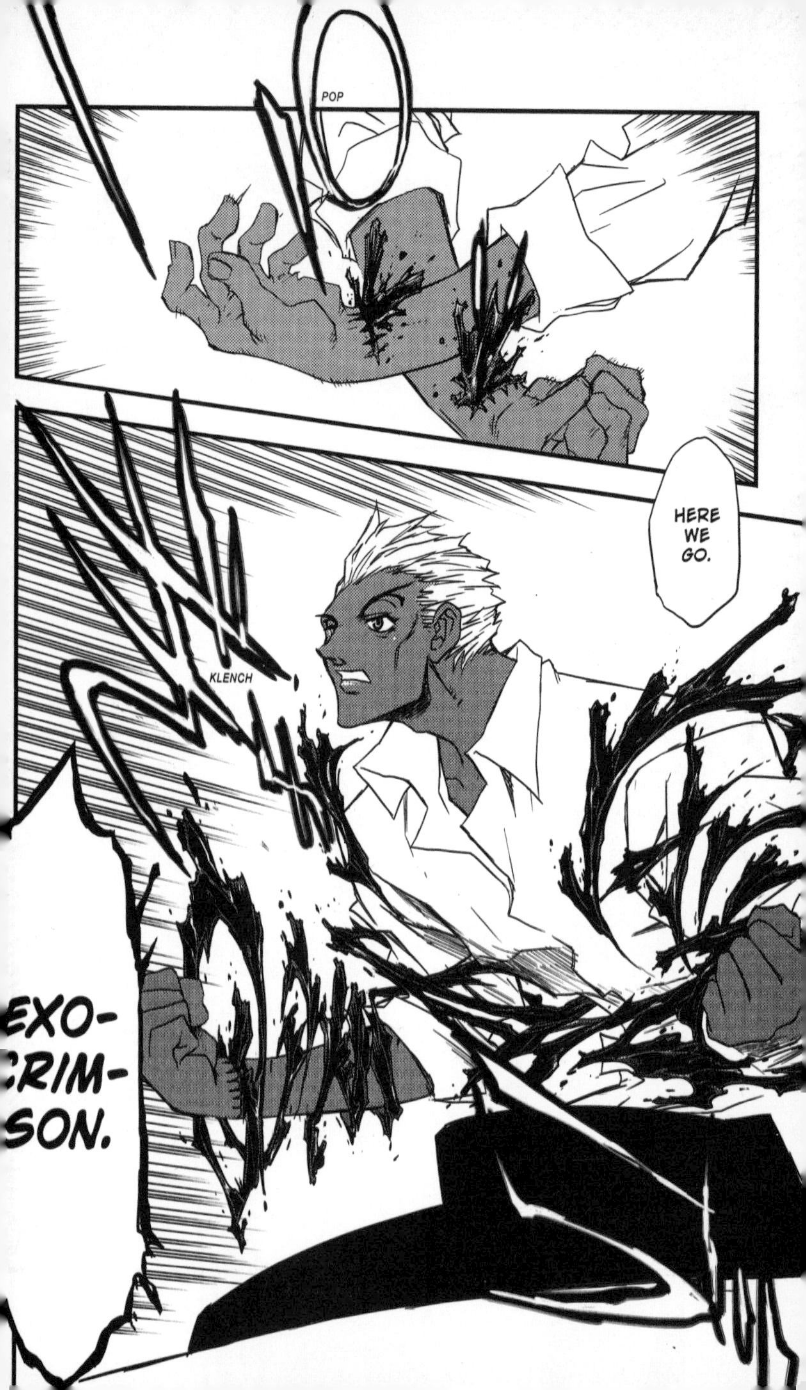
POP
HERE WE GO.
KLENCH
EXO-CRIM-SON.

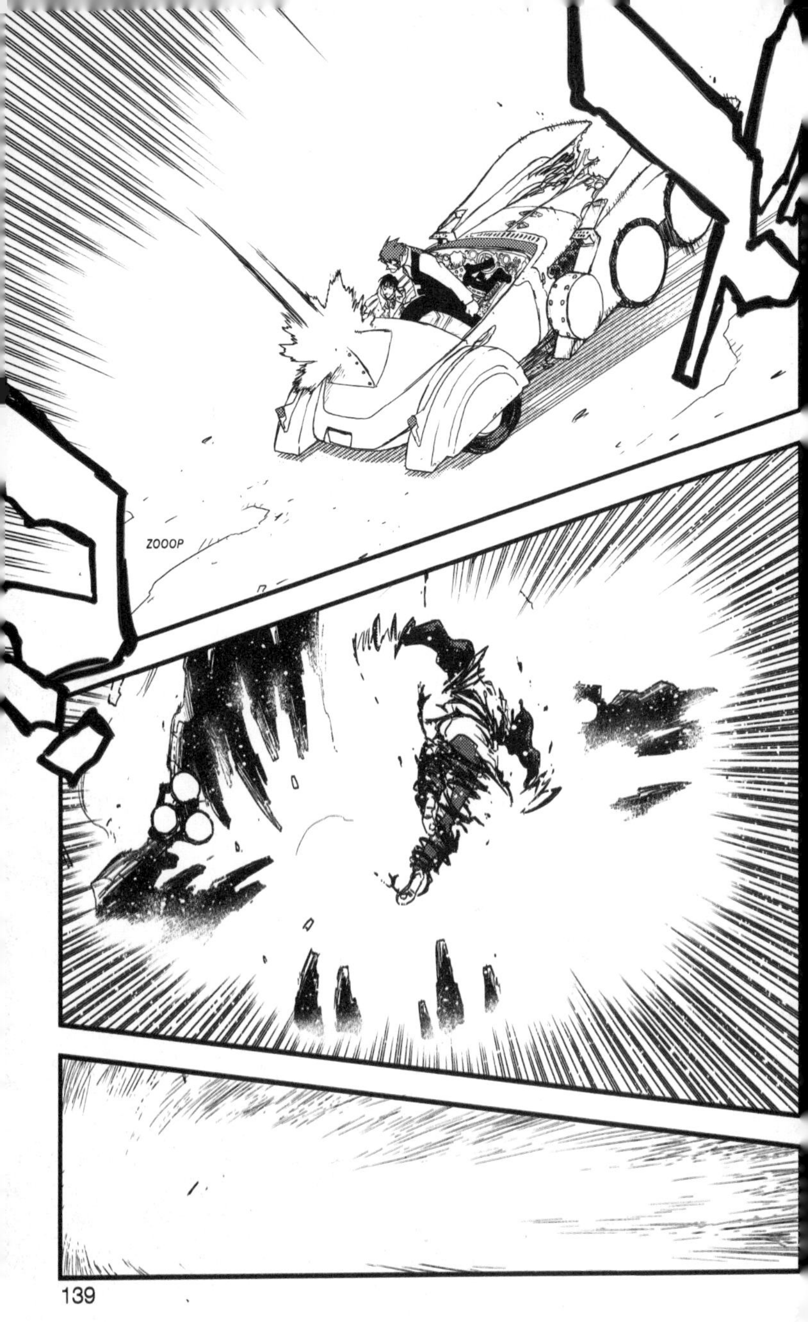
ZOOOP

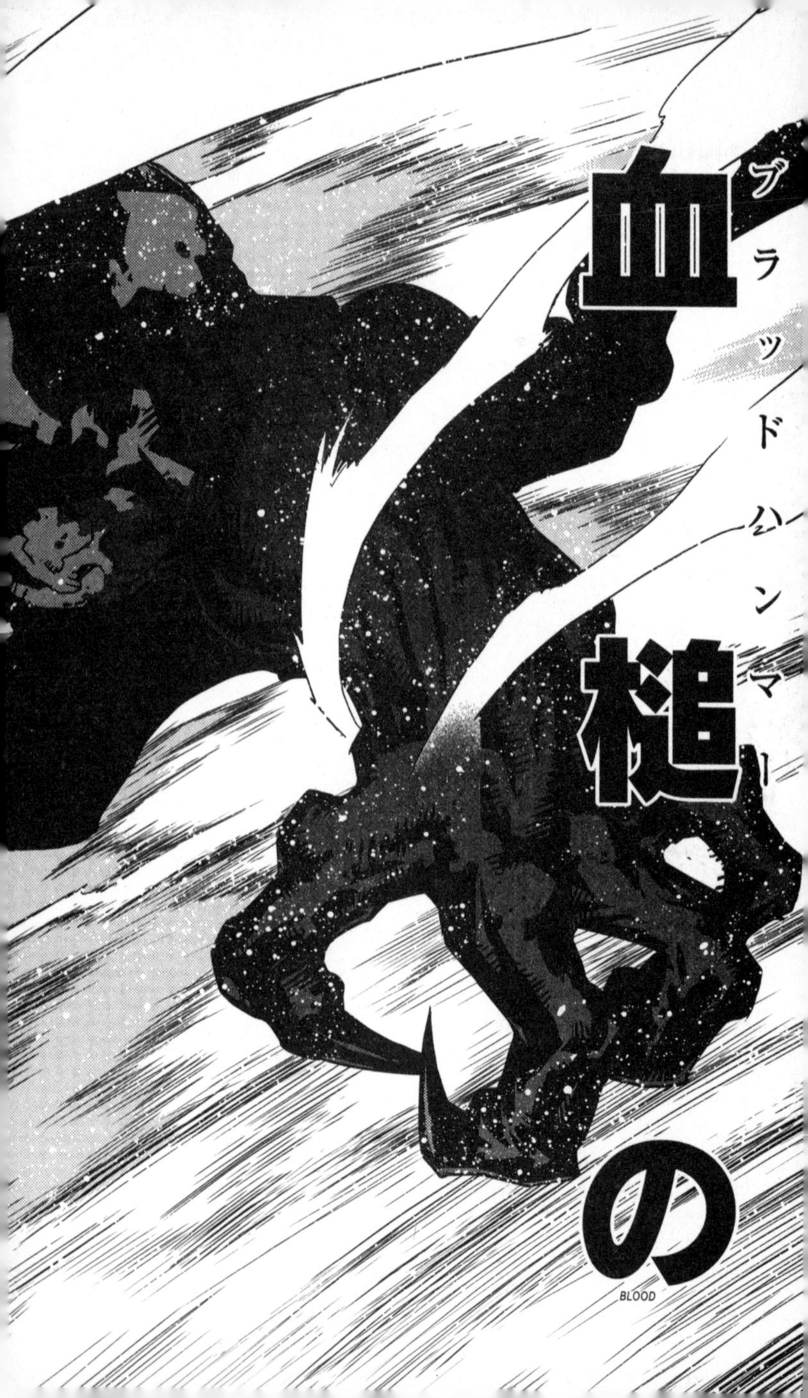
ブラッドハンマー
血槌の
BLOOD

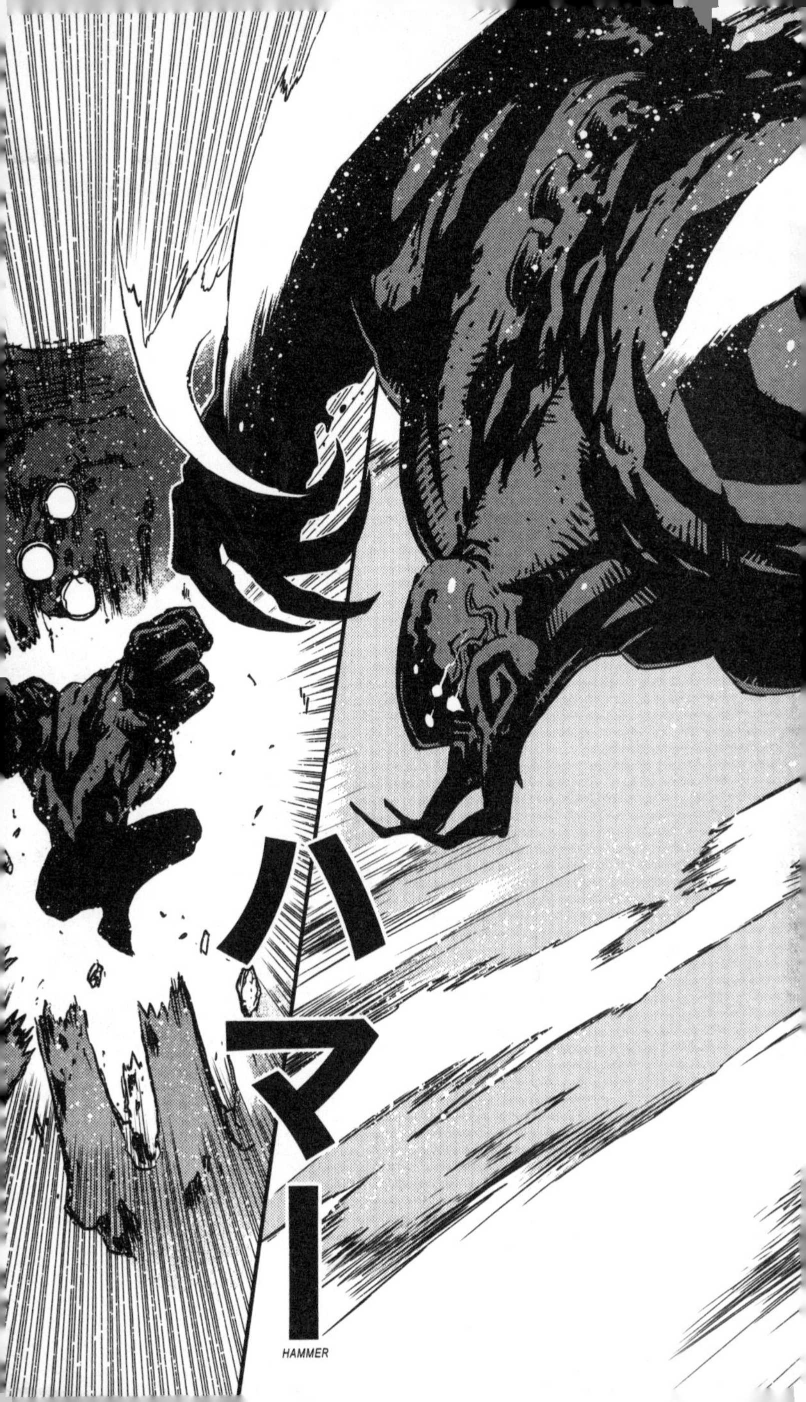
ハマー
HAMMER

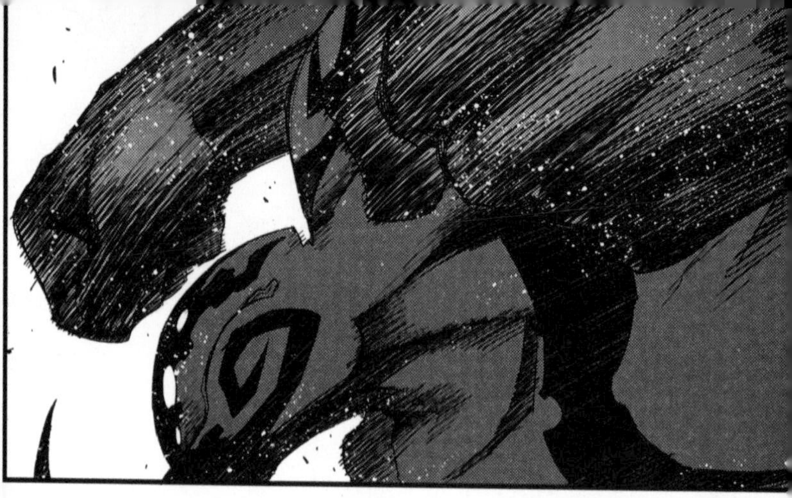

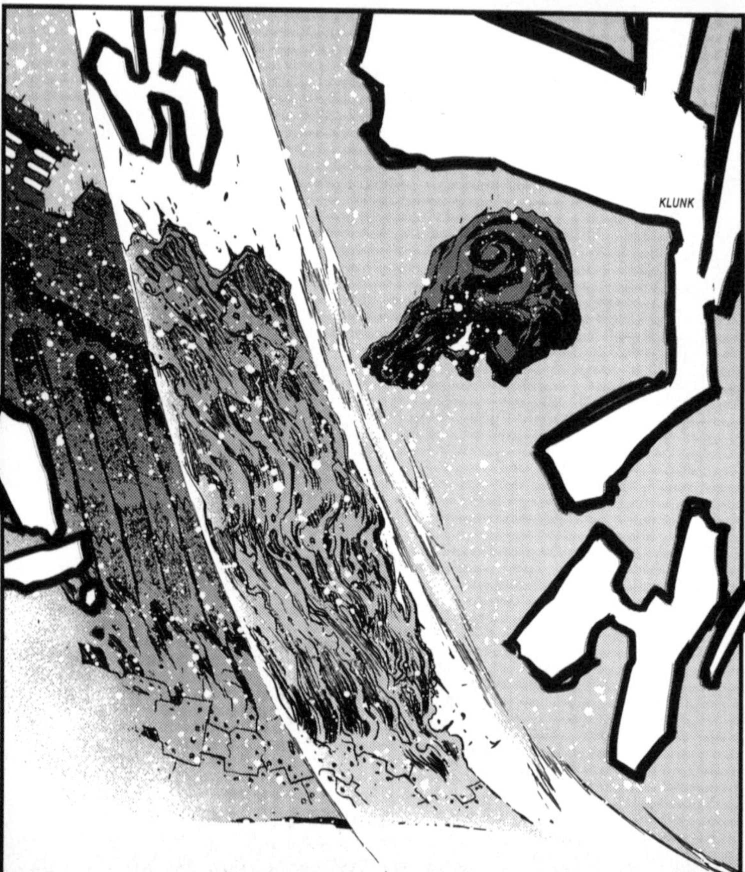
KLUNK

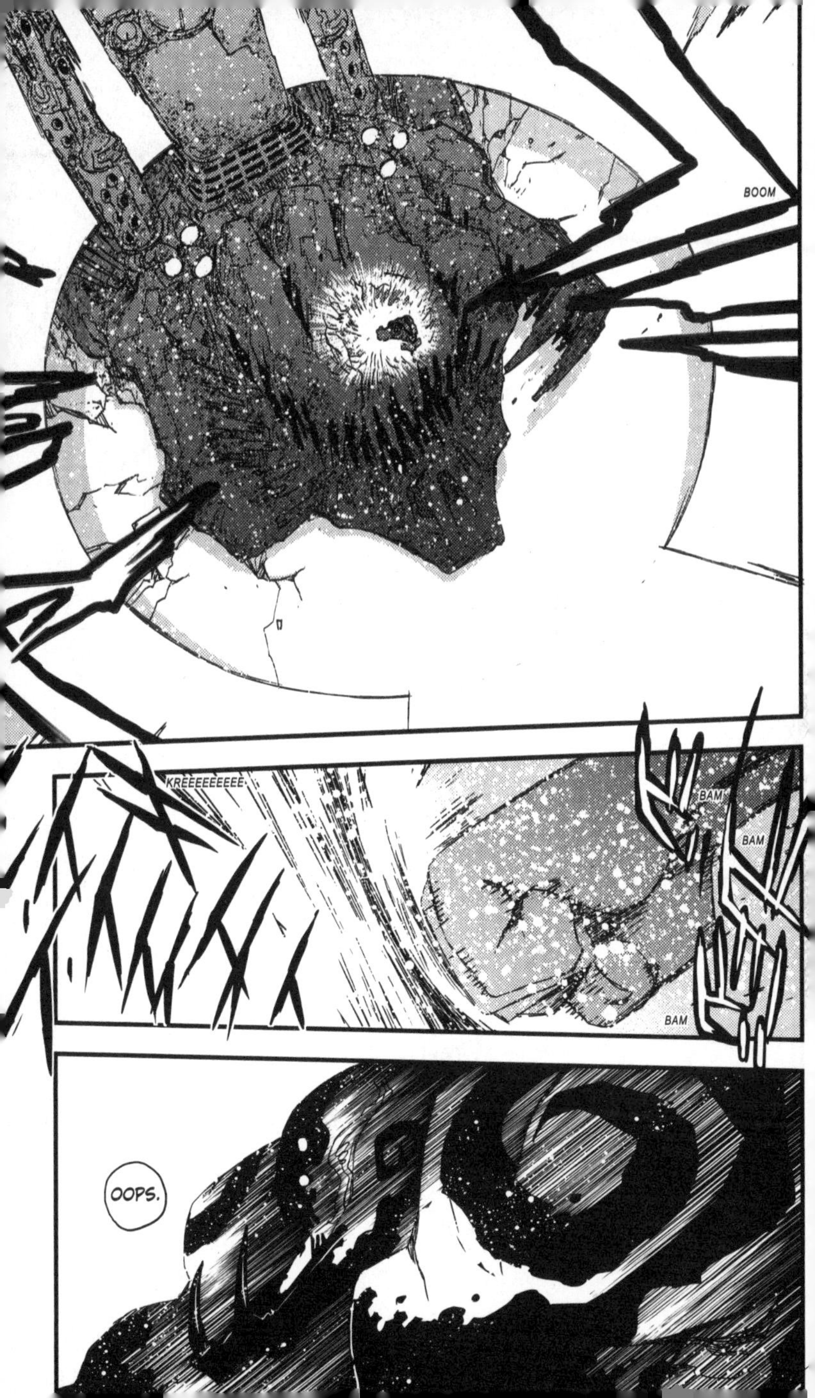
BOOM
BAM
BAM
BAM
KREEEEEEEEEE
OOPS.

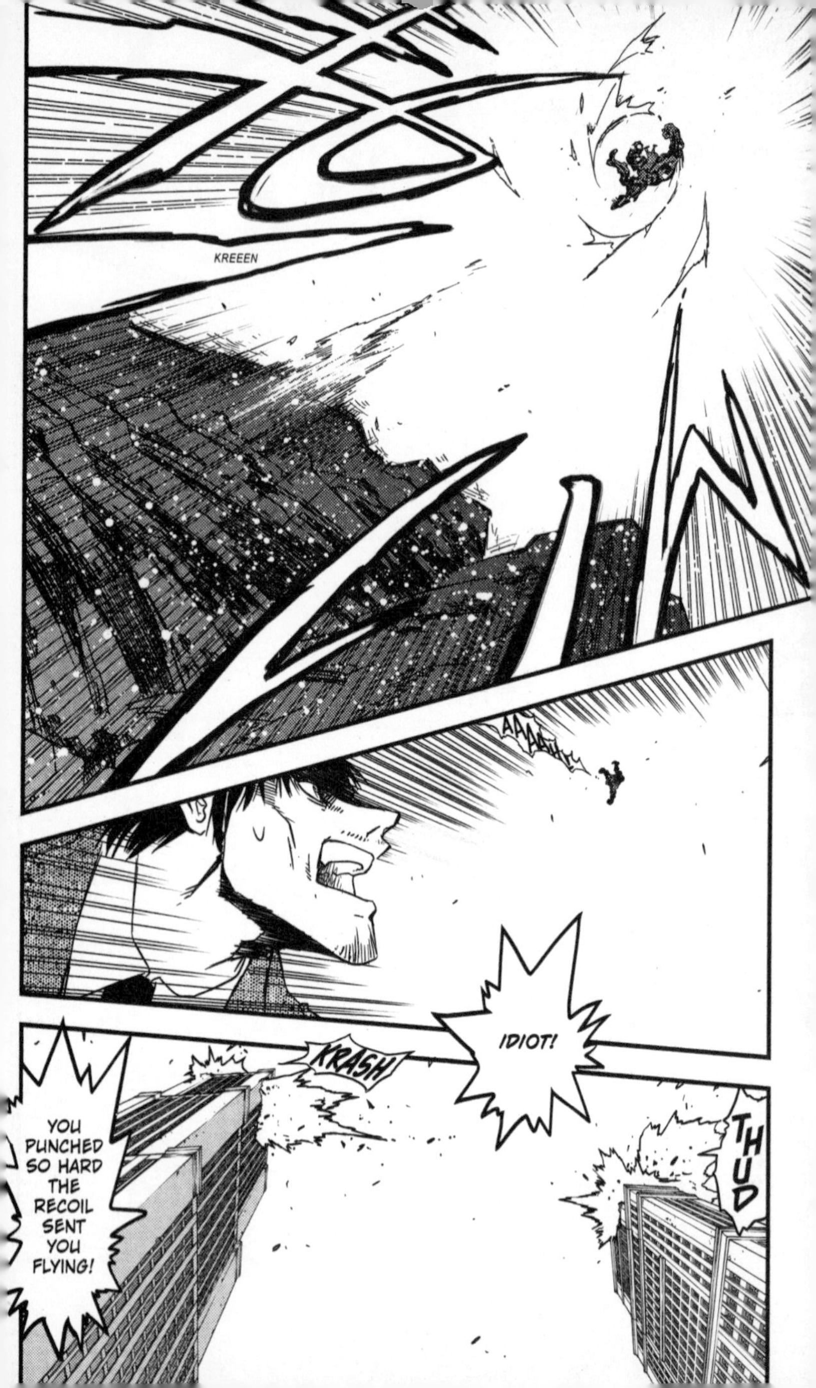
KREEEN
IDIOT!
THUD
KRASH
YOU PUNCHED SO HARD THE RECOIL SENT YOU FLYING!

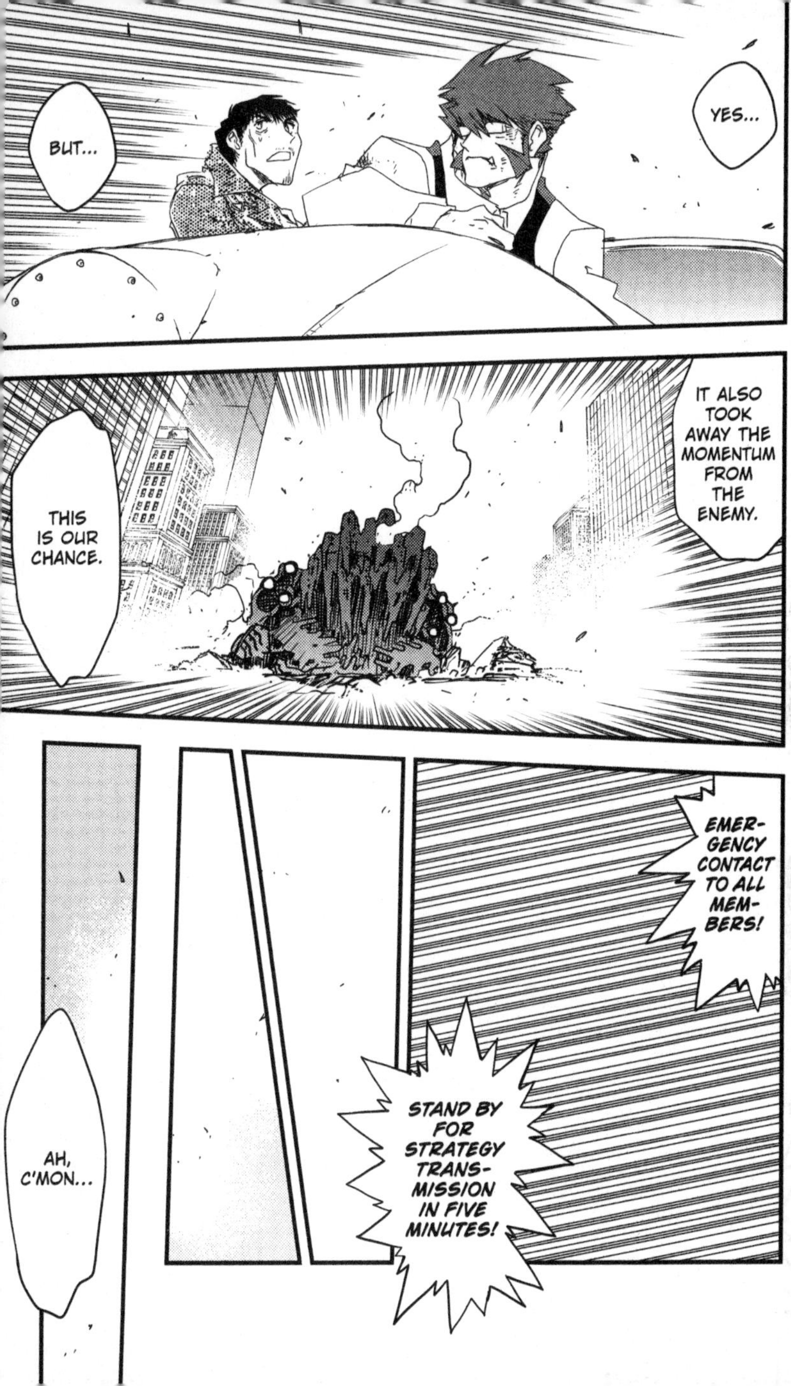
YES...
BUT...
IT ALSO TOOK AWAY THE MOMENTUM FROM THE ENEMY.
THIS IS OUR CHANCE.
EMERGENCY CONTACT TO ALL MEMBERS!
STAND BY FOR STRATEGY TRANSMISSION IN FIVE MINUTES!
AH, C'MON...

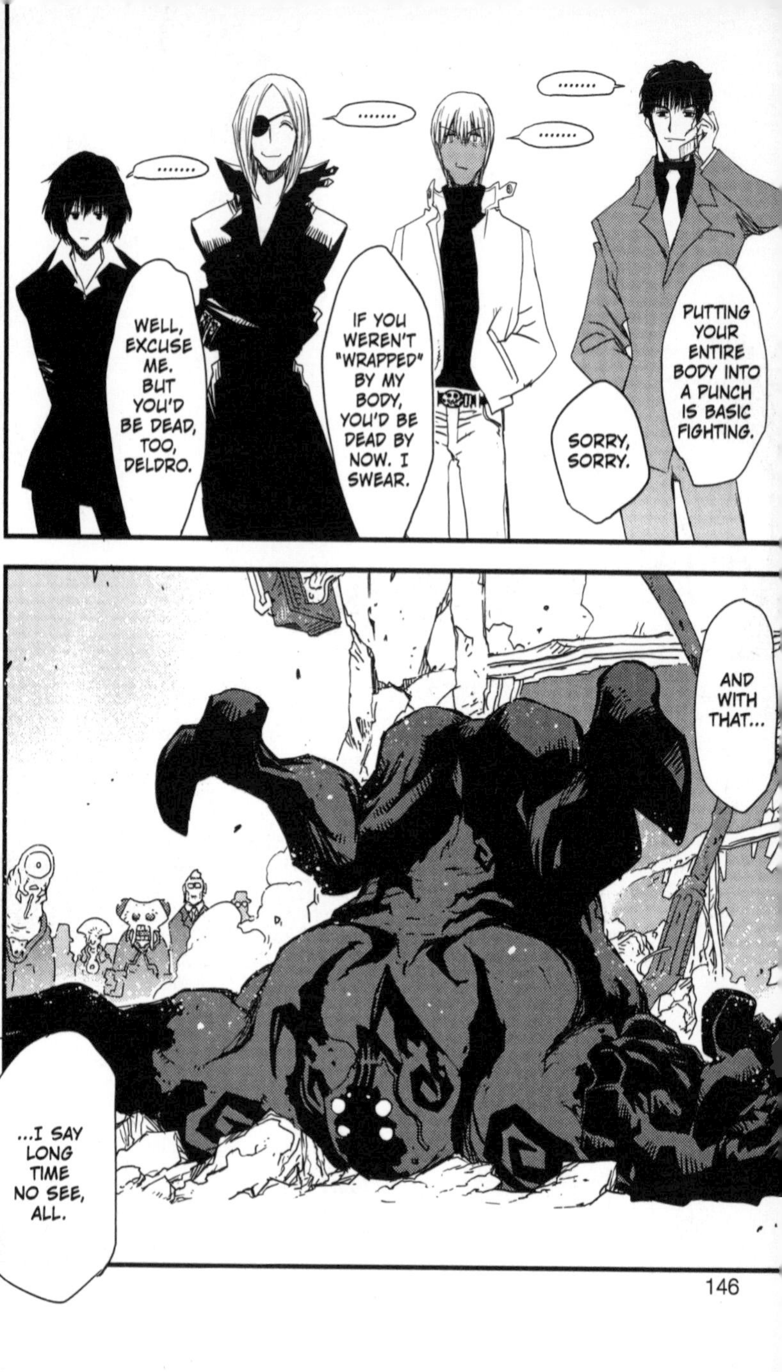
....
....
....
....
PUTTING YOUR ENTIRE BODY INTO A PUNCH IS BASIC FIGHTING.
SORRY, SORRY.
IF YOU WEREN'T "WRAPPED" BY MY BODY, YOU'D BE DEAD BY NOW. I SWEAR.
WELL, EXCUSE ME. BUT YOU'D BE DEAD, TOO, DELDRO.
AND WITH THAT...
...I SAY LONG TIME NO SEE, ALL.

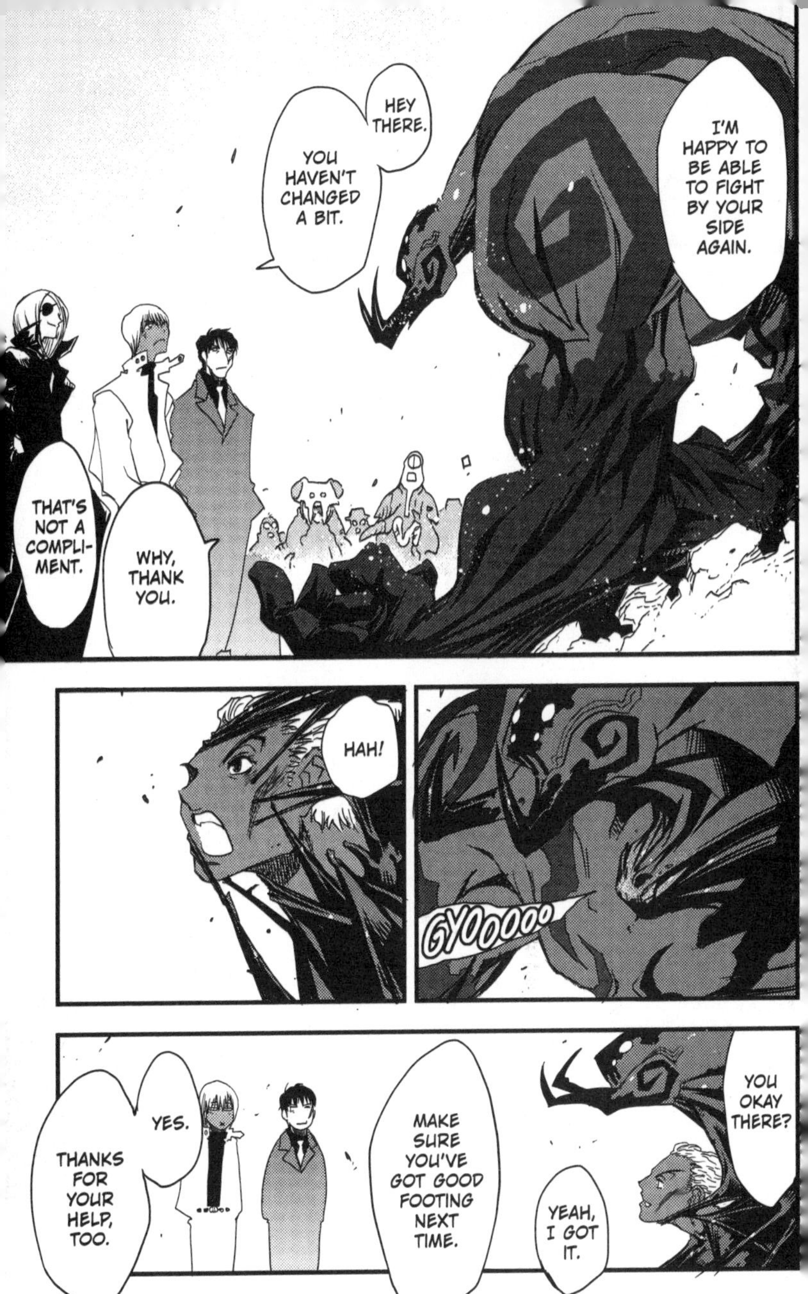
I'M HAPPY TO BE ABLE TO FIGHT BY YOUR SIDE AGAIN.
HEY THERE.
YOU HAVEN'T CHANGED A BIT.
!
WHY, THANK YOU.
THAT'S NOT A COMPLI-MENT.
GYOOOOO
HAH!
YOU OKAY THERE?
YEAH, I GOT IT.
MAKE SURE YOU'VE GOT GOOD FOOTING NEXT TIME.
YES.
THANKS FOR YOUR HELP, TOO.

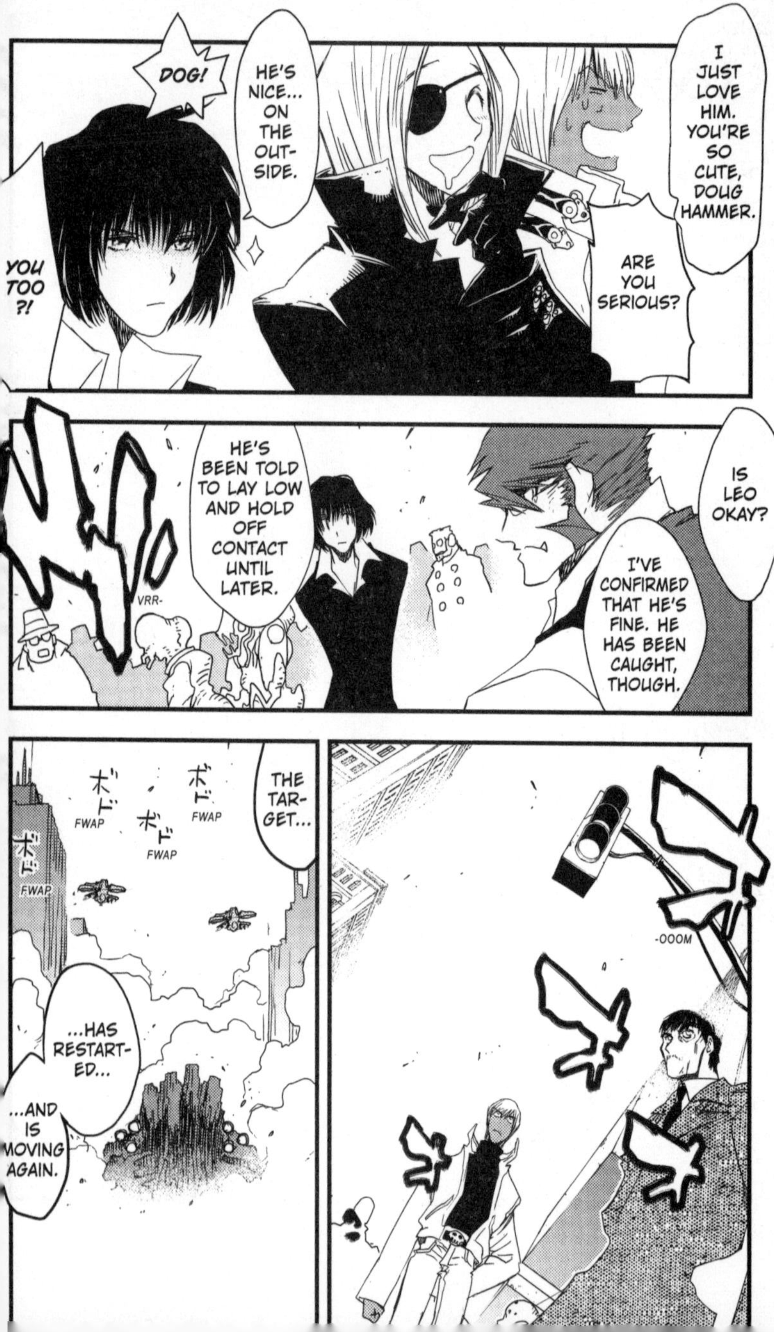
I JUST LOVE HIM. YOU'RE SO CUTE, DOUG HAMMER.
ARE YOU SERIOUS?
HE'S NICE... ON THE OUT-SIDE.
DOG!
YOU TOO ?!
IS LEO OKAY?
I'VE CONFIRMED THAT HE'S FINE. HE HAS BEEN CAUGHT, THOUGH.
HE'S BEEN TOLD TO LAY LOW AND HOLD OFF CONTACT UNTIL LATER.
VRR-
-OOOM
THE TAR-GET...
ボド FWAP
ボド FWAP
ボド FWAP
ボド FWAP
...HAS RESTART-ED...
...AND IS MOVING AGAIN.

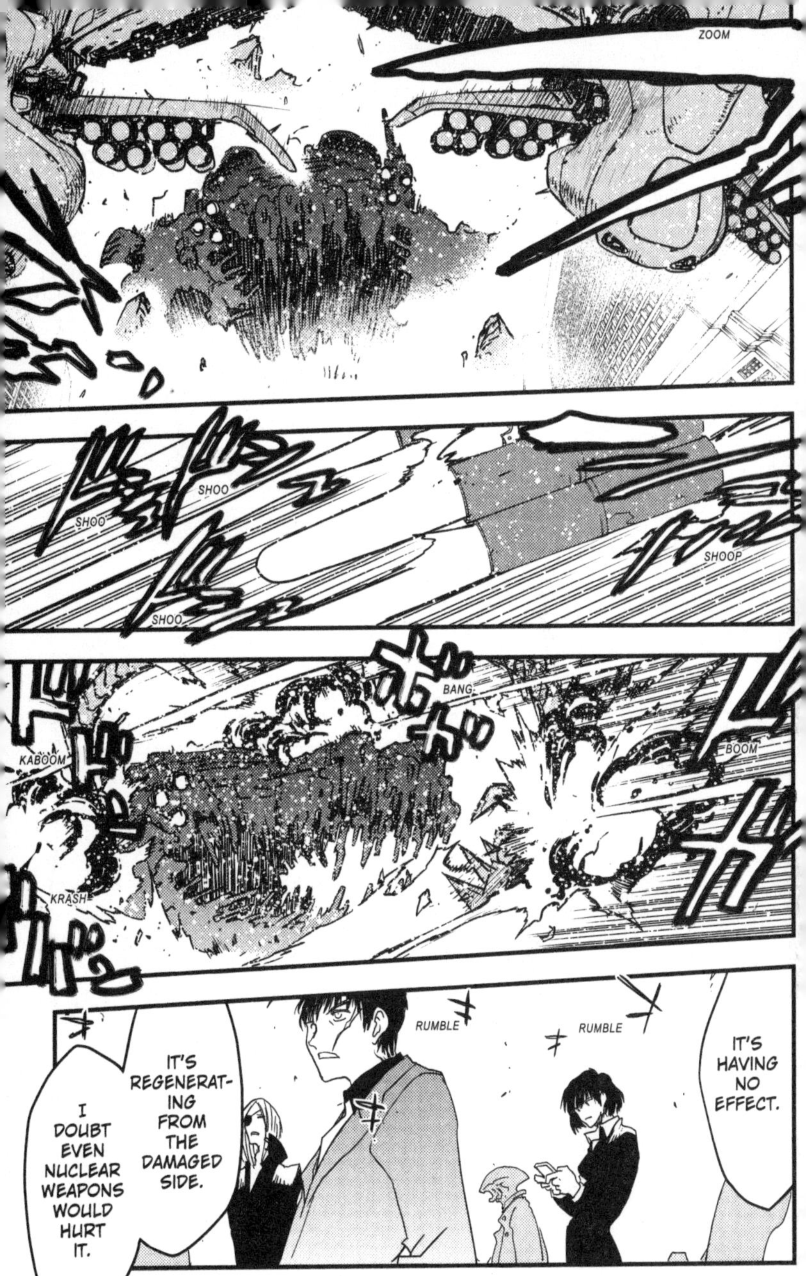
ZOOM
SHOOP
SHOO
SHOO
SHOO
BOOM
BANG
KABOOM
KRASH
RUMBLE
RUMBLE
IT'S HAVING NO EFFECT.
IT'S REGENERATING FROM THE DAMAGED SIDE.
I DOUBT EVEN NUCLEAR WEAPONS WOULD HURT IT.

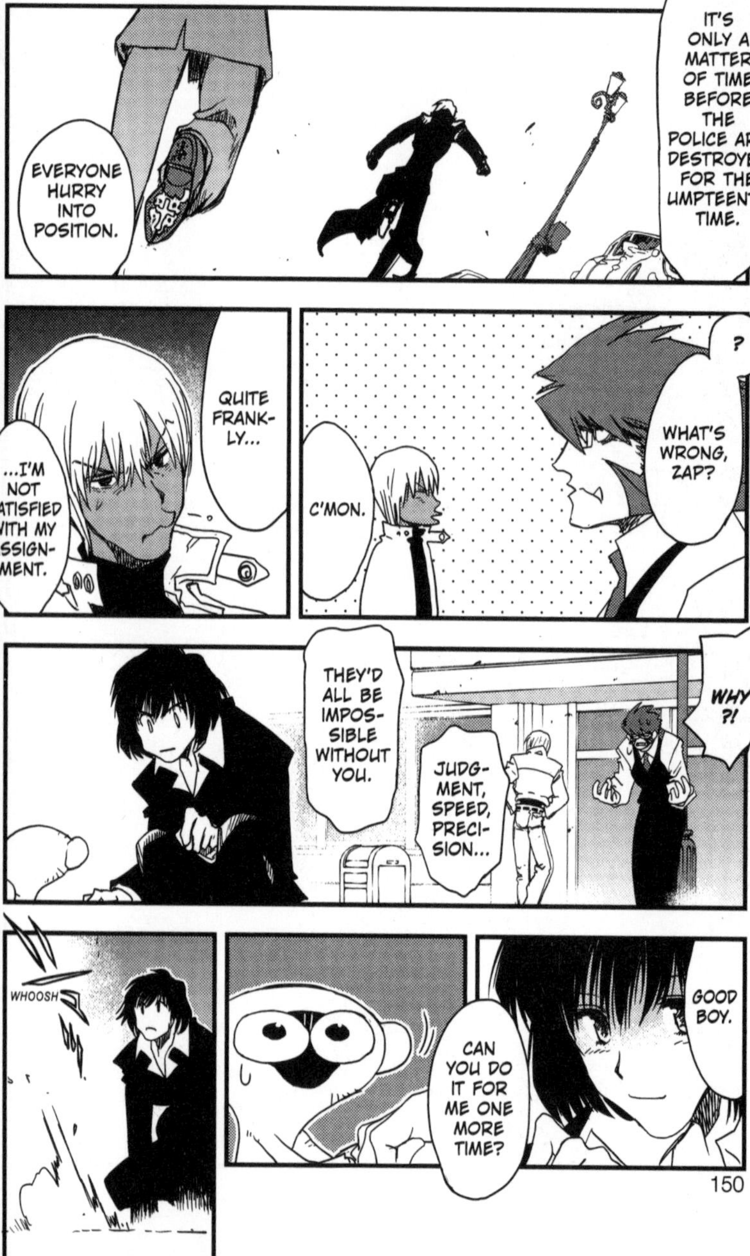
IT'S ONLY A MATTER OF TIME BEFORE THE POLICE ARE DESTROYED FOR THE UMPTEENTH TIME.
EVERYONE HURRY INTO POSITION.
?
WHAT'S WRONG, ZAP?
C'MON.
QUITE FRANKLY...
...I'M NOT ATISFIED WITH MY ASSIGNMENT.
WHY?!
JUDGMENT, SPEED, PRECISION...
THEY'D ALL BE IMPOSSIBLE WITHOUT YOU.
GOOD BOY.
CAN YOU DO IT FOR ME ONE MORE TIME?
WHOOSH

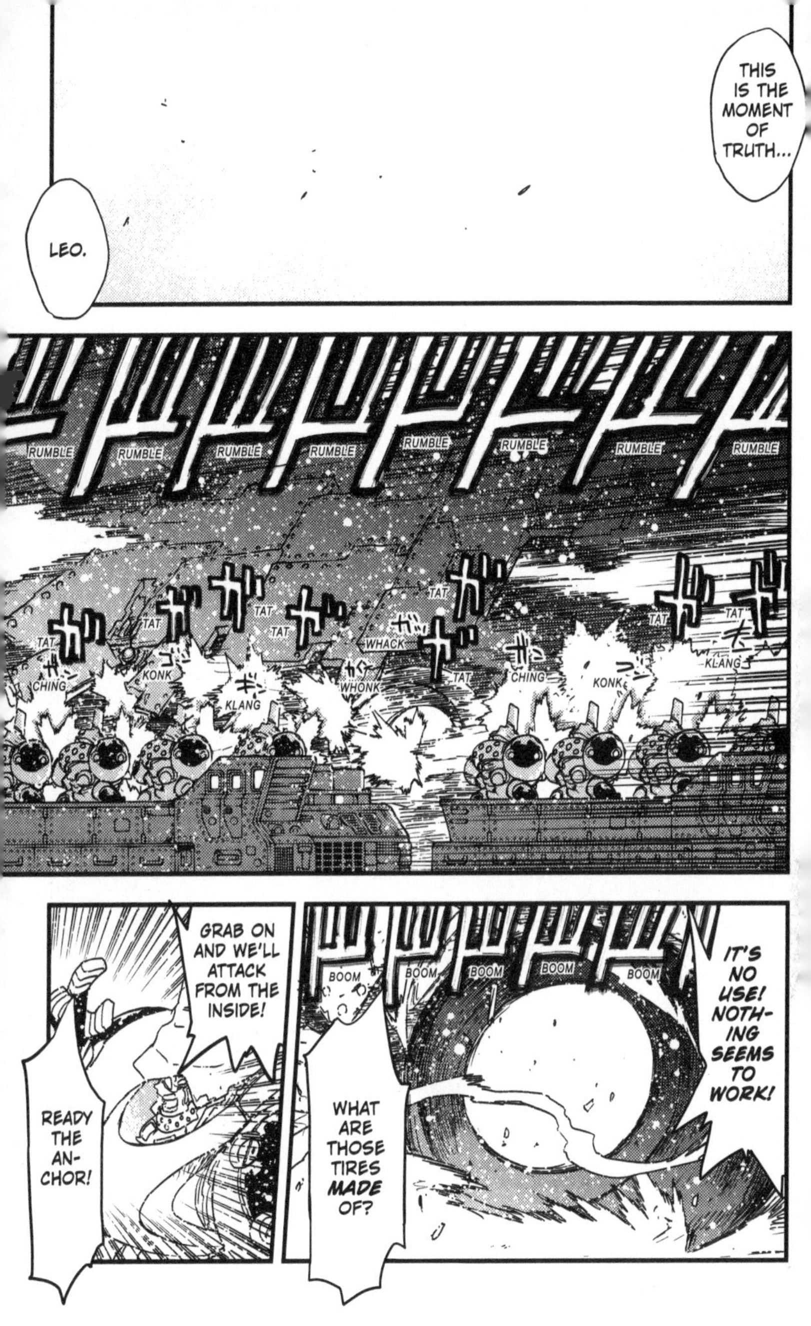
THIS IS THE MOMENT OF TRUTH...
LEO.
RUMBLE RUMBLE RUMBLE RUMBLE RUMBLE RUMBLE RUMBLE RUMBLE
TAT TAT KLANG KONK CHING TAT TAT WHACK WHONK TAT TAT KLANG KONK TAT TAT CHING
BOOM BOOM BOOM BOOM BOOM
IT'S NO USE! NOTHING SEEMS TO WORK!
WHAT ARE THOSE TIRES *MADE* OF?
GRAB ON AND WE'LL ATTACK FROM THE INSIDE!
READY THE ANCHOR!

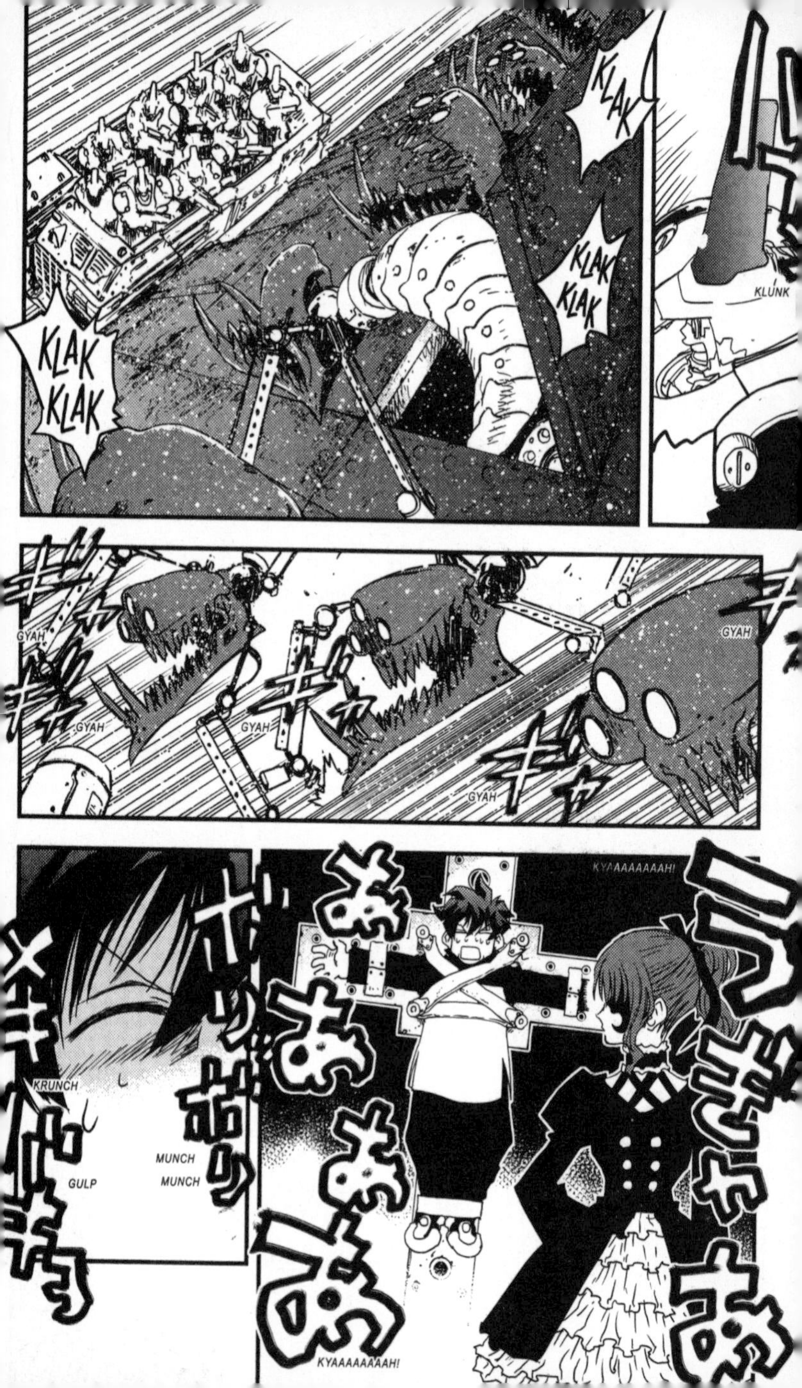
KLUNK
KLAK
KLAK KLAK KLAK
KLAK KLAK
GYAH
GYAH
GYAH
GYAH
GYAH
KYAAAAAAAAH!
KYAAAAAAAAH!
KRUNCH
MUNCH MUNCH
GULP

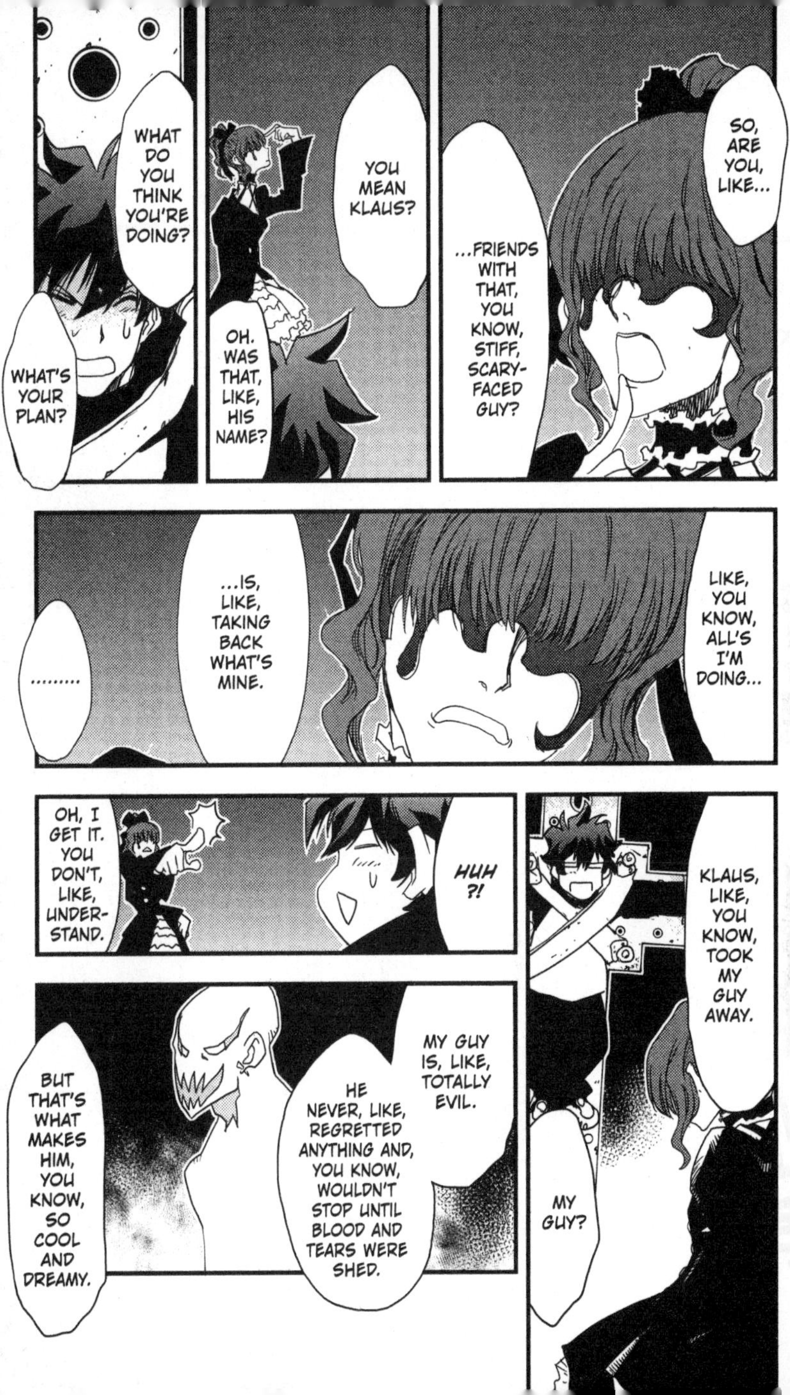
SO, ARE YOU, LIKE...
...FRIENDS WITH THAT, YOU KNOW, STIFF, SCARY-FACED GUY?
YOU MEAN KLAUS?
OH. WAS THAT, LIKE, HIS NAME?
WHAT DO YOU THINK YOU'RE DOING?
WHAT'S YOUR PLAN?
LIKE, YOU KNOW, ALL'S I'M DOING...
...IS, LIKE, TAKING BACK WHAT'S MINE.
....
KLAUS, LIKE, YOU KNOW, TOOK MY GUY AWAY.
MY GUY?
HUH?!
OH, I GET IT. YOU DON'T, LIKE, UNDER-STAND.
MY GUY IS, LIKE, TOTALLY EVIL.
HE NEVER, LIKE, REGRETTED ANYTHING AND, YOU KNOW, WOULDN'T STOP UNTIL BLOOD AND TEARS WERE SHED.
BUT THAT'S WHAT MAKES HIM, YOU KNOW, SO COOL AND DREAMY.

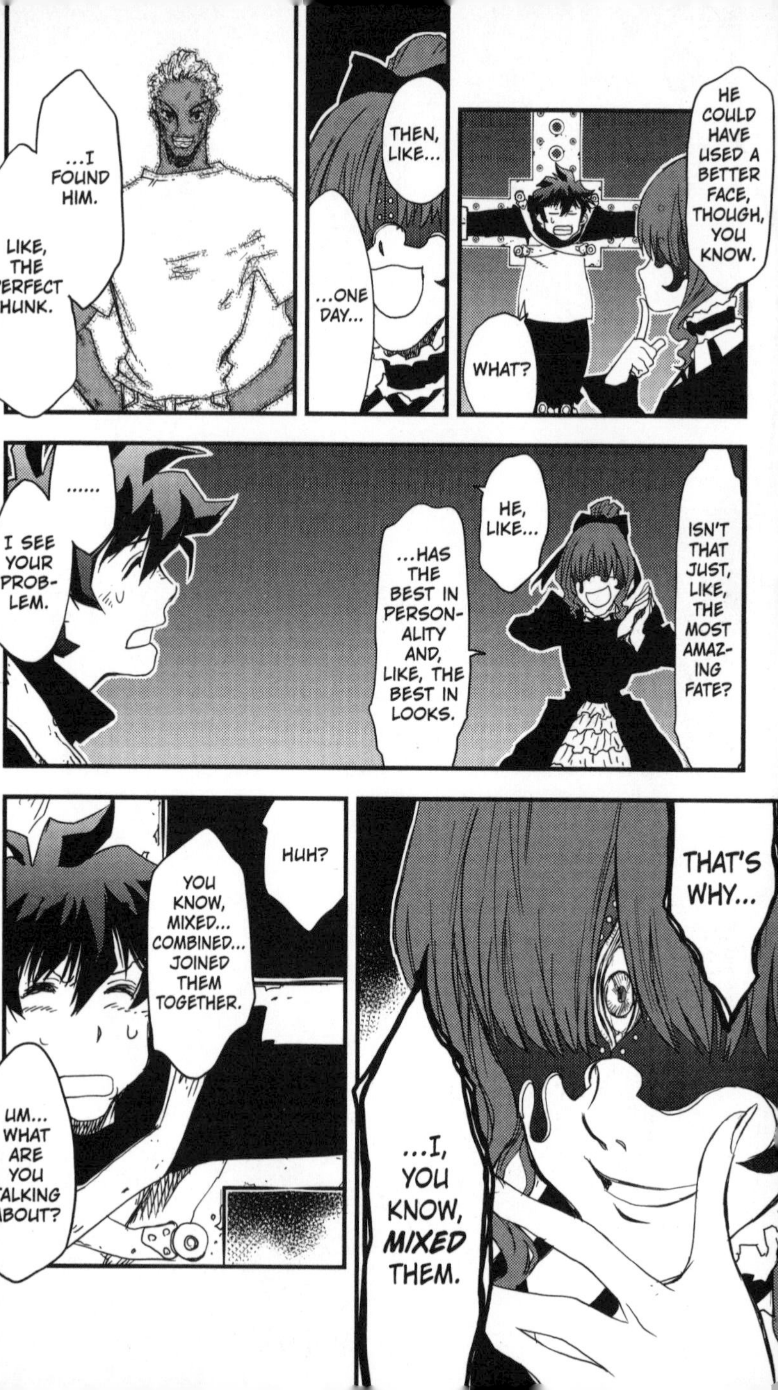
HE COULD HAVE USED A BETTER FACE, THOUGH, YOU KNOW.
WHAT?
THEN, LIKE...
...ONE DAY...
...I FOUND HIM.
LIKE, THE PERFECT HUNK.
ISN'T THAT JUST, LIKE, THE MOST AMAZING FATE?
HE, LIKE...
...HAS THE BEST IN PERSONALITY AND, LIKE, THE BEST IN LOOKS.
......
I SEE YOUR PROBLEM.
THAT'S WHY...
...I, YOU KNOW, *MIXED* THEM.
HUH?
YOU KNOW, MIXED... COMBINED... JOINED THEM TOGETHER.
UM... WHAT ARE YOU TALKING ABOUT?

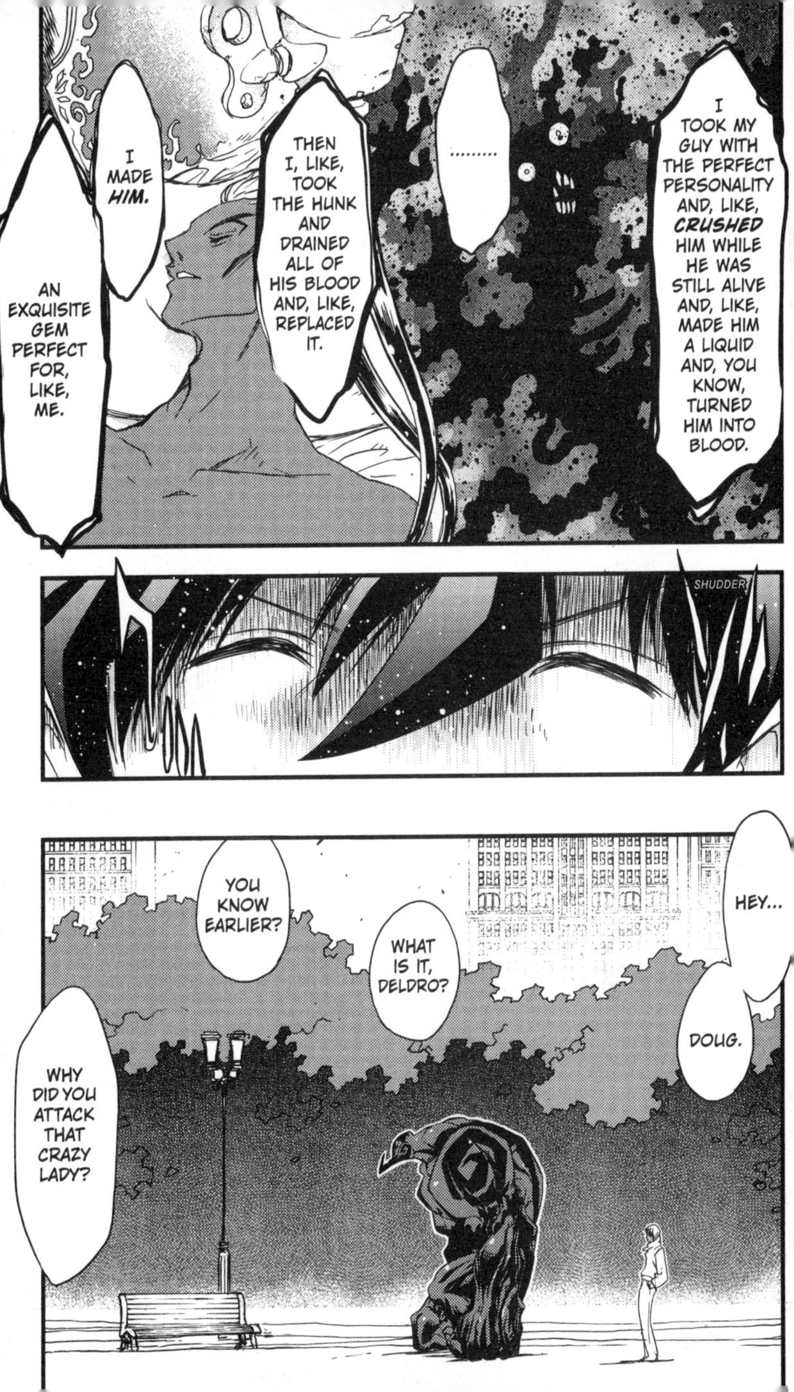
I TOOK MY GUY WITH THE PERFECT PERSONALITY AND, LIKE, **CRUSHED** HIM WHILE HE WAS STILL ALIVE AND, LIKE, MADE HIM A LIQUID AND, YOU KNOW, TURNED HIM INTO BLOOD.
....
THEN I, LIKE, TOOK THE HUNK AND DRAINED ALL OF HIS BLOOD AND, LIKE, REPLACED IT.
I MADE ***HIM.***
AN EXQUISITE GEM PERFECT FOR, LIKE, ME.
SHUDDER
HEY...
DOUG.
WHAT IS IT, DELDRO?
YOU KNOW EARLIER?
WHY DID YOU ATTACK THAT CRAZY LADY?

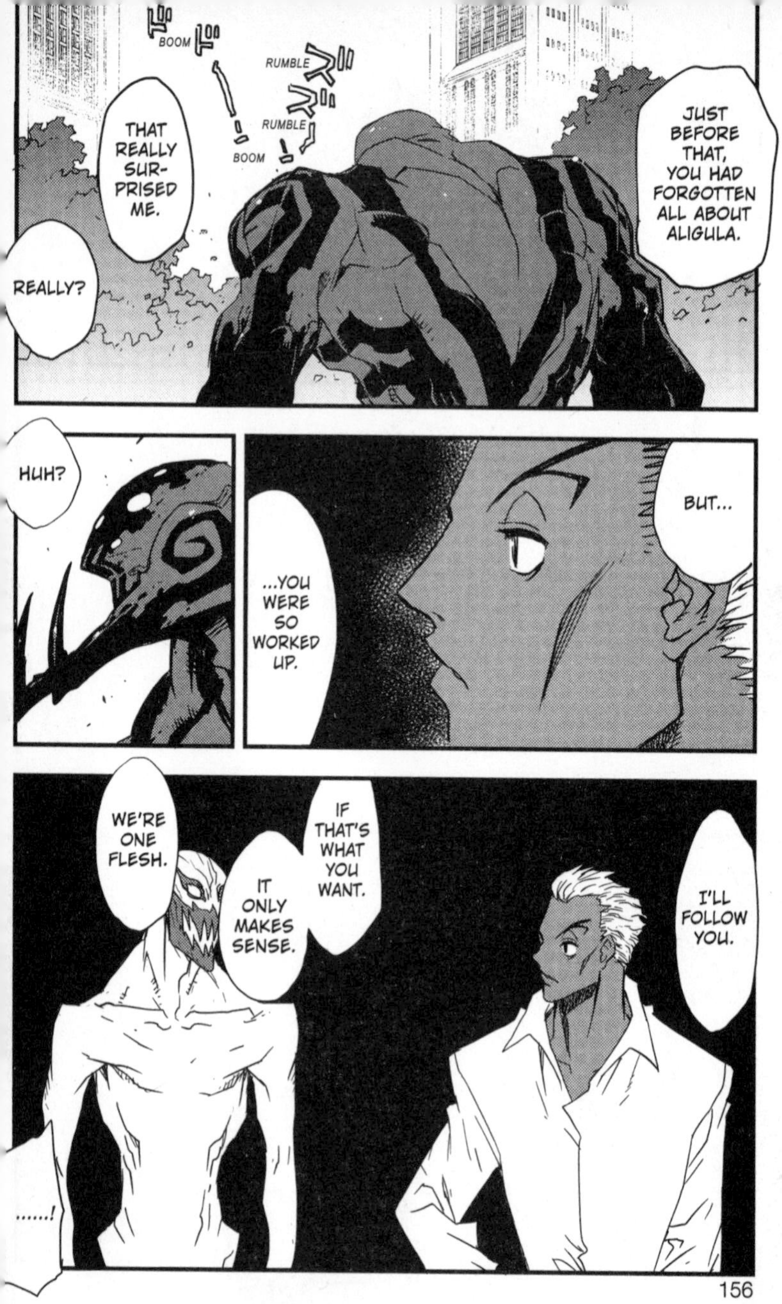
JUST BEFORE THAT, YOU HAD FORGOTTEN ALL ABOUT ALIGULA.
RUMBLE
RUMBLE
BOOM
BOOM
THAT REALLY SUR-PRISED ME.
REALLY?
BUT...
...YOU WERE SO WORKED UP.
HUH?
I'LL FOLLOW YOU.
IF THAT'S WHAT YOU WANT.
IT ONLY MAKES SENSE.
WE'RE ONE FLESH.
......!

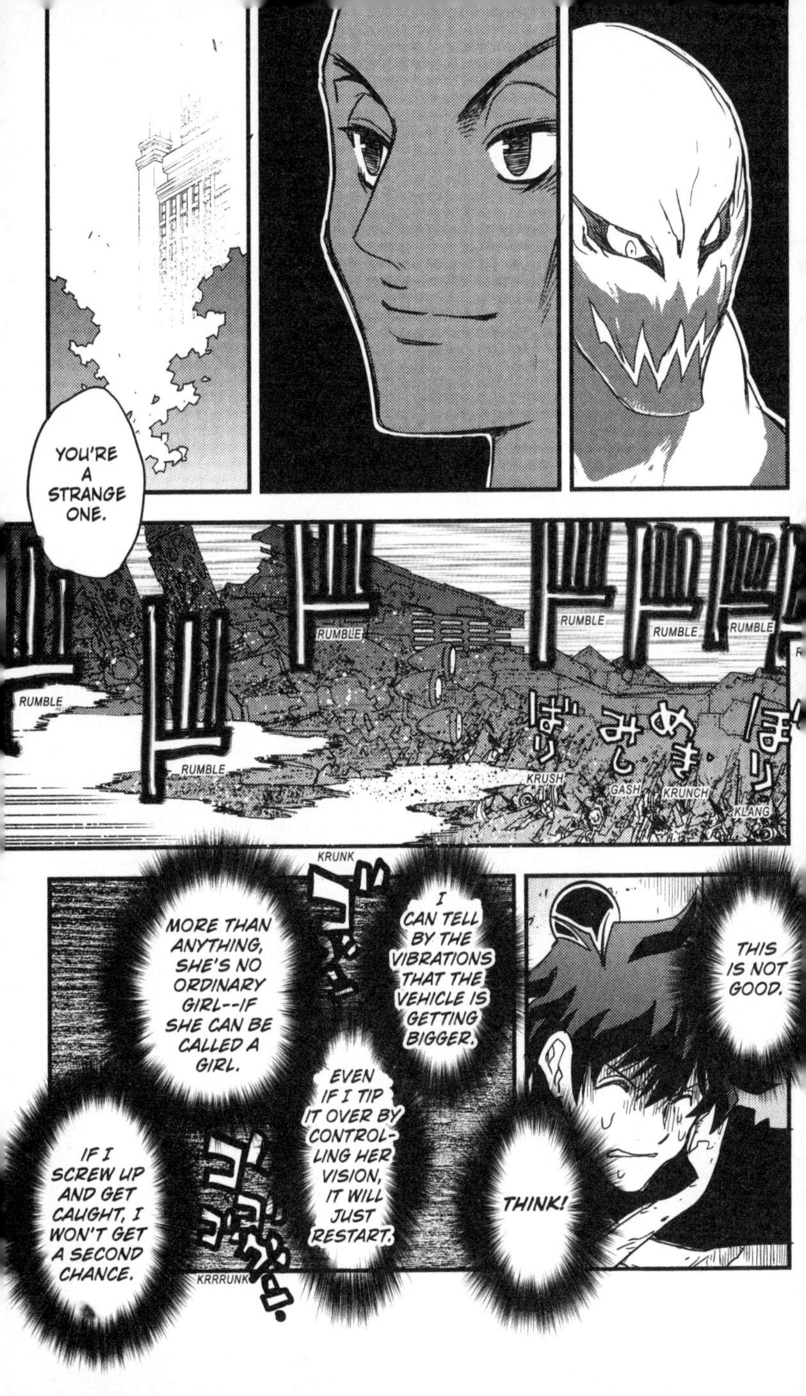
YOU'RE A STRANGE ONE.
RUMBLE
RUMBLE
RUMBLE
RUMBLE
RUMBLE
RUMBLE
KLANG
KRUNCH
GASH
KRUSH
THIS IS NOT GOOD.
THINK!
KRUNK
I CAN TELL BY THE VIBRATIONS THAT THE VEHICLE IS GETTING BIGGER.
MORE THAN ANYTHING, SHE'S NO ORDINARY GIRL--IF SHE CAN BE CALLED A GIRL.
EVEN IF I TIP IT OVER BY CONTROL-LING HER VISION, IT WILL JUST RESTART.
IF I SCREW UP AND GET CAUGHT, I WON'T GET A SECOND CHANCE.
KRRRUNK

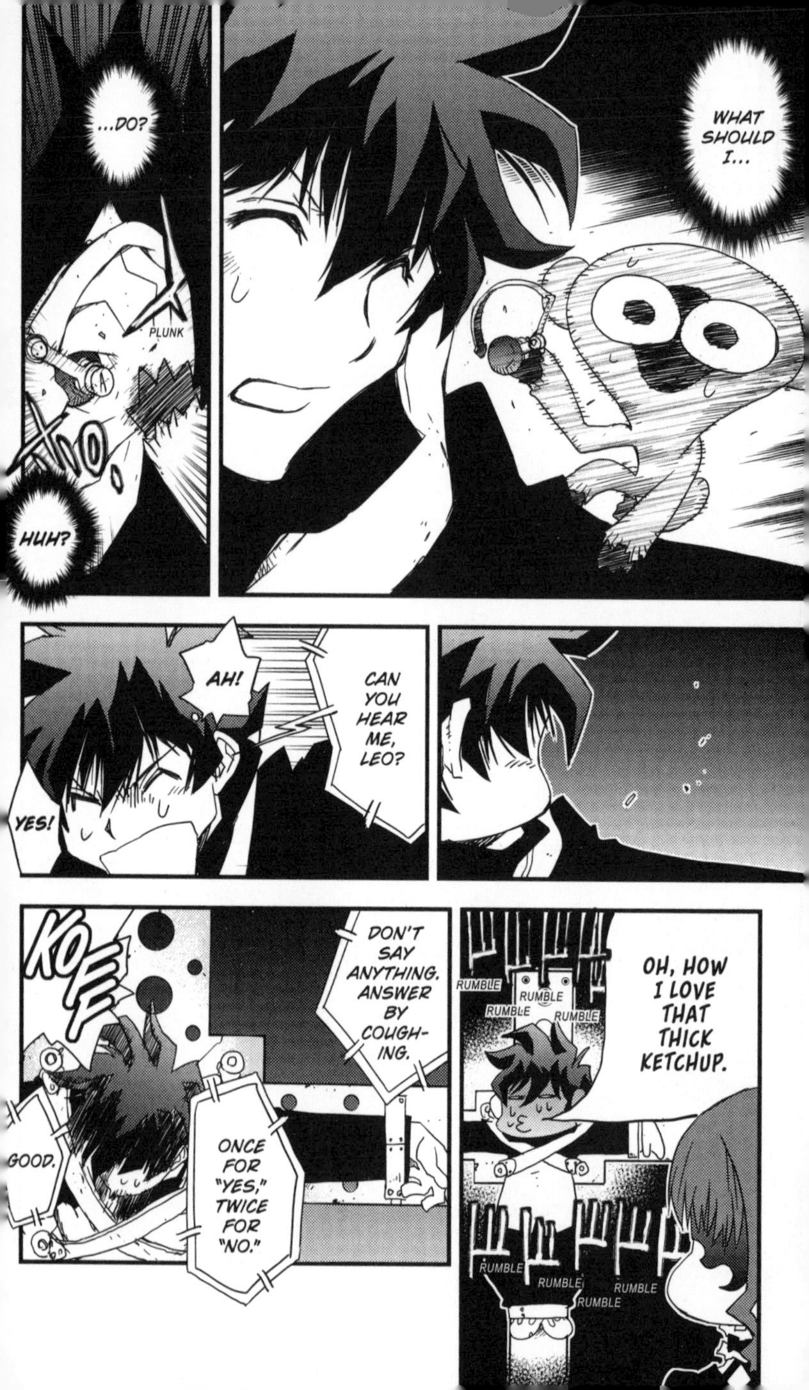
WHAT SHOULD I...
...DO?
PLUNK
HUH?
CAN YOU HEAR ME, LEO?
AH!
YES!
OH, HOW I LOVE THAT THICK KETCHUP.
RUMBLE
RUMBLE
RUMBLE
RUMBLE
RUMBLE
RUMBLE
RUMBLE
RUMBLE
DON'T SAY ANYTHING. ANSWER BY COUGHING.
KOFF
ONCE FOR "YES," TWICE FOR "NO."
GOOD.

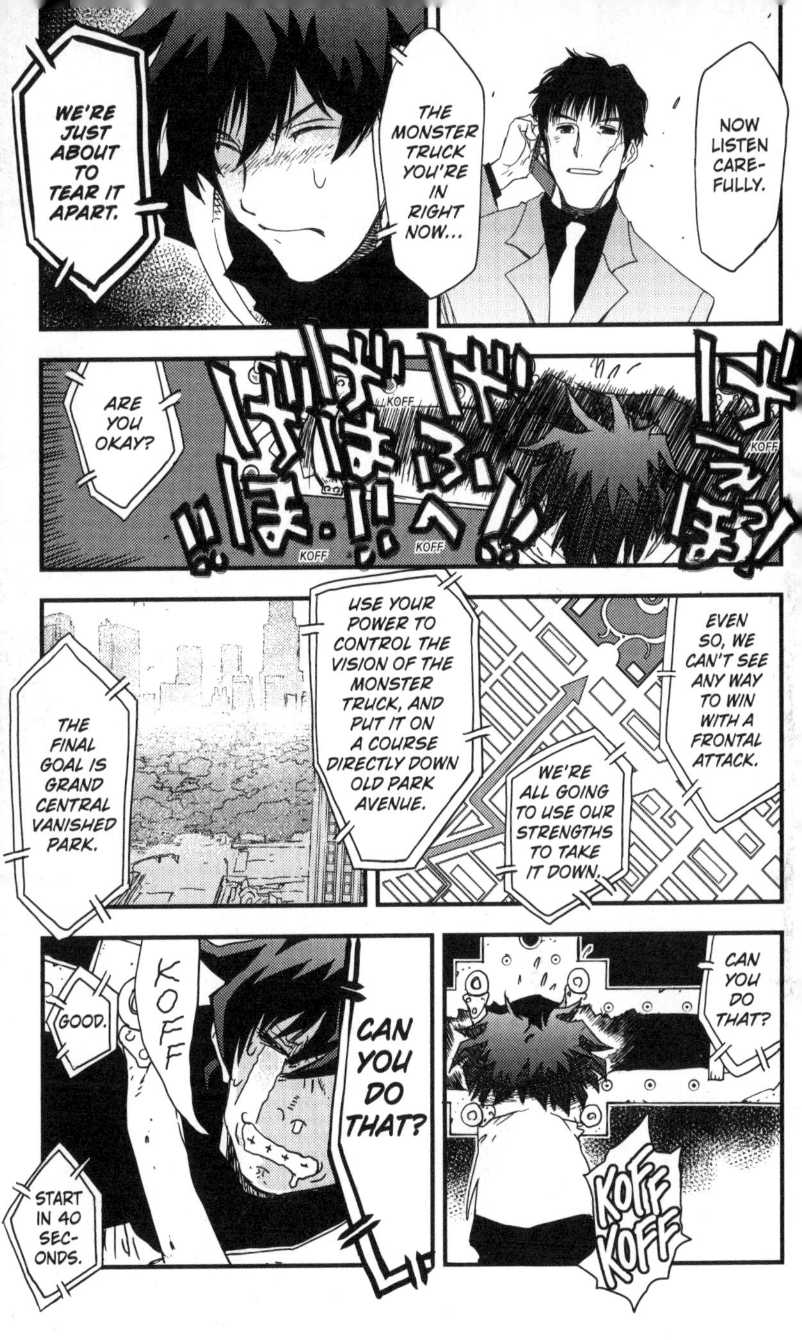
NOW LISTEN CARE-FULLY.
THE MONSTER TRUCK YOU'RE IN RIGHT NOW...
WE'RE JUST ABOUT TO TEAR IT APART.
KOFF
KOFF
KOFF
KOFF
ARE YOU OKAY?
EVEN SO, WE CAN'T SEE ANY WAY TO WIN WITH A FRONTAL ATTACK.
WE'RE ALL GOING TO USE OUR STRENGTHS TO TAKE IT DOWN.
USE YOUR POWER TO CONTROL THE VISION OF THE MONSTER TRUCK, AND PUT IT ON A COURSE DIRECTLY DOWN OLD PARK AVENUE.
THE FINAL GOAL IS GRAND CENTRAL VANISHED PARK.
CAN YOU DO THAT?
KOFF KOFF
CAN YOU DO THAT?
KOFF
GOOD.
START IN 40 SEC-ONDS.

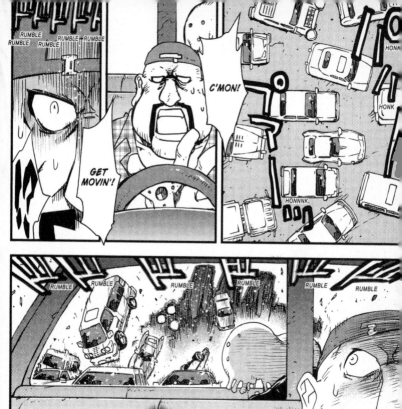

RUMBLE RUMBLE RUMBLE RUMBLE
RUMBLE RUMBLE

HONK

C'MON!

GET MOVIN'!

HONK

HONNK.

RUMBLE RUMBLE RUMBLE RUMBLE RUMBLE RUMBLE

...AND MAKE IT...

CONTROL ITS VISION...

AH!

RUMBLE RUMBLE RUMBLE

AH!

RUMBLE

RUMBLE

AH!

RUMBLE RUMBLE

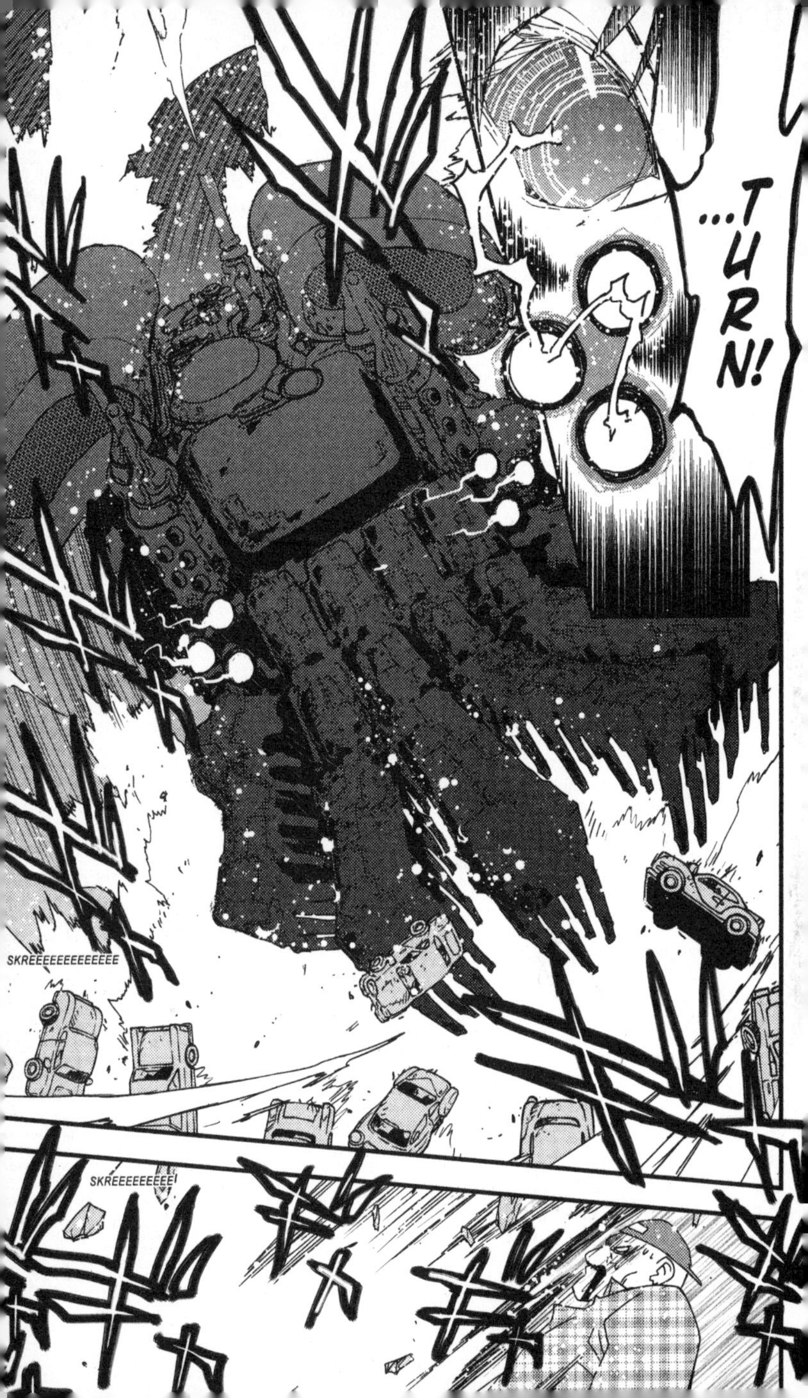
...TURN!
SKREEEEEEEEEEEEE
SKREEEEEEEEEE!

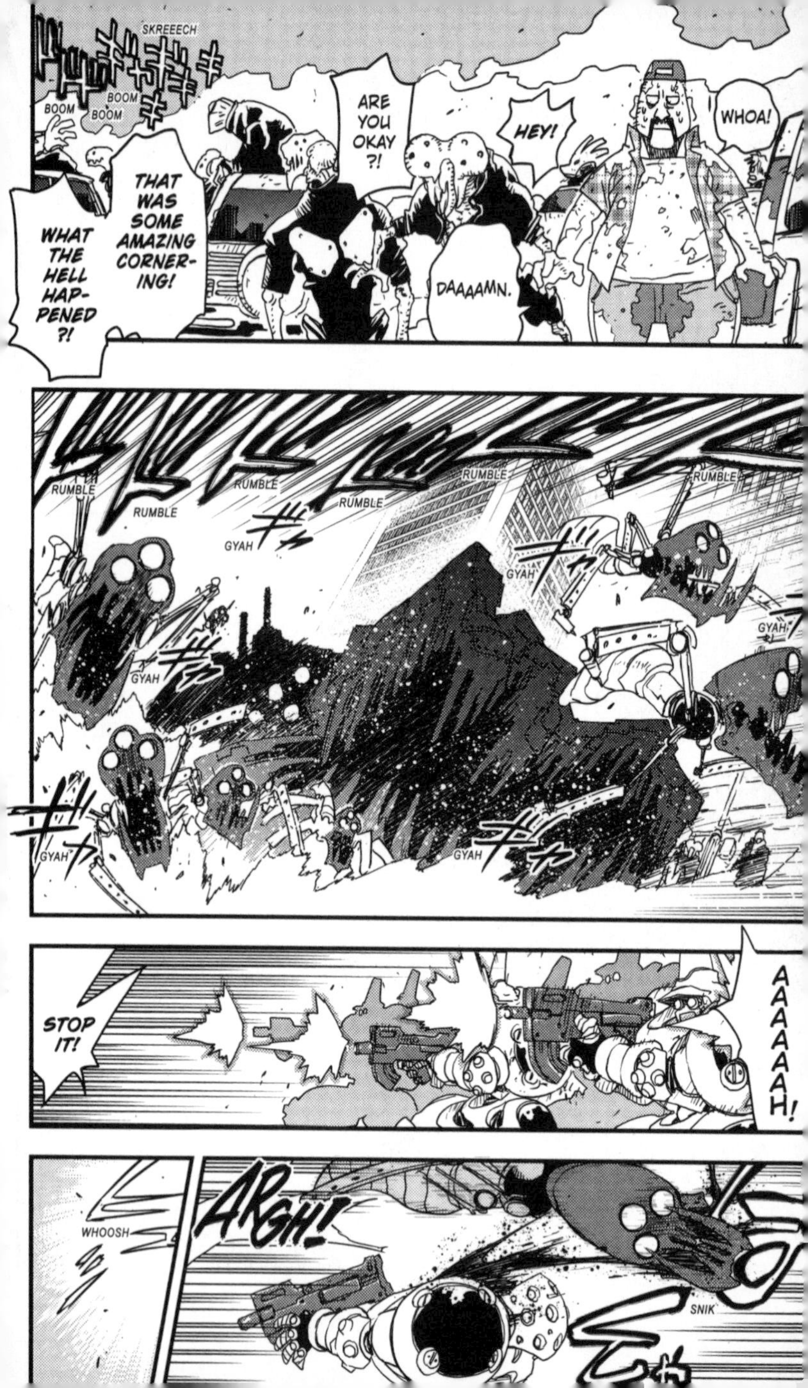
WHOA!
HEY!
ARE YOU OKAY ?!
DAAAAMN.
THAT WAS SOME AMAZING CORNER-ING!
WHAT THE HELL HAP-PENED ?!
SKREEECH
BOOM
BOOM
BOOM
RUMBLE
RUMBLE
GYAH
GYAH
RUMBLE
RUMBLE
RUMBLE
GYAH
GYAH
GYAH
GYAH
AAAAAAAH!
STOP IT!
SNIK
ARGH!
WHOOSH

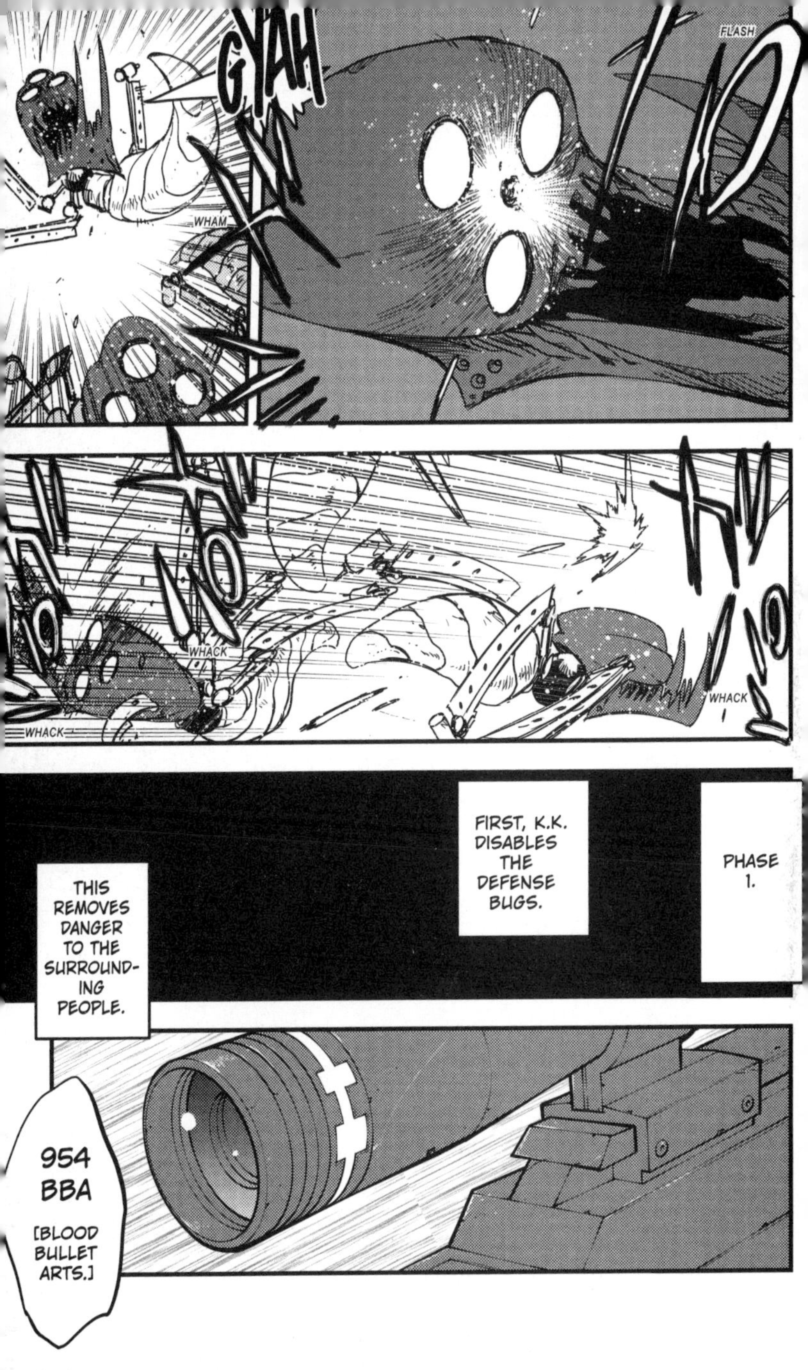
FLASH
GYAH
WHAM
WHACK
WHACK
WHACK
PHASE 1.
FIRST, K.K. DISABLES THE DEFENSE BUGS.
THIS REMOVES DANGER TO THE SURROUNDING PEOPLE.
954 BBA
[BLOOD BULLET ARTS.]

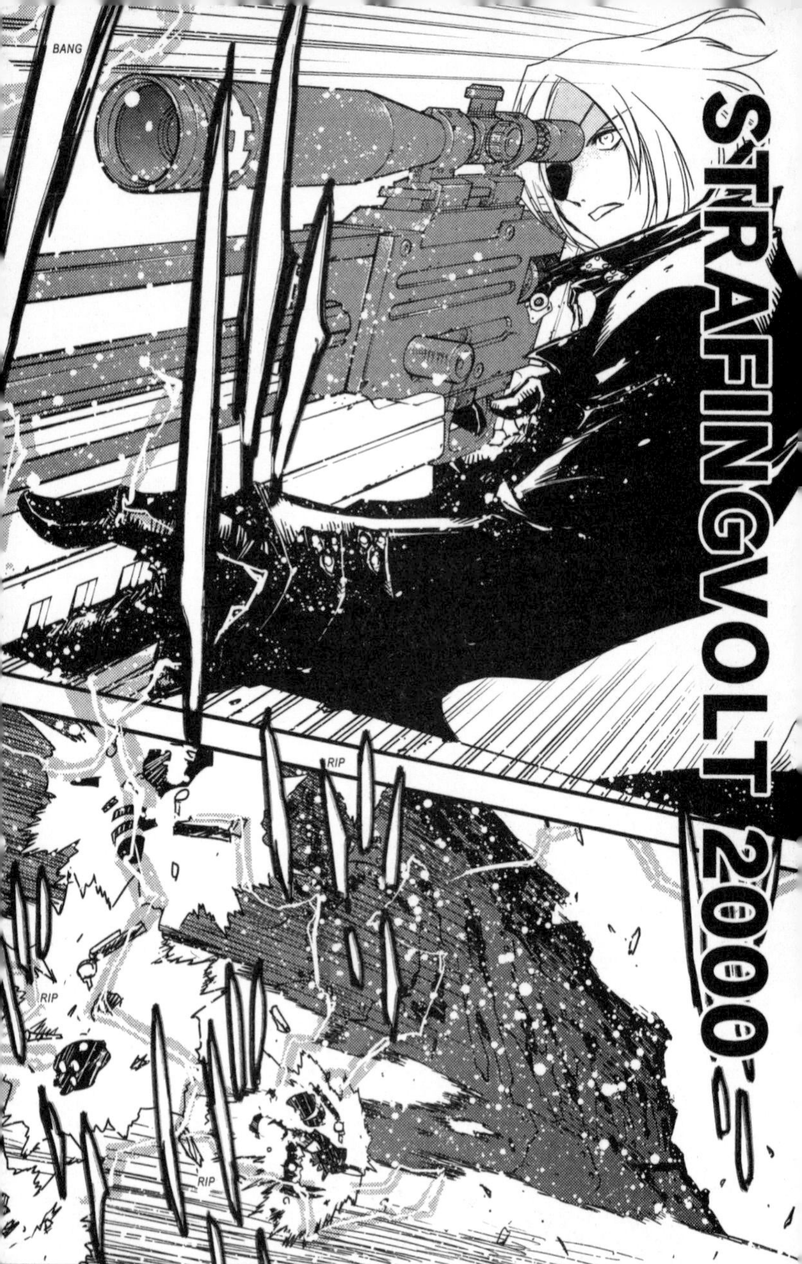
BANG
STRAFING VOLT 2000
RIP
RIP
RIP

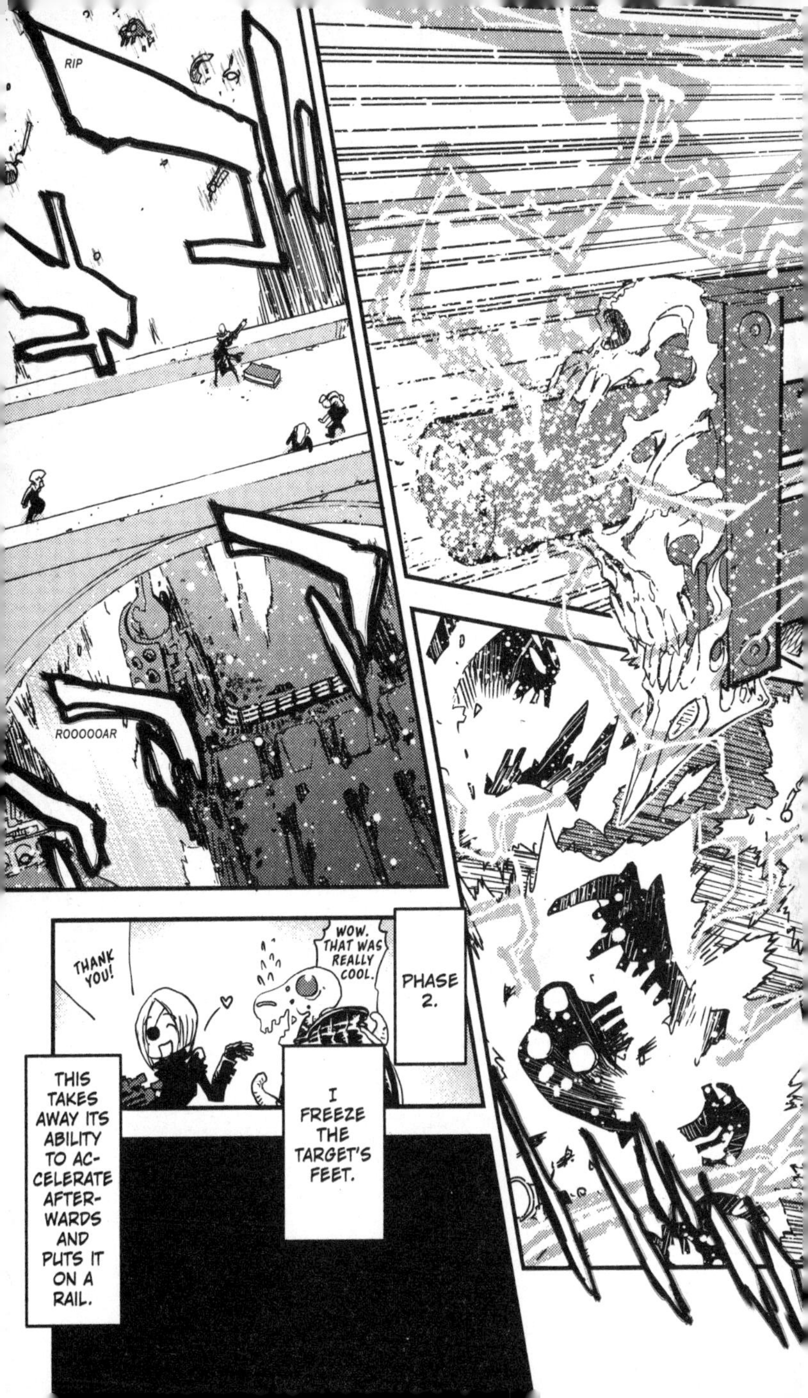
RIP
ROOOOOAR
PHASE 2.
WOW. THAT WAS REALLY COOL.
THANK YOU!
I FREEZE THE TARGET'S FEET.
THIS TAKES AWAY ITS ABILITY TO ACCELERATE AFTERWARDS AND PUTS IT ON A RAIL.

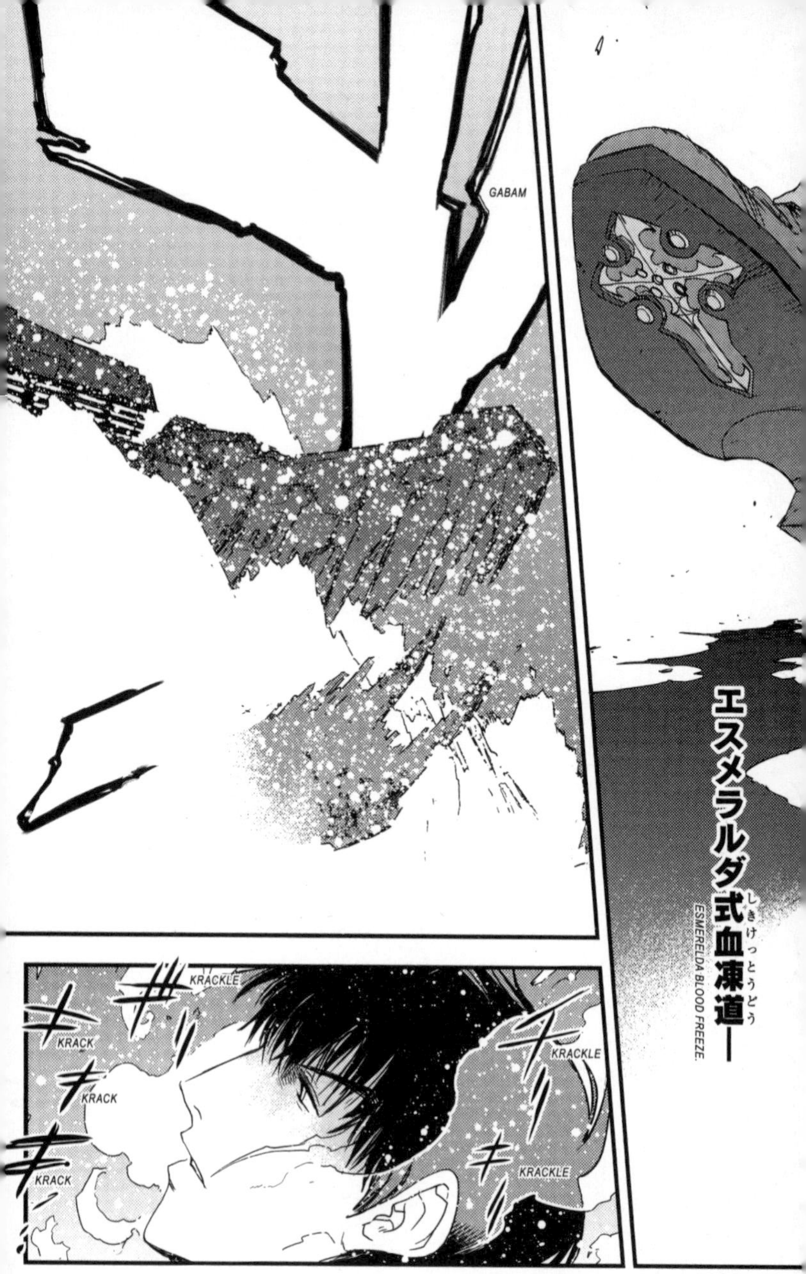
エスメラルダ式血凍道—
ESMERELDA BLOOD FREEZE.
GABAM
KRACKLE
KRACKLE
KRACKLE
KRACK
KRACK
KRACK

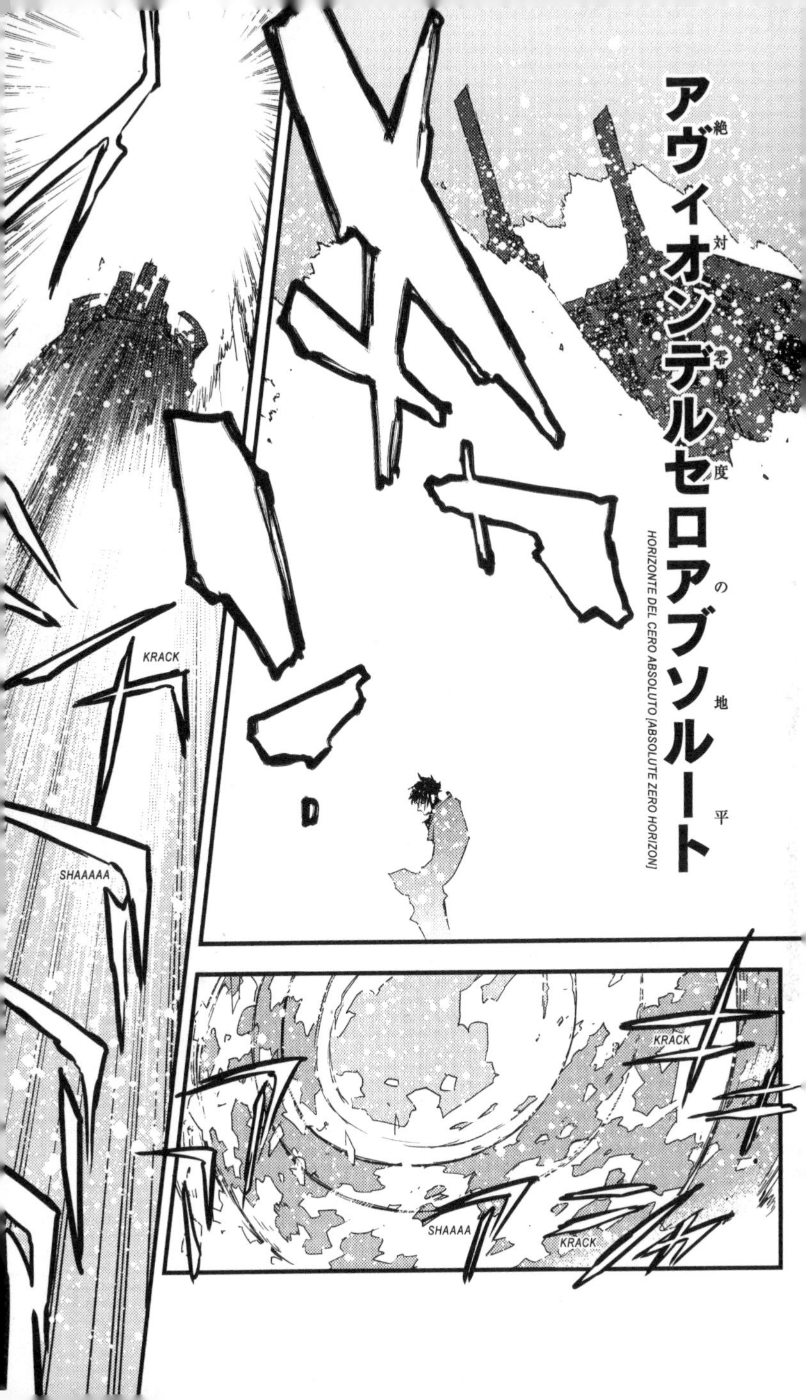
アヴィオンデルセロアブソルート
絶対零度の地平
HORIZONTE DEL CERO ABSOLUTO [ABSOLUTE ZERO HORIZON]
KRACK
SHAAAA
KRACK
KRACK
SHAAAAA

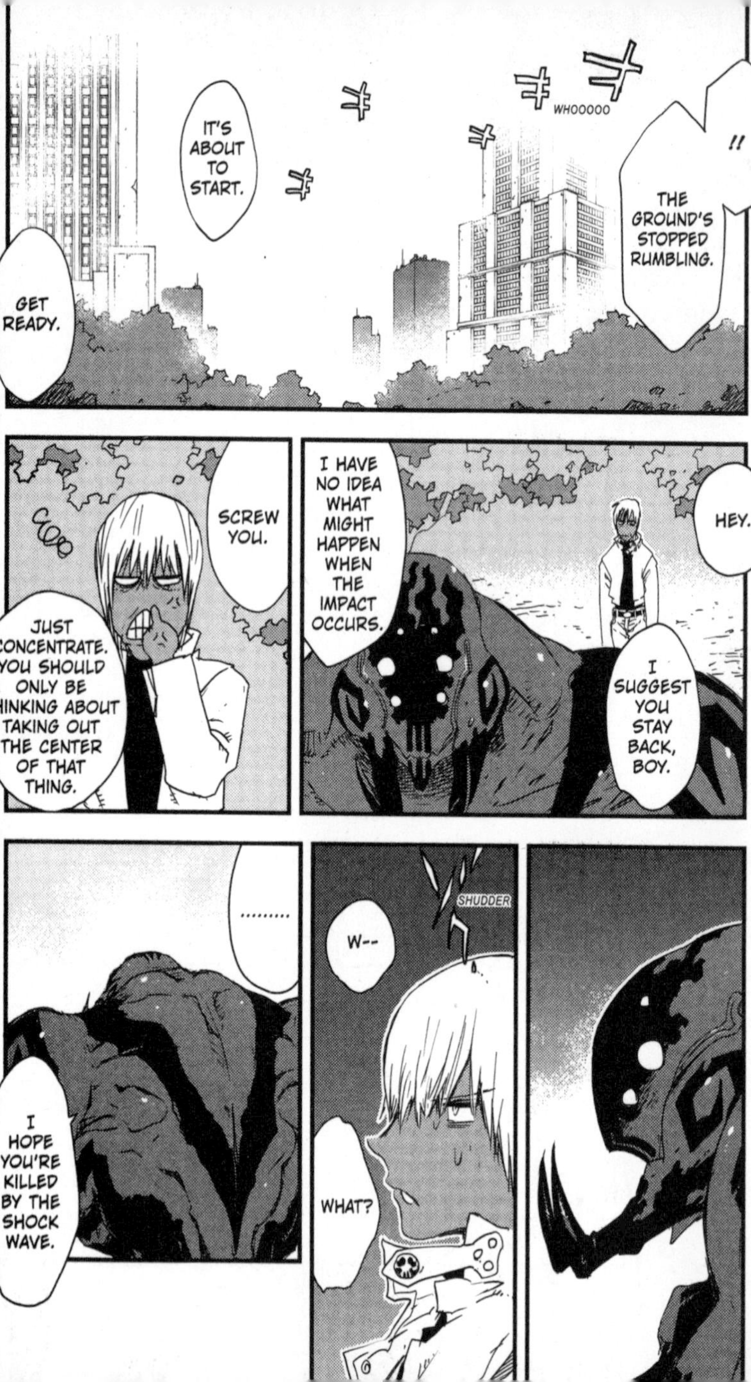
!!
THE GROUND'S STOPPED RUMBLING.
WHOOOOO
IT'S ABOUT TO START.
GET READY.
HEY.
I SUGGEST YOU STAY BACK, BOY.
I HAVE NO IDEA WHAT MIGHT HAPPEN WHEN THE IMPACT OCCURS.
SCREW YOU.
JUST CONCENTRATE. YOU SHOULD ONLY BE THINKING ABOUT TAKING OUT THE CENTER OF THAT THING.
SHUDDER
W--
WHAT?
....
I HOPE YOU'RE KILLED BY THE SHOCK WAVE.

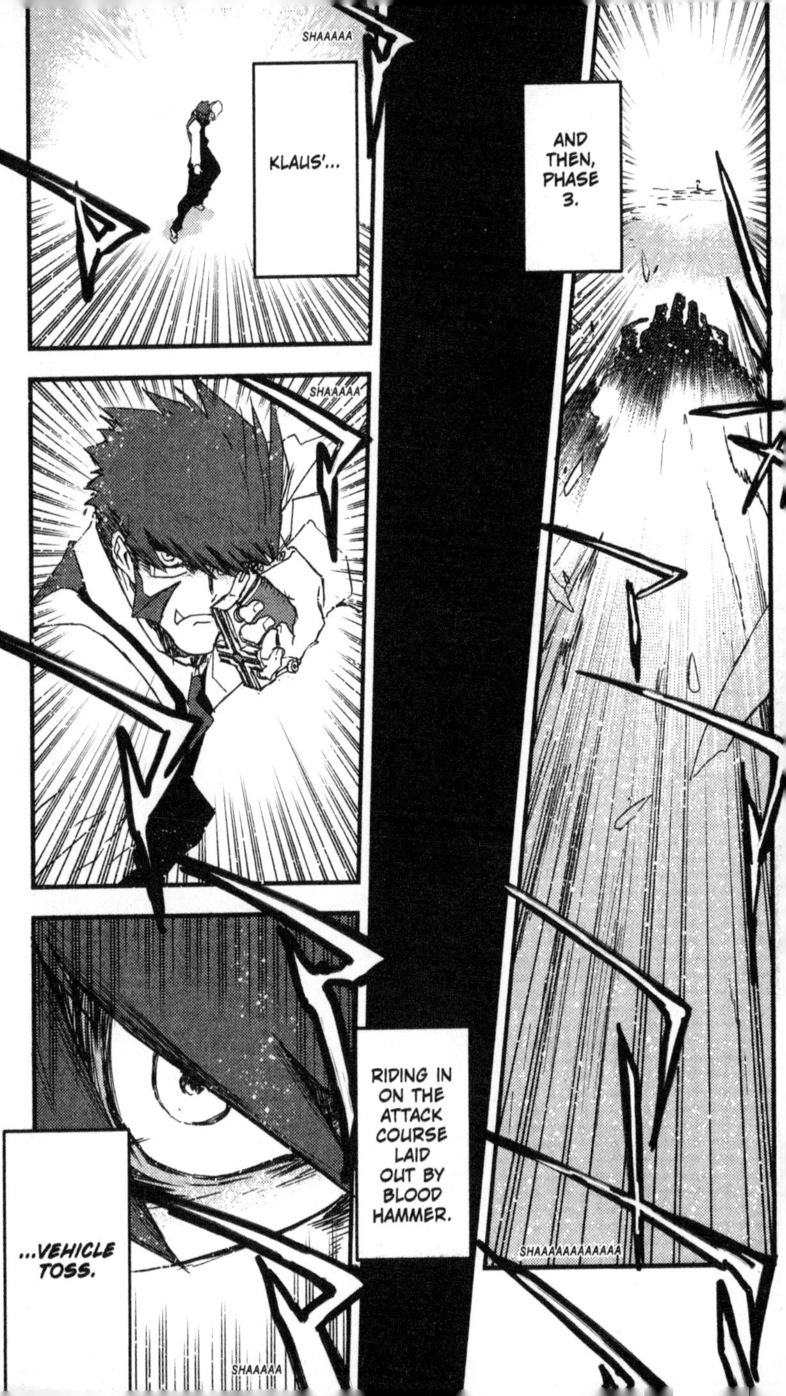
AND THEN, PHASE 3.
SHAAAAAAAAAAAA
SHAAAAAA
KLAUS'...
SHAAAAAA
RIDING IN ON THE ATTACK COURSE LAID OUT BY BLOOD HAMMER.
...VEHICLE TOSS.
SHAAAAAA

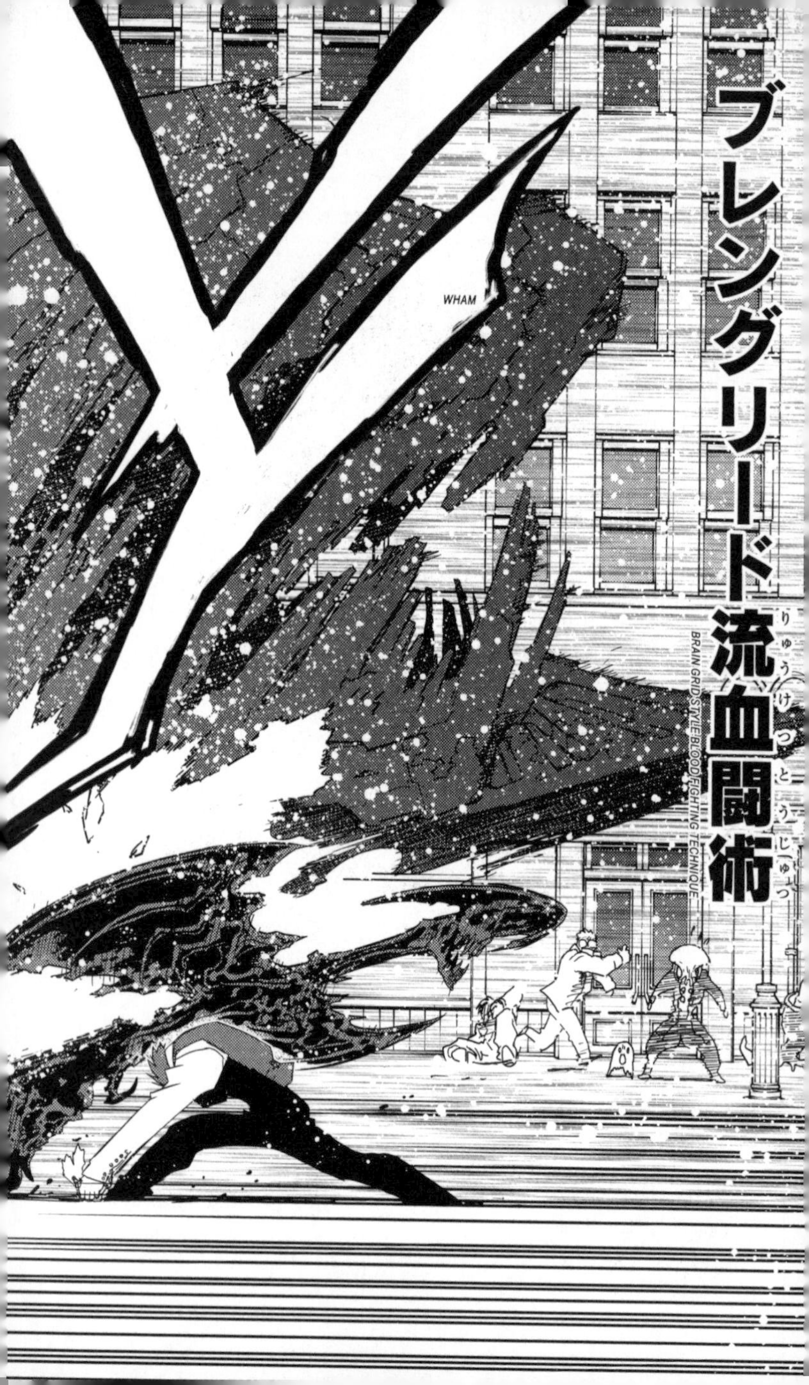
ブレングリード流血闘術
BRAIN GRID STYLE BLOOD FIGHTING TECHNIQUE
WHAM

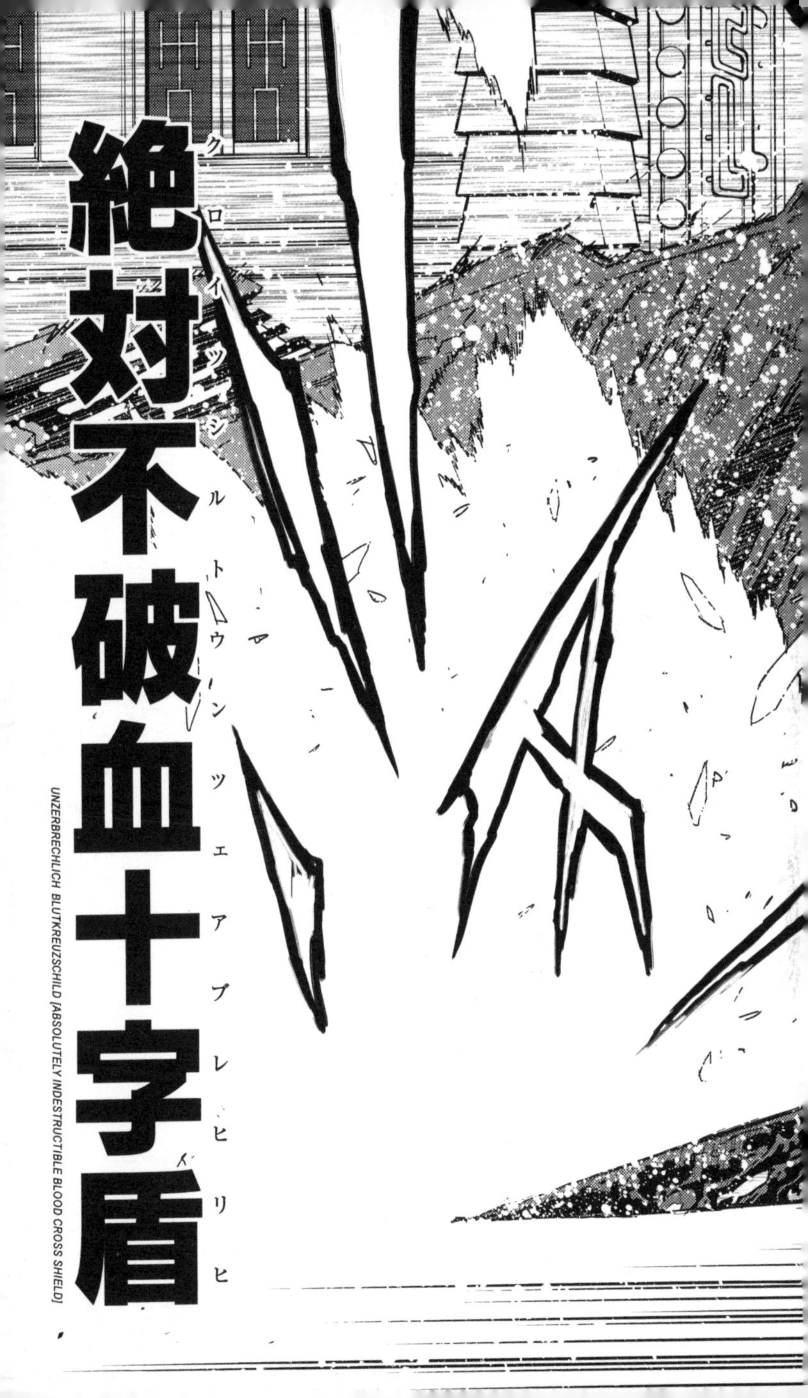
絶対不破血十字盾
クロイツシルトウンツェアブレヒリヒ
UNZERBRECHLICH BLUTKREUZSCHILD [ABSOLUTELY INDESTRUCTIBLE BLOOD CROSS SHIELD]

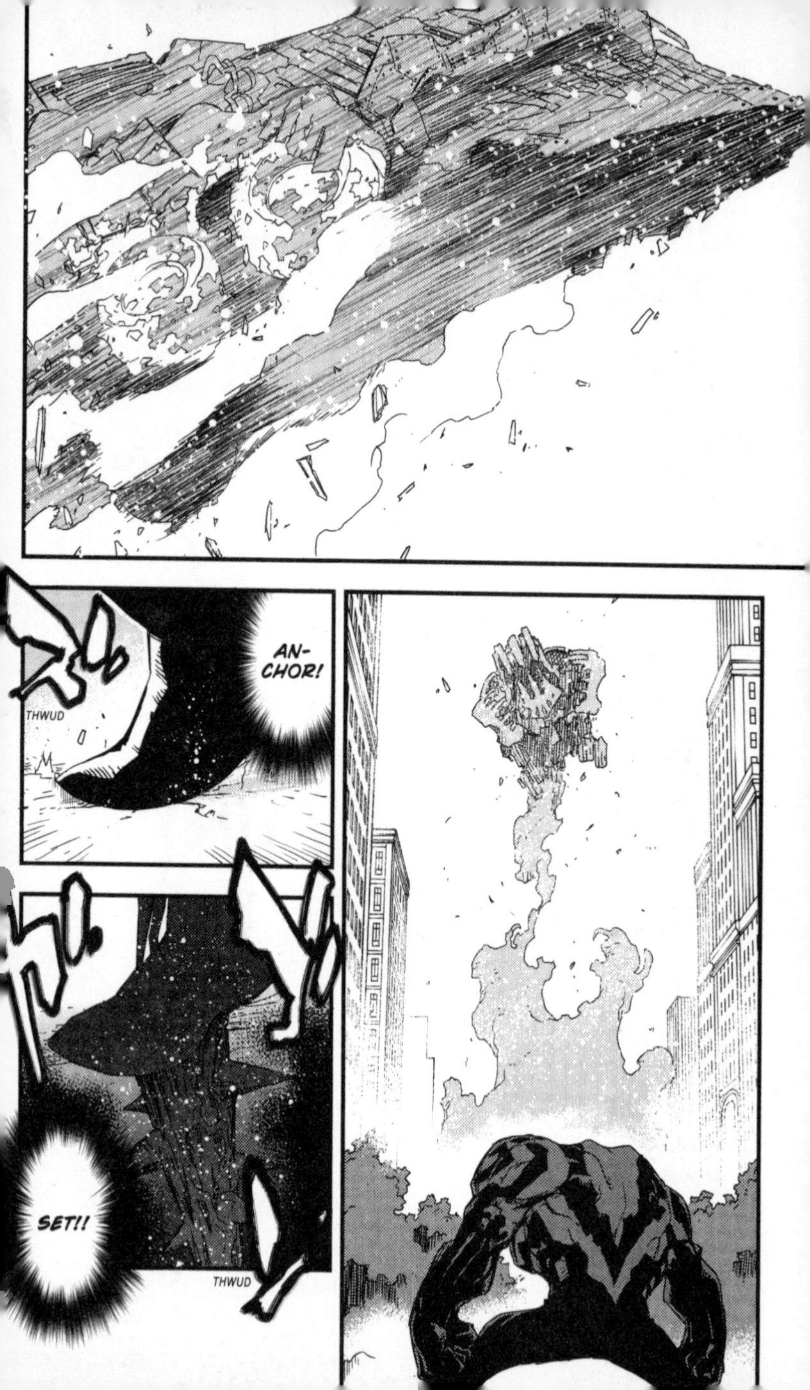
AN-CHOR!
THWUD
SET!!
THWUD

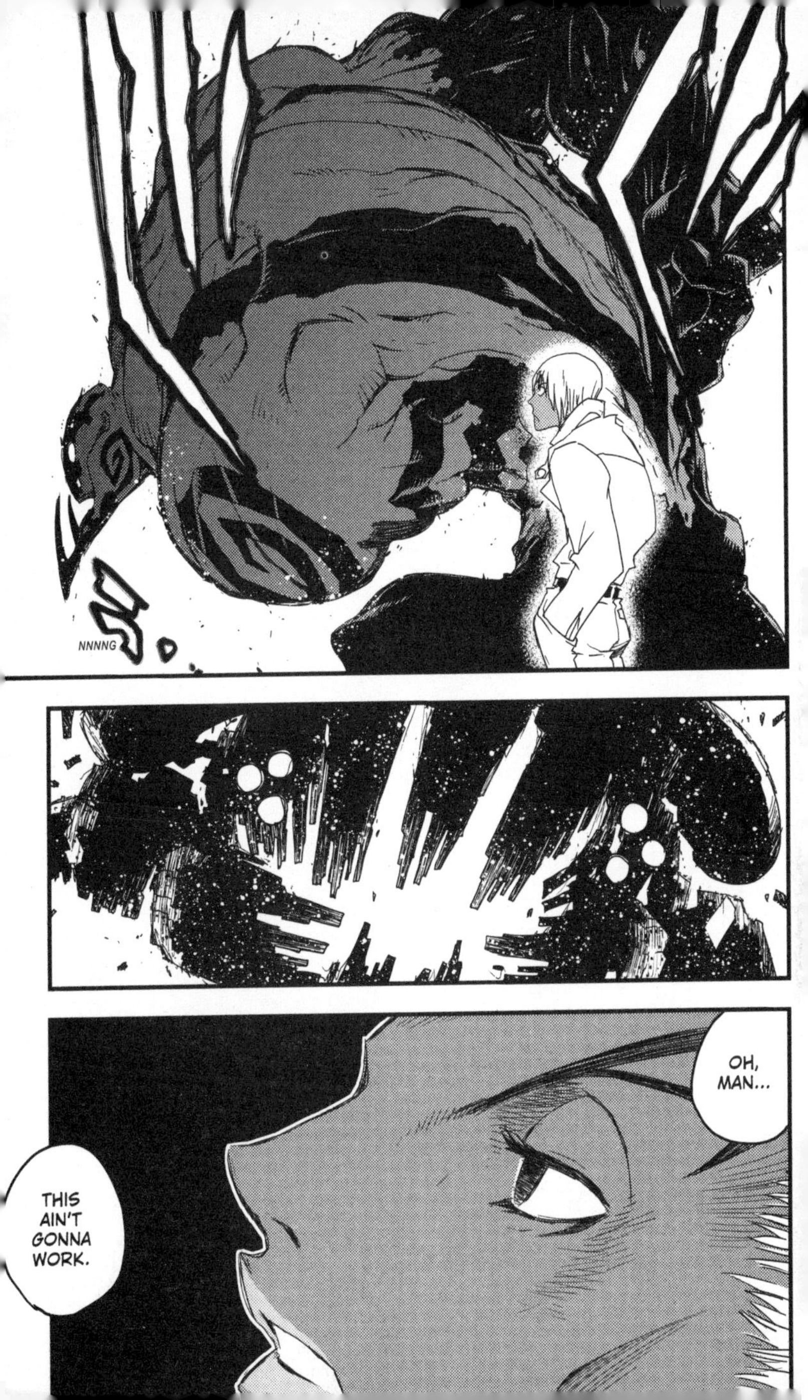
NNNNG
OH, MAN...
THIS AIN'T GONNA WORK.

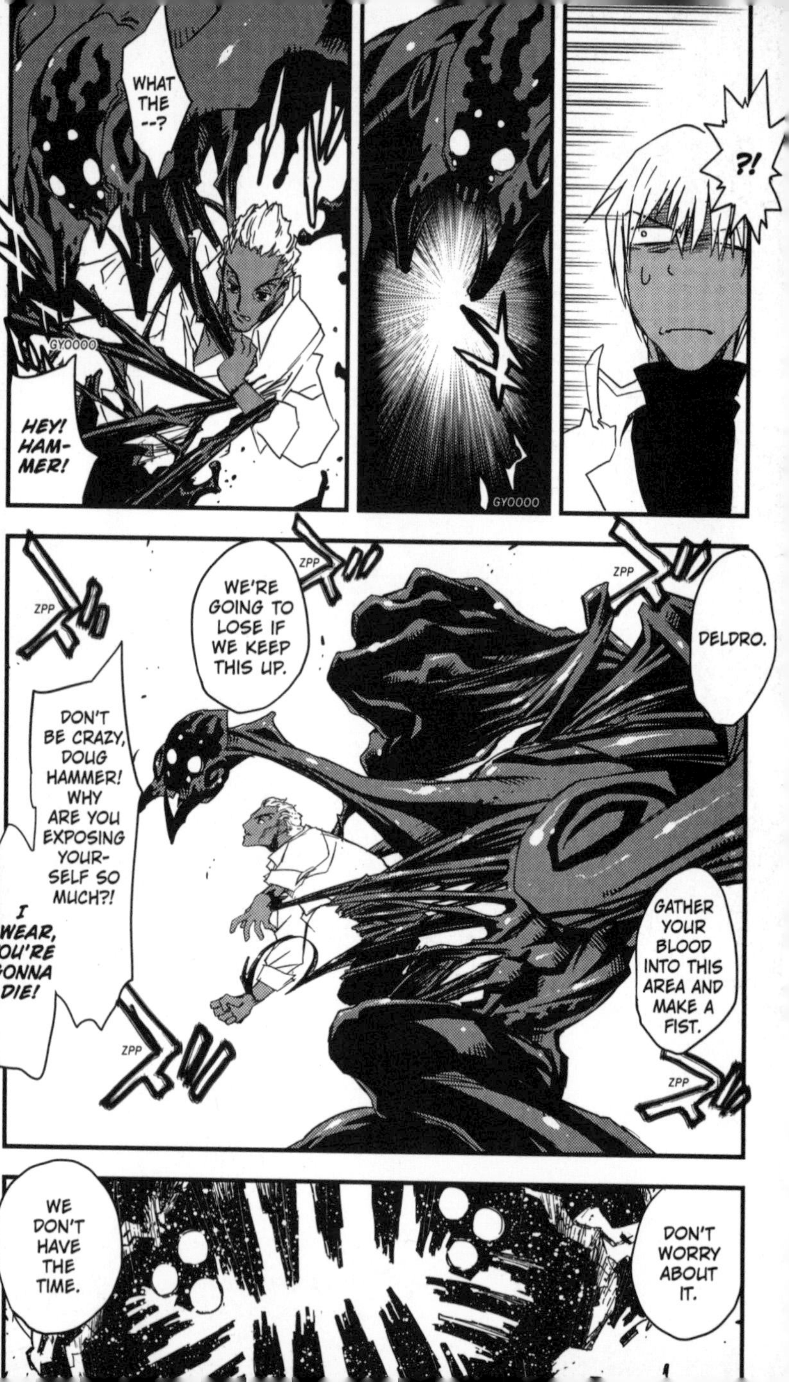
?!
GYOOOO
WHAT THE --?
GYOOOO
HEY! HAMMER!
DELDRO.
ZPP
WE'RE GOING TO LOSE IF WE KEEP THIS UP.
ZPP
GATHER YOUR BLOOD INTO THIS AREA AND MAKE A FIST.
ZPP
DON'T BE CRAZY, DOUG HAMMER! WHY ARE YOU EXPOSING YOURSELF SO MUCH?!
I SWEAR, YOU'RE GONNA DIE!
ZPP
DON'T WORRY ABOUT IT.
WE DON'T HAVE THE TIME.

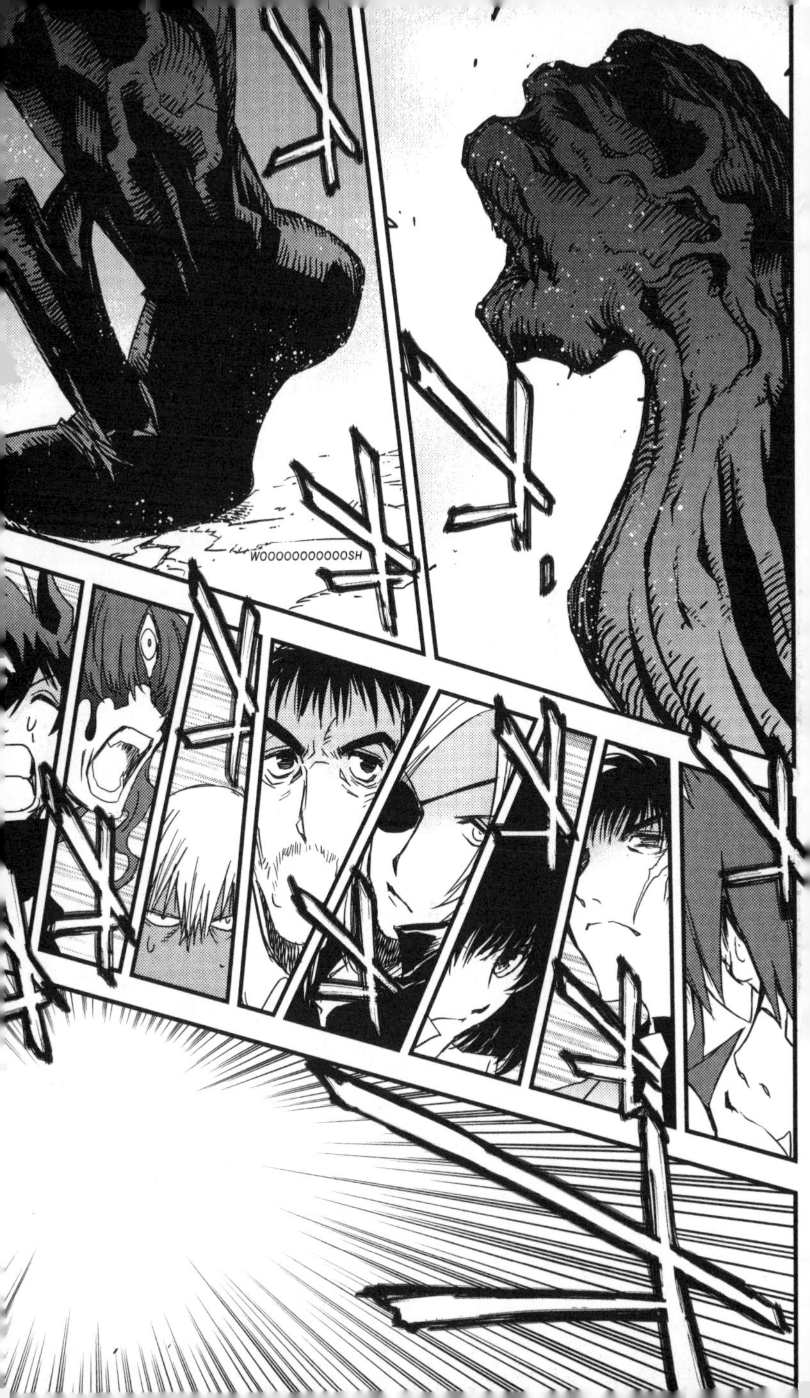
WOOOOOOOOOOOSH

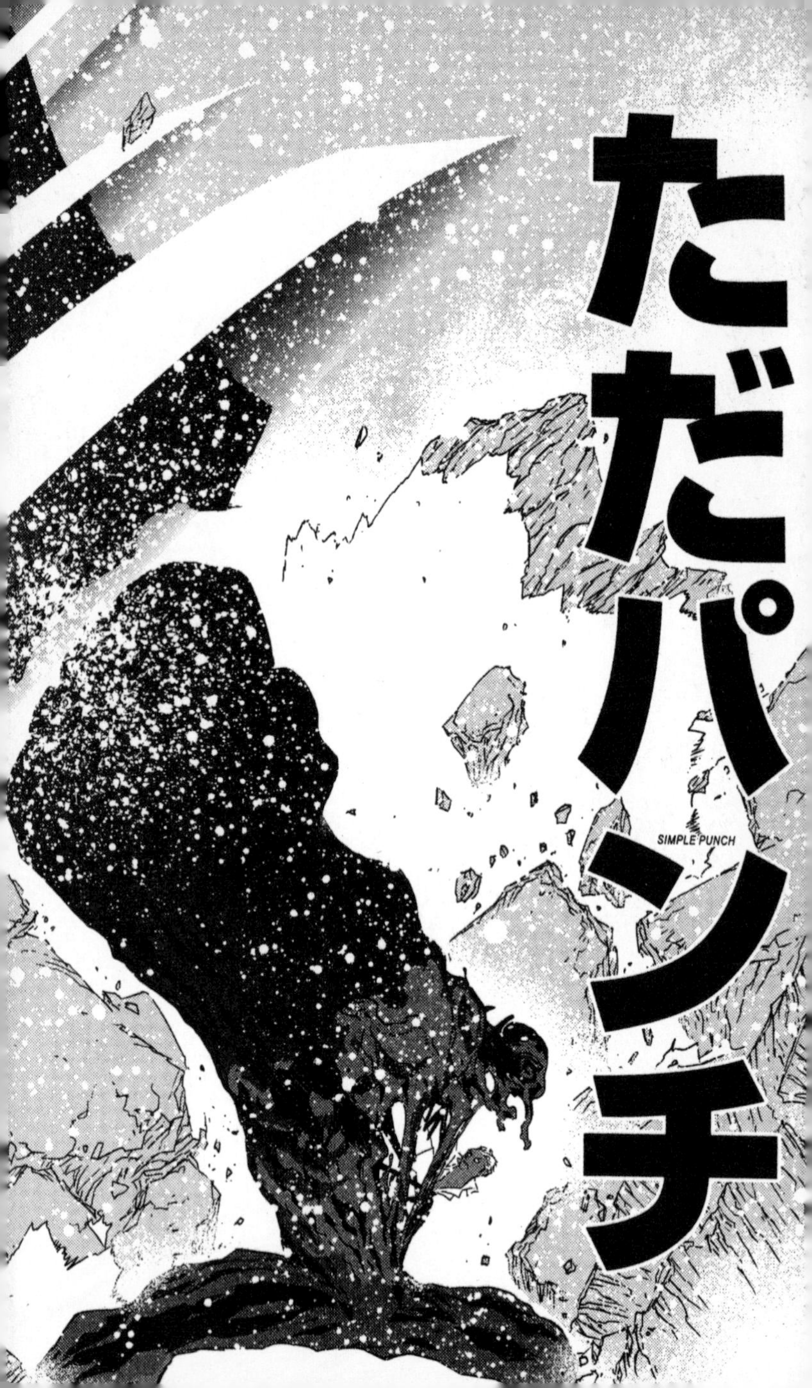
ただパンチ
SIMPLE PUNCH

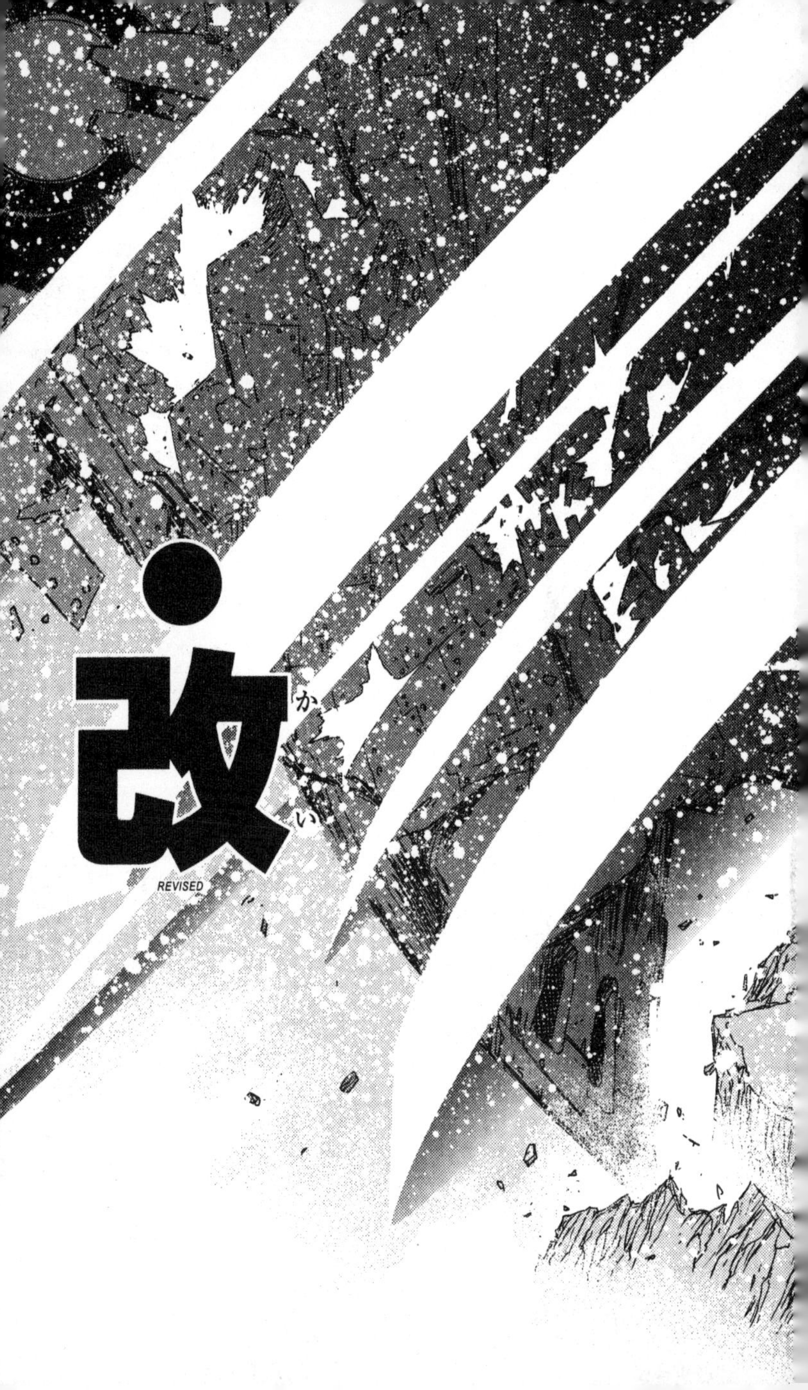

改
かい
REVISED

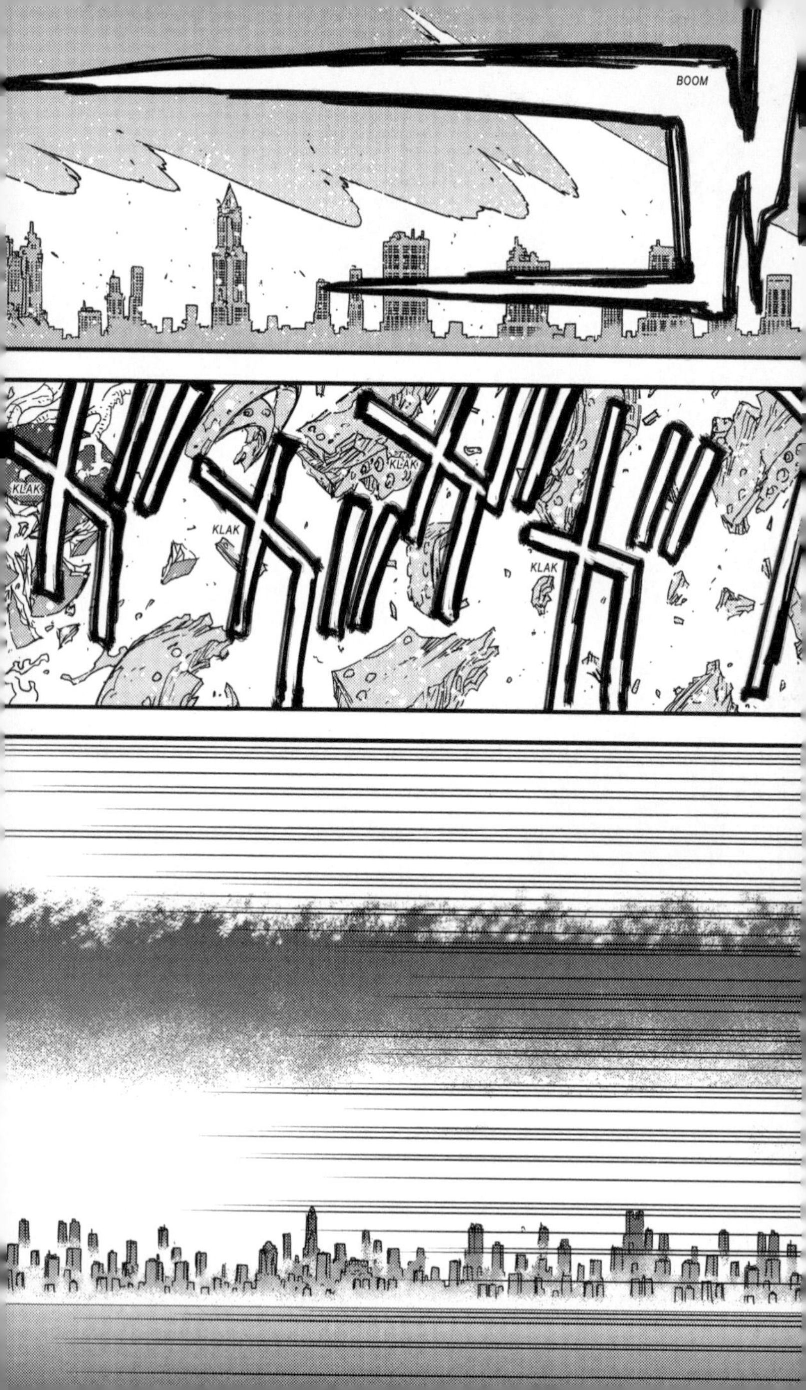
BOOM
KLAK
KLAK
KLAK
KLAK

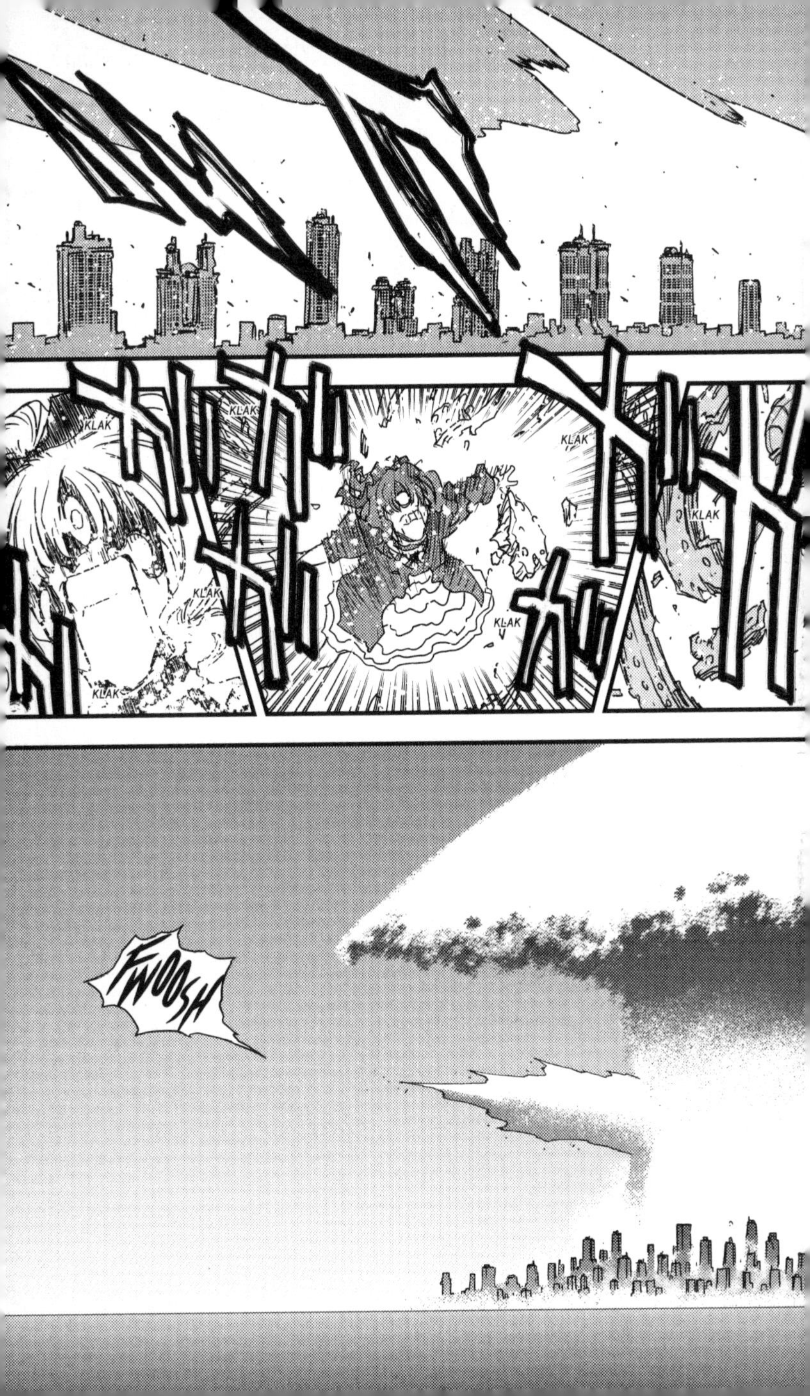
KLAK
KLAK
KLAK
KLAK
KLAK
KLAK
KLAK
FWOOSH

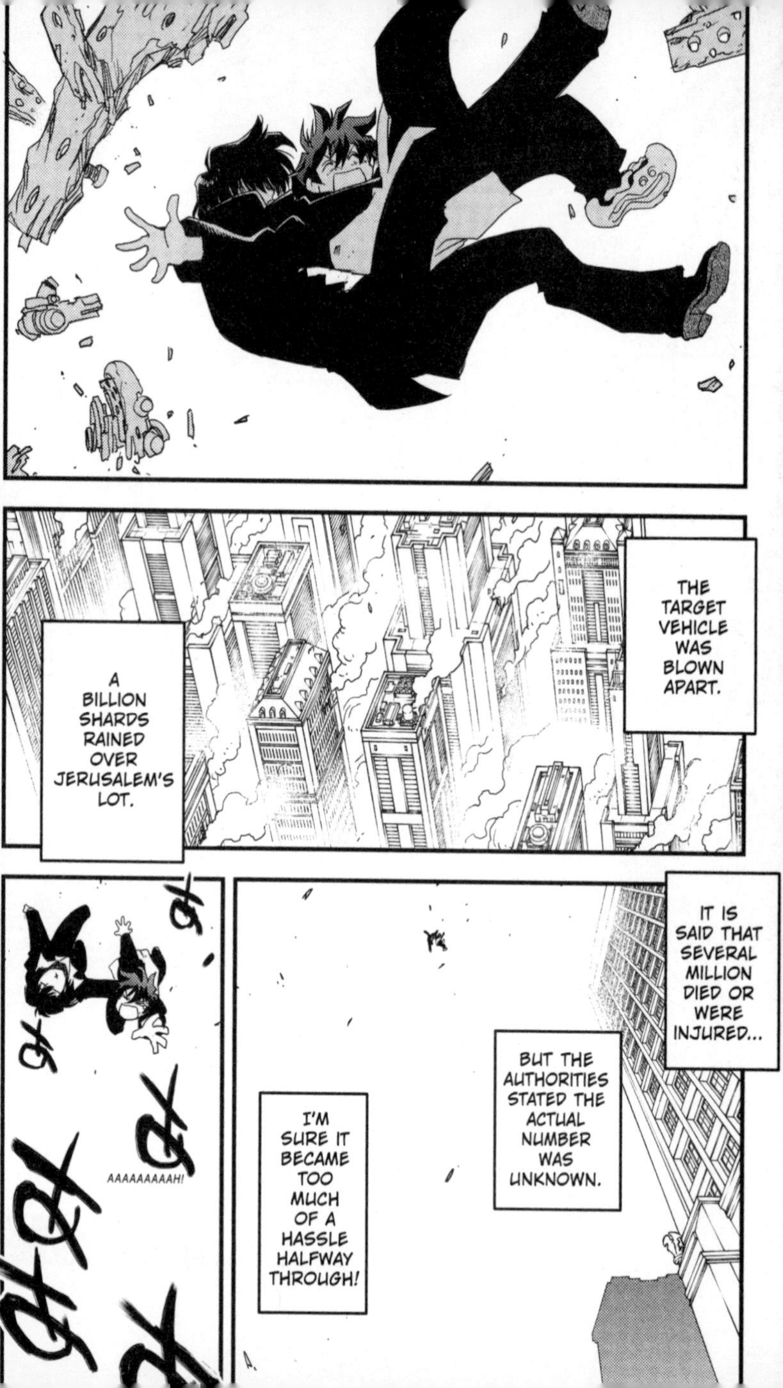
THE TARGET VEHICLE WAS BLOWN APART.
A BILLION SHARDS RAINED OVER JERUSALEM'S LOT.
IT IS SAID THAT SEVERAL MILLION DIED OR WERE INJURED...
BUT THE AUTHORITIES STATED THE ACTUAL NUMBER WAS UNKNOWN.
I'M SURE IT BECAME TOO MUCH OF A HASSLE HALFWAY THROUGH!
AAAAAAAAAH!

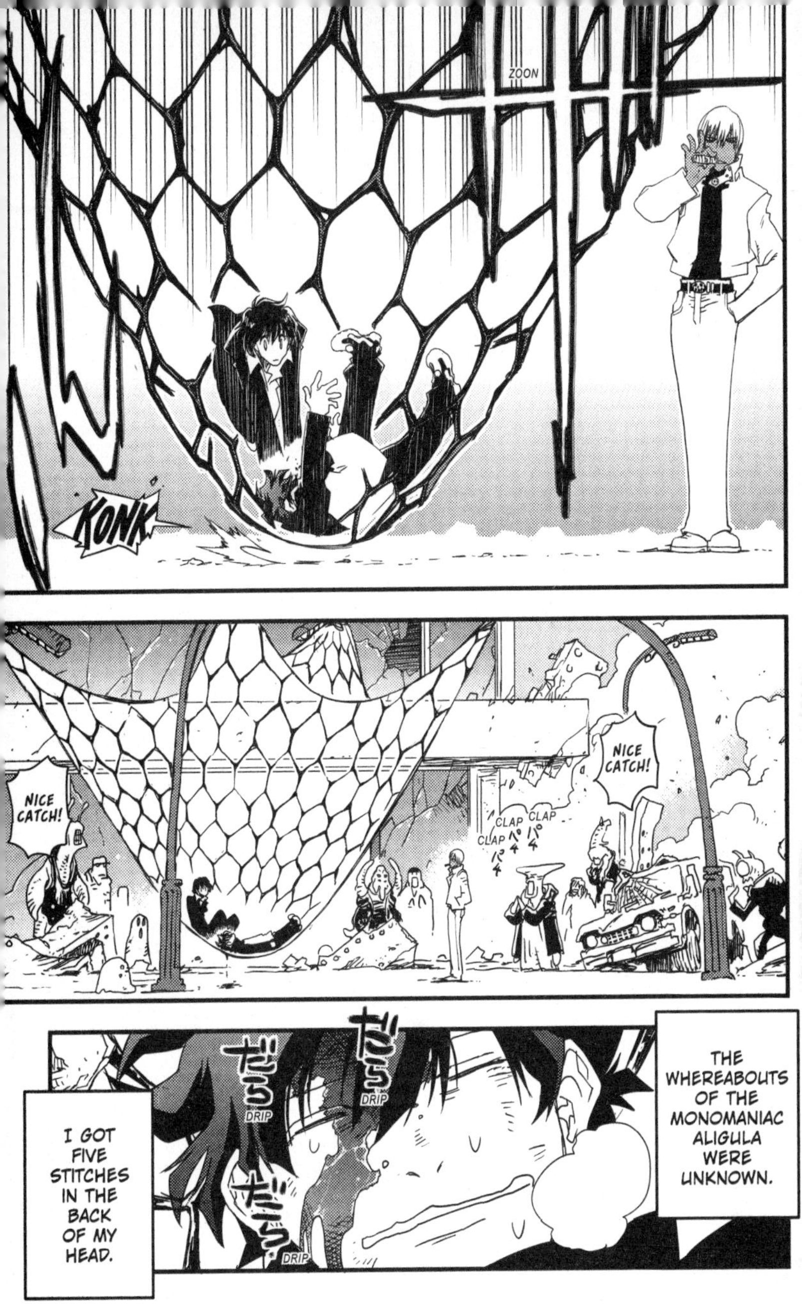
ZOON
KONK
NICE CATCH!
CLAP CLAP
CLAP
NICE CATCH!
THE WHEREABOUTS OF THE MONOMANIAC ALIGULA WERE UNKNOWN.
だら DRIP
だら DRIP
だら DRIP
I GOT FIVE STITCHES IN THE BACK OF MY HEAD.

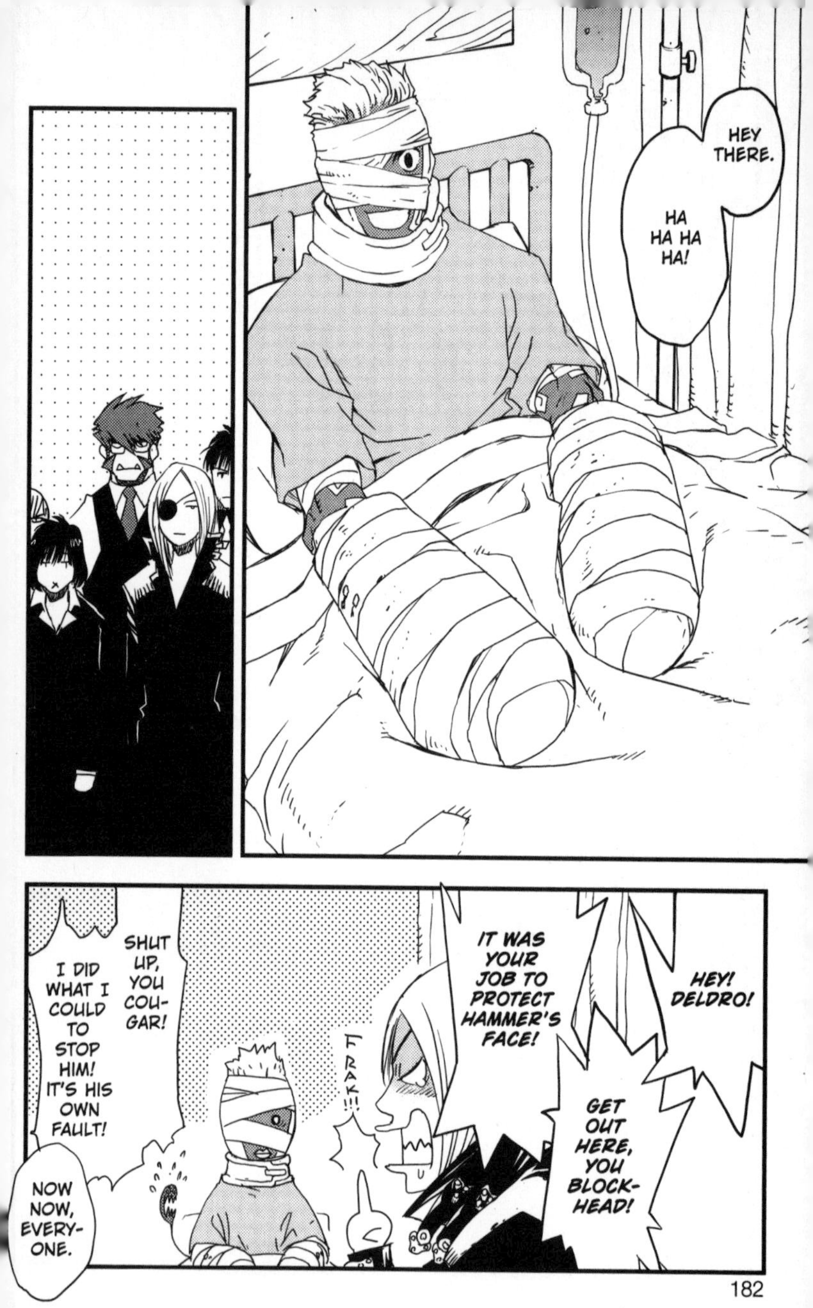
HEY THERE.
HA HA HA HA!
HEY! DELDRO!
IT WAS YOUR JOB TO PROTECT HAMMER'S FACE!
GET OUT HERE, YOU BLOCK-HEAD!
FRAK!!!
SHUT UP, YOU COU-GAR!
I DID WHAT I COULD TO STOP HIM! IT'S HIS OWN FAULT!
NOW NOW, EVERY-ONE.

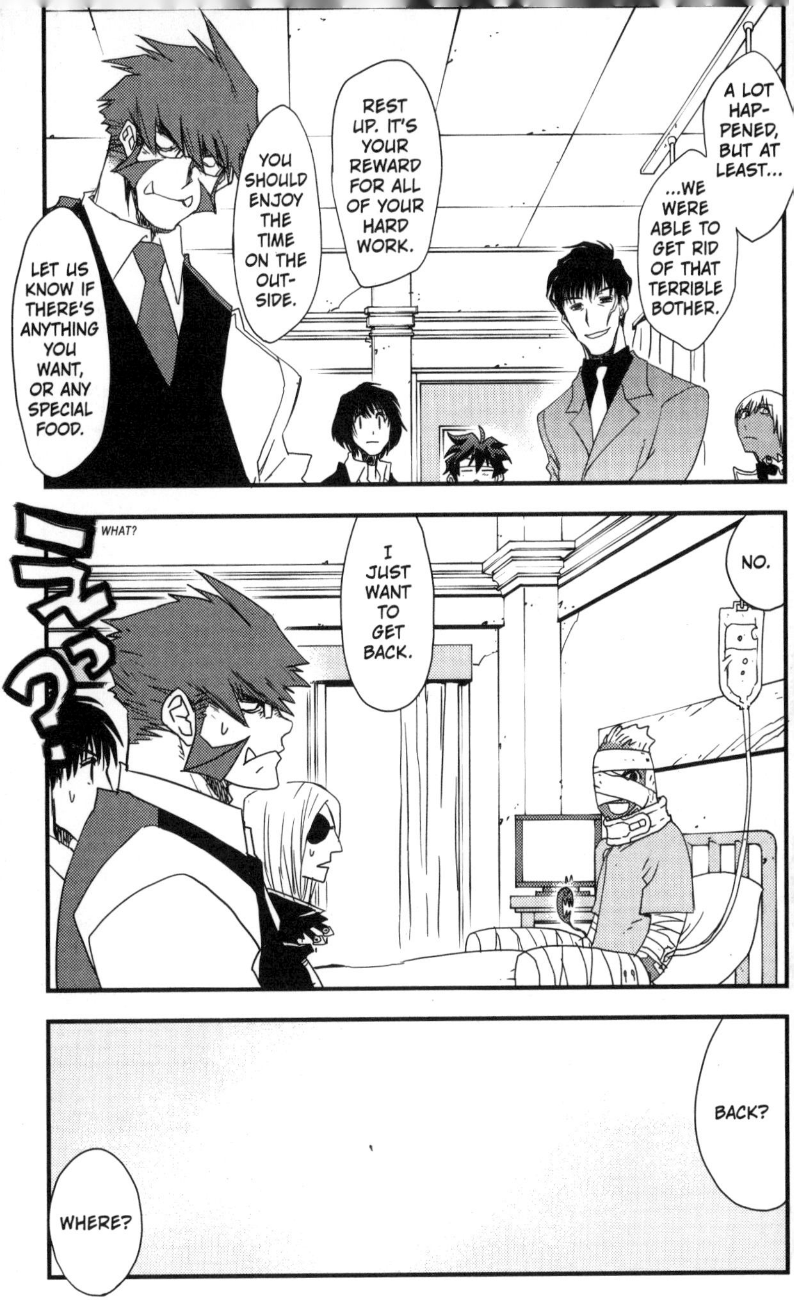
A LOT HAP-PENED, BUT AT LEAST...
...WE WERE ABLE TO GET RID OF THAT TERRIBLE BOTHER.
REST UP. IT'S YOUR REWARD FOR ALL OF YOUR HARD WORK.
YOU SHOULD ENJOY THE TIME ON THE OUT-SIDE.
LET US KNOW IF THERE'S ANYTHING YOU WANT, OR ANY SPECIAL FOOD.
NO.
I JUST WANT TO GET BACK.
WHAT?
BACK?
WHERE?

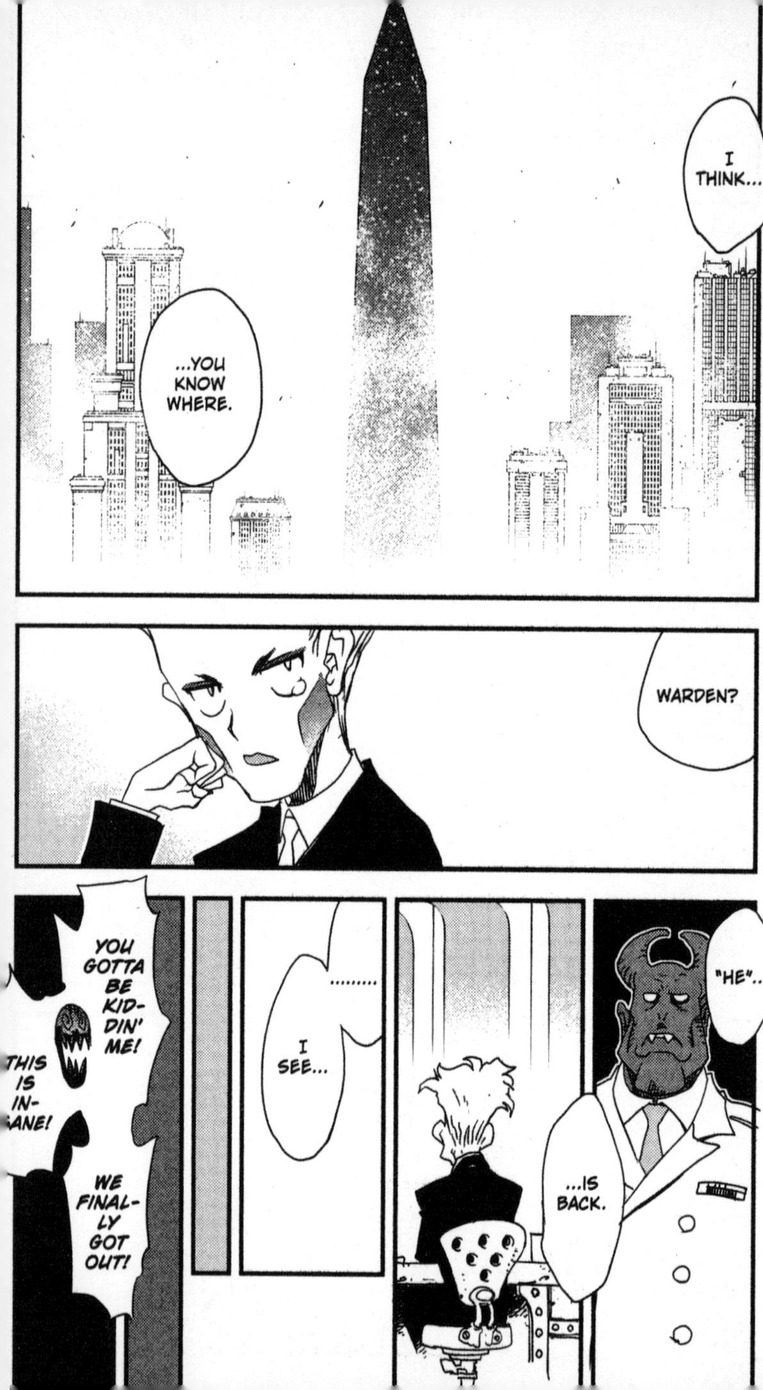
I THINK...
...YOU KNOW WHERE.
WARDEN?
"HE"...
...IS BACK.
....
I SEE...
YOU GOTTA BE KIDDIN' ME!
THIS IS INSANE!
WE FINALLY GOT OUT!

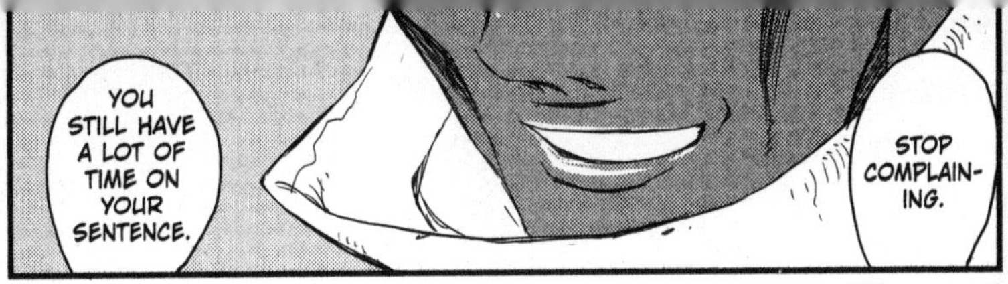
STOP COMPLAIN-ING.
YOU STILL HAVE A LOT OF TIME ON YOUR SENTENCE.

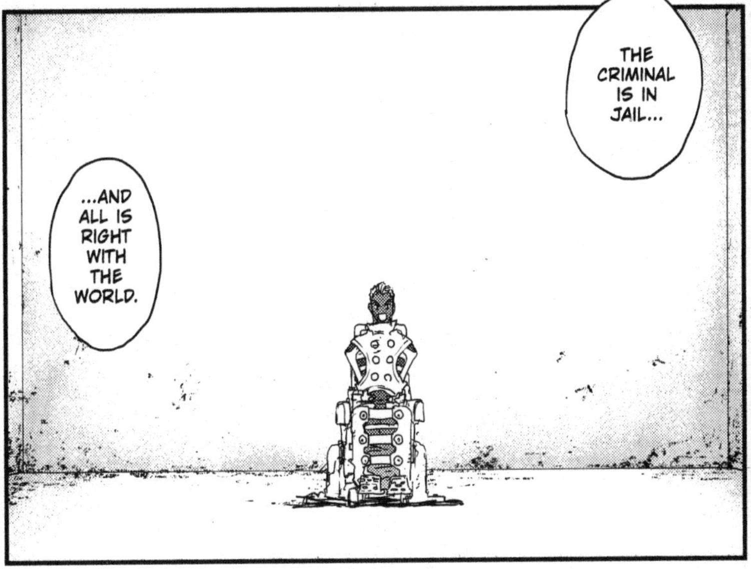
THE CRIMINAL IS IN JAIL...
...AND ALL IS RIGHT WITH THE WORLD.

BLOOD BLOCKADE BATTLEFRONT

DAY IN DAY OUT

END

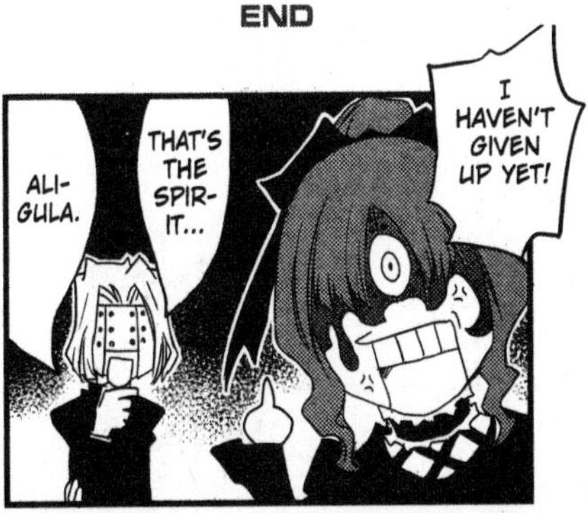
I HAVEN'T GIVEN UP YET!
THAT'S THE SPIR-IT...
ALI-GULA.

BLOOD BLOCKADE BATTLEFRONT

– TREMOR OF THE HAMMER –

3 END

WASSUP? IT'S ME, LEO.
THANK YOU FOR BUYING AND READING *BLOOD BLOCKADE BATTLE-FRONT.*
WHAT?
OH, MY --!
OH, NO!
SOMETHING TERRIBLE HAS HAPPENED TO JAPAN!

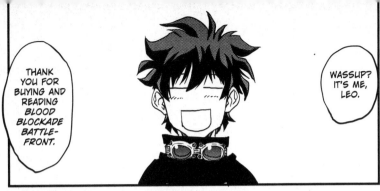

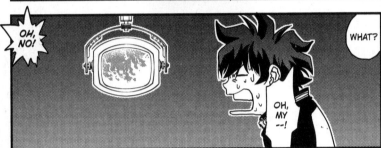

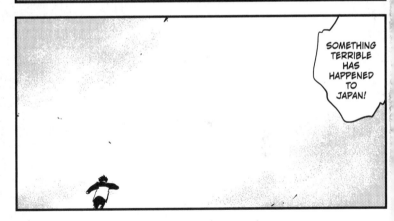

(IN PLACE OF A POSTSCRIPT)

BBB TWO SCENE.

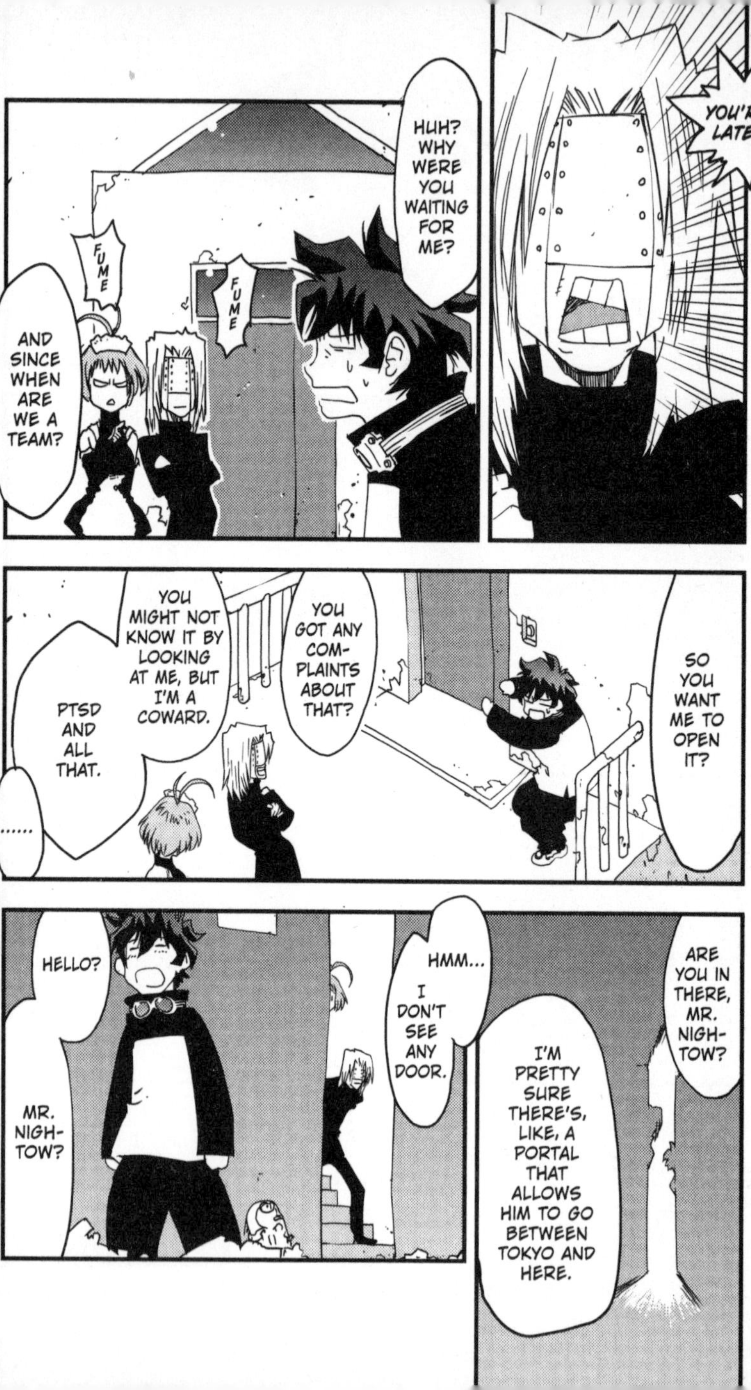
YOU'RE LATE!
HUH? WHY WERE YOU WAITING FOR ME?
FUME
FUME
AND SINCE WHEN ARE WE A TEAM?
SO YOU WANT ME TO OPEN IT?
YOU GOT ANY COM-PLAINTS ABOUT THAT?
YOU MIGHT NOT KNOW IT BY LOOKING AT ME, BUT I'M A COWARD.
PTSD AND ALL THAT.
......
ARE YOU IN THERE, MR. NIGH-TOW?
I'M PRETTY SURE THERE'S, LIKE, A PORTAL THAT ALLOWS HIM TO GO BETWEEN TOKYO AND HERE.
HMM... I DON'T SEE ANY DOOR.
HELLO?
MR. NIGH-TOW?

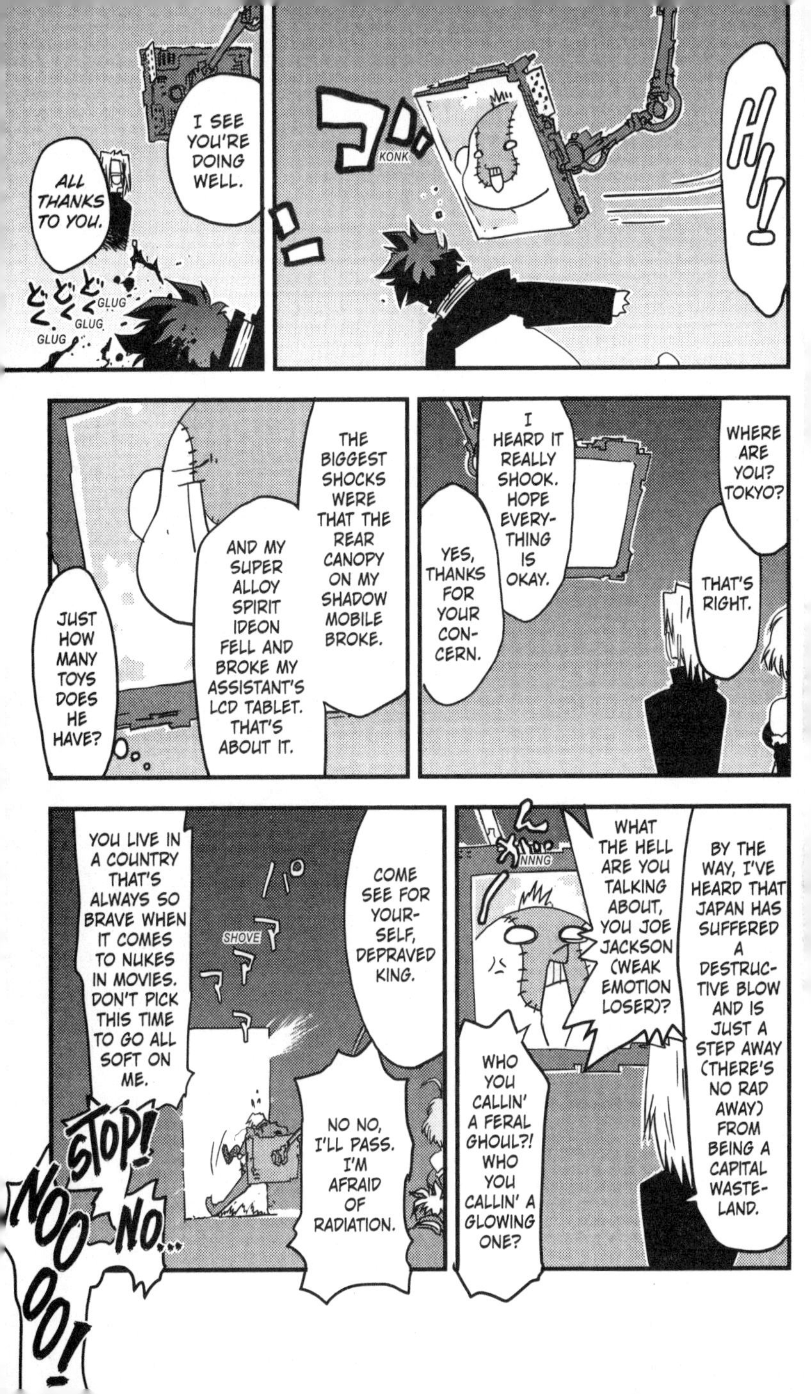
HI!
KONK
I SEE YOU'RE DOING WELL.
ALL THANKS TO YOU.
GLUG
GLUG
GLUG
WHERE ARE YOU? TOKYO?
THAT'S RIGHT.
I HEARD IT REALLY SHOOK. HOPE EVERYTHING IS OKAY.
YES, THANKS FOR YOUR CONCERN.
THE BIGGEST SHOCKS WERE THAT THE REAR CANOPY ON MY SHADOW MOBILE BROKE.
AND MY SUPER ALLOY SPIRIT IDEON FELL AND BROKE MY ASSISTANT'S LCD TABLET. THAT'S ABOUT IT.
JUST HOW MANY TOYS DOES HE HAVE?
BY THE WAY, I'VE HEARD THAT JAPAN HAS SUFFERED A DESTRUCTIVE BLOW AND IS JUST A STEP AWAY (THERE'S NO RAD AWAY) FROM BEING A CAPITAL WASTELAND.
NNNG
WHAT THE HELL ARE YOU TALKING ABOUT, YOU JOE JACKSON (WEAK EMOTION LOSER)?
WHO YOU CALLIN' A FERAL GHOUL?! WHO YOU CALLIN' A GLOWING ONE?
COME SEE FOR YOURSELF, DEPRAVED KING.
YOU LIVE IN A COUNTRY THAT'S ALWAYS SO BRAVE WHEN IT COMES TO NUKES IN MOVIES. DON'T PICK THIS TIME TO GO ALL SOFT ON ME.
SHOVE
NO NO, I'LL PASS. I'M AFRAID OF RADIATION.
STOP!
NO...
NOOOOO!

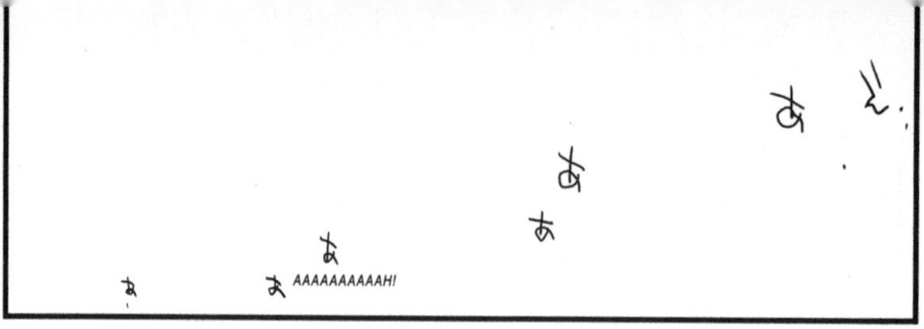
AAAAAAAAAAAH!

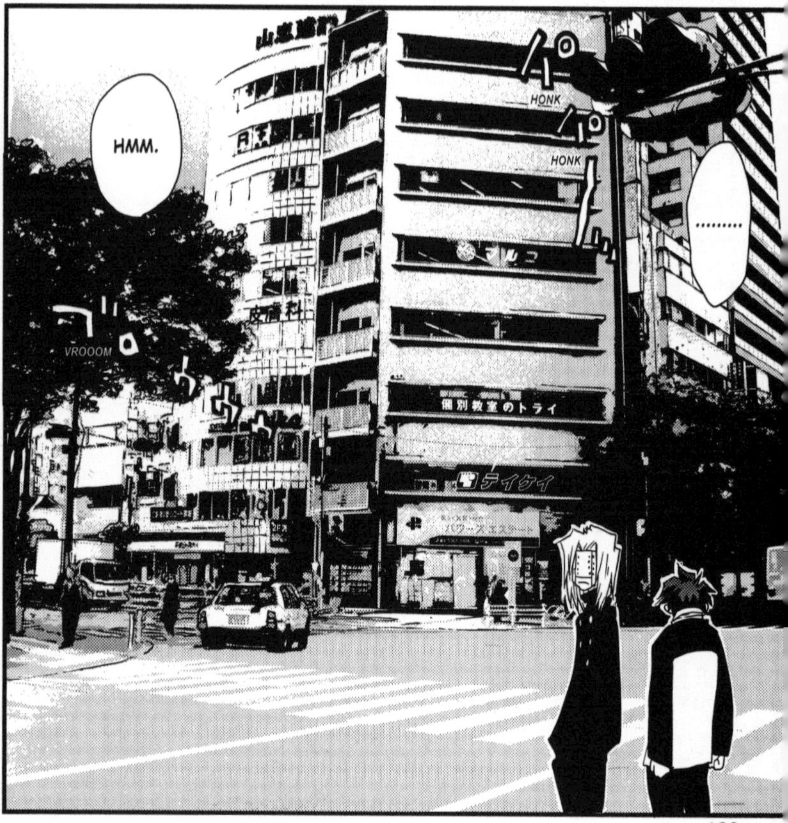
....
HONK
HONK
HMM.
VROOOM

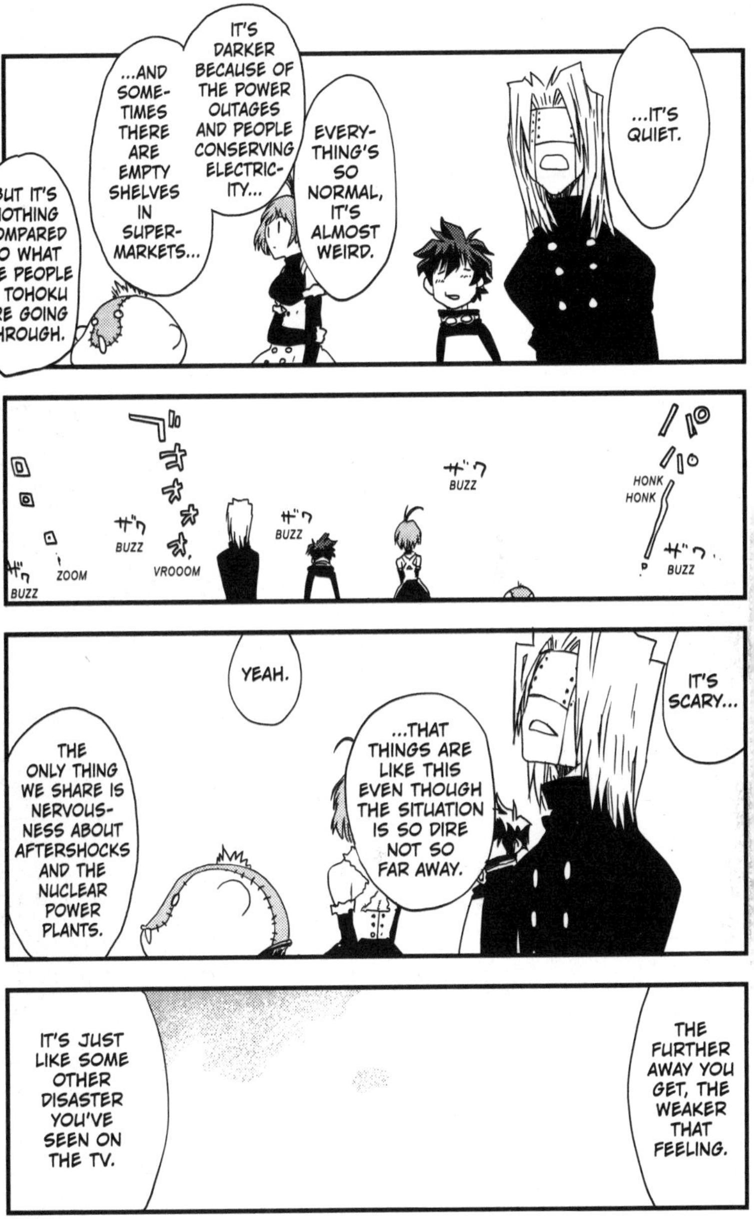

...IT'S QUIET.
EVERYTHING'S SO NORMAL, IT'S ALMOST WEIRD.
IT'S DARKER BECAUSE OF THE POWER OUTAGES AND PEOPLE CONSERVING ELECTRICITY...
...AND SOMETIMES THERE ARE EMPTY SHELVES IN SUPERMARKETS...
BUT IT'S NOTHING COMPARED TO WHAT THE PEOPLE IN TOHOKU ARE GOING THROUGH.
HONK HONK
BUZZ
BUZZ
BUZZ
VROOOM
BUZZ
ZOOM
BUZZ
IT'S SCARY...
...THAT THINGS ARE LIKE THIS EVEN THOUGH THE SITUATION IS SO DIRE NOT SO FAR AWAY.
YEAH.
THE ONLY THING WE SHARE IS NERVOUSNESS ABOUT AFTERSHOCKS AND THE NUCLEAR POWER PLANTS.
THE FURTHER AWAY YOU GET, THE WEAKER THAT FEELING.
IT'S JUST LIKE SOME OTHER DISASTER YOU'VE SEEN ON THE TV.

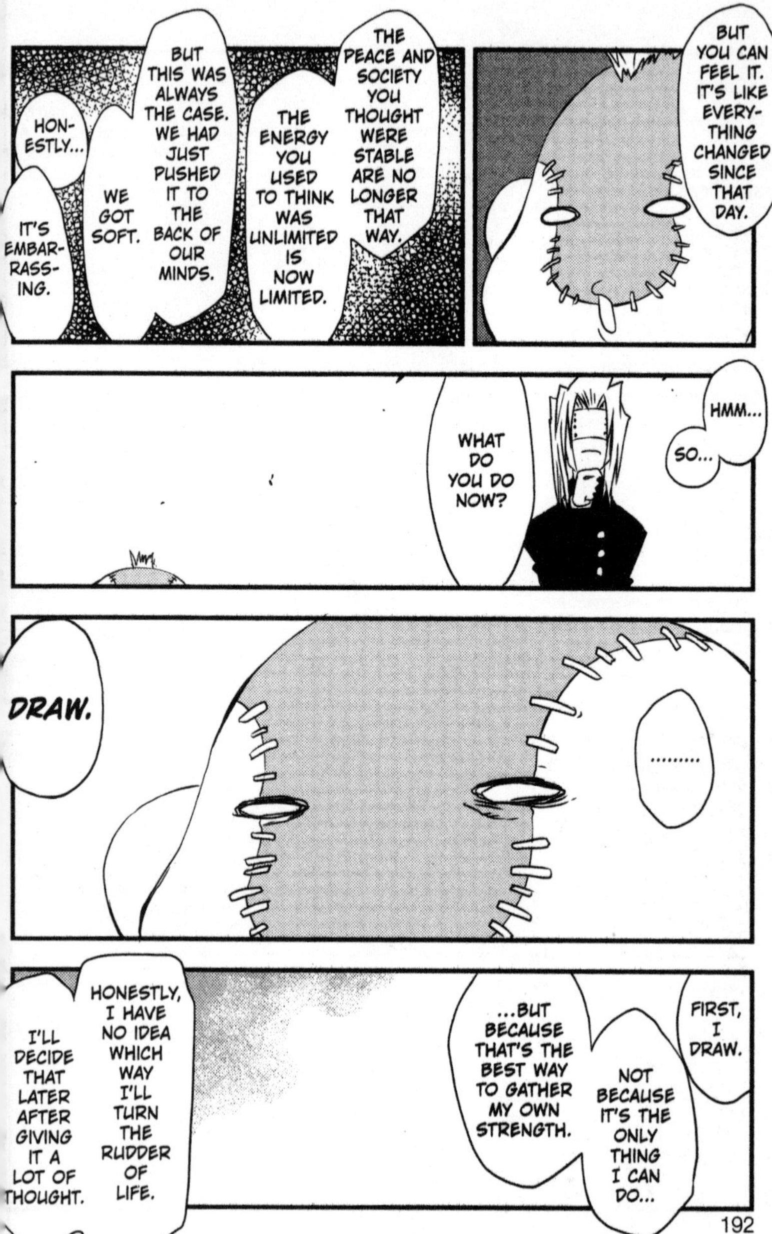
BUT YOU CAN FEEL IT. IT'S LIKE EVERY-THING CHANGED SINCE THAT DAY.
THE PEACE AND SOCIETY YOU THOUGHT WERE STABLE ARE NO LONGER THAT WAY.
THE ENERGY YOU USED TO THINK WAS UNLIMITED IS NOW LIMITED.
BUT THIS WAS ALWAYS THE CASE. WE HAD JUST PUSHED IT TO THE BACK OF OUR MINDS.
WE GOT SOFT.
HON-ESTLY...
IT'S EMBAR-RASS-ING.
HMM...
SO...
WHAT DO YOU DO NOW?
....
DRAW.
FIRST, I DRAW.
NOT BECAUSE IT'S THE ONLY THING I CAN DO...
...BUT BECAUSE THAT'S THE BEST WAY TO GATHER MY OWN STRENGTH.
HONESTLY, I HAVE NO IDEA WHICH WAY I'LL TURN THE RUDDER OF LIFE.
I'LL DECIDE THAT LATER AFTER GIVING IT A LOT OF THOUGHT.

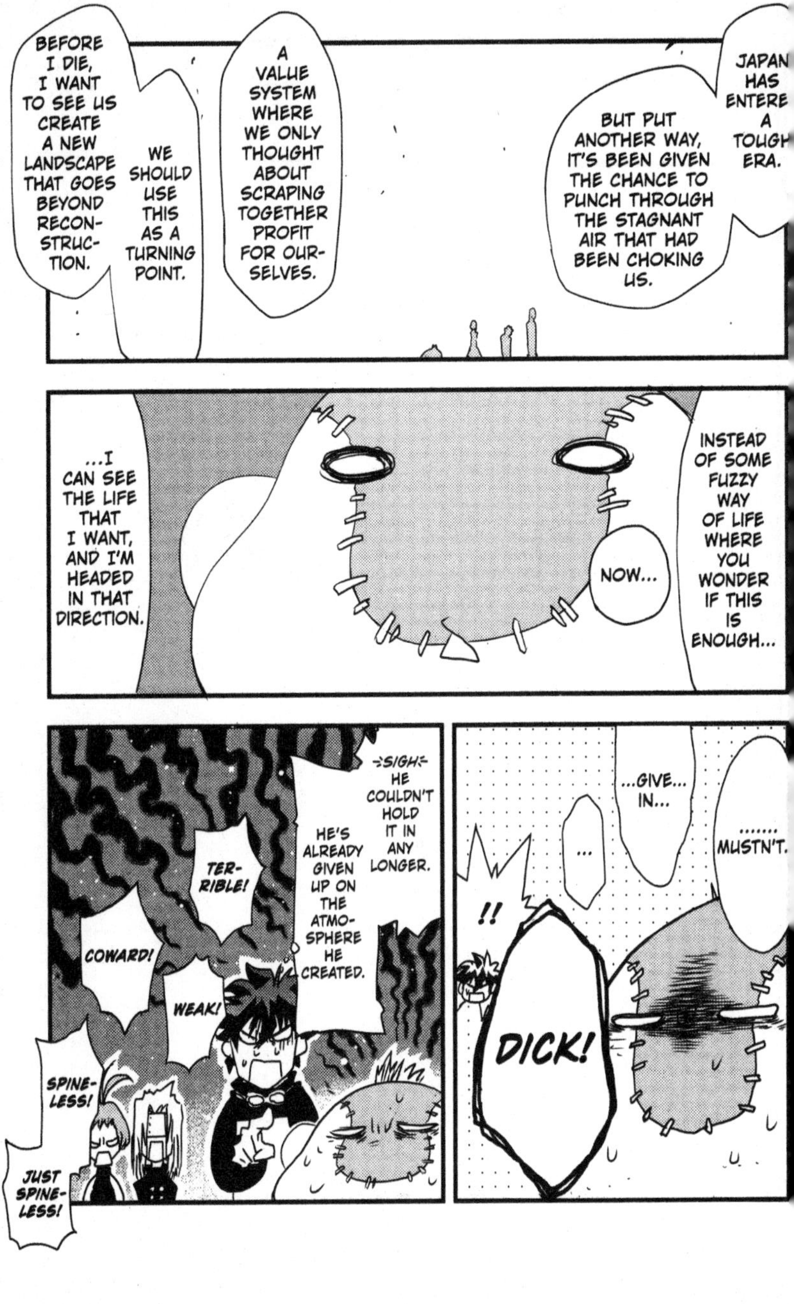
JAPAN HAS ENTERE A TOUGH ERA.
BUT PUT ANOTHER WAY, IT'S BEEN GIVEN THE CHANCE TO PUNCH THROUGH THE STAGNANT AIR THAT HAD BEEN CHOKING US.
A VALUE SYSTEM WHERE WE ONLY THOUGHT ABOUT SCRAPING TOGETHER PROFIT FOR OURSELVES.
WE SHOULD USE THIS AS A TURNING POINT.
BEFORE I DIE, I WANT TO SEE US CREATE A NEW LANDSCAPE THAT GOES BEYOND RECONSTRUCTION.
INSTEAD OF SOME FUZZY WAY OF LIFE WHERE YOU WONDER IF THIS IS ENOUGH...
NOW...
...I CAN SEE THE LIFE THAT I WANT, AND I'M HEADED IN THAT DIRECTION.
.... MUSTN'T.
...GIVE... IN...
...
!!
DICK!
-SIGH- HE COULDN'T HOLD IT IN ANY LONGER.
HE'S ALREADY GIVEN UP ON THE ATMOSPHERE HE CREATED.
TERRIBLE!
COWARD!
WEAK!
SPINELESS!
JUST SPINELESS!

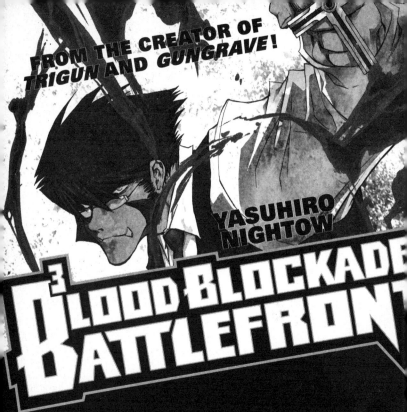

FROM THE CREATOR OF
TRIGUN AND *GUNGRAVE*!

YASUHIRO NIGHTOW

³BLOOD BLOCKADE BATTLEFRONT

Three years ago, a gateway between Earth and the Beyond opened over New York City. In one terrible night, New York was destroyed and rebuilt, trapping New Yorkers and extradimensional creatures alike in an impenetrable bubble. New York is now Jerusalem's Lot, a paranormal melting pot where magic and madness dwell alongside the mundane, where human vermin gather to exploit otherworldly assets for earthly profit. Now someone is threatening to breach the bubble and release New Jerusalem's horrors, but the mysterious superagents of Libra fight to prevent the unthinkable.

Trigun creator Yasuhiro Nightow returns with *Blood Blockade Battlefront*, an action-packed supernatural science-fiction steamroller as only Nightow can conjure.

VOLUME ONE
ISBN 978-1-59582-718-0 | $10.99

VOLUME TWO
ISBN 978-1-59582-912-2 | $10.99

VOLUME THREE
ISBN 978-1-59582-913-9 | $10.99

DARK HORSE MANGA

Kekkai Sensen © Yasuhiro Nightow. All rights reserved. Original Japanese edition published by SHUEISHA, Inc., Tokyo. English translation rights in the United States and Canada arranged by SHUEISHA, Inc. (BL7099)

ALSO FROM YASUHIRO NIGHTOW

TRIGUN MAXIMUM

Go beyond the story available in the *Trigun* anime and the first two top-selling manga volumes with *Trigun Maximum*!

$9.99 each!

VOLUME 1: THE HERO RETURNS
ISBN 978-1-59307-196-7

VOLUME 2: DEATH BLUE
ISBN 978-1-59307-197-4

VOLUME 3: HIS LIFE AS A...
ISBN 978-1-59307-266-7

VOLUME 4: BOTTOM OF THE DARK
ISBN 978-1-59307-314-5

VOLUME 5: BREAK OUT
ISBN 978-1-59307-344-2

VOLUME 6: THE GUNSLINGER
ISBN 978-1-59307-351-0

VOLUME 7: HAPPY DAYS
ISBN 978-1-59307-395-4

VOLUME 8: SILENT RUIN
ISBN 978-1-59307-452-4

VOLUME 9: LR
ISBN 978-1-59307-527-9

VOLUME 10: WOLFWOOD
ISBN 978-1-59307-556-9

VOLUME 11: ZERO HOUR
ISBN 978-1-59307-674-0

VOLUME 12: THE GUNSLINGER
ISBN 978-1-59307-881-2

VOLUME 13: DOUBLE DUEL
ISBN 978-1-59582-167-6

VOLUME 14: MIND GAMES
ISBN 978-1-59582-262-8

DARK HORSE MANGA

AVAILABLE AT YOUR LOCAL COMICS SHOP OR BOOKSTORE!
TO FIND A COMICS SHOP IN YOUR AREA, CALL 1-888-266-4226.

For more information or to order direct visit DarkHorse.com or call 1-800-862-0052 Mon.-Fri. 9 A.M. to 5 P.M. Pacific Time. *Prices and availability subject to change without notice.

Volume 1:
ISBN 978-1-59307-052-6

Volume 2:
ISBN 978-1-59307-053-3

$14.95 each!

AVAILABLE AT YOUR LOCAL COMICS SHOP OR BOOKSTORE!
To find a comics shop in your area, call 1-800-266-4226.

For more information or to order direct visit darkhorse.com or call 1-800-862-0052 Mon.-Fri. 9 A.M. to 5 P.M. Pacific Time.
Prices and availability subject to change without notice.

darkhorse.com

DARK
HORSE
MANGA

DMP
Digital Manga
Publishing

dmpbooks.com

BERSERK

Created by Kentaro Miura, *Berserk* is manga mayhem to the extreme—violent, horrifying, and mercilessly funny—and the wellspring for the internationally popular anime series. Not for the squeamish or the easily offended, *Berserk* asks for no quarter—and offers none!

Presented uncensored in the original Japanese format!

VOLUME 1
ISBN 978-1-59307-020-5

VOLUME 2
ISBN 978-1-59307-021-2

VOLUME 3
ISBN 978-1-59307-022-9

VOLUME 4
ISBN 978-1-59307-203-2

VOLUME 5
ISBN 978-1-59307-251-3

VOLUME 6
ISBN 978-1-59307-252-0

VOLUME 7
ISBN 978-1-59307-328-2

VOLUME 8
ISBN 978-1-59307-329-9

VOLUME 9
ISBN 978-1-59307-330-5

VOLUME 10
ISBN 978-1-59307-331-2

VOLUME 11
ISBN 978-1-59307-470-8

VOLUME 12
ISBN 978-1-59307-484-5

VOLUME 13
ISBN 978-1-59307-500-2

VOLUME 14
ISBN 978-1-59307-501-9

VOLUME 15
ISBN 978-1-59307-577-4

VOLUME 16
ISBN 978-1-59307-706-8

VOLUME 17
ISBN 978-1-59307-742-6

VOLUME 18
ISBN 978-1-59307-743-3

VOLUME 19
ISBN 978-1-59307-744-0

VOLUME 20
ISBN 978-1-59307-745-7

VOLUME 21
ISBN 978-1-59307-746-4

VOLUME 22
ISBN 978-1-59307-863-8

VOLUME 23
ISBN 978-1-59307-864-5

VOLUME 24
ISBN 978-1-59307-865-2

VOLUME 25
ISBN 978-1-59307-921-5

VOLUME 26
ISBN 978-1-59307-922-2

VOLUME 27
ISBN 978-1-59307-923-9

VOLUME 28
ISBN 978-1-59582-209-3

VOLUME 29
ISBN 978-1-59582-210-9

VOLUME 30
ISBN 978-1-59582-211-6

VOLUME 31
ISBN 978-1-59582-366-3

VOLUME 32
ISBN 978-1-59582-367-0

VOLUME 33
ISBN 978-1-59582-372-4

VOLUME 34
ISBN 978-1-59582-532-2

VOLUME 35
ISBN 978-1-59582-695-4

VOLUME 36
ISBN 978-1-59582-942-9

$14.99 each!

DMPBooks.com DarkHorse.com

AVAILABLE AT YOUR LOCAL COMICS SHOP OR BOOKSTORE
To find a comics shop near your area, call 1-888-266-4226. For more information or to order direct:
•On the web: darkhorse.com •E-mail: mailorder@darkhorse.com •Phone: 1-800-862-0052 Mon.–Fri. 9 AM to 5 PM Pacific Time.

GANTZ
HIROYA OKU Works.

The last thing Kei and Masaru remember was being struck dead by a subway train while saving the life of a drunken bum. What a waste! And yet somehow they're still alive. Or semi-alive? Maybe reanimated . . . by some kind of mysterious orb! And this orb called "Gantz" intends to make them play games of death, hunting all kinds of odd aliens, along with a bunch of other ordinary citizens who've recently met a tragic semi-end. The missions they embark upon are often dangerous. Many die—and die again. This dark and action-packed manga deals with the moral conflicts of violence, teenage sexual confusion and angst, and our fascination with death.

Dark Horse is proud to deliver one of the most requested manga ever to be released. Hang on to your gear and keep playing the game, whatever you do; *Gantz* is unrelenting!

VOLUME ONE
ISBN 978-1-59307-949-9

VOLUME TWO
ISBN 978-1-59582-188-1

VOLUME THREE
ISBN 978-1-59582-232-1

VOLUME FOUR
ISBN 978-1-59582-250-5

VOLUME FIVE
ISBN 978-1-59582-301-4

VOLUME SIX
ISBN 978-1-59582-320-5

VOLUME SEVEN
ISBN 978-1-59582-373-1

VOLUME EIGHT
ISBN 978-1-59582-383-0

VOLUME NINE
ISBN 978-1-59582-452-3

VOLUME TEN
ISBN 978-1-59582-320-5

VOLUME ELEVEN
ISBN 978-1-59582-373-1

VOLUME TWELVE
ISBN 978-1-59582-526-1

VOLUME THIRTEEN
ISBN 978-1-59582-587-2

VOLUME FOURTEEN
ISBN 978-1-59582-598-8

VOLUME FIFTEEN
ISBN 978-1-59582-662-6

VOLUME SIXTEEN
ISBN 978-1-59582-663-3

VOLUME SEVENTEEN
ISBN 978-1-59582-664-0

VOLUME EIGHTEEN
ISBN 978-1-59582-776-0

VOLUME NINETEEN
ISBN 978-1-59582-813-2

VOLUME TWENTY
ISBN 978-1-59582-846-0

VOLUME TWENTY-ONE
ISBN 978-1-59582-847-7

VOLUME TWENTY-TWO
ISBN 978-1-59582-848-4

VOLUME TWENTY-THREE
ISBN 978-1-59582-849-1

VOLUME TWENTY-FOUR
ISBN 978-1-59582-907-8

VOLUME TWENTY-FIVE
ISBN 978-1-59582-908-5

$12.99 EACH

DARK HORSE MANGA

AVAILABLE AT YOUR LOCAL COMICS SHOP OR BOOKSTORE
TO FIND A COMICS SHOP IN YOUR AREA, CALL 1-888-266-4226

For more information or to order direct:
On the web: darkhorse.com E-mail: mailorder@darkhorse.com Phone: 1-800-862-0052 Mon.–Fri. 9 A.M. to 5 P.M. Pacific Time.

publisher
MIKE RICHARDSON

editor
CHRIS WARNER

book design
JUSTIN COUCH

Dark Horse Manga
A division of Dark Horse Comics, Inc.
10956 SE Main Street
Milwaukie, OR 97222

DarkHorse.com

First edition: November 2012
ISBN 978-1-59582-913-9

10 9 8 7 6 5 4 3 2 1

Printed at Lake Book Manufacturing, Inc., Melrose Park, IL, USA

BLOOD BLOCKADE BATTLEFRONT VOLUME 3

To find a comics shop in your area, call the Comic Shop Locator Service toll-free at 1-888-266-4226.

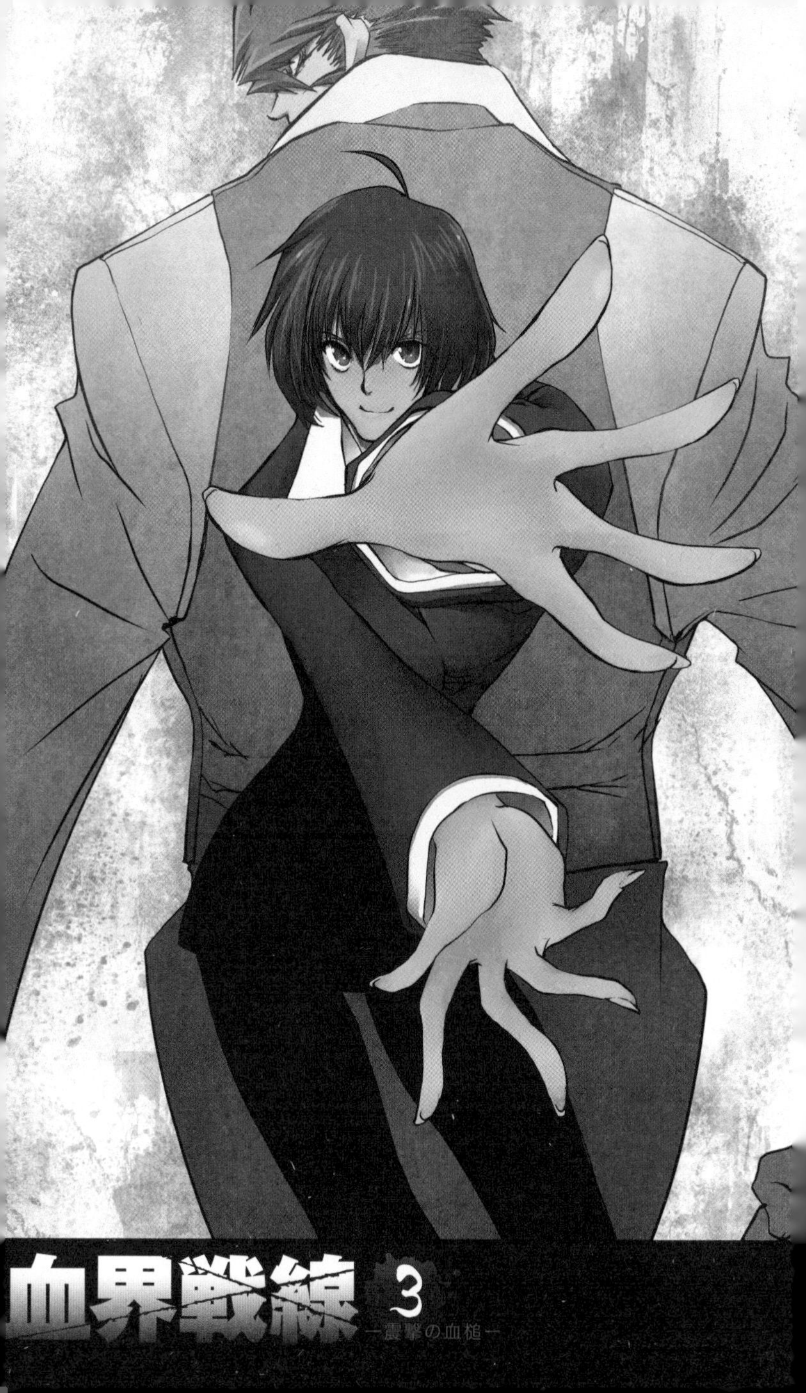

血界戦線 3
—震撃の血槌—

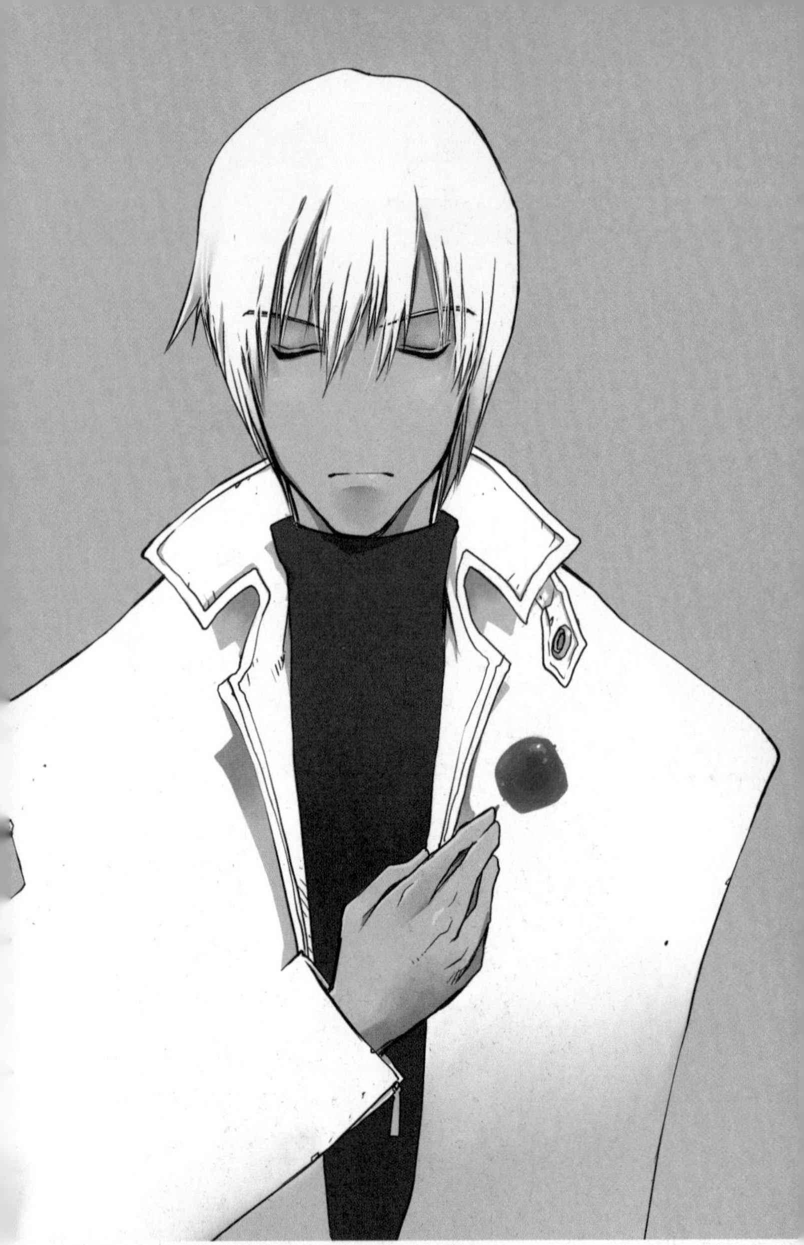

血界戦線 3

—震撃の血槌—